Mother of Oscar

Other books by the author

Ellen and Edy: A Biography of Ellen Terry and Her
    Daughter Edith Craig
Lost Children of the Empire (co-authored)

Mother of Oscar

The Life of Jane Francesca Wilde

JOY MELVILLE

JOHN MURRAY

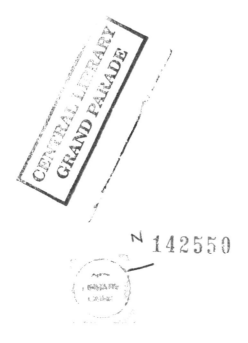
© Joy Melville 1994

First published in 1994
by John Murray (Publishers) Ltd,
50 Albemarle Street, London W1X 4BD

The moral right of the author has been asserted

A catalogue record for this book is available from the British Library

ISBN 0-7195-5102 1

Typeset in 11/13 Times by Colset Private Limited, Singapore.
Printed and bound in Great Britain by The University Press, Cambridge.

To my sister

Contents

viii   *Contents*

Illustrations

(*between pages 148 and 149*)

1. Jane as 'Speranza of the *Nation*'
2. William Wilde, 1847
3. Oscar as a child
4. Oscar as a young boy
5. Portrait of Lady Wilde by Bernard Mulrenin, 1864
6. An idealized rendering of the Mulrenin portrait
7. Jane as Madame Recamier by the *Punch* artist Harry Furniss
8. Jane and her husband William caricatured by Furniss
9. William Wilde, 1875
10. Jane Wilde, 1882
11. Oscar during his 1882 tour of America
12. Oscar being comforted by his brother Willie after the failure of his play *Vera*
13. Willie Wilde's first wife, Mrs Frank Leslie
14. Constance with the Wildes' eldest son Cyril, 1889
15. Jane in old age

The author and publishers would like to thank the following for permission to reproduce illustrations:

Plate 1, Brown University Library; 2 and 6, National Library of Ireland; 3, 4, 9, 11, 14 and 15, William Andrews Clark Library; 5, Boston Public Library; 7, 8, 10 and 12, British Library; and 13, Madeleine Stern and the British Library.

Acknowledgements

I SHOULD LIKE, above all, to thank Merlin Holland for his permission to use Lady Wilde's unpublished letters and Oscar's letters (edited by Rupert Hart-Davis) as well as giving me his most generous encouragement and support.

So many people have helped me that it is impossible to mention them all. But my particular thanks go to John Holland for his permission to reprint letters from the Holland family, as well as to Edith Elgee, Mrs Catherine Elgee, Davis Coakley, Kevin O'Brien, Antony Sellers, Anthony Tuohy, Winnie Mulligan, Eileen Pollock, Nicholas Furlong, Walter Nelson, Bengt Holmquist, Horst Schroeder, Walter Nelson, John Wyse Jackson, Dr Krishnamurti, George Newkey-Burden, Tony Gould, Nina Reid, David Goddard, Maria Pilar Pulido, Hugh Ruddick-Bracken, James Treanor, Bernadette Masterson, Howard Davies, Andrew McDonnell and Bindon Russell of the Oscar Wilde Society, London, and members of the Oscar Wilde Society, Dublin.

Staff at a number of libraries have given me a great deal of assistance during my research. I am greatly indebted to Dr Michael Halls (then Acting Reference/Acquisitions Librarian) at the William Andrews Clark Library, University of California, Los Angeles, and to Suzanne Tatian, the Reading Room Supervisor; Muriel McCarthy, Keeper of Archbishop Marsh's Library, Dublin; Aine Keegan, Librarian, Early Manuscripts Department, Trinity College, Dublin; Paula Howard, former Librarian of the Gilbert Library, Dublin; David Doughan of the Fawcett Library; Michael Bott, archivist of Reading University;

and the staff of the London Library, British Library, Royal Library of Sweden, National Library of Ireland, Trinity College, Dublin, and the Bodleian Library.

I am grateful to the following for permission to reprint material: to the William Andrews Clark Library for letters from, and to, Lady Wilde; to Reading University for letters from Lady Wilde to an unknown correspondent; to the Royal Library of Sweden for letters from Lady Wilde to Lotten von Kraemer and other Swedish friends; to the National Library of Ireland for letters from Lady Wilde to Rosalie Olivecrona, and to and from Charles Gavan Duffy, William Carleton, John O'Donovan, Sir Thomas Larcom and Sir William Rowan Hamilton; to the New York Public Library for a letter from Lady Wilde and diary comments; to the Division of Rare and Manuscript Collections, Cornell University Library, for passages from Violet Hunt's 1882 diary; to the Houghton Library, Harvard University, for two letters by Lady Wilde to Longfellow; to the University of Oklahoma Press for excerpts from *Purple Passage: the life of Mrs Frank Leslie*; to Terence de Vere White and the *Times Literary Supplement* for excerpts from 'Speranza's Secret'; to the Society of Authors on behalf of the Bernard Shaw estate for excerpts from George Bernard Shaw's 'My Memories of Oscar Wilde'; to Walter Nelson for excerpts from privately published material; to the Royal College of Physicians, Dublin, for excerpts from the Minutes of the Medico-Philosophical Society; and to Horst Schroeder for use of his *Additions and Corrections to Richard Ellmann's Oscar Wilde*.

Finally, I would like to thank Ann Jameson for generously giving me all her material on Sir William Wilde; my agent Sara Menguc of Murray Pollinger; and finally my editor at John Murray, Caroline Knox, for her enthusiasm and patience.

. . . the D[aily] T[elegraph] of yesterday –
truly you are a startling celebrity!!!
I must now pose as 'the Mother of Oscar'!
Come & see me when you can, for a talk.

Addio Mio Caro

Francesca

Introduction

DOES OSCAR WILDE'S mother need an introduction? She was famous for her own. An acquaintance once observed that she always introduced people to each other as if they were world-wide celebrities ('Miss – – , allow me to present you to Mr – – , who has painted that picture that the whole of London is talking about').

In *The Picture of Dorian Gray*, Oscar affectionately parodied his mother in the character of Lady Brandon who introduced one man, in a loud tragic whisper, with the words: 'Sir Humpty Dumpty – you know – Afghan frontier – Russian intrigue: very successful man – wife killed by an elephant – quite inconsolable – wants to marry a beautiful American widow – everybody does nowadays – hates Mr Gladstone – but very much interested in beetles: ask him what he thinks of Schouvaloff.' Lady Wilde herself was unquestionably a celebrity. Her fiery, nationalistic poetry and prose had made her famous in her native Ireland. She wrote it in her twenties during the country's disastrous famine of the 1840s and her work fired the imagination of the Irish people. Never lacking courage, she lambasted the conditions in Ireland at a time when young women of her class normally remained docilely in the background. Her Protestant family staunchly upheld English rule; she rebelliously attacked it. So virulently did she express herself on one occasion that the paper for which she wrote was immediately closed down for sedition.

Her verse, written under the name of 'Speranza', had such a long-lasting, emotional effect on its readers that when Oscar toured

America some forty years later he was hailed by Irish immigrants there not as the renowned aesthete, but as 'Speranza's Son'. She accepted such homage as her due. After Oscar's plays proved so brilliantly successful, she wrote to him only half jokingly to say, 'I must now pose as the Mother of Oscar.'

Her closeness to Oscar shines out from her many letters to him, all of which he kept. For some twenty years, from the time he went to Oxford until the end of her life, she wrote to him constantly. She signed her letters, with a flourish, 'La Madre', adding adjectives according to her mood: in carefree times, it was La Madre Devotissima; but at times of despair she ended with La Madre Dolorosa or La Madre Povera, sometimes with an added threat about taking prussic acid.

When writing to friends, she never used her first name, Jane. It was far too prosaic for such a flamboyant figure. Instead she would sign her letters Speranza or use her second name, Francesca. But flamboyance was only one facet of this complex, vibrant and intelligent woman. Renowned for her wit – W. B. Yeats was to say of her that 'London has few better talkers' – she was brave and honourable, deeply loyal to family and friends and completely without jealousy. A voracious reader in many European languages, she loved solitude, emerging only to hold her celebrated weekly salons.

In both Dublin and London she was at the centre of the closely interwoven Wilde relationships, supporting and defending her husband, providing a lasting home for her elder son Willie, trying to keep her two sons friendly, and consoling Oscar's wife Constance during his absences. Loving them all, she remained the linchpin of the family throughout its extraordinary succession of dramas, comedies and tragedies and died lamented by the Irish nation, who remembered her still as a source of inspiration.

1

Growing Up in Dublin

LADY WILDE WAS born plain Jane Elgee. She preferred the idea of a romantic ancestry, however, and when asked if her family was purely Irish, said, 'No, it originated in the sixteenth century from Italy and Elgee is an Irish corruption of the name [Algiati].'[1] From here it was just a minor step for her to claim relationship with the poet, Dante Alighieri.

With her long black hair and luminous dark eyes, Jane Elgee could well have been of Italian descent. There was no documentation to disprove it. Her birth was not registered as there was no legal requirement to do so, and she was not baptized. She took advantage of this lack of documentation about her birth to re-invent herself and weave romantic mysteries about her background.

The truth about her ancestry is more prosaic (and is recounted in an appendix to this book). Her great-grandfather Charles Elgee was a bricklayer. He was born at Raby, Co. Durham in 1714, and in the 1730s he and his brother sailed to Ireland where there was a building boom. There they quickly prospered.

Charles's youngest son (Jane's grandfather) went into the Church and rose to the position of Archdeacon in Wexford. But the Archdeacon's eldest son, another Charles and the future father of Jane Elgee, opted for the law rather than the Church and became a solicitor.

He practised in Dublin and there, from 1807, he lived at No. 8 Essex Bridge, a bustling, smart area of town near Dublin Castle. Ships came right up to Essex Bridge on the River Liffey in order to moor alongside the spectacular, domed Custom House. The bridge was also the favourite haunt of blind Michael Moran ('Zozimus'), the most famous of all the Dublin ballad-singers. Until his death in 1834, Moran would sit by the bridge in his coarse frieze coat, turning every occurrence of the day – from an unpopular new measure to an abduction – into rhyme, which he sang. Jane would certainly have seen him as a child and his songs could have influenced her future ballad-style poetry. Newsboys also sang the news from the papers they sold while beggars dodged the drivers of the black cart, sent out by Dublin authorities to arrest them.

While working in Dublin, Charles Elgee met his future wife, Sara Kingsbury. She came from a solidly prosperous and well-connected Protestant family. Such middle-class Protestants regarded themselves as 'the gentry' and were traditional supporters of the British government.

Sara and her two sisters, Henrietta and Elizabeth, were considered the most beautiful girls in Dublin. Henrietta married the eccentric young clergyman, playwright and famous writer of terror-tales, the Revd Charles Maturin, while Elizabeth married Sir Charles Montagu Ormsby, a member of the old Irish parliament. Their father, Thomas Kingsbury, was Commissioner of Bankruptcy and owner of Lisle House, one of the finest mansions in Dublin; their grandfather was President of the Royal College of Physicians and an intimate friend of Dean Swift.

Charles Elgee and Sara returned to Wexford for their marriage which Charles's brother conducted at the impressive Doric-style, eighteenth-century Protestant church of St Iberius in the High Street. The close-packed, spidery writing of the church's register of marriages for 1803–1811 records the wedding on 23 December 1809. The wedding celebrations combined with Christmas festivities must have given the couple a great send-off. Wexford was known for its parties, balls and musical evenings – one family even had a small theatre in the top floor of their house for concerts and plays.

After their wedding, Charles and his wife left for Dublin and returned to Charles's lodgings at Essex Bridge. Their first child, Emily Thomasine, was probably born late in 1810. In 1811, the couple moved from Essex Bridge to Leeson Street, and before another year had passed they moved again, this time to 4 St James's Street East. Their second child, John, was born in 1812.

This continual moving may imply a rather unstable family life, and a registered deed of 11 November 1814 reveals that Charles was in debt and that the couple were possibly considering separation. The deed refers to their marriage settlement with its provision that if Sara should ever, after her marriage, live apart from her husband, she should get all the interest and dividends from £839 14s 9d. This amount was her share of the inheritance from her father and was quite a large sum: during the famine in the mid-1840s, for instance, men on relief work in some areas only earned 8d a day.

The deed also specified that Charles Elgee was to be given £130 to discharge his immediate debts. But he had to sign over the future interest of his wife's inheritance and an annuity of £60 for Sara's 'benefit and advantage . . . without the control or intermeddling of the said Charles Elgee'.[2]

Despite that blast across Charles's bows, he and Sara continued to live together. In 1815 they moved back again to Leeson Street, this time to No. 3, and in June the following year their third child, Frances, was born. But she died shortly after at Wexford, where Charles's family still lived. Her interment was recorded briefly by his brother in the burial register at St Iberius' Church: 'September 12th, 1816, Frances, daughter of Mr Charles Elgee of the City of Dublin at Selskar [Wexford], aged 3 months.'

Although Frances's burial is in the register, no other church records have been found of the baptisms of the other three children of Charles and Sara either in Wexford, home of the Elgee family, or in St Peter's Church in Dublin – Charles and Sara's local parish church. As Charles was the son of an archdeacon, it is an unexpected omission.

In 1817, the couple moved a few houses further down, to No. 6 Leeson Street. They stayed here until 1822 and it was during this time that Jane must have been born. After 1822, the Elgees disappear from the street directory for twenty-one years. There was obviously some kind of upheaval as Charles precipitately left Ireland for India – a fact only known from the appearance in Dublin's *Freeman's Journal*, on 4 February 1825, of the following obituary: 'On the 13th August last, at Bangalore, in the East Indies, Charles Elgee, Esquire, eldest son of the late venerable Archdeacon Elgee of Wexford.'

Charles could have gone out to Bangalore to make his fortune; or to avoid the debt collectors. The life of a soldier could not have attracted him as his name did not appear in any Indian Army lists of the time. He was qualified to take a legal position, but would have had a wide choice of employment. India was the land of hope then: the

East India Company alone offered a huge number of jobs. The cause of his death is another mystery. No contemporary Indian paper mentions it.

As Charles died in India in 1824, he could not have fathered Jane if she was born in 1826. But 1826 was widely accepted by her contemporaries as her birthdate and never denied by Jane. There has been speculation that she was illegitimate, but this is most unlikely. Sara Elgee was highly respectable and Jane inherited the unmistakable large-boned Elgee physique – still evident in the Elgees to this day.

Jane's most likely birthdate is 27 December 1821, which she gave in 1888 when applying for a grant to the Royal Literary Fund. The advantage then in giving her real age, rather than claiming to be five years younger, was that she needed the money and as a relatively elderly woman was more likely to get it. The 1821 birthdate is the one I shall keep to throughout this book.

Enquiries into her date of birth and birthplace were dismissed by Jane as impertinence. When asserting her claim to a share in the estate of Sir Robert McClure, her first cousin and the discoverer of the North-West Passage, she wrote imperiously: 'There is no register of my birth in existence. It was not the fashion then, nor compulsory in Ireland as it is now, but I cannot see why it is required when there is no dispute as to my legitimacy as daughter of Charles Elgee.' She claimed that 'all records, bibles and other documents' had been sent to her brother, who had emigrated to America, and that these documents had then (fortuitously?) 'perished in the fire at New Orleans'.[3]

By giving different birthdates on every possible occasion Jane did her best to muddy the waters. She even convinced herself she was younger by slicing a year or so from her son Oscar's age, congratulating him on winning the Newdigate Prize at Oxford 'when only 22', whereas he was actually nearly 24. Oscar copied his mother's tricks, claiming on his marriage certificate to be two years younger than he was and announcing at his trial that he was 39, when he was six months off 41. He also forgot to register the birth of his second son and then could not recall what day he was born. Sympathetic towards his mother's manipulations, Oscar, in *The Importance of Being Earnest*, accorded Lady Bracknell the remark: 'No woman should ever be quite accurate about her age. It looks so calculating.'

Whether or not Charles had gone to India with Sara's blessing, his death left her under the necessity of raising the three children without his support. Jane was too young to have established any real bond with her father and was never to mention him. She may have agreed with Oscar's comment in *An Ideal Husband*, 'Fathers should neither be seen nor heard. That is the only proper basis for family life.'

Jane's childhood must have been rather solitary, given the large gap in age between her and her brother and sister. In 1823, when her father left for India, Jane was two, her elder brother John was 11, and her elder sister, Emily Thomasine, was 13. Jane had little time to grow close to the two older ones as they soon left home. At 19 Emily married a Captain Samuel Warren, a Lieutenant-Colonel in the 65th Regiment and a member of a leading Dublin mercantile family. His grandfather had been Lord Mayor. John, when a young student at Trinity College in 1829, went to live in rooms in town. He signed the marriage settlement of his sister, Emily Thomasine, that year: 'John Kingsbury Elgee of 33 French Street, Gent, aged 18 years and upwards.' He married a Dublin girl called Matilda Duff shortly after and in 1831 he, his wife and their infant daughter emigrated to Louisiana. He was admitted to the bar there and became a prominent lawyer. Curiously, in his will he left a legacy to his sister Emily Thomasine and to his old nurse, but Jane is not mentioned.

In which precise district of Dublin Jane grew up after her father went to India remains a mystery. In later years, writing to the author John Gilbert about his book, *History of the City of Dublin*, Jane told him how familiar the names of the streets were: 'all those you give in Molesworth Street were my mother's friends – I have heard them all talked of so often.'[4] Her aunt Henrietta's husband, Charles Maturin, died in 1824 and it would have been natural enough for the two widowed sisters and the children to share accommodation.

The sisters undoubtedly got on very well together. According to the preface of a republished novel of Maturin's, to which Jane contributed details, Sara was often at her sister's house when Maturin was alive. Maturin, the first literary figure in Jane Elgee's family, had liked people to be in the room when he was writing, 'especially if they were arguing', and so Henrietta 'and one of her sisters, Mrs Elgy [Elgee] or Lady Ormsby, to both of whom Maturin was much attached', would sit with him. He would paste a wafer over his mouth to stop himself joining in the conversation.[5]

Jane was a bright, alert child. No portraits of her as a child exist but she must have been unusually tall as she ultimately reached nearly six foot in height. Jane's sons were to inherit her towering, Junoesque figure. She also had black hair which, even when elderly, she still wore loose on her shoulders or thickly coiled round her head.

She had the same forcefulness of character her mother had shown in rearing a young family alone. Her strong will became evident in her twenties when she refused to give way to powerful family pressure to change her political views. But she was also a compassionate, generous-spirited girl, with a lack of malice that stayed with her all her life. Her family background gave her an abiding belief in social hierarchy and Oscar shared her love of high society. He once remarked, 'To get into the best society nowadays one has either to feed people, amuse people, or shock people – that is all', and both he and his mother followed his maxim.

Formal education for girls in Ireland was rare, though some attended the few boarding schools that then existed. Jane was taught by tutors and was given an excellent grounding in literature and contemporary European writing. She was particularly stimulated by the classics and she passed on her fervent delight in these to Oscar. She once said, 'I was always very fond of study, and of books. My favourite study was languages. I succeeded in mastering ten of the European languages. Till my eighteenth year I never wrote anything. All my time was given to study.'[6] In later years, she translated books from the French and German and poems from an extraordinary range of languages, including Russian, Norwegian and Spanish. When adult, she taught herself Swedish for pleasure.

A major flaw in her education was her handwriting. She admitted that her writing master 'said I was the only one that he could not teach to write. He was very cross with me.' A future editor of her work complained that 'Her handwriting was still a marvel of unsightliness, which she made painful efforts to amend, without much success.'[7]

Jane's mother would have had no trouble in finding tutors for her daughter. The seaport of Dublin in the 1820s and 1830s was a melting-pot of nationalities. Considered one of the more important capitals of Europe, newcomers were attracted by its thriving, commercial growth. A third the size of London, it was home to some 200,000 people. And when Jane was young, Dublin was pulsing with talent. It was one of the great medical centres of Europe and its doctors and scientists were renowned for their wide interests in art and literature.

The city had grown up haphazardly around an ancient castle which overlooked the low mud banks of the River Liffey. The Gaelic name of the city was *Dubh Linn*, meaning the dark pool: in the Middle Ages most of lower Dublin was covered by the tide. A grey city, built mainly of greyish yellow bricks, its colour came from the Dubliners who gave the city vigour.

Students had flocked to Dublin from the sixteenth century, when Trinity College was founded. Early in the eighteenth century rich traders still lived in the narrow streets of the old city; but then came the great age of Georgian building, when the Wide Streets Commissioners were set up and revolutionized the look of Dublin. The wealthy promptly moved from the narrow streets of the old city to the elegant, newly built Georgian houses set in stately boulevards and magnificent large squares. A traveller in those times said of fashionable Dublin: 'The houses were lofty and elegant . . . the whole possesses an air of dignified retirement – the tranquillity of ease, affluence and leisure.'[8]

Jane would have enjoyed a life of comparative comfort in Dublin while growing up in the 1820s and 1830s, taking gentle exercise in the shaded walks of St Stephen's Green or visiting the elegant shops of Grafton Street. There were lunch parties, tea parties, bazaars in aid of charities, and the military displays at Dublin's pleasure ground, Phoenix Park. Here soldiers with white knee breeches and long black gaiters marched in formation, and galloping cannoneers blazed away right and left. The Vice-Regal Lodge was also in the Park and during the 'Castle season' fashionable society flocked in from country and town to attend the drawing rooms, levees and court presentations held at the Lodge by the Lord Lieutenant, the monarch's representative.

In the evenings there were plays at the two Dublin theatres, as well as concerts and ridottoes. Musical soirees were very popular then, with Italian singers being much in demand. Jane would also have gone to private balls where dragoons swept their partners into decorous quadrilles. The Royal Barracks in Dublin was one of the largest in Europe and its dashing officers were asked everywhere. As Charles Lever wrote in *Jack Hinton the Guardsman*, 'Don't tell me of your insurrection acts, of your nightly outrages, your outbreaks, and your burnings, as a reason for keeping a large military force in Ireland – nothing of the kind. A very different object, indeed, is the reason – Ireland is garrisoned to please the ladies.'[9]

Jane was too young to attend the famous Kildare Street salons of Lady Morgan – author in 1806, under her maiden name Sydney Owenson, of *The Wild Irish Girl*, a novel which romanticized the feudal trappings of rural society. What Jane admired about Lady Morgan was the way she selected her guests. 'When a celebrity arrived

in Dublin whom she was desirous of entertaining, she sent out no formal notes of invitation, but simply stood at her open window in Kildare
Street, just opposite to the fashionable club, watched the passers-by,
beckoned over the suitable atoms, stepped out on the balcony, and
called down the name and the hour . . .'[10] As well as literary guests,
there were radical politicians, singers, dancers and a host of Europeans
attracted by Dublin's thriving growth.

Maturin was a constant visitor to Lady Morgan's salons, sometimes
absent-mindedly turning up in dressing-gown and slippers. Oscar,
on leaving prison, took the pseudonym Sebastian Melmoth from
Maturin's terror-tale, *Melmoth the Wanderer*, published in 1820. Jane
grew up at a time when such Gothic tales were highly popular and later
she herself translated a terror-tale from the German.

Although Maturin was Jane's uncle only by marriage, there were
striking similarities between them. Perhaps, knowing all about his
habits, Jane deliberately copied him. Maturin also came from a respectable family background – his father was an Inspector of Roads for
Ulster – but he opted, as Jane did, for a more romantic pedigree. He
claimed that when an infant, before the French Revolution, he was
found clad in rich clothes in a Paris street, was later thrown into the
Bastille and finally escaped to Ireland.[11]

Both Jane and Maturin preferred to keep the room shutters
closed – which Maturin did to indulge his passion for daytime dancing – and both had an extravagant taste in clothes and a love of
declaiming verse. Once a church dignitary called on Maturin and was
kept waiting until Maturin entered wearing a fantastic dressing-gown,
with his hair stuck all over with quill pens, reciting passages from his
new play.

Politically, Maturin was an ardent nationalist, as Jane was to be. His
writing expressed his regret that the Act of Union in 1800 between
England and Ireland had ever been passed and in *The Wild Irish Boy*
(1808) he deplored how few benefits it had brought.

Other contemporary novels also stirred up nationalist feeling, even
though this caused political difficulties for their authors. In 1806, when
Sydney Owenson wrote *The Wild Irish Girl* on existing social conditions, no Dublin publisher dared touch it. Even the English publisher
Phillips, who finally took it up, had originally written to the author
of the manuscript saying, 'The sentiments enunciated are too strongly
opposed to the English interest in Ireland, and I must withdraw from
my original offer.'[12]

The Irish poet Thomas Moore attacked the English anonymously in 1808 with *Corruption, and Intolerance: Two Poems: Addressed to an Englishman by an Irishman*. His volumes of sentimental *Irish Melodies*, written between 1807 and 1834, also served to remind readers of Ireland's illustrious history. Maria Edgeworth, in 1812, had been one of the first to stigmatize English landlords with her novel, *The Absentee*, and William Carleton, who came from peasant stock in County Tyrone and arrived in Dublin with two shillings and ninepence in his pocket, wrote of the evils of landlordism in *William Reilly* and *Dear Colleen Bawn*, followed later by *Black Prophet*, a bleak tale of the Irish famine. With these, and other novels such as Michael Banim's violent story, *Crohoore of the Billhook*, and *The Croppy*, a dark tale of the uprising of 1798, Jane – an omnivorous reader – would have been presented with the harsh reality of Catholic peasant life.

The growing sense of nationalism, based on these dark events, formed an ominous background to Jane's childhood and youth and ultimately shaped her political consciousness. Although the vast agricultural population of Ireland was almost entirely Catholic, the Protestants were the governing class and no Catholic was allowed by law to hold an official post. Agitation to end this discrimination against Catholics had been led, since 1807, by the formidable, flamboyant Daniel O'Connell – 'King Dan'. He organized and mobilized his Catholic followers and in 1829 succeeded in getting the Emancipation Act passed: Catholic as well as Protestant representatives could now be sent to Westminster.

But the Irish rural problem remained. The peasantry were Catholics: impoverished, poorly educated and oppressed. The ramshackle Irish land system to which they were bound had long been a disaster. Catholics, forbidden to purchase land, were mostly tenants of Protestant landlords. Some of these were recent settlers, others had inherited the land from ancestors who acquired it after the Cromwellian conquest of Ireland. The large landowners were mainly English, preferring to live in their native land but collecting rents from their Irish tenants.

These absentee landlords were a serious grievance. They assiduously demanded rents but cared nothing about developing the land. In order to provide for their families farmers had to subdivide their holdings into smaller and smaller plots. Tenants were not only evicted without notice but also, to their fury, forced to pay tithes – a tax levied on farm produce to support the Established Church which was Protestant. Land rents were often so iniquitous that almost everything grown on the plot had to go in payment. Tenants could barely live on the final scrapings from their tiny potato patches and many ended up as beggars. As William Cobbett wrote of Limerick: 'In one street . . . I saw more misery than any man could have believed existed in the whole world. Men sleeping in the same wisp of dirty straw, or weeds, with their mothers, sisters and aunts; and compelled to do so, or perish; two or three families in one room, that is to say a miserable hole 10 feet by 8 or 9; and husbands, wives, sons, daughters, all huddled together, paying 6*d* or 8*d* or 10*d* a week for *the room*; and the rent paid to a "*nobleman*" in England.'[13]

Anger against the English increased when George IV, on a state visit to Ireland in August 1821, arrived drunk and stayed that way. The following year, when his representative, the Lord Lieutenant, the Marquis of Wellesley, visited the Theatre Royal in Dublin, a quart bottle and a heavy log of timber were flung at him from the upper gallery.

Because of her family's pro-government politics, Jane remained largely unaffected by the conditions in the countryside. Speaking of this she admitted having been 'quite indifferent to the national movement and if I thought about it at all, probably had a bad opinion of its leaders. For my family was Protestant and Conservative and there was no social intercourse between them and the Catholics and Nationalists.'[14]

In the spring of 1840, Daniel O'Connell started his campaign to repeal the 1800 Act of Union with England and restore the Irish parliament. The passionate debate on nationalism sparked off by his oratory at vast, so-called 'Monster Meetings' attracted idealistic young men from the Protestant as well as Catholic middle class. This group thrust the repeal issue into the forefront of Irish thought by creating the Young Ireland movement – a movement which was to rock Jane out of her cushioned ignorance. Known as the Young Irelanders, this group like O'Connell wanted to dissolve the union with England; but unlike him many were willing to use violence to achieve their ends.

The inspiration behind the movement was Thomas Davis, a Protestant barrister and poet. Davis, a highly cultivated young man with a cheerful nature and a sanguine philosophy, had a magnetic quality of leadership that attracted others to his cause. His father was Welsh and his mother Anglo-Irish, which made him, he said, a 'real Irishman', and he wanted above all to break down religious differences and create a

higher sense of nationalism in a united Ireland. To do this, he set out
to show his countrymen that it was England who was guilty of destroy-
ing Ireland's peace.

Davis had two close colleagues. One was Charles Gavan Duffy, a
modest man but a liberal and capable Catholic journalist and poet, who
had a great admiration for Davis. The other was John Blake Dillon,
a Catholic barrister and impassioned orator who resembled, Jane later
said, 'a magnificent Spanish Hidalgo, with his dark eyes and raven
hair'.[15] Dillon had helped Davis transform the dull Dublin daily
paper, the *Morning Register*, a paper originally deferential to the
British authorities, into one that burned with impatience at the status
quo.

In 1842, the three young men, all under thirty, strolled along to
Phoenix Park and sat under a 'noble tree' to discuss Duffy's latest
scheme, 'the establishment of a weekly newspaper which we three
should own and write'. Unknown to Jane, it was to bring her nation-
wide fame.[16] The three men decided to call the paper the *Nation*.
Duffy would finance it and be its editor, while Davis, with his passionate but impersonal patriotism, was elected chief writer. One of his
colleagues said of him, 'Much of his verse [was] mere rhymed journalism, but his depth of thought and his passionate love of Ireland gave
to some of his work the quality of real poetry.'[17]

The first number of the *Nation*, published on 15 October 1842, was
a sell-out before noon: newspapermen even broke the window of the
office in their eagerness to get more copies. In the first year its average
circulation was 10,730 a week, far more than any other national paper,
and its country-wide readership was estimated as a quarter of a million.
Duffy remembered the way banks of listeners would sit around forge
fires or in chapel yards on Sundays: 'Old men still describe the fever
with which they waited for its weekly issue and the delight with which
they lingered over it.'[18] Such enthusiastic scenes were the subject of a
painting by H. McManus, called *Reading 'The Nation'*, now in the
National Gallery of Ireland. Jane's future work in the paper became
known in this way throughout the country.

In the mid-1840s, the *Nation* was preoccupied by the desperate state
of rural Ireland. It gave out a weekly barrage of savage information
about conditions there. In the south and west of Ireland, in particular,
there was appalling unemployment and poverty. Starving families lay
on the floors of their cabins 'for the hunger', as their bodies needed
less food that way. Unripe potatoes were desperately torn up by the

tenants from their pathetic patches of ground in the summer, despite the prospect of facing the winter both famished and freezing. Hungry men working on the roads would sit down exhausted by the ditches at lunch break, having no food to eat.

The potato blight, responsible for the widespread failure of the potato crop and the great famine it caused, first showed up in 1845 as black spots and a white mould on the leaves of the plant. This fungus did not die off but lay dormant each winter, reviving year after year to infect new potato plants. Between 1845 and 1851 some 800,000 people died – about a tenth of the entire population. Dead bodies rotted where they fell, without prayer or mourning, or were thrown into an adjoining ditch to be eaten by starving dogs. The poorhouses contained spectral troops of men and women, who would soon join the others in the poorhouse hospitals. Destitute, weak from hunger and susceptible to disease, many died from typhus, cholera, dysentery, influenza and fever. Typhus, spread by lice, ravaged the workhouses and hospitals. Even the middle and upper class succumbed, catching the disease from the starving poor when, in desperation, they came to the towns seeking food.

There was none to find. Jane may have known little, except through her reading, of conditions in the countryside, but poverty was on her own Dublin doorstep. Right behind the elegant façade of Georgian houses were the slums – broken down, shabby houses, with windows patched with paper, full of the ragged and hungry. The alleyways were festooned with clotheslines and the poor huddled over their tiny potato patches almost within hearing distance of the fishmongers' cries of 'Dublin Bay herrings' on the quays of the Liffey. Beggars sat or lay on the Dublin pavements: the famished were everywhere. It was all too common to go for a walk and come across a starved family, all dead. Sights like this were no exception: anger became explosive, something had to be done.

In 1843, Sara Elgee reappears in the Dublin street directory as the tenant of 34 Leeson Street. The house was over a tallow chandler's shop. Leeson Street was on the south side of St Stephen's Green, a quiet, respectable part of town. Jane, now 22 years old, was still living with her mother. It was a tranquil household and Jane claimed that her awakening to current events happened almost by accident: 'One day, a volume of *Ireland's Library* issued from the *Nation* office by Mr Duffy happened to come in my way. I read it eagerly and my patriotism was kindled.'[19] The *Ireland's Library* volumes were on the lives of dead patriots: it is more likely that Jane was inspired by a collection of the *Nation*'s poetry, published in 1843 and called *The Spirit of the Nation*.

In a speech he made in Dublin on the centenary of Thomas Davis's birth, W. B. Yeats gave a different account of Jane's conversion, saying that it was Davis's early death from scarlet fever in 1845, when only 30, that roused Jane's interest in politics. According to Yeats, Jane had told him:

Once when she was a young girl and walking through some Dublin street, she came upon so great a crowd that she could go no further. She waited in a shop that it might pass, but it seemed unending. She asked a shopman what brought so many people into the streets and he said, 'It is the funeral of Thomas Davis.' And when she answered, 'Who was Thomas Davis, I have never heard of him?' he said, 'He was a poet.' She was so struck to find so many people honouring a poet and one she had never heard of, that she turned Nationalist and wrote those energetic rhymes my generation read in its youth.[20]

Oscar himself described his mother's political awakening in slightly different terms. In San Francisco during his lecture tour of America, he was asked by the Irish community to talk about the stars of the Young Ireland movement. Referring to his mother, he said:

The other poetess of this movement was a young girl who had been brought up in an atmosphere of alien English thought, among people high in Bench and Senate and far removed from any love or knowledge of those wrongs of the people to which she afterwards gave such passionate expression. But one day in 1845, standing at the window of her lordly home, she saw a great funeral pass in its solemn trappings of sorrow down the street and followed by crowd after crowd of men and women in bitter and unrestrained grief. Wondering much what man had died whom the people so loved, she asked who it was they were burying and learned it was the funeral of one Thomas Davis, a poet of whom till then she had never heard. That evening she bought and read his poems and knew for the first time the meaning of the word country.[21]

It is surprising that Jane should have remained unaware of such a public figure as Thomas Davis - even if her family's politics were opposed to his. But she had a sharp, receptive mind and was now quick to study his essays, philosophy and verse. One of his constant themes was the need for reconciliation between Protestant and Catholic, to avoid England taking advantage of the split. His poem 'The Orange and Green Will Carry the Day' began:

> English deceit can rule us no more;
> Bigots and knaves are scattered like spray –
> Deep was the oath the Orangemen swore,
> 'Orange and Green must carry the day!'

Davis also tried to inject his countrymen with pride in Ireland's past by writing about heroic and historical happenings. His hostility towards the landlords, another theme, came out strongly in ballads like 'A Scene in the South':

> 'God of justice!' I sighed, 'send your spirit down
> On these lords so cruel and so proud,
> And soften their hearts and relax their frown,
> Or else,' I cried aloud –
> 'Vouchsafe thy strength to the peasant's hand
> To drive them at length from off the land!'

Jane's sense of injustice was fired by Thomas Davis and the Young Irelanders of the *Nation*. She found Davis's verse 'a tocsin of revolution', and said of the contributor Denis Florence McCarthy that 'he wrote patriot verse that clashed like cymbals.'

Nationalism in those times was no idealistic fancy, but forged by coruscating anger. It aroused in Jane a passionate dedication to all things Irish, causing her to pursue a deep interest in Gaelic history, legends and folklore, and for the rest of her life she retained a deep pride in being Irish.

The *Nation*, edited by Charles Duffy, was currently attracting a host of new poets and writers. Their passionate views not only radicalized Jane's political thinking but gave her the incentive to express her own views. As she herself said: 'Since I had caught the National spirit, all the literature of Irish wrongs and sufferings had an enthralling interest for me; then it was that I discovered I could write poetry.'[22]

At 24, Jane was a confident young woman. Still unwed, in an era when girls married young, she was not the type to sit and sew samplers:

her intellect, chafing under small-talk, needed a challenge. Once she started to write verse she was anxious to have it published and the *Nation* was clearly a natural home for her work. In 1846, courageously rejecting her family's pro-government politics, she put her fiery thoughts into her poetry and wholeheartedly took up the *Nation*'s battle-cry.

2

Speranza of the Nation

WHEN JANE FIRST sent her verse in to the editor of the *Nation*, she signed it 'Speranza', the Italian for 'Hope'. With her mythical Italian ancestry in mind, she liked to foster the Italian connection and later had the motto 'Fidanza, Speranza, Constanza' (Faith, Hope, Constancy) engraved on her writing paper.

Her covering letter, enclosing the verse, was signed under the name of 'John Fanshawe Ellis'. When she began to write prose as well as verse for the *Nation*, she continued to write under this pseudonym. She would sometimes write anonymously, too, or sign her articles with the letter 'A' or 'Albanus'. Her family, arch-Protestant and pro-English rule, would have been shocked at her writing for a journal which attacked all their beliefs. As Jane explained: 'In sending my verses to the editor of the *Nation*, I dared not have my name published so I signed them Speranza and my [covering] letters John Fanshawe Ellis instead of Jane Francesca Elgee.'[1]

Jane's first poem for the *Nation*, signed 'Speranza', was published on 21 February 1846. It was a cautious venture into print, being a translation of a German poem, 'The Holy War', which called for a hero to lead the people who were now 'rising in pride'.

Despite her double disguising of her name, it proved impossible to hide her activities from her family. 'One day my uncle came into my room,' she said, 'and found the *Nation* on my table. Then he accused me of contributing to it, declaring the while that such a seditious paper was fit only for the fire.'[2] The uncle Jane refers to must have been one of her father's three brothers – possibly Captain John Elgee, who was paymaster of the 67th Regiment; or William Elgee, a Major in the Artillery, who was to die three years later; or the Revd Richard Waddy Elgee, Rector of Wexford. Both her uncles by marriage on her mother's side (Sir Charles Montagu Ormsby, the husband of Jane's aunt Elizabeth, and Charles Maturin, her aunt Henrietta's husband) were already dead.

The editor of the *Nation*, Charles Gavan Duffy, had made several attempts to meet the author of the verse he had been receiving, putting in a request to see Speranza in the 'Answers to Correspondents' section of the paper. And as Jane masked her identity by enclosing Speranza's verse with covering letters signed 'John Fanshawe Ellis', Duffy naturally expected to meet a man. 'Each time "Mr Ellis,"' said Jane, 'had to excuse himself from doing so.' Now she felt at last she could meet him. As she said, 'The secret being out in my own family, there was no longer much motive for concealment and I gave my editor permission to call upon me.'[3]

In his memoirs, written some forty years after the event and with some inevitable errors of memory, Duffy recalled this first meeting, probably some time in the late summer of 1846:

[Speranza's] virile and sonorous songs broke on the public ear like the plash in later times of a great wave of thought in one of Swinburne's metres . . . I was greatly struck by the first contribution, and requested Mr John Fenshaw [*sic*] Ellis to call at the *Nation* office. Mr Ellis pleaded that there were difficulties which rendered this course impracticable, and invited me to visit him in Leeson Street. I did so immediately, not without a secret suspicion of the transformation I was about to witness.

A smiling parlour-maid, when I inquired for Mr Ellis, showed me into a drawing-room, where I found only Mr George Smith, publisher to the University. 'What!' I cried; 'my loyal friend, are you the new volcano of sedition?' Mr Smith only answered by vanishing into a back drawing-room and returning with a tall girl on his arm, whose stately carriage and figure, flashing brown eyes and features cast in an heroic mould, seemed fit for the genius of poetry, or the spirit of revolution. He presented me to Miss Jane Francesca Elgee, in lieu of Mr John Fenshaw Ellis. Miss Elgee . . . had probably heard nothing of Irish nationality among her ordinary associates, but as the strong and generous are apt to do, had worked out convictions for herself.[4]

Most of Jane's best-known poetry was written in the two years
between 1846 and 1848. Her verse reacted to events and hammered home
the misery of the people at that time. As the *Dublin Review* rightly said,
her poems needed to be read as a running commentary on the history
of the tragic years before, during and after the famine: '[Her] gloomy
series of images recalls to us the awful state of the country – the corpses
that were buried without coffins, and the men and women that walked
the roads more like corpses than living creatures, spectres and skeletons
at once; the little children out of whose sunken eyes the very tears were
dried, and over whose bare little bones the hideous fur of famine had
begun to grow; the cholera cart, with its load of helpless huddled
humanity, on its way to the hospital; the emigrant ship sending back its
woeful wail of farewell from swarming poop to stern in the offing; and,
far as the eye could search the land, the blackened potato-fields, filling
all the air with the fetid odours of decay.'[5]

Critics, summing up Jane's work in later years, derisively called her
a 'mere versifier' and mocked her melodramatic style. Reading a paper
to the Royal Society of Literature in 1895, a member said her poems
were 'especially marred by the intense strain she subjected herself to,
which prevents her ever approaching naturalness'.[6] But her critics
failed to appreciate the tempestuous emotions in Ireland at the time of
the famine or that Jane had chosen a deliberately heroic mould for her
poetry. They have also not compared her verse with other contemporary work, which was equally impassioned.

Jane's gift was that of being able to write popular verse and prose
with which her readers deeply identified. She was above all the people's
poet. Although writing from her drawing room in Leeson Street, she
intuitively and powerfully tapped into the feelings and reactions of
those suffering appalling privation. As the *Irish Fireside* said, whether
she was writing prose or poetry, her language 'in its passionate ardour,
in the advocacy of liberty, in denunciation of tyranny, rose to the
majesty of Demosthenic eloquence'.[7] In her poem, 'The Voice of the
Poor', Jane spoke out for the starving:

> Before us die our brothers of starvation:
>   Around are cries of famine and despair.
> Where is hope for us, or comfort, or salvation –
>   Where – oh! where?
> If the angels ever hearken, downward bending,
>   They are weeping, we are sure,

> At the litanies of human groans ascending
> From the crushed hearts of the poor.

Her 'A Lament for the Potato', taken from the Gaelic of 1739, showed equal compassion. It began:

> There is woe, there is clamour, in our desolated land,
> And wailing lamentation from a famine-stricken band;
> And weeping are the multitudes in sorrow and despair,
> For the green fields of Munster lying desolate and bare.

Many wrote to thank her for writing as she did. One man, a John MacCorry, told her, 'From early boyhood I have learned to revere your Queenly poetic name and read your songs and burning Lays of Ireland . . .'[8]

After Thomas Davis's death in 1845, Charles Duffy had asked the Ulster Protestant John Mitchel, one of the firebrands of the Young Ireland party and previously a country lawyer, 'to undertake the chief editorial conduct' of the *Nation*. This gave him the task of writing leaders and nearly all the political articles in the paper, though Duffy himself remained editor. Mitchel was a handsome man with dark hair and moustache, strong features and a dynamic personality. A rebel by instinct rather than reason, he was the most radical of the Young Irelanders. Watching his countrymen starve in conditions of misery created in him a volcanic hatred and he used the *Nation* to stir up rebellion.

Committed to revolution, the paper under his guidance began vociferously and angrily to hold England responsible for all Ireland's ills. Mitchel admitted that 'a kind of sacred wrath' took possession of a few Irishmen at this point. Unable to endure matters any longer, they decided to attack the British 'car of conquest, though it should crush them to atoms'. Youngsters attracted to the Young Irelander cause by his vehement arguments joined the Mitchel Clubs, named after him.

His heated articles aggravated the *Nation*'s already hostile attitude towards England. One article on 'English Rule', a couple of weeks after Jane's first poem in 1846, typifies the constant barrage levelled against the English: 'The Irish people [know] that "hungry ruin has them in the wind" – and they ascribe it, *unanimously*, not so much to the wrath of Heaven as to the greedy and cruel policy of England . . . their starving children cannot sit down to their scanty meal but they see the harpy-claw of *England* in their dish . . ."[9]

Writing about Mitchel to a friend, Jane recalled the leaders of the French Revolution – she later translated a book on the subject – and confessed that on meeting him, her first impression 'was a shrinking as if I could not bear to touch his hand; his face is handsome but the expression the most sinister I ever beheld – the cold metallic blue eye of Robespierre was drawn for him – the man has nothing noble in him, he was ambitious from envy of those above him – he would assuredly have had a Reign of Terror in Dublin had he succeeded to power.'[10]

Nevertheless, she was quick to respond to the increasingly agitated mood. Even though she initially considered that 'There is an earnestness almost amounting to fanaticism in the Patriotism of all the Young Ireland Party', as so often with those who have been converted, she later became more militant than the militants.

In May 1846 the *Nation* published the famous patriotic poem 'My Dark Rosaleen' by Clarence Mangan, in which he pictured Ireland as a sorrowful woman. James Joyce was to say of Mangan that he 'sums up in himself the soul of a country and an era'. Jane could consider herself highly praised by the *Nation* when, in the summer of 1846, it commented on one of her poems: 'Our new contributor promises to rival Mangan in the melody and fullness of his verse.'

Most of Jane's work for the *Nation* in 1846 consisted of translations of verse from German, Spanish and Portuguese. The poetry she chose came from different centuries, but almost all expressed nationalistic sentiments or urged nations on to war against an oppressor. But in the 5 December issue of that year Jane wrote 'The Lament', a criticism of Daniel O'Connell for his lack of leadership and his weakness in dealings with the Whig administrations. It began in swinging style, 'Gone from us – dead to us – he whom we worshipped', and continued scornfully, 'Hush! 'tis the Sassenach ally you greet.'

The famine in Ireland was worsened by the scarcity of corn. Every country in Europe menaced by the potato blight had forbidden the export of corn and had also established public granaries. The Irish harvest of 1846 had been one of the best ever, but instead of giving it to the starving, the landlords reacted greedily by exporting to London and Liverpool in the November of that year more grain than ever before over a similar period. John Mitchel wrote in outrage in the *Nation* about the 'greedy and cruel policy of England . . . with every grain of that corn there goes a heavy curse.'

Jane, too, wrote one of her angriest poems, 'The Stricken Land', later reprinted as 'The Famine Year'. Published in the issue of 21 January 1847, it attacked the injustice of the English in taking the corn:

Weary men, what reap ye? – Golden corn for the stranger.
What sow ye? – Human corses that wait for the avenger.
Fainting forms, hunger-stricken, what see you in the offing?
Stately ships to bear our food away, amid the stranger's scoffing.

The last two lines of the poem ended:

A ghastly, spectral army, before the great God we'll stand,
And arraign ye as our murderers, the spoilers of our land.

Jane might equal Mitchel's passion, but she admired the editor, Charles Duffy, for being 'the calm philosopher of the party and the best Poet. He has the most cultivated mind I know of in Dublin and Patriotism with him has the elevation of religion.'[11] She wrote to him on many occasions and he found 'her little scented notes, sealed with wax of a delicate hue and dainty device, represented a substantial force in Irish politics, the vehement will of a woman of genius'.[12]

Scented notes and vehemence are uneasy partners, and Jane's letters were an odd mix of teasing, archness and forthright views. She admired Duffy and the style of her letters might have been an attempt to intrigue her new editor. Preoccupied with her writing, Jane sought his approval and Duffy assured her that she had 'never written anything wanting vitality'. He later recalled his embarrassment when John Mitchel, whom Duffy regarded as being an imperfect judge of poetry, disliked one of Jane's poems and put a message in the paper's 'Answers to Correspondents' on 27 June 1846 to that effect, telling her: 'against such erotics we are hard as quartz.'[13] Believing this comment was from Duffy, Jane wrote to him saying: 'My Lord Critic, I enclose a pretty trifle from my favourite poet, illuminate your paper, or your Cigar with it, which you please. If you don't like my Erotics perhaps you are right. We are more at home in a War song . . . I'm not angry, only revengeful, therefore I shall instantly set about inventing another for next week – this will be excellent practice for me and embitter your existence by making you read it . . .'

Jane took the opportunity to make a side-swipe at Mangan, asking why one of his poems, 'The Stricken Brothers', was no more than 'a rechauffé from old University Magazines' and if his brain was exhausted. This was youthful arrogance on Jane's part, given that Mangan was the *Nation*'s chief poet. She ended, 'Yours as ever with profound respect, John Fanshawe Ellis, under which appellation please publish me.'[14]

Duffy lent Jane the first volume of Thomas Carlyle's biography of Cromwell, along with the revised 1845 version of the poet Philip James Bailey's 40,000-line narrative verse, *Festus*, which was based on the Faust legend. The first edition was a favourite of Tennyson and the Pre-Raphaelites and Jane loved it, writing to Duffy to say, '*Festus* is superb – lofty as heaven and deep as inspiration. I read two scenes to-day that, as the French say, made me grow pale with wonder. I complained of his metrical faults, but in the "Festival" scene the measure dances like Bacchantes.'[15] In later years she wrote a long essay about Bailey's *Festus*, calling it 'less a drama than one long monologue of the author's soul'.

In another letter to Duffy from Leeson Street, she returned the volume of Cromwell, 'which has been travelling about with me for the last four months', and asked him for the remaining two, 'though not even Carlyle can make the soulless iconoclast interesting. It is the only work of Carlyle's I have met with in which my heart does not go along with his words.' She continued flatteringly:

> I cannot forbear telling you, now the pen is in my hand, how deeply impressed I felt by your opening lecture to your club. It was the sublimest teaching, and the style so simple from its very sublimity – it seemed as if Truth passed directly from your heart to ours without the aid of any medium – at least, I felt that everywhere the *thoughts* struck you, nowhere the *words*, and this, in my opinion, is the perfection of composition. It is soul speaking to soul. I never felt the *dignity* of your cause so much as then – to promote it in any way seemed an object that would ennoble a life. Truly, one cannot despair when God sends us such teachers.

She then laughingly admitted he would wish her away for another four months if she wrote such long notes, though added a postscript to say that she had only read his lecture and that some time 'I would like to *hear* you'.[16]

As the famine tightened its grip, the choice for many in 1847 lay between death and emigration. The pages of the *Nation* chronicled the deaths from starvation in different counties, as well as the number of Irish who had left that week for America. In 1847, 60,000 arrived in New York alone. Almost all rural areas of Ireland lost half their population: and it was the young men who went. Between 1850 and 1887, about 66 per cent of the emigrants were aged between 15 and 35. Many never arrived. In one year, out of 100,000 Irishmen who fled to Canada, 6,100 perished on the voyage, 4,100 on arrival, another 5,200 in the hospitals and a final 1,900 in the towns they went to. The Emigrant Society of Montreal reported that: 'from wherever the tide of emigration has extended, are to be found one unbroken chain of graves, where repose fathers and mothers, sisters and brothers, in a commingled heap, no stone marking the spot. Twenty thousand and upwards have gone down to their graves!'

Jane was at her best when writing verse on emotional themes such as the waste of young men through death and forced emigration. She took up this subject in her poem 'The Exodus':

> A million a decade! – of human wrecks,
>   Corpses lying in fever sheds –
> Corpses huddled on foundering decks,
>   And shroudless dead on their rocky beds;
>   Nerve and muscle, and heart and brain,
>   Lost to Ireland – lost in vain.

The magazine *Irish Readings* stirred up readers further by reporting that the English press 'rejoiced over the process of depletion: they prophesied that in a few years Catholic Irishmen would be as rare in Munster or Connaught as Red Indians on the plains of Manhattan.'[17]

Many of the Irish depended for their lives on the money sent back to them from family members who had emigrated to America. The amount was substantial. A letter to the *Dublin Evening Post* from New York in 1847 revealed that over one million dollars was sent to Ireland in 1846 in small drafts by Irish labourers and servants from the cities of New York, Philadelphia and Baltimore. 'The *heart* of the poor Irishman does not change by expatriation,' said the letter, '. . . the very first use he makes of his surplus wages is to assist those loved ones whom he left behind.'

Jane believed the Irish should emigrate to the New World – though by choice rather than as an enforced escape from starvation. She kept

her views. Writing nearly forty years later, in 1882, she argued that
Australia had an immense amount to offer: 'There is room for all
classes and many Irelands, and no one need stand on the dead to clutch
at rent-rolls . . . The poor Irish settler who now treads his dreary round
of life in the furrows of his scanty potato-field would there find tracts
of the finest land . . . while all the political dreams would be actually
realized that in Ireland seem now but the vain hope of despairing men;
land without the incubus of a landlord; a true Republic . . .' The same
article called on the Irish to compare the wealthier condition of the
emigrants with those left at home 'working like convicts on the daily
treadmill, joyless and hopeless, till they drop from exhaustion into
the grave; others, strong and stalwart men, standing idle in the
market-place because no one has hired them . . .'[18]

During 1847 Jane was writing verse several times a month. The
historian John Gilbert pointed out that it was all credit to her 'that
she worked persistently and disinterestedly for the *Nation* without
receiving that remuneration which was her due'.[19] Along with her
three other women poets also worked regularly for the paper: Eva
(Mary Anne Kelly), Mary (Ellen Mary Patrick Downing) and
Thomasine (Thomasine Olivia Knight). Like Jane, they wrote in the
intense, defiant style favoured by the *Nation*, as a stanza from Eva's
poem, 'The People's Chief', shows:

Come forth, come forth, O Man of men! to the cry of the gathering
    nations;
We watch on tow'r, we watch on the hill, pouring our invocations –
Our souls are sick of sounds and shades, that mock our shame
    and grief,
We hurl the Dagons from their seats, and call the lawful Chief!

Despite these militant sentiments, Duffy called Eva's verse 'pensive
and sympathetic', Thomasine's verse 'thoughtful', and Mary's verse
'as passionate, spontaneous, and native as anything in the circle of
song'. But he agreed with A. M. Sullivan, a later editor of the *Nation*,
that Speranza 'was incomparably the most brilliant of the galaxy'.[20]

Jane's poems ring with exhortations like 'Liberty! Truth! Vengeance!
Freedom!' and 'Oh Courage!' They were in the heroic mould of poetry,
like Byron's 'Oh Rome! my country! city of the soul!' She liked slipping
in biblical, classical and mythological references, would write of
Ierne's harp, call on Cassandra, fling in Latin tags or bring a line of

poetry to an abrupt halt by a phrase like 'phylacteries of misery' or 'mystic-eyed Hierophant'. She was experimenting with verse, in love with language, and it was an exhilarating time for her.

Her work is best read aloud, in the old oral tradition, as happened throughout the country in those days. One contemporary, who praised Jane's verse for being 'full of ardour, trumpet-calls to action, not feminine wailings for the past', remembered her verses being taken up by the street ballad singers.[21] A likely candidate for this honour would have been Jane's poem, 'The Brothers', published in March 1847. It was based on a true story of a trial and execution in the 1798 rebellion, which was long remembered in Irish history. One verse alone shows the powerful content:

> All eyes an earnest watch on them are keeping,
>   Some, sobbing, turn away,
> And the strongest men can hardly see for weeping,
>   So noble and so loved were they.
> Their hands are locked together, those young brothers –
>   As before the judge they stand –
> They feel not the deep grief that moves the others
>   For they die for Fatherland.

Fifty-one years later, Oscar was to write *The Ballad of Reading Gaol*, another tale of a prisoner about to die which had a certain echo of Jane's verse:

> Or else he sat with those who watched
>   His anguish night and day;
> Who watched him when he rose to weep,
>   And when he crouched to pray;
> Who watched him lest himself should rob
>   Their scaffold of its prey.

An established contributor to the *Nation* by 1847, Jane had become very much involved with the Young Ireland group, thriving on their admiration and remaining friendly with many of them for years. They were intelligent men of character, a stimulating change from her previously restricted life. 'They are all poets,' she wrote once, 'and I

know of no genius outside their circle in Ireland.'[22] Charles Duffy
recalled the weekly supper given at the *Nation* and the immense number
of breakfasts, dinners, dances and excursions there were held at that
time, despite the grave political situation: 'There was much wooing and
some marrying in that day,' he said.[23]

Politics and passion are a heady mix and Jane did indeed particularly
admire one of the patriots, Thomas Meagher. She described him as
being 'handsome, daring, reckless of consequences, wild, bright,
flashing eyes, glowing colour and the most beautiful mouth, teeth and
smile I ever beheld'.[24] Her poem written in 1847 and called 'The
Young Patriot Leader' was based on Meagher and in it she refers to
the way 'a noble madness falls on each spirit he enthralls'. The Young
Irelanders also attracted a number of other eminent men who sympathized with the cause, though they did not wish to be politically
involved. Jane would have met them all. Dublin social circles were
relatively small and in one of her letters she said, in a lordly way, 'I
am acquainted with all the people worth knowing in Dublin.'

Jane's preoccupation with the Young Irelanders and her anti-English
stance horrified and embarrassed her Protestant relatives. Once her
uncle had revealed that she was writing for the *Nation*, the family on
both sides had watched with alarm as her writing became increasingly
militant. They must have worried that Jane would cement her political
change of heart by actually marrying a Young Irelander. None of them
could exert any influence over her and doubtless blamed her mother
for not controlling her.

Jane's brother-in-law, Captain Warren, wrote to his wife Emily from
England, sending his regards to his mother-in-law and to 'the Rebel,
and desire her not to be putting any disloyal thoughts into my
daughter's noddle'. In an attempt to remove Jane from Ireland
altogether he added a hopeful postscript, saying, 'I think your mother
and Jane had better pack up and come over here and let us all live
together.'[25]

On 29 May 1847, the *Nation* appeared with black borders in response
to the death of O'Connell: Jane was later to write a memorial poem
praising him ('His great heart burning still with patriot fire / Tho'
Death's pale shadow rested on his brow'). In the countryside the famine
tightened its stranglehold. There were famine riots in June and the
Nation reported the police taking possession of stores and mills to protect them against attacks from the peasantry. The Young Irelanders
were divided over whether or not to advocate militant action.

In December of that year, John Mitchel, more revolutionary than ever, urged the peasantry through the *Nation* to defy the government, to hold on to the food they grew, and start arming themselves. Duffy at once stopped him from using the paper to put forward his views. 'He greatly injured the cause,' Jane was to say of Mitchel, 'and all the noble minds of the confederation are glad he is silenced though they regret the manner of doing so.'[26]

Although most of the Young Irelanders backed away from the use of force, the issue caused a split. William Smith O'Brien, the Young Irelanders' political leader, called for a resolution committing Young Ireland to constitutional action. Mitchel, though claiming that he was not advocating force – merely not ruling it out – left the *Nation* shortly after to form his own paper, the *United Irishman*, where he could thunder out his views unhindered. He had a decided following and sales of the revolutionary paper leapt up, though the *Nation* still retained its high circulation.

December 1847 also saw the beginning of a correspondence amounting to some fifty letters written by Jane over fifteen years to an unknown Scotsman. She had been away from Ireland for several months that year, and as she refers in these letters to having met this man and his friends in Scotland, it is likely they met at this time. She claimed to feel a strong 'mystic' affinity with the Scots – naturally enough, with their shared Celtic ancestry. These letters, a mixture of intimate detail and spirited discussion – mostly on literary and political topics – reveal Jane as an intelligent, liberated woman. Only occasional clues surface about the man to whom she was writing. Apparently he wrote reviews under the pseudonym of 'Gurth' and worked in a 'counting house', which may have been a bank, or some kind of office.

Jane must have felt more than a mere liking for her Scotsman, as she admits: 'I don't care for a friendship unless fringed with – not quite love perhaps – but something that is always on the point of becoming so.' In an early letter, she writes of his 'clear open brow' and 'disdainful mouth' noticed in 'that only half hour I ever beheld you'. She chides him on one occasion for being so forgetful as to tell a friend she was fair ('why, I am dark as Sappho'), always sends her regards to his 'gentle mother', and once, after a long silence, said, 'Do for Heaven's sake write on the back of an invoice – on a receipt – anything rather than your shrouding yourself like a Hindoo Deity in this vast formless silence . . .'[27] No replies from this unknown deity have survived.

Her first letter, dated 13 December and addressed to 'My Eloquent Friend', is given up to a discussion of writers. Immensely well read, Jane let loose her opinion on a wide spectrum of writers. 'I see your Gods are my Gods. His [Tennyson's] *Locksley Hall* is my greatest favourite of all his poems – of all modern living poets Tennyson and Elizabeth Barrett hold the first place in my affection, leaving, of course, the great God Wordsworth undisturbed on his throne.'

She warned him against too much worship of Carlyle and Emerson, whose doctrines she believed were dangerous to the ignorant masses: 'Infidelity in Religion, Democracy in Politics – to this England is fast hastening; now they labour to destroy all reverence for symbols such as rank, station, etc.' Jane may have been writing revolutionary poetry, but she was no republican and believed firmly in the established social hierarchy. Some of the ideas of proletarian revolution that were currently sweeping Europe were in decided conflict with her views.

Fascinated, as well as gifted, with languages, Jane enjoyed translating verse as well as composing it. However, she told her Scots friend that she was finding it difficult to progress with her language studies: 'Books cannot be had. I have been trying in London and Paris for three years for some Russian books and cannot procure them.' Even without them she managed to translate for publication in the *Nation* a Russian poem called 'The Waiwode', about a Russian slave killing his master.

Jane was also corresponding with William Carleton, whom she was to call her greatest friend. Carleton was author of many stories about the Irish peasantry and the poet W. B. Yeats was to say that modern Irish literature began with him. Carleton, always convinced his fellow Irishmen treated him badly, plunged into periodic fits of depression. Jane told him briskly he had no real cause for this: 'It is distressing in the extreme to see a mind like yours deliberately killing itself by conjuring up imaginary gloom . . . one could live like a prince on £200 a year so try to dissipate the gloom by amusement, change of scene; go to Paris for two or three weeks . . . here I am, this blessed midnight, absolutely writing a sermon to you . . . well, do not let me preach in vain.'

She went on, with a nice sense of irony, 'Let St Speranza, if you will admit my canonization, work the miracle of your restoration . . . I am glad you met my cousin, for no doubt you testified to my merits with some of your emphatic adjectives, and the extreme eminence I shall attain in their opinions in consequence will be truly flattering to my vanity – but have I vanity? I don't know, only the praise of some people is certainly very charming to my ears.'[28] Jane had a number of cousins: and the one referred to could have been Robert McClure, son of her father's sister Jane, or possibly the Revd William Maturin, the son of Charles Maturin and Henrietta.

Carleton at the time was writing weekly to Jane and she told her Scots friend, 'My greatest friend is now Carleton the author, he is the most excitable, passionate, poetical enthusiast you can imagine': she enclosed some of his letters to prove her point. However, the Scotsman disliked their impassioned contents, and told her so. Perhaps he was jealous, considering Carleton an unwanted third in his paper relationship with Jane. She wrote pages back to him in defence of Carleton, saying that he was 50, married and with a grown-up family, and was being misjudged:

> I do not attach the meaning to his phrases which you see in them . . . a poetical passionate Nature will call simple admiration by some extravagant hyperbole . . . but tho' I do not believe that a thought of me ever interferes with Carleton's domestic affections, I can well understand the kind of feeling he entertains towards me . . . all his love as a man is given to his wife, but then no one has been the partner of his higher nature . . . if then he finds an exalted, perhaps an extravagant pleasure, in the acquaintance of one who can sympathize with that diviner nature and appreciate that genius, am I to cloud this faint ray of light in his already too dark existence? . . . the difference of our social position will indeed prevent my name ever being associated with his, as you fear . . . No – no – people may say he worships me if they choose, a woman cannot help that, but they will never dream of adding anything further . . .'[29]

This was true. Jane's rather intense friendships with literary men were usually confined to letter-writing; there was never a breath of scandal. She accepted their homage as her intellectual due and in turn admired their intelligence and ability. Her sense of morality was strong, and not being a woman with a strong sexual nature she felt little temptation to stray. Although not cold, her emotions were directed to her work and her literary connections. Men appreciated her liveliness and knowledge and were quick to realize that she appreciated compliments directed at her intellectual accomplishments rather than her feminine attributes.

Another lengthy and undated letter of hers to Carleton was in reply to his suggestion that there be a woman's page in the *Nation*. Jane was vehemently against this, her arguments sharply similar to those of many women today. 'If a page of the *Nation* were devoted to feminine contributions,' she said, 'it probably would be the only page left unread. If women teach or preach politics, they should do so unasked to produce any effect . . . If indeed any are so gifted the columns of the *Nation* are open to them now . . .'

Jane also pointed out that Irishwomen 'are nationally the lowest in Europe as regards patriotism', and if the *Nation* as a whole had failed to kindle 'this divine flame', then a single page would be unlikely to do so. 'I could never consent to any portion of the *Nation* becoming "A Lady's Newspaper", though I highly approve of all Ladies who have the ability [to] disseminate their views through its columns.' Few women it seemed, in Jane's view, qualified. Although she liked the idea of editing a literary weekly paper, she stated dismissively that such a publication would never appeal to the ladies of Dublin, who 'care more for one valse with a moustachiod Dragoon than for all the literature of Europe put together'.[30]

Those living in the countryside had no thought for dancing. In January 1848 the *Freeman's Journal* reported a great number of deaths from fever among the teachers and children attending the boys' school at Castlebar. The *Nation* claimed that Galway's jail was more of a pestilent hospital than prison, with 115 inmates dying within two weeks in February, while a chaplain was reported as having seen 'living persons lying on the same bed with a corpse, whose fetid condition renders it dangerous to approach'. Horrific stories of starvation appeared daily in all the papers. Of one man sentenced for sheep steal-ing, the judge said, 'The prisoner and his family were starving; one of his children died and he was credibly informed that the mother ate part of its legs and feet . . .'

Many desperately searched the seashores for food. One man in County Mayo was found on the roadside, dead, with 'a portion of the grass and turf on which he lay masticated in his mouth'. The statistics for 1848 were numbing: in all, 178,159 of the Irish emigrated, while the total number of deaths was 208,252 – including 97,076 from epidemic diseases, 4,678 from starvation and 123 suicides.

No other country in Europe suffered the ravages of famine to the same extent as Ireland, and with the outbreak of nationalist insurrec-tions in the rest of Europe, Ireland too was set alight.

The first of these foreign uprisings took place in Palermo in January 1848, with the Sicilians demanding separation from Naples and forcing the King of Naples, Ferdinand II, to promise a constitution. The King of Sardinia had to follow his example. The Paris revolutionaries, wanting more liberty, rose up in February 1848, overthrowing Louis-Philippe and declaring a republic. On 2 March, a public meeting of some 3,000 people at Wiesbaden fired off the German unity movement; and in Austria-Hungary the Vienna revolution broke out on 13 March, causing the despot Metternich to resign and flee for refuge. During the German uprising Karl Marx was editor of a revolutionary paper and in that same year, 1848, he issued the Communist Manifesto, which ended with the celebrated words, 'The workers have nothing to lose but their chains. They have a world to win. Workers of all lands unite.'

Mitchel, in the *United Irishman*, urged his readers into action. 'Let the man among you who has no gun sell his garment and buy one,' he said, and was promptly arrested on a charge of treason. Jane wrote various reviews and articles in the *Nation* in the early months of that year. Caught up in the general revolutionary fervour, she ended a review of a book about Pope Pius IX with the words, 'If *all* other means fail by which we could carry light into this chaos of misery, depredation and untold agonies around us *then*, in God's name, let us fling away the scabbard and illumine it by the light of our unsheathed swords.' Her poem 'Courage' (later retitled 'The Year of Revolutions') in the issue of 22 April 1848 started:

> Lift up your pale faces, ye children of sorrow,
> The night passes on to a glorious to-morrow!
> Hark! hear you not sounding glad Liberty's paean,
> From the Alps to the Isles of the tideless Aegean?

and continued with a strong call for action:

> We'll conquer! we'll conquer! No tears for the slain,
> God's angels will smile on their death-hour of pain.
> On, on in your masses dense, resolute, strong
> To war against treason, oppression, and wrong . . .

Jane may have encouraged the people to fight but her belief in the social order remained as strong as ever and she wrote to her Scots friend to say, 'No Democracy. Why should a rude, uncultured mob dare to utter its voice? Let the best reign, Intellect and Ability – you and I if they choose and an admirable world we would make of it – but not the machine masses.' She was to react indignantly when the popular Young Irelander Smith O'Brien addressed a meeting and encountered a crowd stirred up to angry mood by the Young Irelander John Mitchel, who had written against the pacifism of Daniel O'Connell. A stone hit O'Brien and Jane wrote to Gavan Duffy saying: 'What can be done with such idiots and savages? . . . This noble Smith O'Brien who has sacrificed *all* for the people, and who could gain nothing in return, for no position, however exalted, could add to his dignity, whose whole life has been a sacrifice to his country – a self-immolation – and this is the man who has to be guarded by [the] *English* from *Irish* murderers! I cannot endure to think of it. We are disgraced for ever before Europe, and justly so. Adieu!'[31]

The *Nation* meanwhile was publishing inflammatory tips for its revolutionary readers, including 'How to break down a bridge or blow one up' and 'How to buy and try a rifle'. The atmosphere was one of fear and unease and there was talk of rescuing Mitchel from prison in case the verdict went against him. Placards all over Dublin told the people to bide their time. The formidable scholar John O'Donovan wrote to his friend the poet Daniel MacCarthy on 27 June 1848 to say that, despite being content himself with the golden link of the Crown, he was afraid that 'our people here will run amuck and get themselves slaughtered in tens of thousands while they cut down her Majesty's army by street fighting.' After commenting on the exceptionally fertile crops near Dublin, O'Donovan went on to say he was afraid that nature would only 'enable us to shed blood the more efficiently in atonement for the many carcases which manure the surface of Ireland. This is the opinion of Dr Nuttal of Dublin and of the Gigantic Lady, Speranza, of the warlike songs, the daughter of a Protestant Dean [*sic*] who thinks that the *sins* of the Liberator must be atoned for by blood.'[32]

Jane wrote to her Scots friend of the political ferment reigning in Dublin. 'I have been incapable of even opening a book,' she said. 'It is awful to contemplate the result of this unnatural struggle going on between a government and all that is eminent or admirable for genius, gifts, purity, enthusiasm and deep love of country in our ill-fated land. I believe an insurrection is certain – the confederates contemplate it calmly but the other day Mr Duffy talking of it asked me to sit for my picture saying he would like to have it before his turn came to die, for truly, death is certain, either by the bayonet or on the scaffold.'[33]

Politics then touched all lives with danger: not merely those giving voice to the debate. The Young Irelanders, as Duffy said, were all in danger of arrest for treason, transportation or even execution. Jane herself, though, a member of a firmly established Protestant family, was in no fear of arrest; neither were the other women poets of the *Nation*: treason, in those days, was regarded as men's work. Regardless of this, 'John Fanshawe Ellis' wrote a review of two books on O'Connell which, despite the editorial disclaimer, was clearly an attempt to stir readers into action: 'If a government stands in the path of that people, and refuses those demands which it was only placed in office to execute (for a government is not organized to control, but to execute a people's will), that government must be overthrown . . . The country, therefore, is now in the position which O'Connell himself avowed would *justify* armed resistance to tyranny, and an armed enforcement of the people's rights.'[34]

Alarmed at the growing possibility of revolt, the government took the initiative. On 15 July 1848, a dozen policemen turned up at Charles Duffy's home, arrested him on the new charge of treason-felony, for which the penalty was transportation, and took him off to jail. Other leading agitators arrested included Thomas Meagher who was charged with using seditious language. The police then went to the offices of the *Nation* and took possession of its files and papers.

Despite Duffy's arrest, the *Nation* refused to be intimidated. The editorship was taken over by Margaret Callan, Duffy's cousin and sister-in-law, and the next issue (22 July) contained a militant poem by Jane, 'The Challenge to Ireland', again calling for action:

> And are there no men in your Fatherland
> To confront the tyrant's stormy glare
> With scorn as deep as the wrongs ye bear –
> With defence as fierce as the oaths they swear,
> With vengeance as wild as the cries of despair
> That rise from your suffering Fatherland?

This was only a prelude to the famous, unsigned and inflammatory leader, written by Jane, which appeared in the issue of 29 July 1848 called '*Jacta Alea Est*' ('The Die is Cast'). Jane had promised Duffy, still in prison, an article 'suitable to the occasion' and Duffy admitted she provided one which might have been issued 'from the headquarters of the National Army'. He smuggled out his own article, 'The Tocsin of Ireland', which appeared in the same issue.

Jane's leader, with its trumpet call to arms, caused a sensation and resulted in the government immediately seizing the issue and suppressing the paper for sedition. It began:

The Irish Nation has at length decided. England has done us one good service at least. Her recent acts have taken away the last miserable pretext for passive submission. She has justified us before the world, and ennobled the timid, humble supplication of a degraded, insulted people, into the proud demand for independence by a resolved, prepared, and fearless Nation.

Now, indeed, were the men of Ireland *cowards* if this moment for retribution, combat, and victory, were to pass by unemployed. It finds them slaves, but it would leave them infamous.

Oh! for a hundred thousand muskets glittering brightly in the light of heaven, and the monumental barricades stretching across each of our noble streets, made desolate by England – circling round that doomed Castle, made infamous by England, where the foreign tyrant has held his council of treason and iniquity against our people and our country for seven hundred years.

Courage rises with danger, and heroism with resolve. Does not our breath come freer, each heart beat quicker in these rare and grand moments of human life, when all doubt, and wavering, and weakness are cast to the winds, and the soul rises majestic over each petty obstacle, each low, selfish consideration, and, flinging off the fetters of prejudice, bigotry, and egotism, bounds forward into the higher, diviner life of heroism and patriotism, defiant as a conqueror, devoted as a martyr, omnipotent as a Deity!

We appeal to the whole Irish Nation – is there any man amongst us who wishes to take one further step on the base path of sufferance and slavery? Is there one man that thinks that Ireland has not been sufficiently insulted, that Ireland has not been sufficiently degraded in her honour and her rights, to justify her now in fiercely turning upon her oppressor? No! a man so infamous cannot tread the earth; or, if he does, the voice of the coward is stifled in the clear, wild, ringing shout that leaps from hill to hill, that echoes from sea to sea, that peals from the lips of an uprisen Nation – 'We must be free!' . . .

It was a volcanic outburst, though not unexpected given Jane's ferocious identification with the cause over the last two years. She was absolutely sincere in what she wrote, seeing herself as a revolutionary figure, cheering on the troops to storm Dublin Castle. A future editor of the *Nation* admitted that others shared this image of her: 'In 1848 she was the Madame Roland of the Irish Gironde.'[35] The leader revealed Jane's romanticized nationalism and her love of rousing sentiments; but it had little political awareness or common sense. She could not see that there was no real popular wish for an uprising: the decimated population had no strength, energy or interest in fighting.

The Habeas Corpus Act, guaranteeing suspects against unlawful detention, was suspended after Duffy's arrest and associates had to decide between immediate arrest or instigating an insurrection. William Smith O'Brien, who remained free, led some fifty or so men and women against the police at Ballingarry, County Tipperary. In the the resulting fight – known as the Battle of the Widow McCormack's Cabbage Patch – the weapons of the insurgents, according to Duffy, consisted of twenty-two guns, and about as many pikes, pitchforks and stones. William Le Fanu, brother of Sheridan, the writer, claimed that when the 'troops' were ordered to attack a police barrack garrisoned by half a dozen constables, they replied, 'Is it what your honour wants us, to go up there to be shot?' and promptly fled.[36]

Jane was totally cast down by the result, later telling Duffy, 'I do not blame the leaders in the least; in Sicily or Belgium they would have been successful.'[37] The mood of the country was shown in the August of 1849 when Queen Victoria paid a state visit to Ireland and collected cheers instead of hisses. After the débâcle Jane wrote to William Carleton saying, 'My poor friend Mr Duffy seems very ill, I am really uneasy about him, but that Ballingarry killed us all. I have never laughed joyously since.'[38]

'*Jacta Alea Est*' brought Jane to the forefront of the Young Ireland movement, marking her as a revolutionary. The leader remained the talking point of Dublin, as its publication constituted one of the charges against Duffy. Yet as the *Freeman's Journal* pointed out, the awareness that 'a lady' had written this leader, and not Duffy himself, was 'a fact as generally known in Dublin as it is possible for a fact to be'.[39] Contemporaries were quick to praise what Jane had written. A. M. Sullivan, a future editor of the *Nation*, recalling those days, said that '*Jacta Alea Est*' was 'without example as a revolutionary appeal.

Exquisitely beautiful as a piece of writing, it glowed with fiery invective. It was in fact a prose-poem, a wild war-song . . .'[40]

Early in 1849, many of the Young Irelanders were still in jail. Jane was half amused that 'No one knows yet what govt. mean to do with O'Brien & Co. They are all in prison here, writing verses and sitting for their portraits and giving banquets. Everything is in true melodramatic style – the general belief is that all will be pardoned and the scene close with a general embrace.'[41] Jane went to Meagher's trial and said that nothing could exceed the sympathy he excited. 'He was brought to see me at his particular desire.' Although sentenced to penal servitude for life in Van Diemen's Land, Meagher later escaped to America. John Mitchel too escaped and went to America along with many other young immigrants who supported the Young Ireland movement. They were to lay a foundation of Irish nationalism in that country which was enthusiastically followed by future generations of Irish immigrants.

Duffy was kept waiting for months in prison before being brought to trial. The *New York Nation* fiercely criticized this delay, claiming that his 'delicate frame and energetic mind must fret' and angry that he was not even allowed to see his relations, unless in the presence of 'some odious pimping policeman'.[42] The charge against him of seditious libel was based on his use of the *Nation* to advocate armed revolution, with the leader, '*Jacta Alea Est*', being cited as one of the proofs.

Jane need have felt no guilt at being implicated; she knew that Duffy had always strongly supported what she had written for the *Nation*, including her leader; indeed he had been arrested before it was even written. In any case in those days there was no shame in being imprisoned for one's Young Ireland views; it was, on the contrary, a matter of pride. Nevertheless, Jane did not want Duffy to be unjustly accused of having written her leader. In February 1849, the day before he appeared at the dingy-looking Green Street courthouse on this charge, Jane wrote to her Scots friend saying, 'Mr Duffy's trial at last comes on to-morrow. His counsel said they could defend all but the *Jacta Alea*. This was a dreadful position to place me in, so I went to the Solr. Genl., denounced myself as author and prayed to have it removed from the indictment, but without effect. However, I think he will not be *violent* on the subject after my visit, I shall have done that much good. I think this piece of Heroism will make a good scene when I write my Life, but the lesson was useful – I shall never write sedition again. The responsibility is more awful than I imagined or thought of.'[43]

The magazine *Irish Society* was one of the many periodicals and papers that, years later, was still repeating the story that when the Attorney-General read out in court the inflammatory words of '*Jacta Alea Est*', Jane stood up in the gallery and in a soft musical voice exclaimed, 'I am the culprit, if culprit there be.' Listeners, said the magazine, 'saw that the words were spoken by a tall, stately, handsome young lady, whom many of the audience recognized as Miss Elgee, one of the society belles of Dublin'.[44]

It makes a good story, but no contemporary paper quoted these words. One account claimed that the Solicitor-General's speech against Duffy was interrupted 'by the fair writer of one of the articles in the indictment, but her maiden speech was not listened to by the court and her voice was drowned by the police crying "Silence".'[45] Another paper said, 'No way of proving the authorship remained but by producing the lady herself upon the table – a course which Mr Duffy peremptorily refused to take . . .'[46] A third paper described how Isaac Butt, QC, told the jury that the article in question, '*Jacta Alea Est*', was written 'by one of the fair sex – not, perhaps, a very formidable opponent to the whole military power of Great Britain . . . it is not likely that the Crown will institute a prosecution against the respectable young lady whose productions I will prove them to be.'[47]

Referring some years later to the story that she had declaimed her guilt in court, Jane told her Scots friend, 'I was amused at that imputed heroic act of mine becoming historical. Posterity will not believe it and I shall leave it so – it will read well 100 years hence and if an illustrated history of Ireland is published no doubt I shall be immortalized in the act of addressing the court.' At the time, however, as she admitted: 'I was in quite alarm [*sic*] lest I should have to appear as witness, however I wrote a letter acknowledging the authorship and the Court said they must believe me so that there was then really no case against Mr D. Still the whole affair has thoroughly unsettled me against politics – our grand Revolution ending in shielding itself with a lady's name . . .'[48]

No verdict was obtained from Duffy's first trial and a re-trial was ordered.

Dublin was now returning to a more stable social life and Jane's letters were full of her different activities: going to Shakespearean readings by an elocutionist one moment and attending balls the next. 'The Keans are here and I attend the theatre frequently,' she wrote. 'Are you Puritan enough to be shocked at this? I have a passion for fine acting and Kean is up to this ideal. I also go now and then to grand gatherings of the Soullness [family] where they polka and eat and I at least talk.' Talk she did, for despite the balls, she remained Speranza at heart. 'I went to the last Drawing room at the Castle,' she wrote, 'and Lord Aberdeen smiled very archly as he bent to kiss my cheek, which is the ceremony of presentation. I smiled too and thought of *Jacta Alea Est.*'[49]

The fashions of the time were flattering to women: dresses had low-cut bodices and short sleeves ending in flounces of lace, with a profusion of ribbons and bows and full, long skirts. Jane loved them and continued to wear floating ribbons and trailing bows all her life even when the style was outdated, an example of Oscar's remark, 'Fashion is what one wears oneself. What is unfashionable is what other people wear.' She enjoyed dressing up and would tell her Scots friend what she was wearing at the various balls she attended. On one occasion it was 'black lace trimmed with bunches of gold wheat – on the head a small mantilla of black lace fastened with gold wheat to correspond', and another time she wrote, 'I wore pink and silver and talked pearls and rubies' – young enough as she was to escape Oscar's imputation: 'Never trust a woman who wears mauve, whatever her age may be, or a woman over thirty-five who is fond of pink ribbons. It always means they have a history.'

In January 1849 Jane sent her Scots friend a poem she had written in the *Dublin University Magazine* in which she alluded 'to our dear rebels and patriots', and mentioned it had been much praised by the papers. She was not one for hiding lights under bushels and took great satisfaction in being lauded as Speranza in Dublin circles. At an evening's entertainment in the grand, spacious rooms of the Royal Irish Academy, 'a full dress dancing affair', she was gratified to find that over a hundred celebrities were present: 'Poets, artists, astronomers and professors of all kinds, but *clever* ladies are rare in Dublin – at least ladies who write, so when I found they would also make me a celebrity the other evening I consented and resigned myself to introductions most amiably; after all there is something pleasant even in this small tea-table celebrity. In Dublin I have found it easily acquired for I have no rivals amongst these ladies. Beauty is the grand characteristic of the Dublin Belles, so in that department I leave them undisturbed in possession of their domain and am content with undisputed sovereignty in mine.'[50]

Jane knew she had a good brain and what she called a more 'spiritualized nature' than other people. But she claimed it was not her higher qualities that made her a favourite in society, but 'because I *descend* to them with sleek facility; alas how few I meet who make my soul ascend to their higher level. *Mais je suis vraiment égoïste . . .*' Oscar, like his mother, never doubted his own ability. He once claimed: 'I have put my genius into my life. I have put only my talent into my works.'

During the last half of 1848 and early 1849 Duffy was tried no fewer than six times. His trials were abandoned for various reasons such as a point of law or lack of evidence. The authorities were finally forced to abandon the prosecution and on 10 April 1849 he was released. The Young Ireland movement had by now faltered to a halt as, with Duffy in jail since the summer of 1848, there had been no real leadership.

The *Nation* had been suppressed ever since Jane's famous leader, but Duffy on his release decided to restart it. He found it hard work to rouse contributors' enthusiasm, saying of Speranza, 'To my policy and projects she gave a general but tepid assent and sympathy; but the eagerness and impatience of a woman of genius could ill reconcile themselves to the slow road we were bound to travel.'[51]

In the first issue of the re-launched *Nation* on 1 September 1849, pride of place was given to a verse by Jane, who wrote of freedom sending forth her young heroes glowing. But she seemed uncertain of the point she was making and her early fervour had gone. As the *Northern Standard* commented: 'Our readers will perceive . . . the old tone is changed, while they will easily recognize the sweet, saddened music of the instrument which erewhile sang of war and all its horrors.' The *Nation* hit back in its issue of 15 September, with: 'The English and Landlord Press . . . affect to be pleased with the *Nation* on the false assumption that we have postponed or abandoned the struggle for Independence.' But despite the brave words, the spirit had gone.

Jane was left rudderless. She had had an extraordinarily swift rise to fame. From being completely unknown and without any experience as a writer, she had, within three years, become a household name across Ireland. Her contribution to the cause of the Young Irelanders had been crucial and brought her enduring popularity. Now that the heart had gone out of the movement, she must have missed the political excitement as well as her Young Irelander friends, many of whom had been deported or taken refuge in America. Ambitious, aware of her talent, yet with the main thrust of her life removed, the problem Jane now had to face was what to do with her life next.

3

'In Love I Like to Feel Myself a Slave'

JANE MADE IT quite clear to her Scottish correspondent that she missed the challenge and grim upheaval of the last few years. 'I want excitement,' she wrote, 'excitement is my genius. I have none without it and Dublin is bleak of the divine inspirer as a Polar icefield – I should like to range through life – this orthodox creeping is too tame for me – ah, this wild rebellious ambitious nature of mine . . .'[1] She admitted that when she felt bored she became worthless and her energy disappeared.

To counteract her boredom, Jane decided to put her gift for languages to use. She worked hard translating a terror-tale by the German author William Meinhold, called *Sidonia the Sorceress: the supposed destroyer of the whole reigning ducal house of Pomerania*, telling her Scots friend rather dispiritedly that she was submerged in what she called an 'ink ocean', and that 'this daily pen and ink mechanical employment is rapidly killing the divine within me.' Her hard work paid off, however, and over the next decade she was to be acknowledged as a translator of some importance.

Sidonia was published in 1849. Set in the seventeenth century, it tells the story of the cruel Sidonia von Bork, Abbess of the Convent of Marienfliess, whose fatal beauty lures young men into her power. Practising witchcraft as a sideline, she renders them sterile by sorcery. Even the ponderousness of the original German prose – Meinhold was a Lutheran clergyman – cannot disguise its sensationalism. Sidonia tortures geese, whips young men out of pure evil-mindedness, dances merrily on the coffin of a young girl and is finally carried off in chains to public execution. A ferocious story, not for the timid, it has the high-born Sidonia fighting to the last for power and spiritedly arguing in court for her life.

The grisly details took two volumes to relate and one would have expected Jane to have been highly amused by it. But she told her Scots friend not to read the book and made it clear that she had written it for money rather than love: 'It is a disagreeable book. I disliked it greatly, but would not refuse a first offer.' Jane had a kind nature: perhaps she found Sidonia's activities too cruel and too removed from the nobility of spirit that always appealed to her. She did not put her name on the title page to prove, she said, 'that I am not writing for celebrity'.

Until Jane came across it, presumably as part of her wide reading in European languages, Meinhold's book had made little impact. As the critic Sir Edmund Gosse was to say, 'this German romance did not begin to exist until an Irishwoman revealed it to a select English circle.'[2] Even then the translation might have attracted little long-term interest, had not the poet and painter Dante Gabriel Rossetti become obsessed by it in later years. Gosse, who thought the book 'obviously retains far more vitality than any other work of that fervid authoress', said Rossetti quoted from it incessantly, 'until he inoculated the whole Pre-Raphaelite circle with something of his own enthusiasm'. Edward Burne-Jones's portrait of Sidonia in 1860 was one of his finest early watercolours.

Oscar was to claim that *Sidonia the Sorceress* was his favourite romantic reading when a child. His delight in the story could have sparked off his interest in the macabre and supernatural, evident in stories like 'Lord Arthur Savile's Crime', 'The Canterville Ghost' and *The Picture of Dorian Gray*. *Sidonia* could have had a particular influence in the creation of *The Picture of Dorian Gray*. In the castle of the Count von Bork, in Meinhold's story, there is a portrait of Sidonia which shows her as a beauty, dressed in azure velvet, with her golden hair in a gold net. Behind, a terrible spectre looks over her shoulder: another portrait of Sidonia, but as a sorceress. Charles Maturin's *Melmoth the Wanderer*, likely reading in the Wilde household, could also have inspired Oscar. In it the young student Melmoth is sent to collect some wine from a long unused room full of lumber – a room very like the schoolroom where Dorian was to conceal his picture. In it the student sees a portrait of an evil Melmoth ancestor who had made a bargain with the devil whereby he could live 150 years without showing any sign of ageing.

After the publication of *Sidonia*, and her contribution of a verse to the first issue of the newly revived *Nation*, Jane took up again her work for that magazine. In the issue of 15 September 1849, she wrote an admiring review of a book called *Beauties of Boyne and Blackwater* by Dr William Wilde, saying: 'Few men indeed could be more fitted than the accomplished author to render such subjects popular by their mode of treatment, combining as he does profound and varied erudition, and the subtle acuteness of a practised critic, with vivacity, feeling, and the most genial sympathies . . .' In one of the chapters in the book, describing the monuments upon the River Boyne, Dr Wilde had quoted a verse beginning 'By the cromlech sloping downward', a verse signed 'Speranza'. It is very likely that he and Jane had already met. Both were well-known, even famous, within Dublin circles. At 34 William Wilde was a brilliant figure, ambitious and proud of his success. From his early beginnings as an apprentice at Dr Steevens' Hospital in Dublin, he had risen to be a leading eye and ear surgeon, with a growing reputation throughout Europe. He came from a medical background. His father, Thomas, had been a doctor in the county of Roscommon and even when nearly 80 years old could be seen doing his rounds on horseback, jumping hedges in his many-caped riding coat.

William first made a name for himself in 1845, at the age of 30, when he successfully reopened and ran the old St Mark's Hospital as an Ophthalmic Hospital and Dispensary for Diseases of the Eye and Ear for the Poor. It was the only hospital in Great Britain which taught aural surgery and students from round the world gathered there to learn from his teaching. William was highly skilled, once performing a difficult tracheotomy with the only instrument to hand, a pair of scissors. About the only adverse comment on his work came from Bernard Shaw, who claimed that after his father was treated by William for a squint, he 'squinted the other way for the rest of his life'.[3]

William was also a contributor to medical and literary journals; editor of the *Dublin Quarterly Journal of Medical Science*; a leading authority on Irish ancient history; a highly praised archaeologist; and medical commissioner for the Irish census, in which he provided moving medical evidence of the results of the famine; and author of three highly admired books: *Narrative of a Voyage to Madeira, Teneriffe, and along the shores of the Mediterranean, Austria: Its*

Literary, Scientific, and Medical Institutions and *The Closing Years of Dean Swift's Life*. He was close friends with a number of literary men, including the authors Charles Lever and Sheridan Le Fanu.

Full of vitality, with a lively personality, William shared many interests with Jane. Though a Unionist, he was sympathetic to the cause of the Young Irelanders. A compassionate man, his work on the medical census had brought home to him starkly the conditions under which so many Irish people died. He wrote of the way 'bankrupt landlords, pauperizing poor-laws, grinding officials and decimating workhouses have broken up the very foundations of social inter-course'.[4] Jane's passionate verse would have aroused his sympathy and both had contributed individually to the *Dublin University Magazine*. They liked going to the theatre, and the Shakespearean actress, Helen Faucit, was a mutual favourite: in fact it was said that William Wilde had once proposed to her.

In her letters to her Scots friend in the course of 1850, Jane made no mention of William Wilde. But she gave her views on love when she scolded him for telling her he had 365 lady correspondents. 'What! dispose fractions of your heart in this manner over the world and only offer the remainder to your Sultana Queen. Why, I would grow jealous of sun, moon and stars had I a lover – I would not let him love mid-night or the moon, nor seem conscious they existed. I must be his Universe, terrestrial and celestial . . . When I meet with a Baronet of £5,000 a year with the Athenian's soul and your good heart – why, I'll fall in love with him . . . in love I like to feel myself a slave – the difficulty is to find anyone capable of ruling me. I love them when I feel their power . . .'[5]

Here was the type of man that attracted her. Not a sensual woman, Jane made no secret of the fact that she admired men of ability. It was the calibre of a man's mind that attracted her and the 'soul-music' a man and woman could create. She was used to mixing with the Young Irelanders and the man who ruled her would have to do so by intellect: in this regard William Wilde was eminently qualified. Once, mention-ing a friend of his, Oscar was to say, 'Between his mind and mine there is no *intellectual friction to rouse me up to talk or think* . . .'[6] Jane herself believed that 'no woman without intellect ever yet gained permanent influence over a man's life.' And she undoubtedly stimulated William. If he was to choose a wife from the middle classes, he would not find many who had her brains and force of character. He must have been impressed by her exceptional literary knowledge, her gift for languages and her wit. A.M. Sullivan of the *Nation* called her 'Young, beautiful, highly educated, endowed with the rarest gifts of intellect; her cultivated mind, her originality and force of character, made her the central figure in Dublin society . . .'[7]

Although both had active minds and were well matched mentally, this was not the case physically. Jane was a good six inches taller than William, who was of less than average height and slight. His dark hair, brushed back from a high forehead and descending to side-whiskers, framed an oval, scholarly face whose gentle expression was at odds with his unexpectedly full, sensuous lips and receding chin. Like many brilliant men, he took no heed of his appearance; as a result, he was the target of endless jokes about his slovenliness. W.B. Yeats recalled the insulting Dublin riddle, oft-repeated – 'Why are William Wilde's nails so black.' The answer? 'Because he has scratched himself.' Harry Furniss, the Wexford-born artist, later drew a malicious caricature of the couple, showing a small, scruffy William being towered over by Jane – her exceptional height emphasized by her hair being piled high on her head. Of her Furniss commented unkindly that she had 'the appearance and air of a tragedy queen of the Mrs Crummles type'.[8]

Others did not share Furniss's jaundiced view. Jane was praised for her 'symmetry of form, loveliness of countenance, gracefulness of motion, gentleness of demeanour and modesty of look'.[9] Jane's view of herself was equally idealized. Her favourite portrait was painted by Bernard Mulrenin for the Royal Hibernian Academy Exhibition of 1864. The portrait emphasizes her large eyes, dominant under well-marked eyebrows, her straight nose over full, shaped lips and her determined chin; in it she wears a tiara, with pearls looped around thickly coiled hair which is centrally parted and smoothed down severely in the style of the young Queen Victoria, to reveal a high, patrician brow. 'Noble,' Jane would have called it: a word of which she was particularly fond.

Her leisured lifestyle in 1850 hardly seemed to include time for serious courtship. Writing of her activities in Leeson Street then, she said:

> I rise at ten or often eleven, glide down to breakfast which mamma has all ready arranged for me, find letters, papers, notes on the table awaiting me, sometimes a Scots postmark, *very* welcome that. Breakfast over, I plunge into my ink-bottle. Silence and solitude

reign in the Drawing Room till 2 o'clock, for everyone knows I admit no visit before that hour. It strikes – up go books and papers, a general clearance of the table of all literary activities and I vanish to my chamber to dress. At three I descend, but visitors call at that hour, knowing I am visible. From that till five the day is utterly wasted, either with visitors, or visiting or shopping or some promenading. Complete idling in fact, for I never can write effectively unless in the unceintured comfort of a peignoir. We dine between five and six, after which I have the whole evening to myself. Mamma takes a siesta till tea at eight o'clock. I read or write in my own room, descend to tea, the eternal pen again or book until eleven o'clock when Mamma departs to rest – I to my room where the midnight lamp is seen burning by observant neighbours till two or three. In fact I have never the least inclination to lie down at night or to rise in the morning.[10]

There were exceptions to these ordinary days. Jane would go on riding parties for up to four hours or so, which she found 'very exhilarating to my spirits'. Then there were the evening parties, which started at ten or eleven at night, and from which she did not get home until three or four in the morning. She confessed these made her feel very wretched the next day 'and wholly unfit for thought'. It could not have been a particularly exhilarating life for her mother, but then Jane admitted to having 'numerous faults in my nature; selfishness especially is remarkably large.'

Her favourite days were rainy ones. 'These are enchanting. No going out, no visitors, a delicious feeling of safety comes over me. The peignoir stays on all day, the writing proceeds like improvisation. The only other variety I have to mention is the depressed days when I am miserable, I don't know why. Would be glad even for the society of a cat. I could do nothing on these days but drown myself. They are very frequent, too. Black, bleak, and unutterably desolate, isolation, gloom, a horrible sense of loneliness, a despairing feeling as if all the world else were standing in Sunlight, I alone condemned to darkness.' She admitted that 'Spring utterly takes away all power from me. It is so full of life and hope and joy and youth that I sink subdued . . . I feel nothing in my heart, seared, saddened, disillusioned to re-echo its hymns of coming joy, but a starless midnight, a gloomy muttering tempest – a sunless noon like our November, a saddened creation that does not sing.'[11]

Jane was now 28. Perhaps she needed the excitement of a real, rather than paper relationship. Work helped to quell her loneliness and depression and in 1850 she was busy translating Alphonse de Lamartine's *Pictures of the First French Revolution*. She said that she liked the work as it concerned history, but admitted to her Scots friend that 'writing for money is a very dull thing compared to writing for a Revolution. I am longing to light up another. Will you help me?'

She wrote again with relief to say that the book was finally finished and in type. It was published that same year in the Parlour Library series, although again her name was not on the book as translator. The subject was dear to her heart and she wrote with verve, giving lively descriptions of Madame Roland ('Young, beautiful, and radiant with genius') and the crowd's reaction to the royal family's attempted escape ('a never-ending yell of insult and opprobrium'), as well as sympathetically outlining the aims of the Girondists ('pure republicans, but they dreamed of a rule in which intellect and talent should hold the place of conventional rank and supplant the fictitious pretensions of royalty and aristocracy').

With the book behind her and having 'given up all my essayings and poetizing for the present', Jane decided to spend some time in the country, near Monaghan so that she could 'live wholly with nature, glorious nature'. Jane had never shown much interest in nature, but William Wilde was passionately keen on the Irish countryside and may have influenced her decision. However much she may have intended to be at one with nature, she was quick to ask her Scots friend to send on papers or notes while she was there, telling him that Monaghan was a Sahara as regards literature, having 'neither library, nor book, Society, nor Institute, nor living men with souls in them. Neither papers nor periodicals ever gleam across its murky darkness.'

The letter she received in return must have contained the news that her friend was thinking of getting married, for in her reply she commented acidly, 'Who is the sublime Semiramis has led you captive? I should think your heart more a tender than a loving nature . . . do forgive me if I am not very enthusiastic. I shall have to wait ten years now I suppose before your ardour is sufficiently cooled down to give a rational opinion on any point literary or psychological . . .'[12] Jealous perhaps at finding his affections involved elsewhere, she writes again rather waspishly, 'The truth is, I hate men in love, the heart holds but one at a time at least in that transition state between the "rippling friendship" as you call it and the authorized Version of the Rubric, and

I do not care to have my image only an intrusive guest. One thing amused me in your eulogy. You say she has no *Ambition* – so then this is the opposite of me with whom it is the strength of all feelings . . .'[13]

At this time Jane was still living with her mother in Leeson Street. But in the following year, 1851, her mother died. She left what property she had divided between Jane and her sister Emily, but Jane was placed in a quandary. Up to now her mother had looked after her and provided her with a home, and women of 29 did not live alone. Jane's only option was to move in with her pro-English rule relatives, who would hardly have welcomed an erstwhile revolutionary.

Despite the claim made to her Scots friend that she disliked men in love, and the emphasis she laid on professional ambition, later that same year, 1851, Jane Elgee accepted William Wilde's hand in marriage.

4

'Genius Should Never Wed'

A BRIEF ANNOUNCEMENT appeared in all the Dublin papers in November 1851: 'Married on the 12th inst. at St Peter's Church by the Reverend John M. Wilde, A.M., Incumbent of Trinity Church, Northwich, William R. Wilde, Esq., F.R.C.S., to Jane Francesca, youngest daughter of the late Charles Elgee, Esq., and grand-daughter of the late Archdeacon Elgee, of Wexford.'

It was a quiet wedding. The bride and groom both had a large number of friends but none was invited as Jane was still in mourning for her mother. Jane's uncle, John Elgee, attended the wedding and wrote an account of it to Jane's sister Emily after returning from seeing the couple leave for the Holyhead steamer – possibly for a honeymoon in London:

> Everything went off remarkably well, the carriage called for me this morning a little after eight . . . as soon as Wilde came I drove to Leeson Street for Jane, and *found her ready*, so that no time was lost and at nine precisely we entered the church – a brother of the Dr's who is a clergyman residing in Cheshire was the chief priest – William 'assisting' – We fairly stole a march on the Town, no one was expecting the affair till tomorrow, and so nobody were present save our own party and the old hangers on of the church . . . Jane looked and comported herself admirably – she wore a very rich dress of Limerick lace with very rich lace veil, a white wreath in her hair etc. – by ten we were at breakfast at

the Glebe and by eleven Jane had resumed her mourning and had driven off for Kingstown.[1]

He added a postscript in reply to a letter from Emily he had just received. His comments reveal a certain tension between the sisters, no doubt caused by Jane's political views. Emily would hardly approve of her rebel sister: like her family she upheld English rule in Ireland, had married a soldier and was now living in England. John Elgee wrote:

> I am compelled to agree with you entirely in your estimate of Jane's character and it was only coming from the wedding this morning and talking to Wright [unknown acquaintance] about her that I expressed myself to the effect that whether it would be a happy marriage was problematical – my hope rested in Wilde's good sense but he will have I think [?] a major [?] ordeal to pass through – she likes him, which I think a great point – she respects him another – his intellectual and literary standing is superior to hers which is also very material, had she married a man of inferior mind he would have dwindled down into insignificance or their struggle for superiority would have been terrific – Jane has some heart, she has good impulses, but the love of self is the prominent feature of her character – as to caring for either of us, I don't believe that our fortunes cost her a thought – however, I don't want to see open war between you and them – I did not wish to hurt Wilde's feelings therefore I have agitated myself and I hope successfully to bring matters round between you to a decent state of intercourse.

There was one side of William Wilde of which John Elgee, living in Wexford, was probably unaware: he had a notorious reputation as a womanizer. Indeed, according to popular rumour he was a man 'with a bastard in every farmhouse'. His dynamism had always attracted women and prior to his marriage he had three known illegitimate children.

The first of these was Henry Wilson, born in Dublin in 1838 to a woman who remains unknown. William, 23 at the time, paid for his son's education and medical training and Henry, though lacking his father's brilliance, became an able ophthalmologist. Henry was 13 when William married and was commonly referred to as William's nephew. William ultimately took him on as his medical partner and

Henry was to live in Merrion Square near to the family, with whom he was on familiar terms. It is not known which woman, or women, bore William's two illegitimate daughters: Emily, born in 1847, and Mary, born in 1849 – only two years before William married Jane. If the two daughters were born to the same woman, this implies a relatively long relationship. How often William saw them, or how deeply he was involved with them, remains a mystery.

There was a great deal of sexual freedom in Dublin then, though the double standard over male and female behaviour still remained and women were expected to behave with propriety. William would certainly not have been socially ostracized for fathering these children: illegitimacy was accepted. Other friends of his, like the lawyer Isaac Butt, also had illegitimate children. William didn't marry until he was 36, which gave him a long time to sow wild oats. Only later in the century was a man expected to marry the woman bearing his child; before then it was sufficient for him to take financial responsibility for them. As Oscar was to say in his play, *Vera*: 'A family is a terrible encumbrance, especially when one is not married.'

William had two brothers, Ralph and John, both of whom had entered the Church. The Revd Ralph Wilde, the eldest, came to William's assistance and took his two daughters on as wards. Their surname was therefore Wilde.

Jane may well have heard the Dublin gossip about her future husband's sexual prowess. But she was a strong-minded 30 year old, more likely to shrug off whispers than have an attack of Victorian vapours. She must certainly have learned in time that Henry was William's son. She would have known he was not a nephew and there seems to have been little secrecy about his paternity. Although Oscar in later years referred to Henry as a cousin rather than half-brother, this could have been more a casual way of referring to a member of the family than a deliberate euphemism.

Even if William did not at first tell his new bride about the long and relatively recent affair that had produced two illegitimate daughters, he may well have done so when he discovered his wife's easy tolerance. And Jane would have known Ralph was unmarried and made an educated guess about the girls' paternity. She probably didn't care. She was in love with William, admitting to her Scots friend that this had overthrown her feminist leanings: 'for myself I died long ago – the old original Ego that you used to know. I love and suffer – this is all I am conscious of now and thus at last my great soul is prisoned within a *woman's destiny* – nothing interests me beyond the desire to make *him* happy – for this I could kill myself.'[2]

After their honeymoon, Jane and William Wilde returned to Dublin to William's house at 21 Westland Row. Until three years previously, when his mother died, he had lived at No. 15 – the house in which, in the early 1840s, he had first set up his practice as an eye and ear specialist.

No. 21 was an unpretentious three-storey Georgian terraced house, near to Dublin's large railway station and with a pleasant view of Trinity Park from the back windows. The rooms were small but it offered a comfortable home for the Wildes. And William, thanks to his large and lucrative practice, was by now quite wealthy.

The couple had a wide circle of friends and entertained them to supper – among them were Samuel Ferguson, the barrister cum scientist, archaeologist, artist and poet, and his wife, who was one of the Guinness family; the young archaeologist and historian, John Gilbert; Charles Lever, who had abandoned medicine for literature and now edited the *Dublin University Magazine*; the lawyer Isaac Butt, who had acted as counsel for Gavan Duffy; the sculptor John Hogan and William's close medical friend, Dr William Stokes, who was to become President of the Royal Irish Academy.

Jane must soon have realized that she was not to see much of her husband. He was extremely busy. His daily work running clinics at St Mark's, visiting patients and performing minor operations continued until early evening. Then he might have a paper to read at the Academy or Royal Dublin Society. At home, he was putting together his 600-page conspectus of the medical census of 1851. These medical findings were a general history of Irish medicine, which included a graphic description of the famine and its aftermath. They were to bring him further fame.

He was also working hard on his book, *Irish Popular Superstitions*, which was published the following year, 1852, and dedicated 'To Speranza'. The book is a compendium of Irish folklore, touching on such subjects as ancient ceremonies, the fairy people, folk medicine, festivals and Irish characters like Paddy Welsh, who taught young William how to throw a 'red-tackle' or a 'black-and-orange' over the nose of a trout. It was in Connaught, where the Wilde family had lived for over a century, that William first became fascinated by his country's legends and superstitions. He was to ask many people, mainly village schoolmasters who could speak both Irish and English, to collect these for him. Jane later wrote of him: 'There was probably no man of his generation more versed in our national literature, in all that concerned the land and the people, the arts, architecture, topography, statistics, and even the legends of the country.'[3]

William may have worked hard but he still liked to go off with his friends for uproarious supper parties with lavish feasting and hard drinking. A number of convivial Dublin dining clubs were formed during the 1840s and 1850s, like the 'Mystics' of which William was a member along with John Gilbert, the Irish historian. A friend of Gilbert's, who thought the Mystics too frivolous a club, wrote to him in irritation saying that now he was a 'Mystic', he would no doubt 'have sacrificed to the Jupiter–Esculapius and Juno–Minerva [Dr and Mrs Wilde] of Westland Row. I wish you joy of the . . . pleasant anticipations of literary and historical eminence into which you are sure to rise in such company!'[4] There was also always lavish hospitality at Charles Lever's house. Once, before his marriage, when William pleaded work in refusing yet another dinner there, Lever promptly turned up at his home with a bandage over his eyes, which succeeded in bringing William to the door at once and then, amid roars of laughter, on to Lever's dinner party.[5]

Wives were expected to allow their husbands total latitude in pursuing their own entertainments. Jane herself had a curiously dual attitude to marriage: half feminist, half deferential. As a feminist she deplored the fact that, as she wrote in her essay 'The Bondage of Woman', 'women still weep and toil, as they have ever done, that man, the lord of the world, may find existence made easier and pleasanter by the ceaseless devotion and patient self-sacrifice of the inferior, at least, the weaker sex.' She went on to condemn the chief dogma of woman's education being 'simply husband-worship. She was taught that if she studied it was simply to qualify herself as a companion to her husband; if she talked, it should be just enough to show that she appreciated his profounder wisdom.' Jane argued that it was time women broke this political and sensuous bondage, in order that 'a new era may be given to the world of equal rights, equal culture, and equal honours for men and women'.[6]

Yet disconcertingly, she showed signs of this bondage herself. On a number of occasions she came out with statements that would make a feminist flinch. On one occasion she said, 'A good-tempered gay-hearted wife is sunlight in a house, never mind the brains, women don't need them: good sense, patience and love, find these but desire no more.'[7] And when a friend wrote of her own life as being one of 'reading, thinking and writing', Jane replied that in her opinion 'writing is a fatal gift for a woman – I would be a much better wife, mother and head of a household if I never touched a pen. I feel this so strongly that I shall never encourage my daughter to authorship.'[8]

When she was asked in later years if she had remained interested in writing after her marriage, however, Jane said, 'Oh yes; but then I turned to prose and wrote papers on various subjects for the *Dublin University Magazine* . . . I translated a great deal, both poetry and prose, and of translation I have always been very fond.'[9] It was just as well she enjoyed the work as she translated three books between 1849 and 1851 and even though they were commissioned she received very little money for them.

Despite demanding women's rights, Jane also believed in women's duty. She argued in her essay 'Venus Victrix' that women should be a redemptive force, supporting their husbands with sympathy and love and asking nothing in return, 'only the divine joy of sacrifice, the ecstatic sense of self-annihilation for true love's sake'.[10] And in writing on Tennyson's poem *The Princess*, she said: 'Love, as it always does, is turning her woman's nature to a slave's. Still powerful in revolt against all theories of woman's independence was that instinct of her nature which seems satisfied only with self-sacrifice, self-immolation for the one beloved.'[11] Jane's admiration for the Girondiste Madame de Staël was based on her similar ambition to 'become the inspirer, the hidden destiny of some great man, to awaken his energy and be happy in his glory'.[12]

In her essay on 'Genius and Marriage', Jane claimed that women often have 'many and grievous faults in married life, very irritating to a literary husband and a man of genius'. She backed it up with a story about Lady Byron: 'Lady Byron was entirely deficient in this subtle tact that can guide and soothe the wayward, turbulent and terrible temperament of genius. "Am I in your way, Byron?" she asked one day, entering the poet's study while he was at immortal work. "Damnably!" was the answer of the poet-husband. And she deserved it. She had no tact, no fine instincts. She ought to have known intuitively that she was in the way, and effaced herself.'[13]

Next in line for attack was Jane Carlyle, for failing to remain in a subordinate position: 'She ought to have considered that her existence was really of no importance to the universe; but her husband's words and works had power to send the world on its path of progress with mighty tangential force . . .'

Jane's own recipe for domestic happiness, which undoubtedly summed up the Wilde household, was 'when all the family are Bohemians, and all clever, and all enjoy thoroughly the erratic, impulsive, reckless life of work and glory . . .'[14] But her theory that genius should be protected from trivial cares, like domestic duties, meant her household was run in a casual manner, with bills often being neglected even though there was the money to pay them. William never placed his own feelings about domestic happiness on record. But the couple were clearly close. A light-hearted note he wrote to her read, 'Hurrah, hurrah! Well dear Speranza, all has turned out well.'[15] It is not known to what he was referring, but the affection comes through.

In 1852, just before her thirty-first birthday, Jane had her first child. William Charles Kingsbury Wills Wilde was born on 26 September 1852. He was given the name of his own father, Jane's father and the family surname of Jane's mother. He, and later his brother, also took the name of Wills after the family of the playwright W. G. Wills, who were known to the Wildes.

Jane's happy transition from the barricades to the nursery surprised her as much as anyone. Writing to her Scots friend in November, after he himself had had a small daughter, she said: 'She must be married to my son, won't that be nice. Mind I've settled that. My little Willie is 7 weeks odd old. How old is his wife? What an enchanting richness and fullness these young [children] give to one's life. It is like the return of a second youth. Hope, energy, purpose, all awake again and with a nobler object than ever . . . I scarcely know myself, I who lived in lofty abstractions, who loved objects only for the ideas they incarnated, how is it I am enthralled by these tiny hands?'

She still spared a thought for her glory days as Speranza, even if she believed that she had now largely left them behind for a 'truer' life: 'Was there a woman's nature in me after all? Oh Patriotism, oh Glory, Freedom, Conquest, the rush, the strife, the battle and the Crown, ye Eidolons of my youth, where are you? Was I nobler then? Perhaps so, but the present is the truer life. A mere woman, nothing more. Such I am now. The other was an abnormal state. Well, after all it is a satisfaction to have been through the whole circle of human emotion, literature, ambition, love, motherhood, till my wings fall from me at last beside an infant's cradle. How many lives we live in life!'

Jane didn't swim for long in the sea of sentimental motherhood. In fact, even before the end of this letter, she seems to have forgotten the 'truer' life as she goes on to say: 'I think we are all getting stupid since we married, don't you think so? ponderous, heavy, prosy, calculating. All the ethereal vanished. Again I say, Hear it oh ye gifted and fated, *genius should never wed*. You cannot serve two masters . . .' After enquiring what her friend was reading or writing, she admitted: 'I never read now; as someone said seeing me over little saucepans in the nursery, "Alas! the Fates are cruel / Behold Speranza making gruel!" Yes, my friend, to this complexion have I come at last. Well, I will rear Him a Hero perhaps and President of the future Irish Republic. Chi sa? I have not fulfilled my destiny yet. Gruel and the nursery cannot end me.'[16]

Women today would immediately identify with Jane's fluctuating emotions about her role as mother – many new mothers experiencing similar conflict between the desire to submerge themselves in motherhood and the delights of child-rearing, and a longing to return to their professional career and the life they enjoyed before childbirth. Within two years Jane had gone from her status as Speranza, and a relatively carefree life being looked after by her mother, to herself being both wife and mother. It was understandable that her emotions were muddled. Now, though she was never to become a true establishment figure, her revolutionary ideas were fading into the past. She was bewildered by the change in herself, and like many women living with a partner, felt she had lost her original identity without having found another: 'I look back on the past as into a former existence,' she said, 'and wonder at my own self that then was. Now I have gone forth into another life with nothing but memory to make me aware of the identity, for all true identity has vanished.'[17]

To make matters more difficult, her husband was not an easy man to live with and during the early stages of her marriage, she must have had a great deal of adjusting to do. A letter to her Scots friend showed the problems she faced over her husband's depressions and her underlying relief that she had her baby to occupy and interest her:

Well, well, after all talk of Politics, patriots, poetry, love, literature, intellect, nothing fills the heart like a wee, wee child. So sayeth Speranza, and is she not a judge, for hath she not tried them all. And so you know nothing of my husband . . . Well then he is a Celebrity – a man eminent in his profession, of acute intellect and much learning, the best conversationalist in our metropolis, and author of many books, literary and scientific . . . in short he is a man to be proud of as far as intellect goes.

But he has a strange, nervous, hypochondriacal *home nature* which the world never sees – only I and often it makes me miserable, for I do not know how to deal with fantastic evils though I could bear up grandly against a real calamity. In truth my own energy has sunk under what I have gone through – I am not the same – I have lost hope, faith, confidence, energy. My husband so brilliant to the world envelops himself . . . in a black pall and is grave, stern, mournful and silent as the grave itself. Although naturally I have my high spirit and long warred bravely against his gloom, yet at length his despondency has infected me and I am now nearly as gloomy as himself. This is bad, so tell me how best to keep up the bright vivid nature I once had, which made all things possible to me – when I ask him what could make him happy he answers *death* and yet the next hour if any excitement arouses him he will throw himself into the rush of life as if life were eternal here. His whole existence is one of unceasing mental activity . . .[18]

In her essay on 'Genius and Marriage' Jane wrote with feeling on what seemed to be the reality of her married life: 'A woman has a strong tendency to look on a man of genius as a god, and to offer him worship as well as love; but in the fatal intimacy of daily life illusions soon vanish, and she finds that, except in moments of inspiration, his divinity is even weaker than an ordinary mortal, less able to guide or strengthen others; so she resents the knowledge that her idol is only made of clay, and her feelings alternate between contempt and dislike, especially if she is of a passionate, impulsive temperament.'

William had married 'Speranza' and, like many husbands of professional women, still expected her to be unchanged after motherhood. Jane was having to act three parts at once: the bright and vivid poet William had married; the wifely supporter of a depressed husband; and the caring mother. It is not surprising that her depression equalled his. Despite the birth of her first son in 1852, that year saw the publication of Jane's fourth translation, *The Glacier Land*, by Alexandre Dumas père. It is an amusing, descriptive account of Dumas's tour round Switzerland in 1832, in which the translation at times cheerfully departs from the original text. There are anecdotes about historical happenings; conversations with local people on subjects from cholera to the debate about whether or not Napoleon passed that way; and observations on buildings like the German inn in Berne, admirable 'for those who love waltzing and sauerkraut'. Later on, Jane wrote her own travel book about Scandinavia and used the same approach.

The archives of the Swedenborg Society for 1853 note that Jane was working on a revised translation of Emanuel Swedenborg's *Of Heaven and Hell*, originally written in Latin and first translated into English in 1758. Swedenborg, the Swedish philosopher, scientist and mystic, had a strong following throughout Europe, and a society had been set up in London to propagate his works. Jane was particularly interested in his theories, and wrote in a later essay of his 'visionary glance'.

Of Heaven and Hell was subtitled 'Heaven and its wonders and concerning Hell, being a relation of things heard and seen', and the book examined subjects such as angels' clothing, the type of government in heaven; and what is meant by hell fire and the gnashing of teeth.

But a mystery surrounds this translation by Jane. The Revd James Hyde in his 1906 bibliography of Swedenborg's works lists the translation as being published in 1853 under the new title of *The Future Life*. He comments, guardedly, that the work was 'revised, as it appears, by Speranza, Lady Wilde'. Then, towards the end of this same bibliography, he says that Jane did *not* in fact translate the work. In any case the new translation, if it was indeed by Jane, differed only in minute detail from the previous one.

In 1853 William's acclaimed book on *Practical Observations on Aural Surgery and the Nature and Treatment of Diseases of the Ear* was published and became a standard textbook. He also gained his first public honour that year, being appointed to the newly created post of Surgeon Oculist in Ordinary to the Queen in Ireland. It did not require any work, but was a prestigious honour.

His reputation was further enhanced by another book to be published the following year, 1854: *On the Physical, Moral and Social Condition of the Deaf and Dumb*. Despite being so busy that he was having to turn patients away, he was still driven on by work: in the February and March issues of the *Dublin University Magazine* he wrote a detailed two-part article on 'The Food of the Irish', even down to the characteristics of the old Irish pig: 'tall, leggy, arched in the back, remarkably long in the head, with huge pendant ears falling over the sides of the face, a knowing look, and a bright quizzical eye . . .'

Jane also contributed to the March 1854 issue, writing a biographical sketch of her cousin Robert McClure who lived at her grandfather's [Archdeacon Elgee] house in Wexford until he was 4, 'under the care

of his young mother, who had the singular destiny of being wife, widow
and mother in one year and before she had attained the age of 19'.[19]
Jane also reviewed 'The Dramas of Calderón' for the September issue,
discussing the thought and form of his poetry and praising his lyrical
dramas – which had a bloodthirsty appeal recognized by the translator
of *Sidonia*:

> To force a tender damsel to my wish,
> I slew a noble, venerable man –
> Her father. Nay, an honoured cavalier
> I stabbed, through frenzied passion for his wife . . .

Despite these articles, Jane was finding it more and more difficult
to concentrate on writing and wrote to her Scots friend that she envied
those hearts which were still in the fusion state: 'Mine has cooled down
into such a dull mass. I write occasionally, but never poetry. When the
fit takes me I prose in the *University Magazine*. This year there were
two articles of mine, one on Captain McClure and the other on
Calderón, the Spanish dramatist. I am engaged now to write another
on French literature of the eighteenth century, but it is not begun. This
sort of writing brings a great deal of praise and a little small Dublin
fame, just enough to make me remember that I once had an intellect;
and money it brings too . . .' She went on to praise the editor for paying
on time, admitting that she would no longer write without being paid:
'Think of the abysmal bathos into which I have sunk.'[20]

Her Dublin fame, however, attracted envy; so did the success of
her husband. The poet Denis Florence MacCarthy wrote to John
Gilbert that year asking if he had seen the announcement in *Saunders's
News-Letter* that the *Irish Quarterly Review* was owned by Dr Wilde
and that he was not only the editor, but that the leading articles *'are
all written by him and his gifted wife, Speranza!'* (All three allegations
were incorrect.) MacCarthy referred to a critical article in the last
issue by Jane and mocked at 'the idea of Speranza, terrible and
beautiful as an Amazon, with one hand brandishing an enormous steel
pen dripping with the avenging fluid, and then dashing it in the face
of the pallid and collapsed Wilde, who lies drooping and subdued
across the other arm of the heroine!'[21]

Jane became pregnant again early in 1854 and the Wildes' second
child was born on 16 October 1854. It was another son, whom they
named Oscar Fingal O'Flahertie Wills Wilde. The first two names

were from Irish legend and O'Flahertie was from William's family connections.

Emily, Jane's sister, saw the announcement of the birth and sent it to their brother, John Elgee, in America. He wrote back saying, 'Considering the late period at which she married she is doing uncommonly well.'[22] Jane would hardly have appreciated this remark, but – 31 when Willie was born, 33 at the time of Oscar's birth and 36 when she had her third child – she was indeed old for those times to start a family. She was delighted with her two boys, who had brought out a strong maternal side she hardly knew existed. As Speranza, Jane's loyalty had been to her country: now the same loyalty was switched to her children. 'With this duty lovingly laid upon me, what to me are Revolution or the struggle of an uprising Humanity?' she wrote. 'If I can but make them wise and good it seems to me that is all can be done in this brief moment-life of ours.'

After Oscar's birth, her preoccupation with her children increased and she told her Scots friend:

I take an interest now in children beyond all other objects in life. Revolutions may agitate and dynasties fall but I have scarce a thought for them; truly said Jean Paul, 'a woman cannot live for her country and her children.' A Joan of Arc was never meant for marriage, and so here I am, bound heart and soul to the home hearth by the tiny hands of my little Willie and as if these sweet hands were not enough, behold me – me, Speranza – also rocking a cradle at this present writing in which lies my second son – a babe of one month old the 16th of this month and as large and fine and handsome and healthy as if he were three months. He is to be called Oscar Fingal Wilde. Is not that grand, misty and Ossianic?

Despite her delight with Oscar, his birth may have left Jane feeling tired and low. A sense of bleakness pervaded the rest of her letter, as if she had a sudden awareness of what might lie ahead: 'I trust your sweet child may ever continue to be the charm of your life. I can but pray for her as I pray for Willie that he may look upon my grave but I never on his. There is something to take away the horror of death when you think you have a child that will weep for you. Yes, I ought to be happy. God has lavished blessings on me. If I am sad it is because the apprehension of the unknown future sometimes comes over me. Life has such infinite possibilities of woe.'[23]

Among many prospects weighing on her spirits may have been that of the Crimean War which, begun earlier that year, showed no signs of ending. In March 1854, angered by Russia's invasion of Turkey's principalities, England and France had declared war on Russia and the long Crimean campaign had begun. Incompetent Allied administration had led to soldiers dying not only from cholera and starvation but from bungled military engagements such as the famous Charge of the Light Brigade at Balaclava which failed to eject the Russians from their positions of strength. By now, November 1854, Jane told her friend that no one could talk or think of anything but the war and she admitted that she too spent her days reading *The Times*. It made her wonder what future was destined for their children. 'Will the earth be a new Jerusalem after this baptism of blood . . . Watch and pray – this is all we have to do. Willie is my kingdom. I must seek to govern wisely there and leave this world of Futurity to its mystery and Fate . . .'[24]

At a dinner party in April 1855, Jane made the acquaintance of Sir William Rowan Hamilton, who was to become a firm friend. Astronomer Royal for Ireland, world-renowned mathematician, master of European and Oriental languages and winner of the Vice Chancellor's gold medal for English verse at Trinity College, he was one of Dublin's brightest stars. Though a close friend of Jane's husband, whom he knew through the Royal Irish Academy, this was the first time he had met Jane. He found her 'almost amusingly fearless and original and averse', rightly discerned that 'she likes to make a sensation' and had 'a noble nature', and often called her 'the strong-minded lady'.

Despite being firmly on the government side himself, he was impressed by the way Jane had taken up the rebels' banner in 1848, and was delighted too that she liked his dead sister's poetry, which they discussed over dinner. He told Jane in turn that he thought very highly of her own verse. Writing early in May to his friend and fellow mathematician, Professor Augustus de Morgan, he said: 'A very odd and original lady . . . had also lately a baby: such things you know will happen, at least in Ireland; and on my being asked to hand her in to dinner, at a party given by Colonel and Mrs Larcom in this neighbourhood, when I met her for the first time in my life, she told me of this young "pagan", as she called him . . . and she asked me to be a godfather, perhaps because I was so to a grandson of Wordsworth the Poet . . . However, I declined.'[25]

Unperturbed by his refusal, Jane later went to visit him at the

Observatory, staying three and a half hours. They toasted the new baby and Rowan Hamilton told the professor that the baby had been christened with 'a long baptismal name, or string of names, the two first of which are Oscar and Fingal! the third and fourth sounding to *me* as a tremendous descent, but I daresay she prefers them . . . she is quite a genius, and thoroughly aware of it'[26] – a foretaste of Oscar's celebrated retort to the Customs Officer when asked if he had anything to declare: 'Only my genius.'

Rowan Hamilton took Jane to see the Observatory dome and while 'she was professing to admire the house (which she *hoped* was a *haunted* one . . .)' she said to him: 'Let a woman be as clever as she may, there is no prize like this for *her!*'[27] This was an issue on which Jane felt strongly, believing that talented women received far too little recognition, especially public recognition, for their work. 'If men,' she said, 'destined for all the honours the world can give, yet often sink down weary under the burden of their work, how can women keep up a brave spirit without any prospect whatever of honour or reward.' She argued that titles were handed out to men who fight, lawyers who plead and poets who sing and as these ennobled them and symbolized their superior intellect, it was wrong that women were not equally honoured. The Queen, she pointed out, had founded the Victoria Cross for distinguished bravery: why should she not award a royal order of merit for women eminent in literature and art?[28]

Shortly after first meeting Rowan Hamilton in 1855, Jane sent him her lengthy poem, 'Shadows from Life', for his opinion. She may well have been romantically visualizing herself in the following theatrical lines:

So, in lone and lofty beauty, she stood high above the world,
Never heeding, dashing neathward, how life's stormy billows curled;
As a pine upon the mountain, warring tempests raging round,
As an island peak of ocean, with the starry midnight crowned.
How could she who trod the pathway of the spirit's starry zones
Stoop to listen, bending earthward, to a lover's murmuring tones?

The poem went on for sixteen stanzas and Rowan Hamilton was delighted with them all. He wrote back praising 'the gorgeous beauty of many of your descriptions' and the depth of feeling the poem expressed, though was brave enough to query its scansion. Jane, to his surprise, took this well and made some alterations. Rowan Hamilton then sent it to his friend, the poet Aubrey de Vere, that December, who replied that Jane 'certainly must be a woman of real poetic genius to have written anything so beautiful, and also so full of power and grace as the poem you showed me. For the sake both of poetry and old Ireland you must do all you can to make her go on writing, and publish a volume soon. Do not forget to tell her that you showed her poem to a stranger . . . and that he felt a very sincere admiration for it.' Rowan Hamilton sent him a further letter of hers and de Vere, returning it, said: 'It is indeed pleasant to meet that rare thing, poetic genius, in union with a rarer one – the magnanimity . . . which can take censure with gratitude, praise with simplicity, and both with equal grace.'[29]

Rowan Hamilton's letter to Jane was the start of a lengthy correspondence between them. He wrote pages of inconsequential thoughts to her, often in a ponderously flirtatious style. In one of his first letters, he said: 'You must know that Lady Hamilton has been growing very *jealous* about you – not in the sense which might first occur to a sentimental schoolgirl – she did *not* at *all* think that *I* had paid too much attention to you, but often hearing me talk so much about you and knowing that you had favoured me with a long (though not by any means a *too* long) visit, and that I had afterwards sent you my book with an inscription, she asked me about twenty times, "Why does not Mrs Wilde write you a line?" . . . But when I show her, as I shall do in the morning, your charming . . . your *flattering* letter, she will be satisfied.'[30]

He translated bits of Greek prose for her ('unnecessarily for *you*') and in June that year, when Jane had apparently burnt a note of his, he wrote that 'Perhaps too I thought that you wd consider me (though Dr Wilde I am sure wd *not*) to have praised you too much . . . I don't think, after all, that I said *more* than that I thought you a very remarkable, a very interesting, and (if I cd be forgiven for adding it) a very loveable person . . . of course, I never presume to imagine that anything which I may at any time write to you will not be seen by Dr Wilde.'[31]

As Speranza, Jane was accustomed to men paying court to her and she welcomed a new friend who admired her writing. She told Rowan Hamilton on one occasion when he dropped in that she 'led habitually a very retired life with her children', but spoiled this demure effect by telling him she had recently been at the drawing room of Lord Carlisle, 'and rather liked such things'.[32]

Such social invitations were arriving more frequently. The poet and novelist Katharine Tynan said her Dubliner father, who had 'one of his great admirations' for Speranza, had had a shock when he first saw Jane 'fighting her way, like any man' into some banquet or other.[33] Attending another drawing room, the Wildes remained to dine with the Lord Lieutenant. Jane told her Scots friend that she had found Lord Carlisle a good conversationalist, with a great deal of tact and grace as well as considerable knowledge. She went on more frivolously: 'Would you like to know my dress at the Drawing Room? It was entirely of white satin trimmed with silver – there – am I not fallen to a mere woman?'

The summer of 1855 was an anxious one for Jane; her husband was taken seriously ill, as a result of overwork, and for three weeks there was no knowing the outcome: 'I look with terror on all that can ruffle the calm happiness of the home life,' she said. William habitually drove himself to the point of collapse. He suffered from asthma and was prone to bronchial attacks. To recuperate, he took his family to his beloved west of Ireland. They stayed a fortnight in Connemara and Jane was saddened to find it 'grand, desolate and bleak, lofty mountains, rude and bare, interminable bays, no trees and no people. They died of the famine or emigrated. The roofless cabins everywhere made me sick with helpless despair and rage.'[34]

Before her marriage Jane would probably have expressed her rage in poetry. She was only too aware of how much she had altered. 'How marriage changes one, how it fetters us heart and soul to the fragile human being,' she wrote. 'We no longer live in glorious ideas and majestic abstractions – we are prisoned – grand-souled as we were – prisoned to the human and the daily life . . . this is our destiny. Woman's at least.'[35] Although she still occasionally contributed to the *Dublin University Magazine*, she admitted to her Scots friend in the June of that year that 'Since the Doctor's illness a weariness has fallen on me of low unexcitable spirits.' However, she told him she had not put her pen aside indefinitely. 'When I shake off the depression I shall begin writing again. I do not find a day passes quite happy when I have not striven a little with the mental powers within.'

Looking back on her early married life, Jane would surely have agreed with Oscar's comment in 'The Remarkable Rocket': 'As for domesticity it ages one rapidly, and distracts one's mind from higher things.'

5

Feminist Friends

WHEN JANE AND William returned to Dublin from the west of Ireland in the autumn of 1855, they faced the upheaval of moving house. They had decided to leave Westland Row for the more fashionable Merrion Square, a Georgian square whose elegant town houses had been built for the aristocracy. When many of these families opted to live in London after the Act of Union between England and Ireland in 1800, the professional middle classes moved in.

The north side of the square had been designed by the architect John Ensor and completed in 1764. On 24 November Rowan Hamilton sent a packet around to Jane addressed to 'the new house' at No. 1 Merrion Square North. The elite circle of prestigious physicians already living in the square included Dominic Corrigan, William Graves and William's close medical friend, William Stokes.

No. 1 was an imposing, beautifully proportioned corner house, overlooking the square's attractive gardens in the front and another large garden at the rear. Jane now required six servants to run the house, which had a lofty, square hall, wide staircase and large drawing rooms furnished in solid walnut and mahogany. Gas lamps illuminated the oil paintings on the walls, the floors were covered with colourful Turkish carpets, and there were marble-columned mantelpieces and a plaster bust of Maturin and other admired figures.

William's vast collection of medical and antiquarian books formed a formidable library which included books on American fish culture, bound volumes of the *Illustrated London News*, *Irish Academy*

Transactions, and Thomas Davis's poems on *English Misrule and Irish Misdeeds*.[1] Jane had her own library of ancient and modern classics.

The house was ideal for the Wildes, to accommodate their growing family and the increased amount of entertaining they wished to do. Their supper parties, usually for twelve guests, had become well-known for their conviviality and the unconventional and witty conversation they supplied.

The next decade for Jane and William was one of quiet enjoyment: of travel, raising their children, authorship, letter writing and consolidating their social position. Jane was delighted with the new house, telling her Scots friend that 'This move is very much to my fancy as we have got fine rooms and the best situation in Dublin. I trust the two children may flourish there. Oscar is a great stout creature who minds nothing but growing fat. Willie is slight, tall and spirituelle looking with large beautiful eyes full of expression. He is twined round all the fibres of my heart, but what do you think of Mrs Browning's son who at 6 years old composes the most sublime poetry? Poor child, I should die of apprehension if Willie were like this.'[2]

Once he had recovered from his illness, William plunged straight back into work. During 1857, with the help of John Gilbert, he completed Parts I and II of a gigantic undertaking – a catalogue of the antiquities in the museum of the Royal Irish Academy. It required tremendous vigour and ability to bring this to completion. A committee had just spent four years unsuccessfully attempting to finish the catalogue in time for the visit that August of the British Association for the Advancement of Science, the most important school of archaeological research in western Europe. William went on to complete Part III but told the Academy's Council, 'Had I known the amount of physical and mental labour which I was to go through when I undertook the catalogue, I would not have considered it just to myself to have done it; for I may fairly say, that it has been done at the risk of my life.'[3]

Despite this *tour de force*, William occasionally managed to relax. That year he and thirteen other associates revived the defunct medical dining-club, the Medico-Philosophical Society, whose often drunken meetings were devoted to serious discussion of such matters as how to serve snipe.

Jane had other preoccupations. By 1857 she was pregnant again and the whole family was overjoyed when the new baby, born on 2 April, was a girl. She was named Isola Francesca Emily: Isola after the Gaelic

Iseult, Francesca after Jane's second name, and Emily because it was a traditional Elgee family name. Isola was adored by them all: she became a happy whirligig of a little girl, with golden hair, who filled the house with laughter.

Oscar was only two and a half years old when Isola was born. Yet the rumour persisted in later years that, in her longing for a girl, Jane 'caused' Oscar's homosexuality by dressing him as a female when he was a child. The claim was first aired by an acquaintance, Luther Munday, who maintained that Jane told some guests at a party, and 'not in a whisper either', that, in her intense desire for a daughter, she treated Oscar 'for ten whole years' as if he had been her daughter . . . in every detail of dress, habit, and companions'. According to Munday, this turned Oscar into 'a neurotic woman'.[4]

Oscar was indeed photographed as a small boy in an ornate frock, but little boys then were dressed in ruched, feminine clothes by their fond Victorian mamas, who also kept them in fashionable ringlets. Munday's reminiscences were published some twenty-five years after these alleged remarks, in a social climate totally hostile both to homosexuality and to the Wilde family. Another biographer of Oscar's fanned the rumour of Jane dressing Oscar in a feminine style. 'She even used to hang jewels on her little son, which . . . made him look like a miniature Hindoo idol.'[5] Jane hung herself around in jewels, too: she loved the look of them – a taste Oscar inherited, wearing when adult large, noticeable jewels like a turquoise and diamond solitaire, often commented on by his friends.

In July 1857, Baron Robert von Kraemer, the governor of Uppsala in Sweden, and his daughter Lotten came over to Dublin. They had letters of introduction to the Wildes and for Jane the visit became one of great significance. She formed a long-lasting friendship with Lotten who, then nearly 29, was a poet, essayist and editor of a Swedish magazine of modern culture called *Our Time*. Jane admired Lotten for endowing a scholarship at Uppsala University for women, for using her social and literary influence to obtain privileges for them and for helping to fight the legal and social disadvantages which women faced. She was also impressed by Lotten's weekly literary receptions and by her being 'the centre of a brilliant literary set who edit magazines, publish poems, travels and essays, write and act plays, give recitations from all the leading poets of Europe and discuss all the new books and ideas and the latest philosophy'.[6]

Through Lotten she became friendly also with Rosalie Olivecrona, who lived in Stockholm and co-founded and edited *Tidskrift for hemmet, tillegnad den svenska qvinnan* ('A Journal for the home, devoted to the Swedish woman'). The journal worked to give women higher intellectual and social status. Rosalie was married to the Chief Justice and Jane was delighted to have her as a friend: 'She is a wonderful woman to edit and write and take care of such a family.' Full of praise for the two women, Jane told them: 'Sweden ought really to settle handsome pensions on you both for having so raised the character of your nation.'

Lotten and Rosalie were a mirror image of Jane. They were both emancipated women and she admired their ability immensely, finding everything about them stimulating. Her sympathy with their views strengthened her friendship with them: they became important confidantes and Jane's correspondence with them both lasted some twenty-five years. She had no other friends in Dublin who were such strong feminists and shared her beliefs. She was pleased, for instance, to hear from Lotten at one point that a mutual friend, though married, 'still keeps to literature. That is well. We women are progressing in independence.'

She would ask them both about the latest news in Sweden on women's rights and tell them what was happening in Dublin: 'There is to be a lecture on the subject next week in Dublin by Mrs Fawcett, wife of an eminent member of parliament – and there is to be a meeting also at *our* house where she will speak and explain what female liberty means.' She was particularly interested in the content and style of the magazines both women ran. 'I see you have changed the form of your magazine,' she was to write to Lotten. 'You must find the expense and trouble very great – still nothing gives such interest to life as writing and *publishing* and your energy seems untiring and your intellect ever bright and active.'

The two women also fired Jane's interest in Sweden, which she came to believe was the perfect country. She visited it several times and was strongly drawn to the language. When Lotten once sent her a Swedish paper with a translation of her poem, 'Man's Mission', she wrote: 'Speranza transmuted into your fine musical language – am I to thank you for it?' Jane ultimately taught herself Swedish.

Captivated by Sweden's scenery, myths and legends, she also admired its way of life. She was particularly impressed by the way Swedish women had similar educational advantages to men. In a letter to Rosalie, thanking her for sending her essay on 'Women's Work in

Sweden', Jane was to say, 'Even in Dublin scarcely one female servant can read – and few can write – *all* Swedes appear to have university education. This difference of knowledge helps much towards the formation of a fine, self-respecting independent character . . .'

Jane also praised the way all professions in Sweden were 'now open to female intellect and energy, and many of the government offices: so there are thousands of ladies at the present time in Sweden who are not only self-supporting, but in the receipt of good and assured incomes by the exercise of their various talents.' She disliked the absurd idea in Britain that 'politics should not be discussed by a woman, as if the destiny of her country was not a nobler object for thought and subject for conversation than the gossip of a neighbourhood.'[7] She had always argued that intellectual women should be given more recognition and their high standing in Sweden delighted her: 'They are honoured and made much of, and treated with considerable distinction, solely from belonging to the peerage of intellect,' she said. She believed that intellect in England, on the other hand, was 'the least honoured of all God's gifts . . . especially literary power when manifested by a woman.'[8]

When Lotten and her father first called formally at the Merrion Square house, a servant told them that despite it being 1 p.m., 'it was not yet light in his mistress's apartment.' Jane disliked exertion, even the relatively minor exertion of getting up. Her large size made her inclined to move languidly and as little as possible.

The Swedes waited for her in William's study which, with its deep-set windows, was attractively old-fashioned. When William came in, Lotten, who wrote an account of the visit for a Swedish magazine, was impressed by his 'noble and independent personality'. She noticed he stooped slightly, 'less from years than from ceaseless work . . . and his gait seems rather hurried so that he gives an immediate impression that his time is extremely precious. His thick, grey-streaked hair falls around his open, broad forehead in a strange, wilful manner.' He was, she saw, 'carrying a small unruly boy on his arm and holding another by the hand. His eyes rest on them with pleasure.' However hard William worked, he always had time for his children.[9]

On their first night in Dublin the von Kraemers dined with the Wildes and their friends. It was a Sunday and the guests clustered on the balconies of the first-floor drawing room to watch a religious procession pass by, led by a lively orchestra. 'We, like most of the upper classes, are Protestants,' said Jane in her grandest manner, 'but most of the Irish population consists of loyal Catholics.'

It was a casual meal. While roast beef was being served, Jane asked Baron von Kraemer for a Swedish lesson. Oscar (aged three) and Willie (five) were still up and after kissing Oscar ('the small boy with the brown curly hair and the great dreaming eyes'), his father sent him off to get a book he wanted. At the end of the meal, a soprano sang some of Moore's melancholy Irish melodies.

Jane and Lotten instantly admired each other. 'Looking at her,' Lotten wrote in her article, 'the thought comes involuntarily to mind that this is how the Roman matron must have looked at one time, with her classic pure features and with a Junoesque figure and bearing. But here the peace of the ancients has made room for a mixture of soulful and attractive liveliness in her temperament. The fire in her gaze betrays the famous poetess whose lofty songs are so beloved in her homeland. One is tempted to say of her, as of the beauty Deugala, to whom Ossian sang: "She believed in nobility, on the highest/In her heart proud dreams resided."'

The Wildes invited the two Swedes back again for dinner and there was an enthusiastic discussion of Swedish history, legends and antiquities. William, passing round an ancient Swedish drinking horn, said he hoped he would next drink the von Kraemers' health in Sweden. Lotten at once asked if Jane would be accompanying him. 'You must know, dear friend,' William told her, making a quick recovery, 'that I always say only "I" when it means both of us.'

Writing to Lotten after her visit, Jane praised her extravagantly: 'You gained all hearts here – you have so much intellect united with such highbred ease and grace and such sweet natural affectionate manners.' She asked if a poem by Lotten's brother was connected 'with your fine indeed *sublime* old mythology' and ruefully admitted that she was so preoccupied with 'the company pleasures of Dublin' and her three children that she had 'little time for writing or even for thought'.

She could not resist praising her children: 'Willie and Oscar [are] growing tall and wise and Baby – you don't forget little Isola I hope – is now ten months old and is the pet of the house. She has fine eyes and promises to have a most acute intellect – these two gifts are enough for any woman.'[10]

Despite saying she had no time for writing, Jane told Lotten she had begun to translate a German novel 'that fell in my way', called *'Eritis Sicut Deus'* (*Ye shall be as God*). 'Have you met with it?' she asked.

'It has reference throughout to the modern philosophy of Germany.' It was to be five years before the translation was published.

One of Jane's 'company pleasures' in April 1858 was an invitation from Sir William Rowan Hamilton to visit the gardens of the Observatory. The day was dedicated to 'Friendship and the Muse' and poets Denis Florence MacCarthy and Aubrey de Vere were among the guests. The latter, who thanked his host for a 'merry dinner, rambles about the green fields and poetical recitations', knocked in vain at Jane's house over the next few days hoping to see her.[11]

She had taken her children for a six-week holiday in the village of Enniskerry. 'Children bind one down to home with such strong cords it seems unnatural even to leave them for a day,' she wrote to her Scots friend, when she planned a trip to London to find an English nursery governess. 'Their quick kiss and warm hug at parting fill me with remorse for going away at all from them and I long to have Willie's pretty graceful head resting again on my shoulder while I read *The Lady Clare* to him from Tennyson or the scene in *Hiawatha*, two favourites of his.'[12]

However, after 'a delightful month' in England that summer, travel beckoned and Jane admitted: 'Now that I have a governess to leave the children with I hope to make a little tour every summer. Without this, we're apt to fossilize in married state.'

That autumn, Jane and William fulfilled their promise to the von Kraemers and set off for Scandinavia. William's renown as an antiquarian turned their journey into a royal progress. Honours were showered on him: he was given a public dinner in Stockholm and an honorary degree from the University of Uppsala. Jane loved sailing through the Norwegian fiords and stopping at the locks of Sweden's Gotha Canal and made sharply observed notes which she later used in a book: 'The serving-girls were all barefoot, like the Irish peasants, who keep their shoes and stockings for Sundays and festivals only . . . at every station they came down in groups to the steamer – colossal red-haired giants amongst them, probably Finnlanders; dark-haired Swedes; and little elfin Lapps . . . they wore the high-pointed cap, a grey tunic girt round the waist with a leathern belt and looked like dramatic accessories introduced for effect into the scene.'[13]

Jane was particularly fascinated by the wooded islands of the Baltic and their different legends, such as that of the spirit of the eldest son of Gustavus Vasa, the founder of Swedish independence, who was still said to haunt the Uppsala woods. After jealously stabbing his friend he was forced to drink poison and 'In the night-time his shrieks can be heard like the rushing wind through the pine branches, and his ghost sweeps by like the grey floating mist-wraith of a human form.'

But the highspot of the whole journey for Jane was their visit to Baron von Kraemer and Lotten. Jane loved a sense of occasion, grand surroundings and patrician company and she adored the sparkling soirees that were part of the von Kraemers' lifestyle. 'No future ruler can ever surpass the Baron in the grace, the dignity and the noble hospitality with which he did the honours of his distinguished position,' she told Lotten, after her return to Ireland. 'I shall still always think of him as standing, as I last saw him, in the lordly salon of the Castle, with his Star of Diamonds on his breast.' She thought of Lotten too 'in that grand regal castle surrounded by such proud historic memories, with the ancient mounts of Sigtuna and the glorious pine trees, beneath which you told me the story of the son of Gustaf Vasa.'[14]

Once back in Dublin Jane reimmersed herself in the city's social life. 'The world – the world it rushes in on me and seizes me in its grip and flings me down in the low level muddy plains of social pleasures,' she wrote to Lotten, going on to list the number of lords with whom she and her husband had dined lately: 'is not this a pretty string for one fortnight, all dressed out as fine as peacocks.'

She was writing after midnight and explained that 'My husband is dining out with the Chief Justice and I am keeping watch for him in my Bower.'[15] She liked being alone and believed that 'solitude is the only nourisher of the soul.' Solitude at Merrion Square was rare. The children were running around during the day and at night dinner invitations were showered on new friends like Robert Chambers, who reviewed Wilde's Catalogue of the Royal Irish Academy in *Chambers' Journal*, and old friends like Smith O'Brien who, Jane reported, 'likes to talk of the past and calls himself the "Convict"'.[16] Oscar was to remember that 'The earliest hero of my childhood was Smith O'Brien, whom I remember well – tall and stately . . . John Mitchel, too, on his return to Ireland I saw at my father's table with his eagle eyes and impassioned manner.'[17]

Although in December 1858 Jane was claiming that she had given up all literary employment 'since the cares of a household have come on me', she had enough time to write for the *Dublin University Magazine*. She had more than adequate domestic help and her three children were now in the care of an English governess.

In between lessons and church, the children had an easy-going life in the Wildes' casual household. Oscar's memories of that time were happy. He told a friend once he remembered having an evening bath with Willie in the nursery in front of the fire, while their nightshirts were hanging on the high fender to warm. While the nurse was out of the room, a little brown patch appeared on one of the nightshirts which then burst into flames. 'Oscar clapped his hands with delight while Willie shouted to the nurse to come to the rescue, which she swiftly did . . . whereupon Oscar cried with rage at the spoiling of the pageant and the end of the fun.'[18]

Oscar also remembered his love of his toy bear. 'I thought that nothing could make me more unhappy than to lose my bear. Well, one day Willy asked me for it; and I was so fond of Willy that I gave it to him, I remember, without a pang.' For years after, he said, whenever he quarrelled with his brother, he used to ask for his bear back.[19]

In later years Oscar's first biographer, Robert Sherard, in a fit of Victorian prudery, claimed that the 'taint of moral laxness' infected the very air of a house in which 'high thinking did not go hand in hand with plain living'. He considered No. 1 Merrion Square a scene of 'opulence and carouse; of late suppers and deep drinking; of careless talk and example. His father's gallantries were the talk of Dublin. Even his mother, though a woman of spotless life and honour, had a loose way of talking which might have been a danger to her sons.' He condemned Sir William for choosing supper companions who were boozy and boisterous Bohemians.[20]

But there was nothing untoward in this. The atmosphere in the houses of many professional men in Dublin was similar, and provocative remarks of Jane's were hardly likely to create an unedifying example to her children. Willie and Oscar grew up happily in their lively, genial surroundings, unaware and untroubled by the possibility of moral laxness. The Bohemians, scholars and wits at their father's dinner table and in their mother's drawing room only nourished their own brilliance in conversation. As a young boy Oscar 'heard every subject discussed and every creed defended and demolished at his father's table, where were to be found not only the brilliant genius of Ireland, but also celebrities of Europe and America . . . he considers that the best of his education in boyhood was obtained from this association with his father and mother and their remarkable friends.'[21]

The house was the scene of a great many children's parties. John Gilbert recalled William's invitations: 'Tomorrow is Oscar's birthday, and you are such a favourite of his you must be sure to come and dine.' And 'Billy has passed his examination, and you will join us in drinking his health.'[22] Oscar described his father in later years as a man of the greatest social charm and intellectual superiority. Jane too had a loving relationship with her children. Despite maids and governesses, she nursed them when they were ill and delighted in their progress. As Oscar remarked in *The Importance of Being Earnest*: 'All women become like their mothers. That is their tragedy. No man does. That's his.'

Jane was intensely loyal to her husband and when early in 1859 the historian John Gilbert gave her a copy of his first volume of the *History of the City of Dublin*, she promptly fired off a salvo in William's defence: 'I have but one little objection to offer. In the "History of the Philosophical Society" you scarcely appreciated my husband's labours. From the passage one might think he had only compiled a catalogue, where he *first* was the one who wrote the History and told the world all that is known on the subject . . . posterity in 10 or 20 years will certainly think W. R. Wilde was a poor wretch of a clerk who copied catalogues for a livelihood. There is nothing to identify him as a man who has done something in his generation, both for literature and humanity . . .'[23] Gilbert did not repeat the mistake. On receiving a copy of the third volume, Jane told him she was 'glad my grandfather finds a place there, and I must thank you for the very graceful and kind manner you mention my husband.'

In the spring of 1859 William was contemplating another three-week trip to Denmark and Sweden in August to study the antiquities and Jane swore to Lotten that if he did, 'by the nine Gods of Rome' she would go along too. Her husband, she said, had meant to send Lotten his photograph, but had changed his mind, annoyed that it had 'a wisky-wasky look and *no* eyes'.

Jane was also planning a summer of travel, for as well as going with her husband to Sweden, if he went, she hoped to visit Baden Baden, or Vichy, to take the waters for her wrist, which was inflamed and very painful. She told Lotten that it was some comfort that she could at least now use a pen to continue translating the German book, which she had not touched for a year: 'unless I have something of the kind to do I am miserable.'

Dublin was too gay then for misery. 'We were at a ball on St Patrick's night, the 17th March, at the Lord Lieutenant's, of *2,000* people,' she told Lotten. 'Everyone wears shamrock mixed with the artificial trimmings of the dress on that night – and all the ladies wear white feathers and lappets or tulle veils – my dress was three skirts of white silk ruched round with white satin ribbon and looped up with bouquets of gold flowers and green shamrock – a wreath of the same for the hair, plumes of feather and white tulle veil bordered with gold.'

A few paragraphs later in her letter she had forgotten the Dublin Castle ball and insisted she did not go into company: 'That world fatigues me too much. But we have a dinner every Saturday of ten or twelve clever, learned men and that amuses me more and is less fatigue – we dine at 6.30 o/c and part at 11 – and discuss all the current topics and literature and science of the day . . .'[24]

When William could afford the time, he would join Jane and the children for a summer holiday by the sea at Sandymount or Bray; or they would go to Connemara, or to a farm named Crone in Glencree Valley, overlooking the Sugar Loaf mountain, about fifteen miles south of Dublin. Some years earlier, William had also built a small hunting and fishing lodge on the tiny wooded peninsula of Illaunroe on the shores of Lough Fee – Illaunroe meaning the 'red island', though Oscar later referred to it as 'the little purple island' – and there the boys learnt to fish and hunt: Oscar was to tell his own children stories of the 'great melancholy carp' in Lough Corrib. He and Willie always spent a large part of their holidays in the west when they were at school, boating on the lakes and helping their father explore ancient sites.

In the summer of 1859, a young girl of 15 from County Waterford was taken on by Jane as a children's nurse. One of her charges was Oscar and the girl claimed that young Edward Carson, later Wilde's cross-examiner at his trial, was under her care at the same time and the two were playmates.[25] Hearing of this, the actor Michael MacLiammoir said, 'Yes, that would explain it all. Oscar probably upset Edward's sandcastle.'[26]

On one of their holidays around this time, it is alleged that Oscar and Willie were baptized into the Catholic faith. This claim was made by the Revd Lawrence Charles Prideaux Fox, a chaplain at the local reformatory near the Crone farmhouse in Glencree. He often dropped in to the lodgings Jane took there each summer for herself and her children, as the owners were friends, and claimed that Jane finally 'asked me to instruct two of her children, one of them being that future erratic genius, Oscar Wilde. After a few weeks I baptized these two children.' Jane, he said, was present at the ceremony and asked him to call on her husband and tell him what had occurred. William was a strong Protestant believer, but according to the chaplain he merely replied that 'he did not care what they were so long as they became as good as their mother.'[27] The baptism, if there was one, was not registered, though Oscar was to tell friends he vaguely remembered it and in *The Importance of Being Earnest* gave Algernon and Jack the idea of a second baptism.

Jane and William did get to Sweden that year, 1859, and were again overwhelmed by the attention they received from their many friends. Jane said she 'never *loved* anything after leaving Sweden – I vowed not – in fact my heart could not stand it', and thanked Lotten for sending an extract about the 'never to be forgotten Athenian symposium in the brilliant halls of Uppsala Castle'. She told her that neither of them would ever forget her 'enchanting country with all its noble historical associations, its queenly capital throned on her seven hills and robed in her mantle of pine forests and your graceful people'.[28]

Jane was a prolific letter writer and besides her correspondence with Lotten assiduously kept up with a wide circle of friends. Henriette Corkran, who, together with her sister, Alice, a writer, was a long-time Dublin friend of Jane's and daughter of the *Times* Paris correspondent, wrote to her in the autumn of 1859 to say: 'Your splendid letter so dazzled and overpowered me that I have been obliged to take some days to recover from its effect, as from a shock of electricity.' Jane must have received her letter with pleasure: she loved confidences and Henriette poured out her resentment at William Thackeray having 'not treated me as he might have done' in using his influence to get her a job on a weekly publication.[29]

Another of Jane's correspondents at the time was Christopher O'Keeffe, a literary friend and firm Nationalist. Jane had a gift for reducing intelligent men to bemused incoherence and O'Keeffe tied himself up in flowery knots when writing to her in 1859: 'As my mind cooled down after writing to you last it occurred to me with that unspeakable agony of mind which you can appreciate as your exquisitely gifted nature is susceptible likewise of that harrowing pain which surpasses all other agony that what I intended for mere playfulness – un jeu d'esprit – may have awakened your displeasure.'[30]

O'Keeffe wrote to her several times during 1860. In one letter he roused her old passions when he fulminated about the way 'our lords' had mortgaged away whole cities, towns and villages, and went on to castigate Lord Portarlington, whose extensive estates spread over four counties: 'He and his peers were able in this way to exterminate, starve and exile – in short – to murder – several million of people.'

He greatly admired Jane's verse and gave a translation he had finished the following preface: 'To Mrs J. F. Wilde (Speranza), in admiration of her brilliant genius and amiable virtues this volume is dedicated by her devoted humble servant, C. M. O'K.' Equally fulsomely, he told her that 'Maturin's heroine unquestionably resembles you, the same brilliancy of genius and elevation of thought – the same amiability of disposition and lofty aspiration.'

Although he claimed to have profound respect, wonder and admiration for her husband's talents, his opinion cooled when he met William on the stairs of the Catholic University and had him 'growling in my ear bitter complaints of the people of Dublin who did not attend the lectures and complaints of the students who imitated the people of Dublin and complaints of – oh! I did not know what!' A man like that, he told Jane indignantly, 'is a man capable of finding fault with his wife!'[31]

Jane wrote to Lotten that year after hearing of the death of a mutual friend, whose picture she had only just had framed to hang in her library. She and William had cancelled the friends they had coming to dinner: 'Oh, life, life, life! What a mournful mystery it becomes.' Since returning from Sweden she had thought of compiling her travel notes, 'but so many things prevented me commencing until about two or three months ago.' Now she felt she hadn't the heart to go on.

In August 1861, Dublin again hosted the annual meeting of the National Association for the Promotion of Social Science. It was held at the Four Courts, a large and imposing building where the Supreme Court of Ireland met, and Dublin was alive with social events. There was a special dinner at Dublin Castle to which her other Swedish friend Rosalie and her husband Professor Olivecrona, who attended the conference, were invited, and a reception was held there for 1,800 guests.

According to an article by a Swedish woman published in Rosalie's magazine, Jane and William kept open house for the Swedish contingent. The article's author, while walking in Phoenix Park, spotted the enterprising way invitations were handed out: 'I had the opportunity of observing how our kind friend [William Wilde] and his amiable wife, who in her native country is known and valued as a successful authoress, literally went out on roads and paths, encouraging people to come to their table.' The method worked well: everyone joked and talked 'merrily, freely and easily'.[32] It was reminiscent of the way Lady Morgan used to stand on her Dublin balcony and, on spotting a celebrity, call down the hour at which she wished them to visit her.

Jane and William were back in Sweden again in October. From Stockholm, Jane wrote to Lotten to say she would drive down to see her and the Baron: 'I am delighted with your beautiful land, your city and your handsome people.' It was the last time she was royally entertained by Baron von Kraemer in the castle, as a year later Lotten wrote to her to say her father had retired from the position of Viceroy of Uppsala. In a letter to Lotten the following April, she said, 'I quite mourn when I think of your living in sight of your royal castle and not still ruling there.'

Rosalie Olivecrona sent Jane a book of memories of the Wildes' visit to Uppsala, inscribed in gold lettering. Jane was thrilled with scenes of the castle 'and the mounds where we drank mead in honour of Odin', and told her she had 'placed the volume with great pleasure on my drawing room table and it is much admired by our visitors'.

Jane had a high opinion of Rosalie's magazine and told her she wished '*greatly* to have something of mine *contributed*. It is entirely *vanity* on my part – I want to see my name in your magazine.' She asked Rosalie if she should submit an article she had written 'on the condition of women', and said meanwhile she would take all the Swedish magazines she had down to Connemara, on the family holiday, and read them in quiet and solitude.[33]

Both Jane and William were delighted when in 1862 the King of Sweden awarded William Wilde the Order of the North Star. No Swedish order carries title rights but in April of that year the minutes of the Medico-Philosophical Society record that henceforth Dr Wilde was to be addressed as Chevalier Wilde. There were rumours that William Wilde received this honour because he operated on the eye of the Swedish king, Oscar I. But the royal archives in Sweden have no record of any operation; and King Oscar had died from a brain tumour three years previously. More likely, Baron von Kraemer, friend of the Wildes and the prestigious governor of Uppsala, recommended the honour to the then Swedish king, Carl XV.[34]

The next month the World Exhibition opened in London. Jane missed both this and the Social Science meeting there, which, she told Rosalie, 'must have been very brilliant and I regret now I did not go to it'. Instead she and the children went off again to Connemara for a recuperative month, because 'All my children have had whooping

cough and I have passed a miserable time with them.' She confined her
holidays to Ireland that year, explaining to Lotten in October that
Willie had been delicate all summer and that this had prevented her
from leaving home.

Jane was writing from Bray, a seaside town not far from Dublin,
where she was staying with her children and their governess. She
told Lotten that 'Dr Wilde has built four handsome houses there
facing the sea and with the mountains for background – I have taken
one for myself and furnished it . . . I wish that I could receive you there
one sunny day in June when the mountains, sea and sky are radiant
with light and beauty.' The Wildes were doing well out of their Bray
property, renting out the other three houses for £120 a year each.

William Wilde loved owning property. Telling Lotten how hard he
was working, Jane added that she really thought he must have a
building mania: 'He is now going to build a residence on his new property in the County Mayo on the shores of Lough Corrib.' Her husband
was to call it Moytura House, as it was built on the supposed site of
the legendary battle of Moytura. As for herself, Jane said, Willie's
illness had kept her so busy she had never touched a book – but
she hoped to return to her usual life of reading and writing in the
spring.

The Christmas of 1862 was depressing. A Swedish friend, a
Professor Siegfried, who had lunched with them on Christmas Day,
died of a violent brain fever two weeks later and was given a public
funeral in Dublin. Telling a Swedish acquaintance about it, Jane added
that her children had all been ill over Christmas too. 'It was a very sickly
season and Oscar, my second son, was *five weeks* in bed with a fever.'

She was still working at her translation but early in 1863 wrote to
another friend in Sweden to say, 'At last my book from the German
is published – the title is *The First Temptation*, or *Eritis Sicut Deus*.
Try and get it if English books reach you – It will be in the library
next week.'[35]

The First Temptation was a philosophical romance. It was published
anonymously in Germany in 1854, and achieved such a *succès de
scandale* that another edition was published a year later. It was long
thought to have been written by Marie Schwab, but Wilhelmine
Friederike Gottliebe Canz finally admitted authorship.[36] It has a touch
of the Gothic terror-tale about it. Its theme is Satan's first temptation
to man – 'Ye shall be as God' – to which the hero Robert succumbs,
believing man can renounce God and create his own aesthetic world.

The story centres round Elizabeth, his pure and beautiful wife, and Robert's undermining of her faith. To ensure her husband's love, she accepts his arid logic and renounces God. Then a shocking change comes over her: 'She was alive but dead – a galvanized corpse.' Her husband falls under the power of a coquette and he decides to shut up his wife in a madhouse and marry the coquette. Gradually, Robert's moral nature deteriorates and he decides that he alone is fit to be the leader of the age.

Meanwhile, Elizabeth finds she cannot rest in the icy darkness of atheism. She repents and is absolved ('all pain and sorrow fell from her spirit in that moment') while proud, self-worshipping Robert finds that 'his pretensions were lies, his wisdom folly, his strength weakness, his pride blasphemy'.

Despite the unintentional humour, the tale takes three volumes to tell and its style is tedious: a priest admonishes a student for admiring a print of an unclothed Venus, saying, 'Such a shameless picture is calculated to destroy every moral feeling . . . Away with this art worship. It is the most subtle of all poisons because it suits so well the carnal appetite. It is sinful, the lustful idolatry of the age!'

The *Athenaeum*'s reviewer fired both barrels at the book: 'This work is extremely well translated, but few readers will have the patience to wade through three thick volumes of German philosophy and its practical application to the different characters . . . and, whether it be that the puppets are perverse or the author unskilled, the result is a fatal concatenation of madness, badness and general inconvenience . . . all the characters go more or less mad and the reader will find himself inclined to follow their example.'[37]

Further reception was mixed. The *New Monthly Magazine* said the book showed 'the pernicious principles of Strauss and Hegel and their followers in their true colours . . .' while the *Hibernian Magazine* thought it a tale 'full of moral significance, a solemn, almost awful, protest against the spirit of scepticism that devastates the age . . . It is at once a great drama of human passions and a great ethical treatise.'[38] The translator was thought as daring as the book.

An anonymous letter appeared in *Saunders's News-Letter* in vigorous defence of the book (could it possibly have been written by Jane?), saying the writer had read 'with pain' the censures on the book, and was puzzled how any unbiased reader could 'doubt that its object is to do good and not evil'. The letter asserted that the book was the production of a sincere Christian and 'intellectualist of the highest order', and asked, 'Is it fair to dissect a book and, judging merely from isolated passages, cast a slur on the morals of the writer?' It ended angrily: 'Better were our libraries replete with more of such books, and less of modern sensation novels.'[39]

Although by birth a Protestant, Jane was interested in all kinds of religious expression. Oscar was to write of her later, 'Except for the *people*, for whom she thinks dogma necessary, she rejects all forms of superstition and dogma, particularly any notion of priest and sacrament standing between her and God. She has a very strong faith in that aspect of God *we* call the Holy Ghost – the divine intelligence of which we on earth partake. Here she is very strong, though of course at times troubled by the discord and jarring of the world, when she takes a dip into pessimism.'[40]

Rosalie Olivecrona delighted Jane with the news that *The First Temptation* had reached Sweden. 'It is certainly a wonderful book – but too profound for general readers,' Jane told her; 'only *Les Ames d'Elite* will like it.' Jane then wrote to Lotten to say that 'I hope you will read my book – did I understand you that it had been reviewed in a Swedish paper? How I wish I had seen the paper – you should review it in the *Tidskrift for hemmet* . . . I want to subscribe to that journal of Mde. Olivecrona.' She urged Lotten to join her when she was next in Paris, saying that no doubt she was sad and needed a change of scene after her father's retirement. 'We might meet there and you could stay in the same pension with me – but when one has children it is very very difficult to make travelling arrangements and now that mine are growing up I dislike still more leaving them – My sweet boy is now nearly *eleven*, very clever and very high spirited and tho' he obeys me will scarcely obey a governess – I feel it would be a risk to leave him. But we think of sending both boys to a boarding school soon and then I shall be better able to make plans for travel.'[41]

Meanwhile she was enjoying herself in Dublin, telling Lotten, 'I went to a grand Bal costumé the other evening and wore a beautiful dress as Zenobia, Queen of Palmyra.' Jane must have appreciated the clothes as well as the character: the Victorian fashions of the day, crinolines and poke bonnets, were not suited to her tall, statuesque figure.

In April 1863, Jane took the children to Bray again, this time with a new governess, a Swiss one. Jane, anxious to improve her Swedish, had been trying to find a Swedish lady's maid who could also sew for the children. She now asked Lotten again if she could possibly find her a Swedish governess who could speak both French and German as she could teach the children these languages and also read with Jane. She was willing to pay £40 a year.

Jane had also started to learn Danish as she and William planned a further trip that year to Denmark and Sweden. She wrote to Lotten to say she was charmed at the prospect of seeing 'the grand gloomy heroic Scandinavians and the many gifted and valued friends we have there'. She hoped that if they made the trip, Lotten would be 'somewhere within striking distance of the electricity of friendship'.

The years until now had been kind to Jane. She was a celebrated writer and social hostess, lived in a fashionable home in Dublin, could travel extensively, was happily married to a man she admired and had three children whom she loved dearly. It is not surprising that, unaware of the approaching crisis, many envied her.

6

Loyalty on Trial

THE YEAR 1864 started with William Wilde receiving a knighthood and ended with him figuring in a sensational court case.

In January, when he received his knighthood, the future looked glowing. The Earl of Carlisle, the Lord Lieutenant of Ireland, held his first drawing room for the season in the throne room at Dublin Castle and *Saunders's News-Letter* for 29 January reported that the occasion was made still more agreeable when his Excellency 'availed himself of the opportunity afforded by the presence of so brilliant an assemblage to confer the distinction of knighthood upon one of the most eminent men of the medical profession and the scientific associations of Ireland . . .'

It was a deserved knighthood, given to William, in the Lord Lieutenant's words, 'not so much in consideration of your high professional reputation, which is European, as to mark my sense of the services you have rendered to statistical science, especially in connection with the Irish census'.[1] Knighthoods then were relatively rare: in the 1860s, the Viceroy received a deputation from the medical profession complaining that too few titles were being given to doctors.

The new Sir William was congratulated on all sides: the press wrote of his achievements; his friends were delighted. William Carleton wrote effusively to him, ending, 'You have never courted popularity yet you have had it without asking. As for Lady Wilde you know that her fame went before either your title or hers. I shall write to her on the subject . . . I have not yet seen her book but if it is equal to the quaint elegance and purity of style which are to be found in *Sidonia the Sorceress* I will require no more.'[2]

Both William and Jane were overjoyed to make the transition from Dr Wilde and Speranza to Sir William and Lady Wilde. Jane was particularly gratified. She was a favourite with the Dublin crowds, and delighted in hearing them applaud when the linkman called,

'Lady Wilde's carriage stops the way', as her carriage slowed down at the approach to Dublin Castle and its elegant drawing rooms. Oscar must have seen and heard this and it could only have enhanced his admiration for his mother. He was certainly to share Jane's social consciousness: Bernard Shaw said of him that he was 'a snob to the marrow of his being, having been brought up in Merrion Square, Dublin'.[3] Once, at the London house of the Duke of Westminster, Oscar said to a friend of his, Richard Le Gallienne, 'Ah, Richard, this is how a gentleman should live!'[4]

Jane enjoyed social occasions, finding it pleasurable to be deferred to, both intellectually and socially. She especially relished dressing up. The *Irish Times* reported the dress Jane wore when her husband was knighted as having 'a train and corsage of richest white satin, trimmed handsomely in scarlet velvet and gold cord, jupe, richest white, satin with bouillonnes of tulle, satin ruches and a magnificent tunic of real Brussels lace lappets; ornaments, diamonds.'[5] As Oscar commented in *The Picture of Dorian Gray*, 'He atones for being occasionally somewhat over-dressed by being always absolutely over-educated.'

Away from the drawing rooms of Dublin, conditions in Ireland were worsening as unemployment tightened its grip on the country. Jane had not been writing much verse but, as in the old days, she responded to the feelings of the hour and in the March issue of *Duffy's Hibernian Magazine* wrote 'Work While It Is Called To-Day'. The poem had the old Speranza touch and readers would have identified with its opening lines, which began '"No man hath hired us" – strong hands drooping/ Listless falling in idleness down . . .' She followed this up, in the same magazine, with another poem, 'Who Will Shew Us Any Good?', a call for a leader to resurrect Ireland.

It was clearly an attempt to fan old flames and it failed: the poem had a decided sense of *déjà vu*. It was damned by the newspaper, the *Irish People*, which said, 'Speranza's *Who Will Shew Us Any Good* is even more difficult to make out than her verses usually are, and we scarcely know whether we rightly understand its meaning . . .'[6]

At the time of the famine, some twenty years before, Speranza had been above criticism. Her verse was best when she responded to emotional events and, in these circumstances, it was still effective. One man was shortly to write to her after reading 'her admirable lines on the political prisoners in France' to ask if she would get up a petition to the French Empress, 'signed by the ladies of Ireland', to intercede for them. Without a banner to follow, however, Jane's verse lacked direction and her reputation as a poet suffered.

In 1864 she made a bid to revive her past glories by bringing out a collection of her early poetry, called *Poems by Speranza*. The frontispiece read, 'Dedicated to My Sons, Willie and Oscar Wilde', followed by the words,

> I made them indeed,
> Speak plain the word COUNTRY. I taught them, no doubt,
> That a country's a thing men should die for at need!

The collection was mostly well received by the Irish press. The *Freeman's Journal* was full of praise, thinking her poems 'pre-eminently characterized by the beauty of their imagery, their truthfulness to nature and the purity and simplicity of the phraseology in which our gifted countrywoman conveys her musings, her thoughts and her very emotions to the reader'.[7] The *Dublin Review* wrote of Speranza's 'extraordinary influence on all the intellectual and political activities of Young Ireland', though unflatteringly noted her poetry's 'peculiar and powerful but monotonous rhythm, which seems to pulsate on the ear with the even, strident stroke of a Hindoo drum'.[8]

The English *Athenaeum*, which no doubt disliked Jane's verse for political rather than literary reasons, criticized her 'grandiloquent generalities, tricked out with imposing but not striking metaphors of highly-coloured phrases such as "a jewelled-walled city", "the rainbow-crowned angel", "the fatal thanatos", "the rhythmic march of nations" . . .'[9] In a letter to Lotten, mentioning how well her collection of poems had sold in Ireland, Jane admitted that they were 'not suited to *English* tastes you may suppose – oh what an incubus this *English* government is on our country. It strangles all life . . .'[10]

A copy of her volume of poems went to both Lotten and Rosalie. She jealously guarded her reputation as high priestess of verse and was upset if any editor failed to show a similar regard for her work. She took umbrage at any professional slight and her friend Christopher O'Keeffe had to write to her soothingly on one occasion to say that he had told the proprietor of the *Irishman* 'that in your estimation that paper looks unfavourably upon you. He assured me in the most earnest manner that that was not the case . . . He fancied that Sullivan of the *Nation* must have impressed you with that idea and concluded by saying, "I wish Lady Wilde would send us a poem for the *Irishman*."

He and Sigerson [the editor] were entirely unconscious of having said that *Eva* and *Mary* [both poets of the *Nation*] were superior to you. The styles of those ladies are so entirely different that no comparison could well be instituted.'[11]

Jane was further upset by Charles Kickham, the editor of the *Irish People*. This newspaper, which had only started the year before, had echoes of John Mitchel's revolutionary paper, the *United Irishman*, as it too promoted the use of force to achieve national independence. The *Irish People* not only reviewed Jane's poetry collection unenthusiastically but printed a reader's letter that set out a verse of hers as prose, to show it was not poetry. O'Keeffe, again to the rescue, told her that a contributor who wrote verse under the name 'the Kilkenny Man' had been so angry about this that he had told O'Keeffe that 'If there were any deficiencies in Lady Wilde's poems (and there are not) it is our duty to praise them still, shutting our eyes to her shortcomings. She cannot be eulogized too highly . . . Is it possible that Kickham could forget the heroic conduct of Lady Wilde on the occasion of Gavan Duffy's trial? . . . Instead of carping at her productions, we should build her a statue.'[12]

Jane had been preoccupied with deciding which school Willie and Oscar should attend. She and William finally settled on Portora Royal School at Enniskillen, County Fermanagh, known as the Eton of Ireland, where the two went to board in February 1864. She wrote to Rosalie Olivecrona in April to say, 'My two boys have gone to a public school – they are rapidly growing into young men and are both clever and good.'[13]

Jane still had the company of Isola and in thanking Lotten for sending her a photo – friends in those days exchanged photos of each other constantly – told her that she had 'sent it in to Sir William's room by my little daughter Isola to ask, did he know it? She came back saying, "Papa says it is his little love in Sweden."'[14]

Both Jane and her husband were anxious that Lotten come over to see their new house, Moytura, in Connemara, which had been finished that year. Jane wrote of its 'grand wild scenery and the lovely dark eyes of the half-Spanish peasant girls.' Set among the brilliant blues and greens of the Connemara countryside, Moytura House is in a commanding position on the bank of Loch Corrib with the Moycullen hills in the background. A spacious, gabled building, with Connemara and Kilkenny marble fireplaces in the downstairs rooms, it made a

comfortable second home for the family, where they often spent their
holidays. William hunted for antiquities; the boys helped him, fished
or hunted; Isola could play on the banks of the river and Jane languidly
entertained. The private grounds contained a walled kitchen garden
with apple, fig, pear and plum trees; and a rose garden with a sundial.

There is the same sense of peace around Moytura House today that
must have attracted William Wilde over a century ago. Great lakes are
all around: even the nearby market town of Cong is full of water
gushing out of rocks and bubbling up in pools to form the nearby River
Cong.

To encourage Lotten to visit, Jane gave a graphic sketch of her life
there so that she would know what to expect: 'You may do just as
you like in our house, read when you like and take breakfast in bed
and be entirely *sans gêne* – I never come down out of my room till
1 or 2 o/c – then we can go out and drive and enjoy ourselves – and
always a pleasant friend worth talking to drops in to dine . . .'[15]

Dublin was always a social city, but for months after his knighthood
Sir William was positively fêted with dinners. Jane herself was in equal
demand. 'This last year I have been particularly good for nothing,' she
wrote to Rosalie Olivecrona in the summer of 1864, 'so many dinners
and invitations followed on our [*sic*] receiving the title to congratulate
us that we have lived in a whirl of dissipation – now we are quiet –
all the world has left town – and I begin to think of reawakening my
soul . . .'[16]

Her soul was to have an unexpectedly rude reawakening. That
December a woman called Mary Josephine Travers brought a court
case against Jane for libel. Jane hadn't mentioned her in any of her
letters to her friends, but Mary Travers, and William Wilde's involvement with her, had been causing her serious problems. So outrageous
did Mary's behaviour become that Jane had finally written to the
woman's father to complain, and the letter was adjudged libellous.

It had been ten years previously, in July 1854, that Mary Travers,
chaperoned by her mother, had first gone to consult the then Dr Wilde
over a hearing problem. She was an attractive, slim, dark-haired girl
of 19, with a volatile, hysterical temperament that came increasingly
to govern her behaviour.

Her home life was unhappy. Mary's parents (her mother was
Catholic, her father Protestant) did not live together. Her father,
Robert, was Professor of Medical Jurisprudence at Trinity College,
Dublin and in 1854 had been appointed physician to the South Dublin

Cholera Hospital, where he took up quarters. He was also Assistant Keeper of Archbishop Marsh's Library and a portrait there shows him unsmiling in a black, scholastic gown. He immersed himself in books and ignored his wife and children. From 1849 to 1875 he wrote constantly to his friend, Thomas Jones, in charge of Cheetham's Library in Manchester, about his work; he hardly ever mentioned his family. It was months after the spectacular trial involving his daughter, at which he briefly appeared, before he referred to it, writing: 'I have had much of domestic and other annoyance . . .'[17]

Mary's two older brothers had emigrated to Australia and she, two younger sisters and a brother lived in the suburb of Williamstown with their mother – with whom Mary had had a rift. She said later in court that she had not conversed with her mother for three or four years, though 'I have sat at table with her, and addressed her, and she has spoken to me.'[18]

In the autumn of 1854, after his professional treatment of Mary ended, she and William met weekly. 'An intimacy arose between us,' Mary was to say. 'I had conversations on other subjects than medical.' William's interest in her was fatherly. He asked Robert Travers if Mary could correct some of his manuscripts and went on to guide her reading and show concern about how she spent her spare time. He formed what was later called in court 'an acquaintanceship' which lasted ten years. It is a convenient word as there was never indisputable proof they had had an affair, or that he was to rape her, as Mary later alleged.

William's paternal attitude towards Mary undoubtedly changed. He was highly sexed and was not a man to accept indefinitely a platonic relationship. At the time Mary first consulted him, Jane was pregnant with Oscar; her firstborn, Willie, was only two years old; and she devoted any spare time she had to writing for the *Dublin University Magazine*. It was the classic occasion for a husband to look elsewhere for sexual excitement; and as William was twenty years older than Mary, he must have been flattered by her open hero-worship and dependence on him. Mary in turn was lonely and initially susceptible to a surrogate father. She was delighted to attract the attention of such a celebrated man, compensating for the indifference of her father.

The allegation of rape made by Mary took place eight years after they met. Their relationship was a curious, sexually teasing one, which could have provoked William disastrously. Mary was to tell a confused, contradictory story in her allegation of rape, but this does not necessarily exonerate William. No one knows the true story, but Mary was undoubtedly upset by some kind of incident. Given an excitable girl and a highly sexed man, it is very probable that William, sexually aroused, attempted to force himself upon her. Yet Mary went on seeing him afterwards, laying herself open to the charge that she had condoned his behaviour – or that the incident never happened.

Throughout the 1850s William took Mary openly about Dublin with him. He gave her a season ticket to the Dublin Exhibition of 1859 and accompanied her there repeatedly. He took her as well as Jane to the meeting of the British Association when it was in Dublin and he asked her to join him and his children on excursions. Because Mary was kept so short of money by her father, William gave or loaned her small sums of money from time to time, sometimes for clothes that he considered necessary ('Don't you want something . . . boots and underthings for winter?'). Mary would occasionally pay him back in small amounts, sometimes in postage stamps.

William had introduced Mary to Jane, who was kind to her and invited her to the Merrion Square house. On one occasion, after William and Mary had quarrelled, he wrote to her to say, 'If Mrs Wilde asks you to dine, won't you come and be as good friends as ever?' Jane asked her to dinner on Christmas Day 1861 and Mary went to dinner a couple more times in the next few months and also to one of Jane's salons. Jane was not a jealous woman and was unconcerned by her husband playing the role of mentor to Mary.

Unfortunately for William, he had picked the wrong girl for dalliance. When her growing possessiveness caused him to back away, Mary became uncontrolled. By March 1862, William, scenting danger, had encouraged Mary's idea of joining her brothers in Australia and given her money towards the fare. She reached the ship in Liverpool, but returned to Dublin with the excuse that someone else had taken her berth. Two months later she was once again considering Australia. William gave her more money, despite her not having returned the previous amount. She alarmed him by saying that first 'I will see Mrs Wilde and ask her whether it was that she objects to my acquaintance with you, or that you want to carry on a clandestine acquaintance with me . . .'[19] She did leave for Liverpool, but again returned.

Jane would have been saintly if she had not by now become rather irritated by the way Mary clung to her husband and how he, despite his busy schedule, still found time to take Mary around and fuss over her health. She was also becoming aware of Mary's unbalanced behaviour. In June 1862, a close friend of Jane's called to see her and – given Jane's preference for staying in bed all morning – was shown up to her bedroom. Mary was in the house at the time and promptly accompanied the friend upstairs. At this, so Mary claimed, Jane called out, 'Who dares to go into my bedroom?' As Jane stated in court, 'I expressed my surprise. Miss Travers appeared to have taken great offence . . . I don't think she dined at our house afterwards.'[20]

Mary had, however, arranged to take the three Wilde children to the chapel at Dublin Castle a few days later. On arriving at the house late she found Jane had already left with the children. She was angry for a month, cutting Jane when she passed her on the street. 'We were not friends since the quarrel about the church,' said Jane.

Mary wrote to William to say: 'I have come to the conclusion that both you and Mrs Wilde are of the one mind with regard to me, and that is, to see which will insult me most . . . to Mrs Wilde I owe no money; therefore I am not obliged to gulp down her insults . . . You will not be troubled by me again . . .'[21] She then sent William a photograph of her which Jane returned with a note, saying, 'Dear Miss Travers, Dr Wilde returns your photograph. Yours very truly, Jane Wilde.'

According to Mary's evidence, it was in October 1862, during a visit to William's study, that the alleged rape took place. She had kept silent about what happened for two years. Events had begun that month by Mary taking a bottle of laudanum to William's study and recklessly drinking it in front of him. He accused her of acting out of revenge, saying, according to Mary, 'Everyone will say I poisoned you': he sent her off to the first apothecary's she came across for an antidote – following her anxiously to ensure that she did as he said.

A few days after the laudanum episode Mary wrote to him about a corn on her foot she wanted removed, saying, 'I will keep your nose to the grinding stone while your wife is away [Jane was in Bray], and when she returns I will see her; so you had better not make a fool of me this time.'[22]

Receiving yet another visit from her later that month, William said he wanted to examine a burn on her neck. She was later to tell the court:

He came over and took off my bonnet and then he put his hand to pass over it [the burn] as he had often done before and in doing so he fastened his hand rather roughly between the ribbon that was on

my neck and my throat and I in some way, I suppose, resisted;
I believe I said, 'Oh, you are suffocating me' and he said, 'Yes I will,
I will suffocate you, I cannot help it,' and then I do not recollect
anything more until he was dashing water in my face . . .

   I had lost consciousness before the water was flung on my face;
I did not see him throwing the water, but I felt it on my face; he
said to me to 'look up,' because that if I did not rouse myself I would
be his ruin and my own . . .[23]

Her actions became increasingly strange. In June 1863 she filled
Wilde's surgery soap tray with garlic to annoy the other patients and
also handed him a handkerchief soaked in garlic. The same month she
wrote a review of Jane's translation of *The First Temptation* in the
Commercial Journal saying, 'As forbidden fruit is generally the most
prized and the most eagerly sought after, so we fear a condemnation
of the present work will ensure its being devoured with avidity by
prying minds' – but it was so condemnatory of the book's morals
that the editor refused to publish the second half of the notice.[24]
Later in court she admitted she wrote it because 'I had a pique against
Lady Wilde.'

   At the beginning of August 1863, Jane went to Bray with the
children. Mary's next act, on the 3rd of that month, was to send her
a newspaper cutting, specially printed for her by a journalist friend,
which read: 'July 21st, suddenly at the residence of her father,
Williamstown, Mary Josephine, eldest daughter of Robert Travers
MA, MD, FRQUPI.' Underneath was a little drawing which looked to
Jane like a coffin and understandably alarmed her.

   On 13 August, when Jane was back in Merrion Square, the servant
brought up Mary's card to her. Although Jane sent down a message
that she did not wish to see her, Mary remained downstairs two hours.
Jane was to say: 'Finding I was keeping the carriage waiting too long,
I came downstairs where I found Miss Travers seated on the marble
table and staring up the stairs. I passed her without recognition and
was handed into the carriage by a friend whom I met in the hall. As
I was passed out she spoke to one of the children and I put my hand
upon his shoulder and drew him away.'[25]

   The child, of suitable height for the mother to have her hand on his
shoulder, was almost certainly Oscar – who must have been confused
at being pulled away from a woman he had earlier been encouraged
to like. Obsessed by now, Mary at once wrote to Jane, saying, 'Mrs

Wilde – In some of the letters your husband sent me last week he alluded to the circumstance of the coffin, and the notice of my death that you had received. He afterwards told me that the coffin meant a threat. Why any one should think of sending you a threat in connection with my name I cannot understand. Your husband badgered me in such a manner with regard to it that I conceived it due to myself to call and ask what your reason could be for supposing you could receive a threat on my account . . . He [William] blazed at me when you left the house. His abusive language shall not pass unnoticed. M. J. Travers.'[26]

In this vengeful mood, Mary wrote a scurrilous attack on Sir William called *Florence Boyle Price; or A Warning, by Speranza*, thus implying that Jane was the author. It was a rambling story of a Dr Quilp, who chloroformed young Florence [Mary] before, in villainous style, forcing his attentions on her. The various descriptions were fictionalized accounts of the scenes Mary had had with both Jane and William: 'Florence called and sent up her card requesting to see Mrs Quilp. Quilp (who was in the hall when she entered) darted upstairs to the wife. The result need scarcely be told. Mrs Quilp refused to see her visitor. Florence was thoroughly roused at this indignity, her blood boiled at the audacious affront . . .'

The descriptions of Dr and Mrs Quilp were patently William and Jane. Dr Quilp had

a decidedly animal and sinister expression about his mouth, which was coarse and vulgar in the extreme, while his under-lip hung and protruded most unpleasantly. The upper part of his face did not redeem the lower part; his eyes were round and small – they were mean and prying and above all, they struck me as being deficient in an expression I expected to find gracing the doctor's countenance . . .

Mrs Quilp was an odd sort of undomestic woman. She spent the greater portion of her life in bed and except on state occasions, she was never visible to visitors. Therefore, whenever she gave an entertainment, it was perfectly understood by her circle that a card, left by her guests on the hall table, was all she required of those who had enjoyed her hospitality.[27]

Mary had about 1,000 copies of this pamphlet printed and sent them to friends of the Wildes and to William's patients: the artist, Bernard Mulrenin, who was then painting a portrait of Jane for next year's

Royal Hibernian Academy exhibition, remembered Mary calling on him with the pamphlet, full of bile about William. In court, Jane was to say: 'In October, perhaps the end of September, 1863, these pamphlets first came under my notice; one was sent to me through the post anonymously, afterwards several came; some were dropped into my letter-box, others came by post, and others again were brought by friends; we were deluged with them; one came through the post simply folded, so that any one could read it; this continued for many months; I heard in different quarters that they were sent to people; I heard that they were dropped on the Rathmines road . . .'[28]

After Wilde was knighted in January 1864, Mary wrote asking for £20, saying threateningly, 'You will see what will happen if you are not so prompt as usual.' The knighthood, combined with the praise and publicity Jane had received the previous year for her translation of *The First Temptation* and her new 1864 volume of poems, maddened Mary. She became envious of Jane both as wife and writer and her jealous actions became even wilder. She began war in earnest, with more paper weapons. She started to drop scurrilous notes through the Merrion Square house door addressed to William, including the following verse:

> Your progeny is quite a pest,
> To those who hate such critters;
> Some sport I'll have or I am blest,
> I'll fry the *Wilde breed in the west*,
> When you call them *fritters*.
> The name is not equivocal,
> They dare not by their mother's call
> Nor by their father, tho' he's Sir,
> A gouty knight, a mangy cur,
> He dare not even call them Fitz.
> How much he'd wish that I'd say quits![29]

Mary's allusion to the 'Wilde breed in the west' is rather puzzling. It could have referred to Willie and Oscar, who were at school in the north west of Ireland. William's two illegitimate daughters were in the care of his clergyman brother, Ralph, but Ralph's livings were in the north east.

In April 1864 Mary's outrageous actions riveted all Dublin. That month, Sir William was to give a lecture on 'Ireland Past and Present:

the land and the people'. He was a big draw and a distinguished audience was expected. Jane had written to Rosalie Olivecrona about it, saying that she would send a report of the evening. She had no inkling that the newspapers would devote as much space to what happened before the lecture as to the lecture itself.

As guests turned up at the Metropolitan Hall for the lecture, mixing with the sightseers congregating round the entrance, they were faced with boys holding large placards emblazoned with the words SIR WILLIAM WILDE AND SPERANZA, and which advertised a pamphlet called *Florence Boyle Price; or A Warning, by Speranza* – the one which Mary had written some six months previously.

Mary had made the placards advertising the pamphlet; and to make sure it was distributed widely among the crowd, she had recruited five newsboys from outside the *Commercial Advertiser* office and hired a handbell from an auctioneer. On the afternoon of the lecture she came into the city by train and hired a cab to use as her headquarters – sitting in it from seven that evening, when Sir William's audience started to arrive, till half past eight, half an hour after the lecture had started. She watched the five boys take their place outside the lecture hall, one ringing the handbell and each holding a placard and a supply of the pamphlets which included letters from William. All the boys shouted out 'Sir William Wilde's letters' and sold the pamphlets at a penny each. The proceeds were shared equally between Mary and her recruits.

Jane later described the scene to the court: 'When going in, there being a crowd, I saw a boy apparently selling pamphlets; a large number were seized at the door by one of our friends. I did not hear the bell ringing, nor did I see the placards, but my friends did. I have here four pamphlets. I see on the fly-leaf of each a number with the name Speranza on it; the writing Speranza on the pamphlet is so like mine that I would almost say it was my handwriting, but it is not . . . I first saw the placard after the lecture; it was brought to our house by a friend who seized it with a parcel of the tracts.'[30]

The fly-sheet of the pamphlet said: 'The pamphlet contains, in the form of a tale, an altered, curtailed but by no means exaggerated account of Mr, now Sir, William Wilde's conduct . . . he persisted in giving such uncalled for provocation, that even at the risk of appearing under auspices so questionable, the writer parades Sir W. Wilde's cowardice before the public . . .'[31] On further fly-sheets were a series of extracts from seventeen of William's notes to Mary, carefully and dramatically selected from the start of their relationship.

The original letters no longer exist, but they were produced in the court case later that year and showed the progression of the relationship. It was at a calm stage, for instance, in letter No. 1, which William wrote from the Baltic when there with Jane in 1859, telling Mary they had had 'all manner of adventures, all of which I will tell you when we meet'. In letter No. 2, William merely gossips about acquaintances, gives advice on social behaviour, and discusses books: '*Aurora Floyd* I have not read yet, because I am reading *Orley Farm*. Would you like it? . . . I want to do the windmill and bring Willie. What times are you usually there? . . .'

Letter No. 5 asks her to a party, saying, 'Mrs Wilde and I hope you will come in at nine o'clock tomorrow evening, Friday. Do this to please me.' He then talks of bringing baby Isola with him when he meets Mary that Saturday. In letter No. 7, he was apparently trying to end a quarrel: 'Don't throw over your truest friend, one you may never meet again; don't be as rash in one way as he is in the other . . .' By letter No. 11, he is giving her up: 'Yes, you hate and despise. I was wrong to flatter myself to the contrary. Nevertheless, if it is a farewell for paternal intercourse, say how I can serve you. You would not even look back after putting in the letter. God forgive you.' Letter No. 13 showed Mary was still unforgiving: 'You were so angry too when writing last time I had difficulty in reading it. Don't write a cross letter.'

William clearly disliked confrontations and passed this dislike on to Oscar, who hated the rows and recriminations forced on him by his partner, Lord Alfred Douglas. Indeed, William's letters to Mary have a curious parallel with the emotions shown by Oscar and Douglas. Letter No. 16 from William, for instance, begged Mary to forgive him and asked how he could atone, while No. 17 said: 'Yes, dear, you'll injure me, as you did before, and have that satisfaction.'

Such letters publicly revealed a relationship between doctor and patient which was far from professional. In their pleading or angry tone they gave the impression of being from a person in the throes of first love. In response to Mary's haughty announcement that she was not pleased with him, for example, William would write, 'Forgive; I am miserable; do see me.'

Once the contents of the pamphlet were known, there was no shortage of takers. To throw further publicity on the event, Mary had taken a letter round to *Saunders's News-Letter* for publication, signed merely 'Inquirer', which innocently asked the cause of the tumult outside the Hall on the occasion of Sir William's lecture. 'A number of boys were selling a pamphlet,' it said, 'and through curiosity I purchased one in which the knight's name most disreputably figured. Can it be possible the occurrence therein related took place? If untrue, the knight ought to take action and punish the offender. The pamphlet is six months in circulation and its accuracy has not been questioned.'[32]

Mary's rage against the Wildes was still not satisfied. She dropped a further copy of the pamphlet into the Merrion Square house, after the lecture, with a note on it saying, 'Sold at the Music Hall on last Wednesday, the proceeds to pay the expenses of an extended edition.' After publication of her letter in *Saunders's News-Letter*, a number of doggerel rhymes and articles, some signed 'Speranza' (though written by Mary, not Jane), appeared in the *Dublin Weekly Advertiser*. Then came a further series of sarcastic but obscure verses – one addressed to Speranza yet signed 'Speranza'.[33]

A few days after the lecture, Jane and the children fled down to Bray to escape the turmoil. But Mary's jealous spite drove her to follow them to Tower House, where they were staying. Once in Bray, Mary set out to insult and upset Jane to an unacceptable degree: she paid a boy in the town to take a copy of the Quilp pamphlet to every single house in Jane's road, display the placard and shout out Sir William and Lady Wilde's name, and personally supervised his doing so.

To distress Jane even further, Mary then got a boy to go to Tower House itself with the pamphlets. When he first came to the door, Jane threatened to tell the police, concerned above all to prevent her children from seeing them or to give rise to gossip among the servants. But the next morning, Jane was in her bedroom when Isola ('a girl of tender years', said a shocked judge later on) came in and said, 'Mama, there is a boy in the hall with a placard having Sir William Wilde and Speranza on it, that is of course you and papa, what is it all about?' Jane snatched both placard and one pamphlet from the boy and demanded the other three, but as she had not paid for the first one he refused to give them to her.

Mary, brought up in a house full of her father's law books, knew exactly what to do. She immediately took out an action against Jane at the local court in Bray, accusing her of larceny of her property. It was the final straw. On 6 May 1864, Jane sat down and wrote a letter to Mary's father, Robert. It read:

Sir – You may not be aware of the disreputable conduct of your daughter at Bray, where she consorts with all the low newspaper boys in the place, employing them to disseminate offensive placards, in which my name is given, and also tracts, in which she makes it appear that she has had an intrigue with Sir William Wilde. If she chooses to disgrace herself that is not my affair; but as her object in insulting me is the hope of extorting money, for which she has several times applied to Sir William Wilde, with threats of more annoyance if not given, I think it right to inform you that no threat or additional insult shall ever extort money for her from our hands. The wages of disgrace she has so basely treated for and demanded shall never be given to her.

Jane F. Wilde[34]

Robert Travers replied to the letter but did not destroy it. Three weeks later it was found by a delighted Mary. Her needling of William had failed to provoke more than dribs and drabs of money: he was too canny to commit to paper anything that could be legally used against him. Now, at last, she had a weapon. Mary took the letter to the Dublin solicitor Robert H. Irvine and was told what she hoped: that she was in a position to take out an action against Lady Wilde, charging that the letter was a libel reflecting on her character and chastity.

When Jane received a writ claiming damages of £2,000 she refused to pay and her solicitors entered a defence, pleading privilege and justification. Sir William was joined in the action as co-defendant, as a husband was held legally responsible for any civil wrong committed by his wife.

Jane could have agreed to settle out of court; it would have saved her and her husband a great deal of aggravation. But she was essentially a fighter who refused to retreat in front of an offence. Some thirty years later she unhesitatingly urged Oscar to stay and fight *his* court case and not play the coward's part and run away. The trial began on 12 December 1864 at the Four Courts in Dublin, before Chief Justice Monaghan, and lasted six days. The counsel for Mary Travers included Serjeant Richard Armstrong, supposed to be the deadliest cross-examiner in Ireland at the time, and Isaac Butt, QC, the Irish Nationalist MP and, as it happened, a long-time friend of Sir William's. The Wildes were represented by the well-known barrister Serjeant Edward Sullivan, who later became Lord Chancellor of Ireland.

Most of Dublin flocked to the Four Courts while the rest contented themselves with reading the acres of newsprint on the trial. The

Morning Post said that 'a more remarkable case has never been tried here . . . it is alleged that when O'Connell was on his trial there was not a more general anxiety evinced to be present than has been displayed this week to hear the "great libel case".'[35] Although Jane and William had fervent admirers, their very success had created envy and antagonism among a number of people. Mary Travers was not the only one to gloat at their public embarrassment. Oscar encountered similar hostility at his trial.

It is uncanny that both mother and son should have been forced into libel actions by opponents who were so eaten up by revenge that they cared not at all about adverse publicity. Mary wanted only to mortify the Wildes: she gloried in the revelation of the most personal details of her liaison with William, despite the damage done to her own reputation. All Dublin delighted in hearing about William's conduct, Jane's attitude to Mary and the details of their domestic life.

Jane was 44 at the time of the trial, and William 49. William was advised not to go into the witness box to defend his actions – a course which proved mistaken since it made him look cowardly and implied he had something to hide: indeed Isaac Butt in his closing speech accused William of sheltering behind Jane. It was therefore Jane who had to grapple with Butt's cross-examination, spending half a day in the witness box. She made a dignified appearance in court and newspapers reported that 'all through the trying ordeal of her examination, she displayed great self-possession.' Although Jane rarely wore black, she won herself extra sympathy by doing so on this occasion, letting it be known that she was mourning her brother's recent death in America.

Serjeant Armstrong opened the case for Miss Travers. Public interest was focused on the alleged rape of Mary in October 1862 and Mary repeated for the court her story of how William had half suffocated her when examining a burn on her neck. Her claim that he raped her while she was unconscious was made only after prompting:

MR BUTT: Are you now able to state from anything you have observed or know whether, in the interval of unconsciousness you have described, your person was violated?
MISS T: Yes.
MR BUTT: Was it?
MISS T: Yes.[36]

If what Mary alleged had really happened, it is surprising that she should have outlined a different version in her notorious pamphlet:

> The scene is changed to a doctor's study. The patients have been seen, prescribed for, and dismissed – all save one, an intimate friend whose throat requires to be touched with caustic . . . 'You look pale,' the doctor says. 'Here,' and he places a handsome scent-bottle close to her face . . . The bottle contained a strong solution of chloroform; the vapour filled the room rapidly . . .
>
> Florence – for it is she – in utter bewilderment at the scene so suddenly, so unexpectedly enacted, rushes to the door, but is interrupted by the detested Quilp who, flinging himself on his knees, attempts a passionate outburst of love, despair and remorse; but the horror-stricken Florence implores to be liberated from this dangerous place.[37]

The Chief Justice, in his summing-up, pointed out that it was strange that Mary had never reported this alleged rape to anyone. More extraordinary, in his view, was the fact that within a day or so she was 'receiving letters from him, receiving dresses from him and going to the Masonic ball'. A jury might therefore conclude, he said, 'that if intercourse existed at all it was with her consent, or certainly not against her consent . . . and that the whole thing is a fabrication'. Mary didn't help her cause by also forgetting the day on which the alleged assault took place. ('You, a woman representing yourself as a virgin violated, cannot tell the day on which it happened, is that your story?' 'It is.')[38]

She also surprised the court, when asked if there was a further 'transaction', by saying, 'I cannot say yes or no . . . I consider it was attempted.' The date of this attempt, she said, was July 1863, and when asked why she hadn't mentioned it before, she replied, 'Because I was not asked it.'

Jane flatly denied that there had been anything improper between her husband and Mary. 'I did not believe in an intrigue, nor did I accuse her of it; I complained to her father that she had published certain documents which would look to the public that there was an intrigue.' She defined an intrigue as 'an underhand sort of love affair'. Asked if she had any ill will or malice towards Mary, Jane replied coldly, 'Ill feeling? I had no ill feeling; I objected to her conduct; I thought she had behaved very badly indeed.'[39]

She admitted she had seen letters from Mary asking her husband for money, which she called 'the wages of disgrace'. The court was told of several episodes which, if true, pointed to her awareness of her husband's involvement. Once, when William had escorted Mary to a ceremony at the Castle after telling Jane he wasn't going to go, he admitted to Mary that his wife's back 'was a little up'. Mary asked him, 'How up?' and William had replied, 'Oh, the cats get up their backs when you vex them.' Mary claimed he once asked her, 'Did you notice my carriage, as we were coming along the street, coming after us?' Mary was alarmed. 'I had never heard before that Lady Wilde had any jealousy with regard to me.'[40]

Mary also told the court that William had informed her that Lady Wilde 'went into his bedroom one day, and saw in a box a little ornament, in reference to which she said, "Upon my life I have seen this in Miss Travers's bonnet," and he feared that if she quizzed me about this, I being hot-tempered, there would be words between us . . . I afterwards dined at Dr Wilde's house and Dr Wilde assured me that the best proof that Lady Wilde was not jealous of me was that I received from her an invitation to dine at her house.'[41] On another occasion, Mary was in William's room when Jane came in and Mary claimed she said, petulantly, 'Well, where are you going to take my husband now?' Then, only half in joke, had given her cheek a hard pinch.

Juries and the public gallery are sympathetic towards an ill-used wife. Jane would have furthered her cause more if she had broken down in tears. Instead she was clearly indifferent to her husband's and Mary's alleged behaviour, almost to the point of contempt: her composure was not an advantage. Isaac Butt, the opposing counsel, successfully built up the image of Jane as a cold person. He first read out a letter from Mary to Jane, written after the alleged rape, which said, 'I went into your husband's studio and there in his presence I took laudanum with the intention of committing suicide . . .' then continued, 'And what does Lady Wilde write in reply to that awful intimation? Oh! Shame on genius! Oh! shame on the heart of a woman; shame – shame above all on the heart of an Irishwoman – "The intelligence has no interest for Lady Wilde."'[42]

Butt also said of Jane, 'If she had the feelings of a mother, of a wife and of a woman, then it would have been a Christian act in her to endeavour to raise up a fallen woman.' Instead, her reaction was, 'If she chooses to bring disgrace upon herself, that is not my affair.' He tried to blacken her further by reading her translated passages from *The First Temptation* and pointing to the 'immorality' of the work.

Jane's defending counsel, for his part, accused Mary of being 'excitable, furious, uncontrollable, vindictive', and said Lady Wilde was beyond impeachment and that it was a 'grievous thing' to have dragged her into court.[43]

At times Jane's performance in the witness box foreshadowed that of Oscar at his trial. Having told the court about receiving the obituary notice for Miss Travers, for instance, she gave rise to much laughter when, after describing the obituary, she said: 'I think I saw her next in August 1863 – after her death.' Oscar made equally ironic remarks, playing like Jane to the gallery. When challenged by his cross-examiner Edward Carson as to whether he believed the book *The Priest and the Acolyte* was immoral, he replied: 'It was worse; it was badly written.'

The trial lasted a week. The jury was by then numbed by unending details of the extraordinary relationship between William and Mary, confused by Mary still meeting her alleged attacker after the event and puzzled by Jane's cool attitude. The jury remained out for several hours. When they returned, they found in favour of Mary Travers, but in apparent sympathy with the Wildes, set damages at a derisory one farthing. However, costs were awarded against William and these came to £2,000. Neither side had won, though Mary had the vicarious triumph of having dragged the Wildes through the courts.

Oscar was 10 at the time of the trial and together with Willie, now 12, was a boarder at Portora Royal School. Neither was in court, but they must have been aware of the case. (After Oscar's own trial, his two sons had to be removed from their school because of the adverse publicity.) The boys would have known Mary reasonably well. She had come to the house on a number of occasions and joined the three children on excursions. Indeed, William even wrote to her crossly when Willie was ill to upbraid her for not calling to ask after him. In turn, when Oscar was ill, William told Mary that he dreamed that 'he saw her in a most engaging shape nursing his little boy, Oscar, and that the child rapidly recovered.'

In Mary's precarious state of mind, this could well have made her envious of Jane's maternal claim on the child and stoked her dislike. She might easily have expressed to the children the bitterness she felt towards their parents, though Jane may have counteracted this by her air of unconcern. Certainly, when adult neither Oscar nor Willie ever mentioned the woman who so damaged the family, or the fact that their father had brought such a tempest down upon them.

After the verdict, all the papers and medical magazines extolled Sir William and Jane and slated Mary. The only exception was the *Dublin Medical Press*, run by Arthur Jacob, a bitter rival of Wilde's. The *Caledonian Mercury* said of Mary, 'The unhappy girl, though the daughter of a respectable man, has done herself irreparable damage by her vulgar and vindictive attack upon an eminent medical man and his not less eminent and respected partner in life – the "Speranza" of other days . . .' The *Morning Post* considered Miss Travers's persecution of the Wildes to be 'demoniacal', the *London Standard* called her conduct 'scandalous, unwomanly, vulgar and degrading', and the *Lancet* referred to her as a 'poor, wayward woman' and said, 'Of Lady Wilde no one can speak except with sympathy and respect.' The *Dublin Evening Post* condemned 'the absurd and cruel grandeur of the legal machinery which is applied at such an outlay of time, money, heart-burning and heart-breaking, to the extraction of a farthing damages . . .' The *Liverpool Post* took a different line and criticized the Irish in general and their lawyers in particular for endless repetitive talking.[44]

The colourful journalist Frank Harris claimed that after the trial he received a letter from Robert Tyrrell of Trinity College, Dublin, saying that the trial simply established what everyone believed, that 'Sir William Wilde was a pithecoid person of extraordinary sensuality and cowardice (funking the witness box left him without a defender!) and that his wife was a highfalutin' pretentious creature whose pride was as extravagant as her reputation founded on second-rate verse-making . . . Even when a young woman she used to keep her rooms in Merrion Square in semi-darkness; she laid the paint on too thick for any ordinary light, and she gave herself besides all manner of airs.'[45] It is highly unlikely, however, that Tyrrell, always a welcome guest at the Merrion Square house, would have written such a scurrilous letter. Indeed Oscar's friend Robert Sherard vehemently attacked Harris for having invented this letter.[46]

Mary Travers succeeded in her aim of holding Sir William's behaviour up to ridicule. Doggerel rhymes were now set to music and sung by Trinity students. One started:

> An eminent oculist lives in the Square,
> His skill is unrivalled, his talent is rare,
> And if you will listen I'll certainly try
> To tell how he opened Miss Travers's eye . . .[47]

Nevertheless, she failed to get Sir William ostracized. The claims that he was socially disgraced are untrue: his Dublin friends quickly rallied round him and he was submerged in a whirl of social engagements including rumbustious dinners with his Medico-Philosophical Society colleagues.

Jane wrote to Rosalie Olivecrona a fortnight after the trial, refuting suggestions that there had been any adverse professional effects on her husband and told her of the support they were receiving:

> You of course know by this of the disagreeable law affair in which we have been involved. I send you a few extracts from the various papers . . .
>
> The simple solution of the affair is this – that Miss Travers is half mad – all her family are mad too. She was very destitute and haunted our house to borrow money and we were very kind to her as we pitied her – but suddenly she took a dislike to me amounting to hatred – and to endeavour to ruin my peace of mind commenced a series of anonymous attacks. Then she issued vile publications in the name of *Speranza* accusing my husband. I wrote to her father about them and she took an action for libel against me.
>
> It was very annoying but of course no one believed her story – all Dublin now calls on us to offer their sympathy and all the medical profession here and in London have sent letters expressing their entire disbelief of the, in fact, impossible charge. Sir Wm will not be injured by it and the best proof is that his professional hours never were so occupied as now. We were more anxious about our dear foreign friends who could only hear through the English papers which are generally very sneering on Irish matters – but happily all is over now and our enemy has been signally defeated in her efforts to injure us.
>
> I have a book of poems out. I shall try to send them to you. Thanks for two magazines, but your translation of 'The Exodus' [a poem by Jane about Irish emigration] has not arrived yet . . .[48]

The trial at last behind them, Jane returned to her usual preoccupations. She was delighted in March 1865 when Rosalie published 'The Exodus' in her magazine and thanked her for the 'beautiful and vigorous' translation and the complimentary remarks preceding it. The Wildes' social life continued at full spate. Jane wrote to Lotten in June to tell her how crowded Dublin was and how she and Sir William had gone to a ball given by the Lord Mayor to meet the Prince of Wales at which 3,000 people had been presented.

The mud stirred up by Mary Travers had still not finally settled. A leader in *Saunders's News-Letter* after the trial had stated: 'It is not possible to believe the infamous story she concocted as to Sir W. Wilde . . .' – a statement that carried the implication of perjury for which Mary took the paper to court, again demanding damages of two thousand pounds.

The case was heard in June 1865, and the whole story was yet again rehashed. Although Isaac Butt (again defending Mary) said he cared not what Mary did to Lady Wilde 'in the agony of a broken heart', and talked of Mary having wasted her life 'in hopeless passion', it took the jury only twenty-five minutes to decide against her. Afterwards, she disappeared from the Dublin scene. Along with her sister, Mary was to spend the last years of her life in a Protestant home for decayed gentlewomen in Normanstown. She died at the age of 83 in 1919.

Jane considered Mary was 'certainly mad' in suing for libel a second time – hardly surprising, she said, given that her brother was in a lunatic asylum. She complained again of all that they had done for Mary, telling her Swedish friend, 'We tried to get her literary employment as she had *some* ability – she hated me exactly because I was so kind to her and nothing made her so furious as my *literary* reputation, but all this brooded silently in her mind. It was not till I had given up her acquaintance on account of her rudeness that she poured forth her hoarded malignity. However as regards *us* her wicked designs have entirely failed . . .'[49]

This letter was the last time Jane was to mention Mary and she quickly put the whole episode behind her. It was far harder for her husband to do so. The relationship itself had caused him mounting strain for some years and its public conclusion, with accusations of cowardice against him for not going into the witness box along with the humiliation of having his actions laughed at by all Dublin, undoubtedly affected him. Wilde's biographer, T. G. Wilson, believed that despite the support of friends and colleagues, he never recovered from the blow that Mary had administered: 'At the time of the trial he was not quite fifty, and still in the full power and pride of intellect. From that date forward he seems to have degenerated. His originality disappeared. He lost interest in his profession, became dirtier, uglier, more abrupt and intolerant of others. He was not the same physically upright, energetic man he had been. He appears to have burnt himself out, to have shrunk, mentally and physically. Temporary flashes of the old fire only served to heighten the contrast.'[50]

But Sir William had not lost all his relish for life. The strain of the case over, he cheerfully embarked, with John Gilbert, on Part IV of the Academy Catalogue; and although he spent an increasing amount of time at Moytura, he was occupied in researching the ancient battle that took place nearby for a paper he was to read to the Royal Irish Academy, as well as working enthusiastically on a new book about the whole area around Moytura, *Lough Corrib: its shore and islands.*

That year, 1865, to Jane's distress, his health broke down yet again. He recovered, but it was an ominous sign for the future. Jane did not know it, but a Greek chorus of woe was edging itself on to the stage, bringing such a burden of tragedy that it would seem the gods were intent on crushing the Wildes.

7

'A Sword Through My Heart'

'I MYSELF BELIEVE that 1866 will be a year of fate and doom, specially to England,' Jane told a Swedish acquaintance that February. 'We are expecting a great uprising and revolution here and great fear prevails. But as we are both national favourites, I fear nothing personally – still, times of serious trouble are near . . . you are a great nation – I envy you – we are so poor, oppressed and downtrodden.'[1]

The ferment in Ireland was caused by the activities of the Fenian Brotherhood, a secret organization first formed in 1858 in America before emerging in Ireland in 1865. The aim of the Fenians (whose name came from the *Fianna*, a legendary band of Irish warriors) was to end British rule in Ireland: an object which had lain dormant since the failure of the revolutionary uprisings in the 1840s. The Fenian newspaper, the *Irish People*, now demanded the people's right to act according to their own judgement; and plans for a rising were boosted when the American Civil War ended in 1865 and the Irish regiments fighting there returned home loaded with arms.

The Dublin Castle authorities, in a state of alarm, acted fast. They quickly suppressed the *Irish People*, arrested some of the Fenian leaders, seized weapons and cancelled advance military exercises to stop Fenian sympathizers seizing the guns. The action caused a sensation and no one in Dublin talked of anything else. Christopher O'Keeffe, who occasionally contributed to the *Irish People*, was astonished to find himself on trial as a suspect Fenian insurrectionary and wept when he was sentenced.[2]

Jane had no wish to take up cudgels in the present battle: 'The Fenian rebellion engages all thoughts,' she told a Swedish acquaintance, 'but I am not a Fenian and I disapprove highly of their projects – it is a decidedly *democratic* movement and the gentry and aristocracy will suffer much from them – their object is to form a *republic* and heaven keep us from a Fenian republic!'

Her remarks were perceptive. The gentry were indeed to be supplanted by the Fenians. Jane was a firm believer in the social structure and viewed the possible demise of her class with horror. But still showing signs of Speranza's old blood lust, she continued her letter: 'Perhaps a good war with England – with America to help us – might do something for Ireland. At present all life and intellect stagnates here – if Ireland is beaten I'll fly over to Sweden and live there. I suppose no one will travel this summer for a great democratic movement is expected all over Europe.'[3]

In the autumn of 1866 Jane's concern switched to her husband, as he fell ill only a year after his previous breakdown. He had totally ignored his weakened state and had continued to follow a punishing schedule of work. Once well enough to travel, he went to Moytura to recuperate. In the October he wrote to his friend John Gilbert to say he was better 'and able to oversee workmen and take short antiquarian journeys, but nothing more'. His exhaustion was mainly caused by his obsessive work on his book about Loch Corrib, to be published the following year.

But that year, 1867, tragedy overwhelmed the Wilde household. In February, William and Jane's small daughter, Isola, weak from a bout of fever, had been sent to Edgeworthstown to convalesce at the house of her aunt, Margaret Noble, her father's only surviving sister, who was married to the local rector. Within a fortnight, the following brief obituary appeared in all the Dublin papers:

WILDE – February 23 at Edgeworthstown Rectory, after a brief illness in the 10th year of her life, Isola, the beloved and only daughter of Sir William and Lady Wilde.

The whole family bitterly mourned her death. Jane was devastated. Writing to Lotten that April she began:

I write to you in deep affliction. You will see by the paper I send that we have lost our darling *only* daughter . . . She had been a little ill with fever in the winter but recovered – then we sent her for change of air to her uncle's – about 50 miles away – there she had a relapse and sudden effusion on the brain – we were summoned by telegraph – and only arrived to see her die – such sorrows are hard to bear. My heart seems broken. Still I feel I have to live for my sons and thank God they are as fine a pair of boys as one could desire.

But *Isola* was the radiant angel of our home – and so bright and strong and joyous. We never dreamed the word *death* was meant for her. Yet I had an unaccountable sadness over me all last winter, a foreboding of evil – and I ever delayed writing to you till I felt in my heart more of energy and life.

Alas! I was then entering into the shadow which now will never more be lifted . . . But for that glorious promise of scripture, 'The dead shall arise,' I think I would sink down in utter despair.

Sir William is crushed by sorrow. Isola was his idol – still, he goes on with his life work and is even now writing a book to be published very shortly on 'Lough Corrib and its Islands', for the daily work must be done and the world will not stop in its career even tho' a fair child's grave lies in its path . . .[4]

Oscar, 12 at the time, was engulfed by his own bitter unhappiness. The doctor who attended Isola and called her 'the most gifted and lovable child' he had ever seen, recalled Oscar's 'lonely and inconsolable grief seeking vent in long and frequent visits to his sister's grave in the village cemetery hard by and in touching, boyish poetic effusions'.[5] When he died, his possessions included an envelope with 'My Isola's hair' written on the outside, and his sadness shines through the verses of a later poem he wrote, 'Requiescat':

> Tread lightly, she is near
>   Under the snow,
> Speak gently, she can hear
>   The daisies grow.
>
> All her bright golden hair
>   Tarnished with rust,
> She that was young and fair
>   Fallen to dust . . .

> Peace, peace, she cannot hear
> Lyre or sonnet,
> All my life's buried here,
> Heap earth upon it.

The doctor remembered Oscar, at the time, as 'an affectionate, gentle, retiring dreamy boy'. He recalled himself and Oscar's uncle, in a discussion one day, comparing Oscar to his brother Willie, 'a very clever lad, and our assigning the meed of superiority in mental depth to "Ossie" although I believe Lady Wilde was disposed to the opposite opinion'.[6]

That August, Jane took Oscar and Willie to Paris for three weeks to see an exhibition there. She wrote to Lotten to say that no doubt Paris was too 'hot and crowded and noisy' for her to join them and admitted 'exhibitions are vulgar things and not suited to minds of your high tone. Yes I am going there, but it is to amuse my sons during their vacation . . . we all need some change but Sir William prefers his own beautiful place, Moytura, and will not go to Paris.' She thanked Lotten for arranging for Isola's obituary notice to appear in the Swedish papers. 'My little darling was very fond of Swedish,' she wrote, 'and took great delight in reading the Swedish testament with me. She knew German and so Swedish was little trouble to her – could she have thought then that her dear name would ever appear in a Swedish paper within those mournful black borders!'[7]

She wrote again in November 1867 to say that Paris had cheered them all, that it was a brilliant city and that when she returned, 'poor Dublin looked like a little provincial town'. Lotten told her that she had started a ladies' reading class and Jane praised this move. She asked Lotten how her book was getting on but said that, in her own case, 'I *cannot* get myself back into the writing mood and so nothing is left to me but the sorrow – the deep, eternal sorrow for ever and for ever like a sword through my heart . . .'[8]

Jane was now 46, too old to have any more children, and she remained inconsolable about losing her only daughter. For years, she refused all invitations sent to her with the words, 'I do not go out into evening society at present.'

Her husband buried his feelings in work and in seeing his friends. In June the following year, 1868, he invited his colleagues in the Medico-Philosophical Society to Moytura House. The minutes of the society give a vivid picture of a happy, saturnalian outing: 'We

embarked on board the Eglinton steamer to go up Lough Corrib . . .
half an hour before we reached the landing place the flag of the
Chevalier was seen floating majestically from the top of a high tower
in the grounds of Moytura . . . carts, cars and waggons were ready to
convey us to the Chateau and in considerably less than no time we
found ourselves in our most comfortable and beautifully arranged
bedrooms.'

As all guests acknowledged they would suffer from 'obfuscation of
intellect' after the poteen, and forget where their beds were, they
welcomed Wilde's prudence in pinning their name to their pillow. Then,
'soap and water and hairbrushes soon made the party presentable in
the drawing room and before many minutes elapsed we were seated at
the well-known oval table brought from Dublin for the occasion.'

Next day they 'admired the grounds appertaining to the mansion and
the splendid scenery by which we were surrounded'. William took them
around his favourite haunts: they fished in nearby Lough Mask and
went off to see the antiquities at the 'noble demesne of Sir Arthur
Guinness', before getting the steamer home. There was no mention of
Jane being there: it was strictly an outing for the boys.[9]

After Isola's death, and with Oscar and Willie at Portora Royal
School, Jane's life, like the house at Merrion Square, became very
quiet. Although she had initially found it hard to take any interest in
writing, in the end, she told her Scottish friend, it remained her sole
pleasure, 'for I never go into the grey world more but I see my friends
around me at home and have Athenian converse with the best minds.'
Her thoughts were still with Isola and she admitted, 'I have found no
comfort – only a dull resignation to the torture of life and then a dull
resignation to the prospect of coming death . . . my two sons are well.
I have a belief that God will leave them to me for it seems to me as
if I could bear no more sorrow and live.'[10] To Rosalie Olivecrona she
said, 'God grant both to you and to me that we may know no more
sorrow, but have joy in our children henceforth till our last hour
comes.'[11]

She consoled herself by sending hampers off to her two boys and
a letter from Oscar, in September 1868, contained his cheerful thanks:
'Darling Mama, the hamper came today and I never got such a jolly
surprise, many thanks for it, it was more than kind of you. Don't please
forget to send me the *National Review* . . . The flannel shirts you sent
in the hamper are both Willie's, mine are one quite scarlet and the other
lilac . . . You never told me anything about the publisher in Glasgow,

what does he say? And have you written to Aunt Warren on the green notepaper?'[12]

The letter clearly shows Oscar's interest in his mother's affairs. He wanted to see the *National Review* as it had a poem in it by Jane, patriotically called 'To Ireland'. This poem was to replace the dedication to her sons in a new edition of her verse published three years later by Cameron & Ferguson, the Glasgow publisher Oscar mentions. The 'Aunt Warren' Oscar mischievously referred to was Jane's sister, Emily Thomasine, who had married Captain Warren and still frowned on her sister as a nationalist; receiving a letter on green notepaper (green being the nationalist colour) would certainly annoy her.

Jane had easy, close links with both her boys. 'Willie is my kingdom,' she had said when he was two years old. To Lotten in the spring of 1869 she wrote, 'My two sons are at home for vacation and I thank God that he has left me still so much to live for.'

To begin with, Willie easily outstripped Oscar at school, despite his dislike of hard studying. Oscar hated maths but was good at drawing, and only his passion for the classics and modern literature enabled him finally to overtake Willie academically. Oscar himself admitted he 'had nothing like the reputation of my brother Willie. I read too many English novels, too much poetry, dreamed away too much time to master the school tasks . . . the head master was always holding my brother Willie up to me as an example, but even he admitted that in my last year at Portora I had made astounding progress. I laid the foundation there of whatever classical scholarship I possess.'[13]

James Glover, the Master of Music at Drury Lane Theatre, recalled the writer George Henry Moore, father of the novelist George Moore, visiting the Wildes' house at Merrion Square and asking Jane what she thought of the prospects of her two sons. '"Oh!" said Lady Wilde, "Willie is all right, but as for Oscar, he will turn out something wonderful."'[14]

A long blue bill from Portora School has survived, showing that six months' board and tuition for Oscar amounted to £31 10s 0d. Extras included a music master, drawing master and drawing materials, hair cutter, pocket money (40 shillings), ale and eggs.[15]

Louis Purser, a contemporary of the brothers at school, and in Oscar's form, wrote of them both in later years. He remembered Oscar as being 'somewhat reserved and distant in his manners, but not at all morose or supercilious. He had rather a quick temper, but it was not very marked. He never played any games. He paid rather more attention to his dress than did the other boys. He was not what could be called really popular, though he was fairly well-liked and occasionally admired. He had an uncanny gift for giving nick-names which used to stick to his victims, but they did not rankle as there was always a gaiety and no malice about them.' Oscar, he said, was not thought of as academically excellent, but 'on the purely literary side, as distinguished from the scholastic, he was very brilliant . . . he had a real love for intellectual things, especially if there was a breath of poetry in them . . .' Purser recalled him being exceptionally good at steering masters into talking on a subject that interested him.

Willie Wilde was one year Purser's senior at school and Purser thought him 'clever, erratic and full of vitality' even though he never shone at examinations and took very little part in games. He was regarded as something of a character by the boys and was laughed at for being boastful. But Purser remembered him being very kind to the younger boys, particularly in the way he used to play the piano for them.[16]

Sir Edward Sullivan, another contemporary of both boys at school and college, recalled Oscar being extremely boyish in nature, restless when out of the schoolroom, and never taking part in school games. 'Now and then he would be seen in one of the school boats on Loch Erne, yet he was a poor hand at an oar.'[17] According to Sullivan, Willie was never very friendly with Oscar.

Public school is an acknowledged setting for early experiments in homosexuality. But when Oscar was asked if there was 'any of that sort of thing' at Portora in his day he replied, 'No, not as far as I know. There was nothing more than sentimental friendships.'[18]

At the end of the summer term of 1868, Willie left school for university. Jane proudly told a friend, 'My eldest son is in Trinity College and he is a brilliant, fine-souled young man of infinite promise.' She put aside family concerns briefly in January 1869 when her friend, William Carleton, died. In February she wrote an emotional poem about him for the *Nation*, beginning:

> Our land has lost a glory! Never more,
> Tho' years roll on, can Ireland hope to see
> Another Carleton, cradled in the lore
> Of our loved Country's rich humanity.

She also wrote a verse that month expressing her belief that the revolutionary days were finally over ('Has not vengeance been sated at last?').

Her thoughts nowadays were more inwardly concentrated. A poem
written in 1870 showed yet again that she could not forget Isola:

> Dreams – only dreams
> Beguiling my soul in the Night –
> Dreams – only dreams
> That vanish with morning's light.
> Yet sweeter ye be than the thoughts of day,
> And brighter to me than the morning's ray,
> For ye give to my longing heart once more
> The loved and the lost of the days of yore . . .[19]

Jane told Lotten more cheerfully in April 1870 that Willie 'is now
a splendid young man in college who has just, too, got honours in
Classics. He is full of enthusiasm and ambition and brilliant promise – God is good.' But depression took over again mid-letter: 'I have
but my two sons, they are all I have to live for . . . all sorrows recall
my own sorrow which yet seems to me greater than all others. Life is
such a mournful mystery, I cannot see its meaning, but sorrow changes
all to us. Now nothing seems real to me but death. It is well, however,
to be able to live in the higher life of the intellect, there the world does
not meet one with cold unfeeling eyes.'[20]

Jane gave the outside world little chance to be unfeeling. She told
Lotten that after Isola's death she had never gone to a dinner, soiree,
theatre or concert, and that she never would again, 'not even to the
Irish court'. Among friends who instead came to visit her was Henriette
Corkran. She remembered calling at Merrion Square one day to be met
by Jane in a long crimson silk gown with a voluminous skirt over at
least two crinolines: 'When she walked there was a peculiar swaying,
swelling movement, like that of a vessel at sea, with the sails filled with
wind. Over the crimson silk were flounces of Limerick lace, and round
what had been a waist an Oriental scarf embroidered with gold was
twisted. Her long, massive, handsome face was plastered with white
powder; over her blue-black, glossy hair was a gilt crown of laurels.
Her throat was bare, so were her arms, but they were covered with
quaint jewellery. On her broad chest was fastened a series of large
miniature brooches, evidently family portraits . . . this gave her the
appearance of a walking family mausoleum. She wore white kid gloves,
held a scent-bottle, a lace handkerchief, and a fan.'[21]

Jane told her – or so Henriette Corkran claimed in her memoirs written some forty years later – that she could see 'by the form of your eyelids, and the shape of your forehead, that you have decided artistic qualities . . . but I hear that you have a lover, and love puts an end to ambition . . . don't bind yourself till you have seen more of men.' Although Jane had a great deal of perceptive humour, she only applied this to other people. She took herself extremely seriously.

Because her friends complained they never saw her, she decided to hold weekly receptions 'and agglomerate together all the thinking minds of Dublin'. She sent out cards which said: 'At Home, Saturday, 4 pm to 7 pm. *Conversazione.*'[22] It proved a highly successful idea: her rooms were filled with authors, playwrights, musicians, artists, university professors, doctors, clergymen and scientists. She told Lotten that generally about a hundred people came: 'I find them pleasant, for many clever men drop in, who would not come in the evening. We have very good music and often recitations – there is a table for the coffee and wine in the corridor and I have no further trouble – these afternoon receptions are very popular. People come in walking dress and everything is *sans gêne* – then, as I see visitors only on this one day, I have all the rest of the week to myself undisturbed.'[23]

Jane had enjoyed acting as hostess since the early supper parties she had held at Westland Row when first married. The large first-floor rooms at the Merrion Square house gave her far more scope to entertain, easily accommodating a constant flow of guests. The idea of holding salons had always strongly appealed to her. She saw herself as a second Madame Recamier, playing host to the cream of the arts, medical and scientific worlds. It was said that someone would only fail to get an invitation if they were not famous – or not intending to be.

Jane soon came to be acknowledged as the foremost hostess in Dublin. According to the *Irish Times*: 'No. 1 Merrion Square North was known as the house where a guest met all the Dublin celebrities in literature, art and the drama, as well as any stray literary waif who might be either sojourning or passing through the city. The affable and courteous hostess was Lady Wilde . . . the charm in the society to be met in Lady Wilde's salons was that it was wholly devoid of that species of snobbism generally so fatal to social gatherings in Ireland. Talent was always considered by Speranza a sufficient recommendation to her hospitality. We can with justice say that . . . Lady Wilde's literary reunions were as brilliant as any that were ever held in the early part of this century in Kildare Street [by Lady Morgan].'[24]

Jane was fortunate that she and her husband were acquainted with everyone of talent and interest in Dublin. As W. B. Yeats said: '[Lady Wilde] has known most of our '48 poets and novelists – Carleton, Lover, Lever and the rest, and can say something vital and witty of them all. She has a pile of Carleton's letters and can tell many things of our great humorist whose heart was so full of tears . . .'[25] Commenting on Jane's literary salons in Dublin, in August 1880, the *Biograph* said: 'Her passion was for the future, and she surrounded herself with republicans and politicians who put the golden age perpetually into the coming years.' On reception nights the crush of people in the drawing rooms was so great that, according to one account, it was a familiar spectacle to see Lady Wilde 'elbowing her way through the crush and crying out, "How ever am I to get through all these people."'

With her acknowledged *art de faire un salon*, Jane's conversaziones were lively affairs. One report had it that 'Dr Tisdall read his best pieces there. Mademoiselle Gayard Pacini played, and there was talk, such talk as one does not often hear. In fact everyone that was anybody did something or other.'[26] Jane drew out the best in others and was also quick to guillotine boring discussions. In one instance an elderly gentleman was droning on, until Jane took in the situation with a glance: 'My dear Mr so and so,' she exclaimed, 'excuse me for interrupting you, Miss X is going to give us a recitation – *The Bishop and the Caterpillar*.' Miss X did as she was told and all went smoothly.[27]

A guest recalled her being very much the hostess: 'Lady Wilde used to swoop about in huge draperies; she was, like her sons, excessively tall and large, but she had always the manners of a "grande dame" . . . there was some little pretence of tea, but most of the habituees were wise enough to avoid that beverage, for when and where it was brewed was a mystery . . . Lady Wilde had a soul above all the weaknesses of the flesh . . .'[28] Another guest agreed that 'no one seemed to care about eating or drinking.' People came to converse and Jane's conversation was 'remarkably original, sometimes daring and always interesting. Her talent for talk was infectious; everyone talked their best.'[29] With both a mother and father known for their sharp wit, it is no wonder that Oscar was, as Laurence Housman said, 'incomparably the most accomplished talker I had ever met'.

Jane took the duties of a salon hostess seriously and in an essay she wrote in later years, showed she was aware of the difficulties facing a literary hostess: 'The queen regnant of a literary circle must at length become an actress there; she must adapt her manners, her ideas, her conversation, by turns, to those of every individual around her. She must be perpetually demonstrating her own attractions and attainments, or calling forth those of others. She must become a slave to the caprices, envious feelings, contentions, rivalries, selfish aims, ignoble artifices, pretensions of literati, artists, and all the notabilities of fashionable circles.'[30]

Individual friends still dropped round in the evenings. Writing to Lotten in 1870, Jane thanked her for sending a book and said airily that it had arrived after dinner when 'some of the literate were with me'. The fortunate gathering were able to hear some passages from the Swedish which Jane promptly translated for them.

She was writing little poetry then. James Bourke, the editor of the patriotic Irish magazine *Shamrock*, all but went on his knees in 1870, some twenty-five years after Speranza first stormed into print, when asking Jane for a contribution: 'My lady, my lady, don't say No to the poor Shamrock people who ask of you in the name of Ireland to give on Ireland's Day [St Patrick's Day] one more beautiful embodiment of the almost divine thoughts which clothed in lovely and glowing words have made the name of Speranza immortal . . .'[31] Jane was obviously immune to his pleas. He wrote again that November of his unhappiness that she had not laid her 'life-giving breath upon the leaves of the *Shamrock*'.

Jane did, however, write 'The Vendôme Column' for the *Nation* in June 1871 in praise of Napoleon III, starting dramatically, 'Oh! not with the fall of the Column / Can perish his glory and fame.' The editor of the *Nation* wrote to her later that year to ask if she minded her real name being used in a reprint of her notorious leader, '*Jacta Alea Est*'.[32] She did mind; she preferred always to publish under the umbrella of Speranza to avoid further upset to her family.

There was no fierce political activity at the time, though a Home Rule candidate had managed to win an election that year. And when, that August, the Prince of Wales came over to Dublin, the *Cork Examiner* said how favoured Ireland was to receive such a 'truly angelic' visitation.

J.D. Sullivan, the editor of the *Irish Penny Readings*, asked Jane hopefully that year for some personal information: 'We have been saying, whenever the question has been put to us, that "the brave County Wexford" gave you to Ireland. Perhaps you would not object to letting us know whether or not we are right in that opinion?'[33] There is no record of her reply. Jane disliked what she would consider prying.

Oscar left Portora Royal School that summer and in October 1871, shortly after his seventeenth birthday, followed Willie to Trinity College, Dublin. In his last year at Portora he had won the Carpenter prize for Greek Testament, a gold medal in classics and a Royal School scholarship to Trinity. Once there, he won a prize for Greek verse. Willie was doing exceptionally well at Trinity too, winning among other prizes a gold medal for ethics.

Louis Purser, who was also at Trinity with Oscar, said he saw little of Oscar at college, as he lived at home. But after the first year Oscar moved into college, sharing rooms with Willie on the north side of a square known as Botany Bay because the students were as rowdy as the Botany Bay convicts. In Oscar's view, 'Trinity was as barbarian as school, with coarseness superadded. If it had not been for two or three people, I should have been worse off at Trinity than at Portora . . .'[34] Oscar was not particularly interested in oratory but Willie liked debating and once took the floor at the Philosophical Society to speak in defence of prostitutes, with his father acting as guest chairman.

Both brothers were similar in appearance: tall, well-built, languid men, with expressive eyes, sculpted features and an infectious gaiety. George Bernard Shaw, a boy in Dublin at the time, whose family had no social relations with the Wildes, recalled that his sister, an attractive girl who sang beautifully, had met the brothers and made an 'innocent conquest' of them.[35]

Oscar was fortunate in going to Trinity when he did as it was then renowned for its classical scholarship. He was most strongly influenced, both academically and aesthetically, by the Revd John Pentland Mahaffy, Professor of Ancient History. Mahaffy was quick to recognize Oscar's ability and his intellectual stimulus spurred Oscar on to win academic honours.

Further strong support came from Robert Tyrrell, who was to hold chairs in Latin, Greek and ancient history as well as founding and editing the Trinity College magazine, *Kottabos*. Oscar was to say, 'I got my love of the Greek ideal and my intimate knowledge of the language at Trinity from Mahaffy and Tyrrell; they were Trinity to me.'

The winter of 1871, when Oscar went to Trinity, brought another tragedy for his father. His two illegitimate daughters, Emily and Mary, were now 24 and 22 years old. That winter they were staying in the Monaghan area. Although the Revd Ralph Wilde, who looked after them, had no clerical post there at the time, girls in those days were often sent to clergymen for education. The two may have been boarding with the Rector of Drumsnatt, a small village near Monaghan.

They were invited to a ball at Drumaconnor House, off the Clones–Monaghan road, and the parish history records that after the ball, the two girls stayed on until all the guests had gone home. 'The host took one of the girls for a last dance around the floor. As they waltzed past an open fireplace, the girl's crinoline dress caught fire. Her sister, seeing her plight, came to her assistance and her dress also caught fire. The host of the ball wrapped his coat round them and rolled them down the steps in front of the house into the snow. But, alas, it was too late and both young girls died.'[36]

Drumaconnor House is no stately home with a ballroom: it is in fact a small, attractive manor house. The evening's entertainment would have been a party in its medium-sized sitting room. Any attempt to dance there could well have resulted in a girl's crinoline catching fire: it happened all too often in Victorian times. There are also thirteen steps up to the house and if the host had really rolled the girls down them, they would more probably have broken their necks than burned to death.

Another account of the tragedy states that the host took off his coat and wrapped it round the sister he was dancing with, before carrying her outside and rolling her in the snow. 'Her sister, panic-stricken, rushed around in screaming terror until she collapsed, exhausted.'[37]

Emily and Mary were buried in the quiet, ancient Church of Ireland graveyard at Drumsnatt. A large headstone over their grave still stands. Its inscription says, 'In memory of two loving and loved sisters, Emily Wilde, aged 24, and Mary Wilde, aged 22, who lost their lives by accident in this parish, November 10th, 1871. They were lovely and pleasant in their lives and in death they were not divided. II Samuel 1 v 23.'

J.B. Yeats, writing a gossipy letter to his son in later years, told him a story related by a local woman, who had left the dance before the crinolines caught fire: 'While they were dying, their mother, who had a small black-oak shop in Dublin, came down and stayed with them. After all was over, even to the funeral, Sir William came down and old Mrs Hime told me that his groans could be heard by people outside his house.'[38] The tragedy, said Yeats, was all the more intense because 'it had to be buried in silence'. Only the local area paper, the *Northern Standard*, mentioned the deaths in a brief obituary notice which claimed that Mary had died on 8 November and 'Emma' on the 21st – quite possible, if Emily had died later from burns and exhaustion.[39]

Normally a dramatic story like this, involving the name of Wilde, would have reached the Dublin papers; but if the deaths had not been hushed up, William would have faced renewed scandal. The Travers trial had not been forgotten.

A white urn, standing on a block of stone with the words 'In Memoriam' within a laurel-leaf surround, still stands in the walled garden at Moytura. It could have been intended by Sir William to commemorate Emily and Mary's death, as well as Isola's. A picture of him at this time shows him to be a brooding, patriarchal figure, with his long, grey hair swept back and a heavy beard. He was now beginning to reduce his practice in order to spend more and more time in the peaceful grounds of Moytura.

In 1871 Jane had written proudly to Rosalie Olivecrona to say, 'My eldest son is doing well in College and gets honours every examination. He has a fine, vivid, brilliant intellect – and also a fine physique – about six feet high with fine eyes and handsome dark hair.' She went on to give the latest news from London, where her husband was on a visit, telling her of the menacing Republican movement in that city fired by the seclusion of the widowed Queen and the belief that she was a costly figurehead, amassing enormous sums of money for her personal use. The murmurs died down when, early in 1872, the Queen made a public appearance again, driving to St Paul's Cathedral in an open landau for a service of thanksgiving for her eldest son's recovery from illness.

Owing to his reduced practice, Sir William now earned considerably less money and in 1872 was forced to take out a mortgage on the Merrion Square house. His expenses were still high: he had a number of properties to maintain and still had to support both his sons. Although Willie left Trinity that year, he was still costing his father money as he went on to London to study law at the Middle Temple. More cheerful news was the award to Sir William of the Cunningham Gold Medal, on St Patrick's Day 1873, in belated recognition of his work on the Royal Irish Academy Catalogue. It was the highest award of the Academy and he keenly appreciated it.

Sir William Rowan Hamilton's biographer, R. P. Graves, wrote to Jane later that year about the letters the two had exchanged. He wanted to use some, but said tactfully that he could understand her feelings of delicacy about 'giving publicity to such missives of a cordial friendship', and asked if there were any passages she could place at his disposal.[40] Jane allowed him to use some of their correspondence. She frequently inspired adulatory letters from male admirers, but no scandal ever touched her. The Travers case had underlined her total loyalty to her husband.

In June 1874 John Stuart Blackie, the Scottish scholar and Professor of Greek at Edinburgh University, made a month's visit to Ireland and wrote to his wife to say that he was 'beginning to plash about in the wide ocean of Dublin big-wigs'. One of these was Sir William, who was, Blackie found, very easy to get on with and very intelligent. He went off with him on a day trip to Drogheda to see the subterranean chambers of the old pre-Celtic kings. It was, he admitted, a grand catch to be with such 'a restless, keen-eyed old gentleman, like a Skye terrier, snuffing and poking about, who has all the district of the Boyne written in the volumes of his brain'.

He also, he told his wife, 'called on his lady, who is a poetess of the very fervid patriotic stamp, and a giantess to boot – the biggest woman I ever saw, as large as four Jenny Wrens, and who has a furious admiration for my "Aeschylus" [Blackie's translated works of Aeschylus in 1850 were widely praised] and of course for myself!! She is a phenomenon and worth considering, and with more girth on her little finger than some women have in their whole body. They say she is one of those women who love the male as a kindred animal, in whose likeness they should have been created, but failed through the mistake of Nature.'[41]

A few days later Blackie wrote again to his wife to say that he had since had dinner with Sir William, along with various 'Dublin intellectualities', and had sat next to Lady Wilde. He was still preoccupied with her size. 'The presence of amplitude,' he told his wife, 'always impresses me strongly with a certain feeling of awe, which was not absent on the present occasion.' He got on well with Jane, despite his awe, and sent her a copy of his *Lays of the Highlands*. The first of these, 'Columba', was an Irish sacred ballad, and Blackie was delighted when Jane was 'wonderfully pleased' with it.

Bernard Shaw believed that Jane's ample proportions were due to a medical condition called gigantism which causes enlarged hands and feet. He admitted he had never seen her feet, 'but her hands were enormous, and never went straight to their aim when they grasped anything, but minced about, feeling for it. And the gigantic splaying of her palm was [re]produced in her lumbar region.' Shaw also thought that Oscar was overgrown, 'with something not quite normal about his bigness', and airily offered the theory that Oscar 'was a giant in the pathological sense, and that this explains a good deal of his weakness'.[42]

Both Sir William and Jane were immensely proud when in 1874 Oscar won the Berkeley Gold Medal for Greek. Sir William promptly asked some friends to join the family at Moytura 'to cheer dear old Oscar on having obtained the Berkeley Gold Medal last week with great honour'.[43] Oscar prized this medal and kept it with him: after his death, a pawn ticket for it was found among his possessions. Hearing that Magdalen College, Oxford, was awarding two scholarships in classics, he decided to enter and sat for the examination in June. Afterwards he joined his mother and brother in London.

Winning the scholarship was important: it would bring Oscar in £95 a year for five years and meant he could go to Oxford without being too much of a financial drain on his father. When the news of his success came through there was therefore great family jubilation.

Jane wrote to Rosalie Olivecrona from London in late July to say that she and her sons had been there for the past month, amusing themselves and meeting a number of literary people. London, she said, 'is truly a great and mighty city – the capital of the world'. They were now all going on to visit Paris and Geneva. She was sad that she and her husband would not be coming to Sweden that summer – 'that land of culture, intellect, grace and social charm' – but the British Association was meeting in August in Belfast and, as Vice President of the Anthropological Section, William was delivering the opening lecture.

Oscar went up to Oxford on 17 October 1874, a day after his twentieth birthday. 'I was the happiest man in the world when I entered Magdalen for the first time,' he said. 'Oxford was paradise to me.' He was to stand out among the other undergraduates, with his carefully coiffured hair, his resplendent clothes and his habit of filling his rooms with lilies. His remark, 'I find it harder and harder every day to live up to my blue china,' achieved fame, through *Punch*, far outside the university walls.

Jane was equally thrilled for him, boasting to Lotten the following May that her younger son was now a scholar of Oxford 'and resides at that splendid university where so much talent and genius congregate. Amongst his friends he reckons the great *Ruskin*, Max Muller and others who have world-wide names.' She and her husband went over to England to visit Oscar at Oxford in his panelled rooms, where he entertained friends with brimming bowls of gin and whisky punch; an undergraduate friend of Oscar's, David Hunter Blair, 'remembered them as an interesting and delightful family circle'. He also noticed that though Oscar liked to pose as a dilettante, 'trifling with his books', in reality he spent hours assiduously reading, often until early in the morning.[44]

There were plans at the time for letting Merrion Square furnished and removing to Moytura. Jane knew this is what her husband wanted and wrote to Oscar at Oxford saying, 'Amen. I'm content. A great change might do him good. Sir William to Moytura, Willie to Chambers, you in Oxford. I – Lord knows where.' She seemed light-hearted enough at the idea, perhaps guessing it would never happen, and ended her letter, 'O merrily the throstle sings. What is a throstle?'[45]

Willie had been called to the Irish bar in March 1875. He and his fellow examinees celebrated in style and Jane told Oscar, 'All the Corporation got intoxicated and were uproarious. On his return Willie found a brief and cheque waiting him from the faithful Casey and Clay.' She added, 'Of course Willie *must* eventually marry Katy' – the first of dozens of brides whom Jane hopefully chose for him. Her pride in him remained intense. She told Lotten that he was now a barrister-at-law 'ready to spring forth like another Perseus to combat evil. His ambition is to enter Parliament and this hope of his I think may be realized – there is the fitting arena for talent, eloquence and the power that comes of high culture and great mental training – I think I told you that he got the gold medal in Ethics and Logic and also the medal for Oratory and Composition – he . . . is in every sense most suited to shine in society and in Life.'[46] To another friend she said, perceptively, that Willie had 'a good prospect and can be anything if he cares to work'.

Jane's only worry now was Sir William's worsening health. For years he had overtaxed his mind and body and now he was a spent figure. He had been prone to asthma and bronchitis since a young man and the attacks had become severe. The deaths of his three daughters, too, had lowered his zest for life. Jane herself, now aged 53, remained in good spirits and had held her Saturday receptions all winter from 4 p.m. to 6.30 p.m. She told Lotten how crowded they were becoming, 'from 100 to 200 every Saturday. Music, recitation, both French and English – piano, guitar, flute, quartets etc etc . . . they have now ended and I intend going to Bray for a little, before I undertake a Continental tour . . . this summer we hope to see Vienna and some day Willie resolves that he shall visit Sweden.'[47]

In the summer vacation of 1875, Oscar went off to Italy with Mahaffy and William Goulding, the son of a wealthy businessman. Both were implacably Protestant and Oscar may have deliberately chosen them to bolster him against the pull he was feeling towards Catholicism. His father was displeased at his Catholic leanings but Jane merely wrote to say that a mutual acquaintance 'thinks you are really going over to the true and ancient church'.

While in Italy, Oscar wrote to both his parents, cheerfully illustrating his letters. Those to his father were carefully descriptive: a magnificent burial chapel of the Medici, in Florence, was 'of enormous height, octagonal in shape, walls built entirely of gorgeous blocks of marble – all inlaid with various devices and of different colours . . .'[48] His letters to Jane were much warmer and very funny: he told her the countryside near Venice is 'exactly like Bog of Allen, only flatter' and that on arriving in the city they were immediately seized by gondoliers 'and embarked with our luggage into a *black* hearse-like barge – such as King Arthur was taken away in after the fatal battle'. Writing from Milan, after seeing the opera *Dolores*, he said that the applause was followed by 'a frantic rush of all the actors for the composer – who was posted at the side scenes ready to rush out on the slightest symptom of approval – a weak-looking creature who placed his grimy hand on a shady-looking shirt to show his emotion, fell on the Prima Donna's neck in ecstasy, and blew kisses to us all – he came out no less than nineteen times.'[49]

In the late autumn of 1875 Jane went to Paris and wrote from there to Rosalie Olivecrona in the October to say that without such a change of scene she would 'have died altogether' through depression over Sir William's poor health. 'So I went to London first and stayed a short time, then came over here, where I have been for the last month – and have become quite restored by the fine pure clean air and the great interest and variety Paris offers.' Her stay in Paris convinced her that there would soon be a revolution there – 'a rising of *the poor* against *profanity*. There is great discontent . . .' She thought that many regretted the fall of the empire. 'Now the shops are all bankrupt and are selling cheap English goods – pure rubbish – all the glory of fashion is gone. I have not seen a well-dressed woman in Paris – there is no one to lead society and a change of any kind is longed for – but the City is grand and beautiful as ever, with marble and gilding and tree-shadowed boulevards.'[50]

Paris proved an excellent tonic, interesting, amusing and invigorating her. She was pleased to get a couple of letters from the editor of the *Nation*, praising her poem on Daniel O'Connell and hoping that she would contribute to the paper in the future. That year Dublin had celebrated O'Connell's centenary and Sir William had been invited to a public dinner, along with other prominent Irishmen. And Oscar's first published poem, 'A Chorus of Cloud Maidens', also appeared that November, in the *Dublin University Magazine*.

Jane's optimism did not last long and she was soon to write to Rosalie Olivecrona to say, 'the sadness is coming on again – a weariness of all things – and now I long for a glimpse of Italy.' She said, hopefully, that if her husband improved, she might go to Florence with Oscar the following April. The chances, she admitted, seemed slight. 'Sir William's health is *much broken* and I am kept in constant anxiety about him – he is low and languid – scarcely eats and seldom goes out – he complains of gout, but along with this, he seems fading away before our eyes – and has grown so pale and wan and thin and low spirited that I too have fallen like an unstrung instrument and no poet-music can be struck from my heart.' She wished, she said, 'that all who are worth living should live for ever and only the dull and disagreeable pass away – the mystery of life seems sadder to me every day.'[51]

Writing to Oscar initially occupied her time while sitting with her husband, but it began a lifelong habit. She rarely dated her letters and relied on dashes rather than full stops, a method Oscar copied. Her handwriting remained as indecipherable as it was in the 1840s, when the editor of the *Nation* deplored it. Her letters to Oscar were fond ('I trust you are all safe and well – every bit of you. Is the brain in good order? and the heart at peace?') and sometimes positively skittish. 'O darling child!' one began, 'Thy mother loves thee still, her great heart throbs (rhyme to *throbs*?) bobs, sobs? won't do – I better give it up – turn me to prose again! Alas, why don't you go to Moytura, peace, virtue, quiet . . . Willie will be there about the end of the week from circuit . . .'

Her husband was already there, resting, and Jane told Oscar in another letter that he did not talk of coming back. She herself was, she said, 'At home – safe – all right – not damaged but only damp – rain, rain, rain – Willie looking Herculean . . . what of the poem – oh shame – thou art lazy. Let thy nerves rest . . .' She went on to say that Willie's voice was the only refreshing accent she heard. 'He is quite the grand style – not at all Mayo . . . the Irish accent is dreadful – I shudder at *Maurnin Potric* [Morning, Patrick] . . . How refined *we* are . . .'[52] When Oscar went up to Oxford, a friend of his at Balliol reported that he had both a lisp and an Irish accent. Oscar later said that his Irish accent was one of the many things he forgot at Oxford.

In one letter to Oscar, Jane referred to Willie avoiding one of the Dublin families and admitting to her he had behaved like a fool over a girl. Willie's *dégagé* charm caused him to be in and out of involvements with women. Ethel Smyth, who visited Ireland in 1875 and 1876, remembered meeting him and their playing tennis and discussing poetry, the arts and philosophy in remote parts of the garden. Finding him extremely musical and impressed by his cleverness, she was pleased to find he was booked to go to England the next day on the same boat as she was. On deck they sat discussing Auguste Comte and Willie proudly pointed out a tall figure clad in dark blue, leaning over the bulwarks and gazing seawards, as 'my brother, the poet'.

On the train to Holyhead they sat in the loose box, with Willie crouching on a Huntley and Palmer's biscuit tin at Ethel's feet. She remembered how 'he seized my hand and began an impassioned declaration, in the middle of which the biscuit tin collapsed . . . he resumed his tale of passion and before the train steamed into Euston I was engaged to a man I was no more in love with than I was with the engine driver!' She broke off the engagement after three weeks, admitting it was 'probably to his secret relief'. To her relief, he let her keep the engagement ring.[53]

A great admirer of the poet Longfellow and his narrative poems on American legends and folklore, Jane wrote to him in America in November 1875 to tell him the 'beautiful and pathetic lines' of his latest work had touched her deeply. She enclosed a copy of some verses she had written about him in the American magazine, the *Boston Pilot*, saying that he couldn't know if he had touched the universal heart 'unless some human heart throbs back in answering unison'.[54]

Most of Jane's letters in 1875 and early 1876, however, were concerned with her husband's health. 'Sir William is slightly better and this change gives me hope that the worst is over and that he will get on and be himself again,' she wrote to Oscar. On another occasion she asked him to write to his father. 'He is always pleased to get a line from you . . . he is utterly low and languid.'

'Sir William is the same way,' she wrote again, 'weak and low but not worse.' She then told Oscar with evident pleasure that Willie had been invited to the costume ball at the Castle, 'so he was liked evidently by the elite'. Her letters continued to mingle sadness about her husband with a description of Willie's hectic social life. A note telling Oscar that she feared Sir William was now in a very precarious state, went on: 'Willie as usual, balls, rinks, dinners.'

She gave a tolerant account of his outrageous behaviour at Lady Mackay's great ball for 500 people. 'Many could not get in,' she wrote. 'Willie got introduced to Lady Westmeath, young, Greek head, ivy wreath – he *devoted* himself entirely to her and ignored all his nearest and dearest friends of the Corporation lot. "Who are all these people?" asked Lady W. "Really I don't know," said Willie. "Never saw them before . . ." "Oh, of course," said Lady W. "They're not in my lot, but one *must* come to these places sometimes." "Quite so," said Willie, "let us sit down in a corner and look on." So they sat down and loved – deeply – before the night was over.'[55]

Another time, Jane wrote light-heartedly to Oscar laughing at Willie's appearance at a levee wearing a 'velvet suit and steel ornament – Hamlet to the life'. But, she added, 'though I write thus I have become very anxious about Sir William. He was worse than ever yesterday, so low and lifeless . . .' He still saw patients when he could and on 7 February 1876 managed to attend a meeting of the Board of Governors at St Mark's Hospital.

A second poem of Oscar's, 'From Spring Days to Winter', was published in the *Dublin University Magazine* the previous month. He was working on 'Graffiti d'Italia' and Jane wrote to him at Oxford to say, 'Send me yours to read. I feel *neglected* when I only know it in print.' She did not get her advance copy but was delighted when she read it in the *Dublin University Magazine* in March. 'The Magazine arrived last night,' she told him, 'the poem *looks* and reads *perfect* – musical and poetic – the evident spirit of a Poet Natural in it.' She disliked the last line, 'Show to the world my sin and shame,' saying she would have left out the word shame, as it was not 'highly poetical' and found another word that 'expressed moral weakness'. Reporting that 'Sir William carried it off and has it – when I study that poem I'll let you know my opinion,' she said with relief that he seemed slightly better. It was a time of great strain for her. She ended her letter, 'When will you be home? Do tell me so I may reckon the days – I am triste – I want you – come soon.'[56] Writing again, she noted with pleasure that there had been a tremendous run on the magazine and listed the number of people who were 'in ecstasy over the poem'.

A three-page poem of Jane's called 'The Soul's Questioning' was published in the April issue of the *Dublin University Magazine*. It had actually been completed the year before, as during the months of her husband's illness Jane stopped writing. Composed when she already feared that her husband was dying ('The cry of a bitter despair goeth

up through the darkness of night'), she despairingly questions whether
there is an after-life:

Can this be the end of all? – the power of beauty and birth,
The splendours of youth and brain, the laughter and songs of mirth –
A nameless thing of horror, to be hidden away in the earth? . . .

Jane was later to describe the slow ebbing away of William's life to one
of his friends:

> His health was failing with the winter – no actual complaint except
> bronchial attack and we hoped for Spring – but Spring brought no
> strength. He faded away gently before our eyes – still trying to work
> almost to the end, going down to attend professional duties. Then
> he became weaker and further lost his health, never left his bed, he
> himself still hoping and planning as usual for his loved Moytura;
> but still he grew weaker day by day, no pain, thank God, no
> suffering – the last few days he was . . . quiet and still and at the
> last passed away like one sleeping, quietly and softly, no pains or
> struggle – with his hand in mine and his sons beside him . . . I thank
> God that I was with him to the end and that the ministration of love
> and kindness was with him to the last hour.[57]

Sir William's biographer cast a slightly different light on his sons'
behaviour, claiming that 'his end was hastened by the heartless conduct
of his two sons who came in late and filled the house with their friends.
As they tramped noisily up the stairs, their father lay in bed, groaning,
"Oh, those boys, those boys!"'[58]

Oscar's account records yet other events and pays tribute to his
mother's generosity and lack of malice:

> She was a wonderful woman, and such a feeling as vulgar jealousy
> could take no hold on her. She was well aware of my father's con-
> stant infidelities, but simply ignored them. Before my father died in
> 1876, he lay ill in bed for many days. And every morning a woman
> dressed in black and closely veiled used to come to our house in
> Merrion Square, and unhindered by my mother, or anyone else, used
> to walk straight upstairs to Sir William's bedroom and sit down at
> the head of his bed and so sit there all day, without ever speaking
> a word or once raising her veil. She took no notice of anybody in

the room, and nobody paid any attention to her. Not one woman in a thousand would have tolerated her presence, but my mother allowed it, because she knew that my father loved the woman and felt that it may be a joy and comfort to have her there by his dying bed. And I am sure that she did right not to grudge that last happiness to a man who was about to die, and I am sure that my father understood her indifference, understood that it was not because she did not love him that she permitted her rival's presence, but because she loved him very much, and died with his heart full of gratitude and affection for her.[59]

Sir William died at 4 p.m. on Wednesday, 19 April 1876. He was 61, comparatively young for his exceptional achievements. The funeral took place on the Saturday morning, 22 April, at Dublin's Mount Jerome Cemetery, and was hugely attended. The cortège, said one paper, 'was one of the most imposing that has been witnessed in the city for a long time . . . the remains were enclosed in a massive oak coffin, simply though handsomely mounted.'[60] A wreath of immortelles and several bundles of snowy camellias lay on the coffin, which was carried to the family vault (although neither Jane, Oscar nor Willie were ever to lie there).

Some 168 people were present, or had sent carriages, including the Lord Mayor, the Lord Chancellor, the Lord President of the College of Physicians, the President of the Royal College of Surgeons, the President of the Royal Irish Academy, Sir Arthur Guinness, MP, and Isaac Butt. Some thirty-five members of the Royal Irish Academy came, holding the mace of the Academy draped in black crepe.

The Dublin papers devoted columns to his obituary, though London's society paper, the *World*, the following week admitted, 'The London papers generally have given very scanty recognition to the fact that one of the kindest-hearted and most genial of Irishmen has just passed away.'[61] Samuel Ferguson wrote a long elegy to him, starting 'Dear Wilde, the deeps close o'er thee . . .' and there were also many tributes to Jane. A memoir in the *Dublin University Magazine* said, 'In Lady Wilde Sir William found a partner with talents no less brilliant than his own. In poetry and general literature *Speranza* holds a distinguished position; in the former, some of her national pieces are certain to have a vitality so long as the language in which they appear exists.'[62] The *Freeman's Journal* agreed: 'Sir William, ever helped and sustained by the grace and social brilliance of Lady Wilde, dispensed

for many years past a genial and constant hospitality in his house in
Merrion Square, where literary, artistic, and medical re-unions found
a congenial home and where men of letters from other lands were sure
of a cordial welcome. The loss of such a public man cannot but leave
a blank and a gap in Dublin circles.'[63]

But this was nothing compared to the gap that was left in Jane's
own life.

8

The Last Days in Dublin

ALTHOUGH AWARE THAT her husband's health was failing, Jane was still shocked by his death. She had respected and loved him, and their twenty-five-year marriage had endured both the upheaval of the Travers case and the tragedy of their daughter's death without dividing their affection for each other. Two such different lifestyles within one house may have seemed incompatible – with William incessantly working and Jane remaining indolently in bed till lunchtime – but the two of them enjoyed each other's company and Jane was never to be involved with another man.

Without William, she felt rudderless. She wrote to Lotten to say, 'Just now all life to me is discord and every nerve thrills with a dissonance – and the future is all dark and uncertain! When the Head of the House is taken the whole edifice of one's life falls in ruins to the ground. I hate to go on living in Dublin – and if my eldest son Willie was married I would go and live abroad but at present I am as one tossed by tempests in a dark sea.'[1] Jane told another friend that she felt 'like one shipwrecked, for a wife feels the position more fatally than all others – a broken, desolate life, a changed fortune . . . while my eyes are blinded with tears, my brain also is filled with many sad bewildering cares and anxiety for the future and I am very weary.'[2]

She had reason for anxiety. Only on her husband's death did the family realize that he had left them nothing but debts and liabilities. 'Sir William never spoke of his affairs,' Jane wrote, 'but it was now evident that since his health failed during the last three years and he was unequal to professional routine he had been living on capital until all is gone.'[3] The houses at Bray, Moytura and Merrion Square were all mortgaged. Dispositions of the property have to be surmised from letters, as Sir William's will was destroyed in 1922 when the Four Courts building in Dublin holding such public records was blown up. Willie was left No. 1 Merrion Square and also the Moytura estate of some 170 acres – although the rents were to be paid to Jane for her lifetime. These amounted to £100–£150 a year, though they were rarely to be paid in full, if at all. Oscar was left the houses at Bray and a half share, with Henry Wilson, of the lodge at Illaunroe. There was a further complication about a deed Jane had signed, in which she had given up her interest on the £2,500 Sir William had borrowed from her marriage settlement to buy Moytura.

Upset, Jane wrote to Oscar to say, 'Sir William never meant my entire jointure to be on Moytura – only the *interest* of the *money* of *mine* that was sunk in the purchase, that is £2,500. Sir William often said that he would never leave his wife less to live on than £200 a year – of course that sum could not be supplied from Moytura alone . . . you do not seem to understand that my claims are paramount before all others on the property left.' Later, sending Oscar a copy of the agreement of the terms on which she consented to give up her right to the interest, she said: 'I am willing to pay the two guinea fee for counsel's opinion . . . the present uncertain arrangement is very disagreeable to me. *I have no income* and do not even see from what source I am to look for one . . .'[4]

It was indeed a disastrous situation and one that never improved. In later years, writing to Charles Gavan Duffy, she said unhappily, 'My income of £200 a year entirely gone – while my eldest son, who owns the property on which I have a charge has no benefit, for any little sum received is taken for rates and charges.'[5] Jane had never had to deal with finances and she was floundering. Her letters to Oscar are sad and harassed: 'It is all a horrid dream,' she told him in one, and in another she said she had returned from Bray the day before, 'having arranged all I required and shall never see it again while I live . . . I am sorry to say the family affairs grow more dilapidated every day – were I young like you I would take a pupil to read with. Youth can earn, age cannot. But I suppose the consolations of religion and philosophy will be sufficient – at least they cost nothing.'[6]

She wrote despairingly to Sir Thomas Larcom, a friend and former head of the Ordnance Survey, about her financial situation. Her husband, she said, had 'left his affairs in a very involved state, large debts, and very little to meet them, a mortgage of £1,000 on this house and a mortgage of £1,000 on the Bray property, both on 5 June last, and other debts and no funds by which my sons and I can meet these liabilities. Then the expenses of our new life, unaided by the professional income. My sons unhappily are not self-supporting yet . . .'⁷ The following day she told Oscar of her approach to Larcom, amongst others. 'It is so hard *to have to beg*,' she said. Her letter confirmed the confused state of Sir William's finances. In her view, the worst of all 'is when I think of that dreadful debt of £2,000 on you and Willie. How ever is it to be paid? . . . This debt is the *worst of all our affairs* for I see no way of clearing it and what was it for? That I cannot imagine. *The last £1,000* was borrowed in *1874* and all gone – and for what? Who knows – it is a mystery . . . I think it wd be *dis*advantageous to you to sell *one* house at Bray to pay it. You should keep and sell all *together*.' Despite Jane's own fears for the future, she told Oscar that 'Willie seems very jolly – all the county is coming to the auction and Willie is to feast them like Balthazzar.'⁸

In writing to Sir Thomas Larcom her hope was that the government, in consideration of her husband's 'many claims to recognition', would give her a pension. Sir Thomas's reply was disappointing. He told her that a literary pension was entirely in the gift of the Prime Minister and that she should make the approach through an MP.⁹ The rebuff made Jane angry. She failed to see why she could not get a pension when Lady McClure (her cousin's widow) had been awarded one in recognition of her explorer husband's services. A pension to her was crucial; 'we could then continue to live in this house which would be very advantageous to my son when he begins his professional life – and my deep sorrow would be lightened by seeing that he could take his place properly in the world.'¹⁰

She asked Sir Thomas if 'Mr D'Israeli may object to me as a nationalist'. It was a point the *Irish Times* also made: 'We have often wondered that in recognition of Lady Wilde's services to literature the Prime Minister has not placed her name on the civil list; but we fear her poetry is not of that kind which excites sympathy in the breasts of English statesmen.'¹¹ As she wrote to Oscar, 'He [Disraeli] requires the writers to be

– loyal
– orthodox
– moral

and to praise the English! *Jamais* – my descending to this level. Fancy! I have stood a priestess at the altar of freedom!'

In May 1876, Bulgarian freedom fighters staged a revolt against their Turkish overlords and were massacred for their pains. Oscar wrote a sonnet about it, but a twentieth-century critic has pointed out that 'even this poem lacks the revolutionary fervour . . . found in the militant essays and patriotic verses of his mother.'[12] This past militancy, however, was no help to Jane in her petition to the Prime Minister for a civil list pension. One recipient replied to Sir Thomas Larcom's request for support with: 'My dear Larcom, I never admired Lady Wilde and though I did much to help and support Sir William, I never quite liked him either. I tried to: but his intense vanity continually threw me back.'[13] For over a year letters went to and fro, but in the end T.H. Burke, the Under-Secretary, told Sir Thomas he feared the request would be unsuccessful: 'If a Liberal government were in, I think I would get her a pension – somehow or other they are larger-minded.'[14] In the end, Jane had to wait nearly fifteen years to get her pension.

Her general misery was compounded by the thought of having to leave No. 1 Merrion Square, her home for the last twenty years. She wrote to Oscar to say that she thought it had to be given up, otherwise how could Willie live? 'We could not keep up this house and two female servants, fires, gas, food, rent, etc, and mortgage, under £500 a year . . . I am in a very distracted state of mind – what is to be done?'

All Willie's energies and interests were directed towards enjoying himself, and as he remained apparently untroubled by the family's financial plight, Jane continued to pour out her misery to Oscar. 'If I am to be left in mere pauperism,' she announced to him, 'I see nothing for it but to take prussic acid and to get rid of the whole trouble at once – for I would not undertake a wretched struggle for daily bread . . . which I see is my probable future fate.' She ended dramatically, 'So dies Speranza. Goodbye.' Then, in her usual inconsequential style, she added, 'Now I must go and do my tasks in the house.'

Oscar, unworried, spent an enjoyable August and September at Moytura House and Illaunroe, fishing and hunting with a young portrait sketcher, Frank Miles, whom he had met at Oxford and with whom he was later to share a house in London. On Oscar's return to Oxford he announced to his mother that he would have to give up any chance of a college fellowship because he could no longer afford it and would just have to find some paid work instead. Jane wrote back sarcastically, saying, 'I should be sorry that you had to seek a menial situation and give up the chance of the Fellowship but I do not see that, so far, your state is one that demands pity or commiseration – from May last, (just five months), you have received in cash for your own private personal expenses £145 and the rents of Bray and the sale of your furniture may bring you over the year till Spring. Then you can sell your houses for £3,000, £2,000 of which will give you £200 a year for ten years. A very ample provision to my thinking . . . £2,000 is a splendid sum to have in hand – and with your college income in addition I do not think you will need to enter a shop or beg for bread – I am very glad indeed you are so well off . . .'[15] She did not convince Oscar, however, who thought £200 a year impossible to live on and was twice ordered by the Vice-Chancellor's Court to pay his debts to tradesmen.

Willie was also failing to manage. Jane wrote to Oscar to say, 'Willie has spent *all his money* and is now in debt to the bank and all his personal debts are unpaid – so – here's a smash. Of course this house is now his only resource. He says he will wait just for the British Association and then sell off everything – meantime he is jolly and enjoys life.' Though practising on the north-east circuit as a barrister Willie could in no way live on the few briefs he managed to get, and Jane's fond hope was that he would find an heiress, or marry into a family influential enough to bring him some briefs. At the time he was involved with a young, reasonably well-off woman called Maud Thomas: Jane wrote hopefully to Oscar to say that Willie had left for London and had telegrammed to say all was well and he was leaving for Eastbourne to see Maud. She hated being without either son: 'My heart won't stand much more,' she told Oscar, 'and now I am alone in this great house and I have so much to do.'

She wrote again to say that a friend of theirs had rushed to London, to keep an eye – she thought – on Maud and Willie. 'Poor Willie,' she added. 'Will he ever find the right woman? But just now he has no other means of salvation but through a good marriage. I'll let you know what he says after the meeting with Maud – it is quite a drama.'

Willie's engagement plans failed. Jane wrote to Oscar sadly to say, '*As a secret* I must tell you, but don't admit it to Willie – that the whole affair *is off* between him and Maud Thomas. The mother won't consent and she thinks it better to break off entirely at once. So there is an end to my dreams.' This was the first of many times that her dreams ended. Another letter to Oscar was to say: 'Hetty Drew is quite *friendly* and has him [Willie] *to lunch*, but no thought of marriage – so he has given up that idea – and is now a free man, unloving and unloved.'[16]

Jane's loyalty as a wife remained as a widow. Sir William had wanted to erect a memorial cross to the Four Masters (revered as the early historians of Ireland) in Dublin, but after his death there was a move to have the site moved to Donegal. Jane promptly wrote to Sir Thomas Larcom to say that her husband had 'decidedly objected to its being placed in Donegal'. She also drew his attention to the inscription, saying that 'Sir William would never have permitted an allusion to past feuds and hatreds.'[17]

Loyalty again – coupled with the need to occupy her time – made her decide during the summer of 1876 to complete the memoir of the eighteenth-century antiquarian and illustrator, Gabriel Beranger, from her husband's notes. Beranger had travelled around Ireland writing of his archaeological finds and making sketches of ruins before they crumbled. She wrote to Lotten in January 1877 to say she had finished an article for the *Archaeological Journal* 'which was the conclusion of a work by Sir William and it made me so sad to write it'.

Jane was now again contributing regularly to the *Dublin University Magazine* and in January 1877 the magazine published a sentimental poem of hers, 'In the Midnight', recalling the way her husband, who had a deep, attractive voice, used to read to her:

> Read till the warm tears fall my Love,
> With thy voice so soft and low,
> And the Saviour's merits will plead above,
> For the soul that prayeth below.

In a desolate letter to Lotten that month, Jane said, 'I send you by this post two recent poems of mine, sad as my heart, my life, my destiny. I grow more deeply miserable every day, the weight of sorrow is heavier on my life – I cannot begin *now* a new life . . . at times a feeling of ennui and despair comes over me, that I could kill myself – I think writing is the only thing pleases me and in the midst of my tears I write a poem – and am better . . .'[18]

However, another letter two weeks later showed Jane had recovered her astringency. After lyrically praising the Swedes for, in her opinion, having the most 'grace, culture, refinement and social elegance, with the true, noble, high aims of an intellectual existence,' she added waspishly that 'the Germans have the culture without the grace; the

French the grace without the noble aims of life; and the English are deficient in *all*.'[19]

With her usual confidence in tackling any subject she chose, Jane wrote a long essay on 'The Destiny of Humanity' which appeared in the *Dublin University Magazine* in May 1877. She welcomed the daring theories in Richard Proctor's book, *Our Place amongst Infinities*, the 'splendid utterances' of Whewell and Brewster's essays on the plurality of worlds, and 'the earnest, believing tone' of Joseph Hamilton's book, *The Starry Hosts*. She quoted the opinions of St Paul, Aristotle, Kant, Pythagoras, Plotinus, 'the sublime views of Plato' and the religious works of Frederick Faber. Jane was exceptionally well read, though in this case her own prose was heavy-going: 'Sentient or non-sentient, the monads of the universe must exist throughout all eternity . . .'

A further article for the same magazine, on 'The Fairy Mythology of Ireland', dismissed serpent-worship ('as the Irish never could have seen a serpent') and included the legends of the horned woman and of Ballytowtas Castle, which Jane was later to collect in her book, *Ancient Legends of Ireland*.[20]

Jane received no money for these articles. The editor, Keningale Cook, wrote to Oscar that year saying, 'I hope in twelve months the *D.U.M.* may be restored to its true position again, and able to pay its contributors.'[21] Oscar suggested to Cook that he increased sale by advertising the contents of the magazine. 'In Ireland of course any article by my mother is eagerly bought up, but lots of people never hear of them till long after.'[22]

The *D.U.M.* hadn't been the only magazine in difficulties. Jane had told Oscar of another one in Dublin on its last legs and paying no one, when 'even the *Shamrock* [magazine] pays half a crown a page'. She had been pleased at getting a cheque for £1 10s from the *Pilot*, a Boston-based magazine, with a request to write more, but told Oscar, 'I live the spiritual life no more,' being too busy and worried, she said, with a thousand small matters such as how Willie's tailor's bill could possibly be paid.

Willie himself was unconcerned. The whole of Dublin was skating mad at the time and this was his entire preoccupation. 'Willie gives me no rest about the £5 for the rink and I hate the rink,' Jane told Oscar. She must have come to terms with his obsession as in her next letter she said that 'Willie is at the rink daily and is skating superbly.'

Her attitude towards Willie continued to be a mixture of pride and exasperation. She treated him as a large, wayward child over whom one could do nothing but smilingly shake one's head. Her letters to Oscar reveal her eldest son's lifestyle: 'Willie was home at 3 a.m. from the Ball. All the border clans were there – not the *haute volée*. Willie was asked to dine today at the Larkins (solicitor), good that – have a niece, charming girl. They all go to the rink in the evening.' In another letter about the guests who were coming to dine the next night, she added: 'As Willie never pays, he is splendid in hospitality.'[23]

Her sons in her eyes could do no wrong and until her husband's death there had always been enough money to hand out on demand. Now money was short; and while both young men found the transition to self-sufficiency hard, the timing was particularly difficult for Willie. James Holroyd makes the point in his essay, 'Brother to Oscar', that Willie's 'first tragedy was the death of his father before he had been able to establish himself as a barrister in Dublin'.[24] Willie was not prepared to do the hard groundwork himself.

Oscar spent the Easter vacation of 1877 touring Italy and Greece with friends, including his old Trinity College tutor Mahaffy. He missed the first month of term at Oxford and in punishment was rusticated for the rest of it. Writing to Reginald Harding, an Oxford friend, from Dublin he said, 'My mother was of course awfully astonished to hear my news and very much disgusted with the wretched stupidity of our college dons . . . my brother who is down at Moytura at present writes me a letter marked "Private" to ask "what it *really* is all about" . . .'[25]

In another letter to Harding in June Oscar says, 'I am very much down in spirits and depressed. A cousin of ours to whom we were all very much attached has just died.' The 'cousin' was Henry Wilson and his death on 13 June 1877, at the early age of 38, was a general shock. The *Freeman's Journal* said he had been suddenly seized with rigour and the inflammation of the lungs that then developed spread to the heart: 'The occurrence has been the subject of melancholy converse in all circles . . . professionally, socially and personally, Dr Henry Wilson was as thoroughly and genuinely popular a man as our city has known for many a day.'[26]

Both brothers had expected a half of his estate and were gravely disappointed. Wilson, who was Surgeon to St Mark's Ophthalmic Hospital, left some £8,000 to the hospital and £2,000 to Willie. This at least enabled Jane and Willie to stay on at the house in Merrion Square. But Oscar told Harding in disgust that Wilson was, 'poor fellow, bigotedly intolerant of the Catholics and seeing me "on the brink" struck me out of his will'. In fact Oscar was left £100, on condition he remained a Protestant. Wilson had owned the Illaunroe lodge jointly with Oscar, and Oscar only got Wilson's share if he did not become Catholic within five years. Otherwise it would go to Willie.

On 4 October 1877, Oscar signed an agreement over the Esplanade Terrace houses in Bray: 'It was authorized by Mr Wilde to sell his interest in these four houses for £2,900 which he says is the very lowest price he will accept.'[27] Unfortunately, the Bray houses were accidentally sold by two different agents and one of the would-be purchasers sued him. By the time the mortgage and lawsuit had been paid, there was not a great deal left.

Jane was cheered in May 1878 by getting a letter from Longfellow, to whom she had written admiringly three years previously, with a copy of his poem 'The White Czar'. She wrote back to tell him how she was greatly struck by its 'strong, strange music', the 'sensuous music in the refrain' and the way his verses, 'bold, fierce, powerful, have a clang, like the stroke of Vulcan's hammer'. She congratulated him on 'giving words to the music of the march of men on their terrible warpath across Europe' especially when, in her view, other poets only produced 'word-jingle' rather than heroic thought.[28]

Her life was lit up the following month by another poem, for Oscar won Oxford's prestigious prize for verse, the Newdigate Prize, with his composition, 'Ravenna'. She wrote, overjoyed, to 'the Olympic Victor':

Oh Gloria, Gloria! Thank you a million times for the telegram – it is the first pleasant throb of joy I have had this year – How I long to read the poem – well, after all, we have *genius* – that is something, attorneys cannot take that away.

Oh, I do hope you can now have some joy in your heart – you have got *honour* and *recognition* – and this at only *22* [he was actually 23] is a grand thing. I am proud of you – and am happier than I can tell – this gives you a certainty of success for the future. You can now trust your own intellect; know what it can do – I should so like to see the smile on your face now. Ever and ever with joy and pride, your loving mother.[29]

The letter shows that Jane was aware Oscar had been going through a troubled time, beset by doubts over whether to turn Catholic and unsure of his future. Winning the Newdigate did indeed cheer him. Jane, always concerned that her two sons got on together, wrote again to 'the Olympic Victor' to say, 'Willie took a *great interest* about the prize – the moment we got the telegram he took a cab and drove off with it *to all* the Dublin papers . . . Willie really took so much trouble in spreading the news of your glory that he is much down at your not writing to tell him about the Commem in answer to his note and telegram – pray write at once – no one here knows the day . . .' She was delighted, though, to tell Oscar that 'all the world', including Mahaffy, was going over from Dublin to hear Oscar give his public reading of 'Ravenna' on 26 June at Oxford.[30]

Willie wrote poetry too, several examples of which were published in the Trinity College magazine, *Kottabos*. In a late August letter to a new woman friend of his, Margaret Campbell, he said, 'I have, as I told you, some strong poems of mine I would like to send you – I want you to know me as a poet . . .' Margaret Campbell had recently visited Ireland and Willie was anxious for her to come again. She had met Jane, who automatically assessed her as a possible bride for her eldest son; Willie duly told her that his mother had sent 'very kindest remembrances to you – she likes you – and I only wish you knew more of her – she is my greatest friend on earth.'

He went on to say that he and Oscar were just off to 'a little place of ours that lies in far Connemara among purple mountains – we shall be away a week in glorious solitude and I shall paint a sunset for you.' Once there, he wrote again, extolling Illaunroe, the mountains, the heather, the lake, the waterfalls and the splendid salmon fishing, and ended, 'I don't have any *World* paragraphs till I return to civilization – send me some ideas.' Short of briefs, Willie had already started writing short pieces for the *World*, the London weekly 'journal of society', edited by Edmund Yates, which had a larger circulation than any other first-class weekly. 'In last week's *World* I had just a few scraps,' he told her, on his return to Merrion Square.[31]

His letters show his growing boredom with Dublin, fuelled perhaps by seeing Oscar in the more testing atmosphere of Oxford. Although he told Margaret that he had been at one of Dublin Castle's drawing rooms the previous night and that invitation cards were fluttering in 'like a flock of little white pigeons', he declared he wouldn't go to half of them. 'They are all so alike over here – same set, same talk, same ideas, same shallowness. Right, amica, right. Society's almost as deep – well – as a frozen rink – i.e., six inches. Thank God there is a dream world in art and music one can fly to sometimes – out of the worries . . . we all have two lives – the *world life* of combat and fight and hard knocks and rough and smooth places, and the *soul life* – and this we can mould as we will.'[32]

Oscar meanwhile had achieved further academic success, having been awarded a rare double first. But 1878 was not wholly a year of celebration for him as his early love, Florence Balcombe, announced her engagement to Bram Stoker, the new business manager of the Lyceum and later author of *Dracula*. Oscar asked her to return the gold cross he gave her, 'as a memory of two sweet years'.

In the November, having stayed on at Oxford to pass his divinity examination which he needed to take his degree, he left for London. The following year he applied for a classics fellowship and an archaeological studentship. He did not help his chances in the classics examination by publicly telling the other applicants that the paper had been set by 'a very uncultured person'. He failed to get either position.

Jane wrote to him in a businesslike way to say that if he should require money right away, 'I trust you would be willing to sell me the silver Clark jugs. I would buy them from you at a valuation.' She added that Willie wanted to know if Oscar had taken away a print of a woman nursing her child that had hung in his study: 'we miss this and the marble head of *the Pope* and the small head of Guido's "Salperanza", same size as the Cenci, besides all the small china . . .' Perhaps she suspected that Oscar had removed these to decorate his rooms.

Late in 1878 Jane wrote her final blast as Speranza in a pamphlet called *The American Irish*, which resurrected all her old wrath against the English. Its keynote was nationalism: an uncritical hymn of praise to the Irish, at home as well as overseas, and to the stimulation Irish migrants could find in America, 'the mighty mother of freedom'. England, she said, should have counted the cost before compelling the Irish people to migrate, since 'a people who are learning, under the teaching of America, the dignity and value of human rights, are not likely to acquiesce tamely in the degraded position Ireland holds in Europe'.[33]

Reviewing it, the *Sentinel* sharply criticized the way Jane had merely reiterated her rhetoric of thirty years ago: 'We had imagined Lady Wilde would have had something new to tell us, some facts about the Irish in America, how they live, move and have their being. But of this we hear but little. Instead we have endless periods concerning the vain but beautiful dream of independence. She remembers the days of old with a vengeance . . . of 47 pages in the pamphlet purporting to deal with the American Irish, there are 23 taken up with an abstract of mere Irish history.'[34]

Oscar was more partisan. Some three years later he sent a copy of the pamphlet to James Knowles, editor of the magazine *Nineteenth Century*. It was, he said, about 'the reflux wave of *practical* republicanism which the return of the Irish emigrants has brought on Ireland', and was, he told Knowles, 'extremely interesting as a political prophecy'. He went on, 'You probably know my mother's name as the "Speranza" of the *Nation* newspaper in 1848. I don't think that age has dimmed the fire and enthusiasm of that pen which set the young Irelanders in a blaze. I should like so much to have the privilege of introducing you to my mother – all brilliant people should cross each other's cycles, like some of the nicest planets . . .'[35]

Early in 1879 Oscar set up bachelor quarters with the artist Frank Miles at 13 Salisbury Street off the Strand. The only money he had to live on came from his sale the previous year of the four houses in Bray and their 'entirely shattered' furniture – which had brought in an extra £150.

That same year was to be Jane's last in Dublin. She wrote to Oscar to say that Willie now saw he must have 'an attorney of kin to get on – brilliancy won't do – he says he will throw it all up if no work comes in – and he and I will try London – a *small house* . . .' They were finding it hard to manage in Dublin. Willie's £2,000 from Henry Wilson was disappearing and little money was coming in from the Moytura rents, Jane's occasional writings and Willie's even more occasional briefs.

Jane had a dual attitude towards money: she could work herself up to a frantic state about it, but at other times might adopt an attitude of Olympian disdain. A friend who called round to the Merrion Square house, only to find the bailiffs in possession, was amazed at Jane's indifference: 'There were two strange men sitting in the hall, and I heard from the weeping servant that they were "men in possession". I felt so sorry for poor Lady Wilde and hurried upstairs to the drawing-room where I knew I should find her. Speranza was there indeed, but seemed not in the least troubled by the state of affairs in the house. I found her lying on the sofa reading *Prometheus Vinctus* of Aeschylus, from which she began to declaim passages to me, with exalted enthusiasm. She would not let me slip in a word of condolence, but seemed very anxious that I should share her entire admiration for the beauties of the Greek tragedian which she was reciting.'[36]

Jane's tragi-comic existence continued, with her letters to Oscar revealing her complete absorption in the minutiae of daily life. 'Willie has been poorly – swelled face,' she wrote, and then again: 'Dr O'Leary came last evening and was *splendidly agreeable* – quite a delightful talker – then *Mahaffy* dropped in and Willie and O'Leary finally retired to the study to talk business – leaving me and Mahaffy together. It was then 11 o'clock and we had passed a delightful evening. Then O'Leary went and Mahaffy stayed to 12 o'clock – then Willie *went out*, not home till *morning*. He is now (1 o'clock) only going to get up! Is this his ideal of *pleasure*? Well – O'Leary brought his written offer [for the Merrion Square house], £250 for three years – and then £3,250 down. It is *immense*. Willie is to send his answer – and I suppose he will accept.' She went on, obviously flattered, to tell Oscar that 'O'Leary told us that he *knew* Willie would be returned MP for many places, by the mere love of Speranza's name and he advised him to start next election on free liberal principles.'[37]

Despite these excitements, or perhaps because of them, Jane was a tired woman. Financial worries had taken their toll. A friend of Mahaffy's recalled Lady Wilde's 'long, gaunt figure reclining on a horse-hair sofa in her house in Merrion Square'.[38] In the early months of 1879 she was preoccupied with the proposed move to London. 'Willie is still in London, Waterloo Hotel – looking after houses or lodgings,' she told Oscar, 'but all are so dear! – I think a house would be quite beyond us – involving two servants – perhaps we could get the upper part of a house over a wareroom and we could furnish, but it is certain we quit Dublin even if we go into furnished lodgings in London which can be had at any moment – and sell off everything here.'[39]

She was relieved that Willie, who had now decided to give up the legal profession and become a full-time journalist, had reasonably good prospects. To her delight, he had been told that he could easily make £1,200 a year in London. He had gone to see the editor of the *Morning Advertiser* and, she told Oscar, 'The editor of the *Athenaeum* also wanted to see him. He says he wants *young* men, that everyone is tired of the old stagers . . . I think after all Willie is more suited to it [journalism] than anything else, and for this he *must* live in London and I am content.' Willie had two plays printed in Dublin, *French Polish* and *Evening Stream*, and wrote poems for a number of magazines. He was ahead of Oscar in his interest in Salome, writing a poem on her for *Kottabos* in 1878 which ended:

Give me, I pray thee, presently the head
Of John the Baptist. 'Twixt my hands it lies.
Ah, mother! see the lips, the half-closed eyes –
Dost think he hates us still now he is dead?

In later years Jane became more disillusioned with journalism, bewailing the way the 'young and brilliant' would 'fling themselves body and soul to the devouring hydra of journalism, to live and work and die without recognition or honour, distinction or reward'.[40]

The actual move from Dublin was protracted. While Willie was in London looking for lodgings Jane wrote to Oscar in the early spring of 1879, signing her letter 'La Madre Desolata', to say that she had not heard from him. 'He writes seldom – we have only eight weeks more in this house and not an idea where to lay our heads.' Then, in a quick change of mood, she went on, 'Read the last *Whitehall* on the Queen, they insinuate her head is not all right.'

Jane could never resist passing on such items: in the middle of her anxieties and agonizings she would unexpectedly include cryptic news like the death of a friend in Longford who 'left Meg £100 saying he always loved her and wished to marry her'; or the way the Hardy family got £4,000 from America but that 'old Henry keeps it all and never gave Edward sixpence'; or that 'Lady C. Lindsay has taken a house for herself and has written to all her friends to come and see her as she is not to blame but she could not remain with her husband any more'; or the news that 'Nugent Robinson has absconded – a warrant is out for his arrest – great excitement.'

Her letters at this time, however, revolve around the move to London. She wrote again to tell Oscar that Willie had 'telegraphed "All Right" but I know nothing more . . . I don't know what to do. The Bram Stokers have six rooms unfurnished lodging and attendance in Southampton Street for £100 a year.' She asked Oscar if he could get her a suite of rooms in his street, perhaps even next door. 'What am I to do?' she asked him. 'Meanwhile I know nothing of Willie's wishes – is the furniture to be sold or brought over? I know not – I think I'll die and end it – I'm sick and weary – meantime I have a dozen trunks of books to put somewhere – but where?' She ended her letter, appropriately, 'Senza Speranza'.[41]

Willie finally found lodgings in Ovington Square but Jane decided she would not sign a contract until she knew more of Willie's plans, which now apparently included marriage. 'If the marriage is off,' she told Oscar, 'then I better go to Ovington Square and settle it up and share expenses with Willie – So whatever day I arrive I shall drive at once to an hotel. Either Fords, Manchester Street or the newest in Cecil Street – But I cannot fix the day for leaving – for no money has come in from sales or auction.' She was exhausted by how much there was to do, saying she had hardly been out of the house for months. 'Perhaps I'll never go out more till I leave No. 1 for ever.'[42]

The day of leaving Dublin was finally settled. Jane wrote to Lotten on 6 May 1879 to say, 'We leave Ireland tomorrow and our residence for the future is *London*. There we shall take a house.' To her other Swedish friend, Rosalie, she wrote what she called her last note 'from the old family mansion in Merrion Square – both my sons prefer living in London, the focus of light, progress and intellect – and we have taken a house there and disposed of *this* on very good terms. It belongs to my son and he gets £3,500 for it. I may hope to see you in London, which is a much more attractive place than Dublin to foreigners.'[43]

Jane had now convinced herself that Dublin was a small, dowdy city compared to the infinite culture of England's capital. She had visited London on many occasions and had enjoyed it. Nevertheless, to leave all her friends and the familiarity of Dublin life was a great wrench. Jane had never lacked the bravery required to uproot herself from the country of her birth; but in crossing the Irish Sea she lost her base. In Dublin she was a well-known and respected figure, acquainted with nearly everyone of note. She did not realize that her acknowledged talents as hostess there would not automatically be recognized in London, where she was unknown and knew few people apart from her sons. Her early anti-English outpourings, too, were hardly an asset. She was now nearly 58 and her eccentricities of dress and conversation, accepted in Dublin, were only to raise eyebrows in London.

Nevertheless, her mind was made up. Before she left Ireland she wrote to Oscar to say, 'We have done with Dublin – that is what is now in my heart – *times is bad.*'

9

The Two Sons

THE LONDON JANE came to in 1879 was a prosperous, thriving city, where life for those with money was one of relative ease. West End streets were thronged with women with fashionable bustles and bonnets heavily decorated with flowers and feathers, while men sported mutton-chop whiskers, frock coats and top hats. The servants of the middle class busied themselves in the solidly furnished houses, cleaning grates, polishing brassware, carrying up cans of hot water, lighting the fires and oil lamps, watering the aspidistras and draping the chairs with antimacassars to protect them against the popular, sticky macassar hair oil.

Meredith, Hardy and Trollope were the accepted reading in Victorian parlours and Browning, Tennyson and Swinburne were household names. Circulating libraries were thriving, like the select Mudie's in New Oxford Street which carefully protected its subscribers from disagreeable or unpleasant novels. Mudie's was so much part of London's fashionable world that a visit there was as much an afternoon duty as a drive in Rotten Row. Jane, however, had no need to borrow books. Although Sir William's library had been auctioned in Dublin before she left, she had brought over trunkfuls of books from her own library.

Literature and the arts were flourishing in London at the time. During Jane's first summer Sarah Bernhardt and the Comédie Française were being cheered by audiences at the Gaiety while Ellen Terry and Henry Irving were getting an equally rapturous welcome at the Lyceum for their first season, which included *Hamlet* and *The Lady of Lyons*. Ellen's part in the latter play had once been played by the actress Helen Faucit, an early love of Sir William Wilde.

Greatly in vogue at the time was the stylish Grosvenor Gallery, whose vast rooms resembled the interior of an old Venetian palace. It had opened three years earlier in a spirited attempt to undermine the domination of the Royal Academy and its traditional painters like G. F. Watts and Alma-Tadema. The Pre-Raphaelite circle was delighted by the way Edward Burne-Jones – whose drawings adorned Oscar's rooms – constantly stole the show at the Grosvenor. Jane was a great admirer of the Pre-Raphaelites, particularly Rossetti. On one occasion, after going to see an exhibition of his paintings, she told Oscar she thought them beautiful: 'a poem, a drama, a tragedy in each one of them – they are the only modern English paintings that touch my soul.'[1]

After arriving in London on 7 May, Jane stayed a few days with Oscar in town, before she and Willie moved to lodgings at No. 1 Ovington Square, Chelsea. They were to stay there for the next three years. It was not a fashionable area then. As Lady Augustus Fane said, after bumping over the macadam roads in a horse-drawn omnibus with straw covering the floor, 'It was quite an adventure to reach Chelsea.'[2]

Willie was now doing an appreciable amount of work for the *World*. A debonair young Irishman of 27, his failure to make a living as a barrister in Dublin forgotten, he seemed set for a distinguished future. He had quickly established himself with the journal, writing stories, reviews, poems and gossip. Oscar meanwhile, living on the money from the sale of his Irish property at Bray, was putting out feelers for jobs and writing occasional reviews and sonnets.

It was a good time to be a journalist in London: papers and magazines were pouring out of the presses. Jane was to write frequently for the *Pall Mall Gazette*, an evening paper which was a literary and political authority; the *Queen*, a fashionable weekly magazine, considered 'ladies' reading', which ranged from topical leaders to a column called 'The Upper Ten Thousand'; and the *Burlington Magazine*, described by its editor as 'a high-class monthly'. She also contributed occasionally to the *St James's Magazine*, *Tinsley's Magazine* and the *Lady's Pictorial*, all of which shared a similar format combining social news and gossip, short stories – highly popular then – and articles. Jane did not write for the weekly reviews, the

Academy and the *Athenaeum*, the leaders of literary criticism, but her books were reviewed by them.

Both Willie and Oscar wrote for an even wider market: Oscar's short stories appeared in magazines like *Blackwood's* and *Lippincott's Monthly Magazine* while Willie was to be drama critic of *Punch*, the *Gentlewoman* and *Vanity Fair* magazine.

Jane was fiercely proud of both her sons and was convinced they would do marvellously in London. They started off with equal intellectual promise. Oscar, according to family friend Leonard Ingleby, 'always paid a tribute to his brother's brilliant cleverness'. Ingleby added that he was not at all certain that, of the two, Willie was not more intelligent, 'though certainly he never approached his brother from any artistic point of view'.[3]

Willie did well enough at the *World* for the *Daily Telegraph* to offer him the job of its chief correspondent and leader writer. He accepted and Jane was delighted, calling his articles to Oscar's attention and praising his 'bright and pleasant writing'. Willie was also to become a prolific book and drama reviewer and edited a number of prestigious Christmas almanacs in which he wrote about people and events of the year. Despite Bernard Shaw's unkind remark that Willie 'must be ruthlessly set aside by literary history as a vulgar journalist of no account', many thought him not just a good but a brilliant journalist, whose skill was recognized right from his early days on the *World*. 'Willie Wilde,' an observer noted admiringly, 'formulated a paragraph for the *World* which became the type for society journalism: "Baroness Burdett Coutts was in her box with Mr Ashmead Bartlett in attendance; Mr Chamberlain, who was accompanied by his pretty young wife, discoursed of orchids to Archdeacon Sinclair; Mr Theodore Watts brought Mr Swinburne; Miss Braddon outlined her new novel to Sir Edward Lawson; Dr Morell Mackenzie congratulated Sir Edward Clarke on his speech in the Penge mystery trial," and so on.'[4]

Willie could write wittily and succinctly when he chose, but he was exceptionally indolent. Jane once excused her preference for staying indoors, saying, 'It's my indolence, I suppose,' and Willie had inherited more than his fair share of it. But while Jane was always prepared to work hard Willie preferred a slower pace. He never turned up at the *Daily Telegraph* before noon, when the forbearing editor would ask if he had an idea. According to his own account of a working day, he would respond: '"Oh yes, sir, indeed I have. It is the anniversary of the penny postage stamp."'

1. Jane rising to fame as 'Speranza' of the Nation' during the late 1840s: photogravure by Stephen Catterson Smith

2. William Wilde when young, from a drawing by J. H. Maguire, 1847

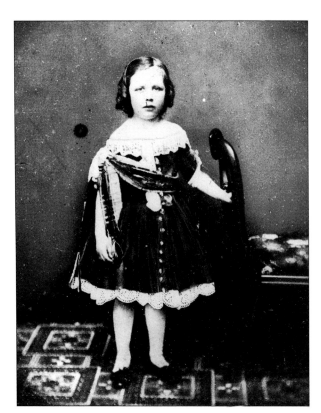

3. Oscar as a child – a photograph which led to accusations that Jane, wanting a daughter, deliberately dressed him as a girl

4. Oscar as a young boy

5. A portrait of Lady Wilde by Bernard Mulrenin, exhibited at the Royal Hibernian Academy, 1864

6. An idealized rendering of the same portrait, which greatly pleased Jane, and appeared in the *Irish Fireside* magazine in September 1885

7. A malicious interpretation of Jane as Madame Récamier at her Dublin salon, by the *Punch* artist Harry Furniss

8. Sir William and Lady Wilde, caricatured by Harry Furniss

9. William Wilde in 1875, the year before his death

10. Jane in 1882, six years after her husband died, painted by J. St. C. Liddell

11. Oscar during his 1882 tour of America

12. Oscar being comforted by his brother Willie when his play *Vera* failed in 1883

13. Willie Wilde's first wife, the formidable Mrs Frank Leslie

14. Constance with the Wildes' elder son Cyril, aged four, in 1889

15. Jane in old age. Her grandson, Vyvyan Holland, recollected her as
'a terrifying and very severe old lady'

Having had his idea accepted, Willie would bow himself out. 'I may then eat a few oysters and drink half a bottle of Chablis at Sweeting's, or, alternatively, partake of a light lunch at this admirable club . . . I then stroll towards the Park. I bow to the fashionables. I am seen along incomparable Piccadilly. It is grand . . . I repair to my club. I order out my ink and paper. I go to my room. I am undisturbed for an hour. My pen moves. Ideas flow. The leader on the penny postage stamp is being evolved. Three great, meaty solid paragraphs, each one-third of a column – that is the consummation to be wished . . . Suddenly someone knocks at the door . . . it is an old friend. We are to eat a little dinner at the Café Royal and drop into the Alhambra for the new ballet.' After sending off his copy by messenger, Willie and his friend go off arm in arm to enjoy 'that paradise of cigar-ashes, bottles, corks, ballet, and those countless circumstances of gaiety and relaxation, known only to those who are indwellers in the magic circles of London's literary Bohemia'.[5]

Often his leaders for the *Daily Telegraph* only just made the first edition. Luther Munday, a family acquaintance, recalled Willie's highly casual attitude towards his job: 'Willie used often to sit until the last minute with his pals round the fire, often at some night club, and then get up to rush away and write his leader; the subject (we sometimes suggested it) appeared in the *Telegraph* only a few hours later. Writing came to him quite naturally . . . At the Owls Club one night George, now Sir George, Power asked Willie to write a couplet as a motto for the club. He wrote this in a minute:

> We fly by night, and this resolve we make,
> If the dawn must break, let the d----d thing break.'[6]

His ability was clear. The *Telegraph* staff admired him for his well-disguised professionalism, despite his habit of working stripped to the waist. They found he was able 'to sum up a situation, political or social, in a single moment. He was able, immediately afterwards, to write a column in the body of the paper, or leading article so succinct, so directly to the point, so informed, with a sort of lambent though cynical Irish wit, that the next morning the words actually seemed to stand out from the printed page . . . There was nothing of the affectation, no hint or trace of the paradox or the epigram employed by Oscar. Clear, witty statement every time and with a pulsing sense of intellect behind it . . .'[7]

After Willie joined the staff of the *Telegraph*, Oscar commented, 'There is a great fascination in journalism. It is so quick, so swift. Willie goes to a Duchess's ball, he slips out before midnight, is away for an hour or two, returns, and as he is driving home in the morning, can buy the paper containing a full account of the party he has just left.'[8] Commissioned by the *Telegraph* to write a story, Willie would often turn up at Oscar's lodgings while he was still in bed and ask him for the outline of a plot or two; then Oscar, 'still puffing his cigarette, would begin to invent stories'.[9] One morning, a friend recalled, Oscar invented the plots of half a dozen short stories for Willie within half an hour.

The two brothers were good friends, with much the same humour. Willie had visited Oscar several times at Oxford, and even though they moved in different sets in London they were always pleased to see one another and were to meet weekly at the salons Jane later held. The style of living the two adopted in London, however, showed up the difference in their characters. Willie continued to share lodgings with his mother, while Oscar's entry into the fashionable world was meteoric: he was the draw of stylish events within two years of his arrival in London in December 1878, fascinating listeners by his sparkling epigrams and outrageous views. Willie had not the desire, energy or thrust of personality to achieve this swift rise to social fame, which Oscar did by diligent self-advertisement and a deliberate fashioning of his public image. But he was happy to help Oscar and gave him useful publicity by writing paragraphs about his activities in the *World*.

Here he had the consent of the editor, Edmund Yates, who had written to Willie in January 1879 to say, 'I wish you would put me *en rapport* with your brother the Newdigate man, of whom I hear so much and so favourably.'[10] It was a significant remark that must have made Willie conscious that Oscar's star was rising. He was unlikely to have seen this as a threat to himself, however. Fond of Oscar, he was pleased at his success. And Oscar took great care to ensure that he was noticed: he would go, for instance, to a private view at the Grosvenor Gallery in a cello-shaped coat. He travelled to Folkestone to welcome Sarah Bernhardt to England with a profusion of lilies, which was noted by the press, and sent Ellen Terry sonnets on her performances as Portia and as Henrietta Maria in *Charles I*. Irving invited him to the opening night banquets at the Lyceum and he profited from Ellen's contacts with the world of art.

In this way he met the right people to launch him on London society. Jane delighted in reading of his activities in the press and Frank Harris recalled continually meeting him in the early eighties at society drawing rooms and first nights at the theatre. His devoted friendship for Lillie Langtry, whom he had met a few years back in his friend Frank Miles's studio, brought him to the fringes of royal society through her association with the Prince of Wales. His reputation was such by then for the Prince of Wales to ask to meet him, saying, 'I do not know Mr Wilde, and not to know Mr Wilde is not to be known.'[11] Dubbing him the 'Aesthete of Aesthetes', the reactionary *Punch* attacked him constantly, portrayed him as a sunflower and merely brought him further notoriety.[12] Oscar was soon being aped in theatrical satires of the aesthetic movement. Gilbert and Sullivan parodied him and his habit of carrying a lily in their operatic skit *Patience*. Jane promptly commented that *Patience* 'though meant to satirize the cultus of beauty, actually gained proselytes to the aesthetic movement, so infinitely charming were the love-sick maidens in their Greek dresses of flowing lines . . .'

Willie, if not the star of social London, was equally interested in its entertainments. Writing to his friend Margaret Campbell, he regretted she was too unwell to go to the Embassy with him and told her that Sarah Bernhardt in *Phèdre* was simply superb – 'You see Oscar has poured out his soul at her feet in the *World*.'[13] An easy-going man, he was prepared to enjoy himself anywhere. 'WCK is off to the Derby,' wrote Jane in a letter: while Oscar had more cosmopolitan tastes, Willie preferred the ebullient, philistine atmosphere of the Pink 'Un (*Sporting Times*) set. As James Holroyd said in an essay on him, 'He established himself among the kind of company which made it a point of honour not to go to bed on the same day they got up.'[14] He may have been living with Jane but she couldn't have seen much of him.

Eating houses like Kettner's and Willis's in the Strand were popular haunts of Willie's and he also devoted an extensive amount of his time to drinking clubs. Like Oscar he went a great deal to the Café Royal whose vast, gilded room with the clink of dominoes and glasses and scurrying waiters was an acknowledged meeting place for Bohemians. An habitué of the Café Royal remembered how Willie would turn up there, 'huge, stooping, high shoulders, always wearing a long, braided morning or frock coat and a rather wide-brimmed silk hat – and peer round short-sightedly till he found a genial coterie.'

After lumbering towards his friends and sitting down with them, his energy then apparently disappeared until he had revived himself with his favourite apéritif: 'He would sip it thoughtfully, looking with dreamy eyes at the people around him. Then suddenly something in the talk would catch his mind, his eyes would light up, the full mouth begin to twitch with merriment, and a flood of talk would come from him – inconsequent but always clever. If Oscar Wilde was wit, his brother Willie was humour – a freakish humour which would take pleasure in the smallest joke, would catch it up, as it were, hold it high to view and embroider it . . . until everyone was laughing heartily and everyone was pleased.'[15] One night when Gus Moore, brother to the writer George Moore, turned up wearing a brilliantly coloured cravat, and asked for an opinion of it, Willie said, 'If you ask me, I should have thought that only a deaf man could have worn it with safety.'

Another favourite haunt of Willie's was the Spoofs Club where nobody made 'the egregious mistake of taking life seriously'. One of its members claimed that, night after night, 'no gentler humorist or more polished gentleman ever entertained the thoughtless patrons of the Spoofs . . .'[16]

Willie's polished appearance included a straggly black moustache and a heavy, pointed beard – which he claimed Oscar paid him to wear to emphasize the difference between the two of them. Similar in build, both brothers shared the long, pale Wilde face and hands that once caused Lady Colin Campbell to describe Oscar as 'a great white caterpillar'. A cartoon by Max Beerbohm shows them embracing, like two giant bears. Both inherited their father's sensuous lips and their mother's heavily-lidded brilliant eyes. One acquaintance said that Willie walked with 'ponderous alertness', while Oscar moved with 'ponderous, and partly assumed languor'.[17] Jane, a large woman herself, moved equally languidly.

Max Beerbohm gave a vivid impression of Willie as a mirror image of Oscar. '*Quel monstre!*' he wrote. 'Dark, oily, suspect yet awfully like Oscar: he has Oscar's coy, carnal smile and fatuous giggle and not a little of Oscar's *esprit*. But he is awful – a veritable tragedy of family likeness!'[18] When Otho Lloyd, the brother of Constance whom Oscar was to marry, met Willie at one of Jane's salons, he had much the same impression. He found him 'a tall straight fellow with a swarthy complexion and an abundance of black hair: an oriental in looks he has a part of Oscar's abilities and something of his manner of speaking but none of his fascination; something about him strikes one unpleasantly, as if there were something within not corresponding to his agreeable discourse; this is not a fancy of my own, others feel it, for he is not a general favourite, and all like Oscar better.'[19]

Not everyone agreed. The brothers' temperament and style was so different that friends liked one or the other. One who preferred Willie considered he was 'generous, witty, kind-hearted to a fault, unconventional and full of courtesy, a stranger to all pedantry and posing, changeable, quick-tempered, and a born journalist'.[20] Frank Harris, too, liked Willie's 'expressive, taking face, lit with a pair of deep blue laughing eyes. He had any amount of physical vivacity, and told a good story with immense verve, without for a moment getting above the commonplace.'[21]

All the Wildes were talented talkers and Willie's conversation in his soft Irish voice was as light-heartedly inventive as Oscar's. On one occasion, meeting Max Beerbohm's sister Dora for lunch, Willie greeted her with: 'Dora, I feel most imperial this morning, rampantly imperial. I like the feeling of getting up in the morning and thinking, Well, I've got Egypt, I've got Ceylon, I've got Singapore, I've got large areas in Africa . . . and now, dear Dora, you are the first to know – I've got India!'[22] It was rumoured that a rich old lady used to pay Willie £300 a year just to come along and talk to her for two or three hours each afternoon and that even when she lost money on her shares, resolved to give up her carriage and take cabs rather than lose Willie.

With his genial charm he attracted less hostility than his brother, who could upset people by pungent remarks at their expense. Max Beerbohm remembered a writer called Lewis Morris complaining about a conspiracy of silence against his poems and Oscar remarking, 'How I wish, my dear Morris, we could induce you to join that conspiracy.'[23] Leonard Ingleby said that after listening to Oscar you would stumble off in mental amazement, but when Willie had talked to you for an hour or so, 'you always went away chuckling with pleasure'. Willie's outlook on life, according to Ingleby, 'was quite unprejudiced and untrammelled by much that the Puritan or the rigid moralist would consider to be necessary confines of talk, but it was eminently kindly and human . . . if he referred to a friend or acquaintance, it was always with an excuse for the failings of that friend or acquaintance, rather than with a bitter, barbed and pointed epigram . . .'[24]

A member of the Spoofs Club observed that Willie was 'the personification of good nature and irresponsibility, and with ten thousand a year would have been magnificent; without other income, however, than that which his too indolent pen afforded, the poor fellow was frequently in straits which must have proved highly repugnant to his really frank and sunny disposition.'[25] But his frank and sunny disposition could turn quite devious when he was short of money. Once, in the Spoofs Club, a member asked if anyone could cash a cheque for two sovereigns. Willie, to everyone's amazement, generously offered to cash him a cheque for five sovereigns. When the man left, Willie followed him and said, 'Would you, as you say two pounds are sufficient for your own needs, grant me the loan of – the other three?' Which the unsuspecting man did.[26]

Another example of Willie's outrageous behaviour over money was related by Max Beerbohm – who said he was more interested in Willie than Oscar because when it came to failures he preferred small ones to those on a heroic scale. Beerbohm recalled the time when Willie became very friendly with a wealthy young widow and her two children. Like Oscar, he was excellent with children and they loved his stories and his frightening pretence of being a bear. 'One day he came – it was just before Christmas – and said, "Now I am a burglar come to rob you, and you must catch me and tame me just as you did when I was a bear." The children had a money bank fixed to the wall, ready to be opened at Christmas, into which adults had dropped some sovereigns. Willie crept towards it, to the children's great excitement. And then, suddenly, obeying some imperious impulse of childhood, Willie ripped the bank off the wall and ran out of the room and out of the house, and was never seen there again.'[27]

It was a childlike action and Willie in many ways remained a dependent child. Jane regarded him indulgently, resigned to him being constantly in some financial or emotional scrape. His loyalty to Jane, like Oscar's, was unshakeable. The Dubliner Jimmy Glover, who thought Willie 'a delightful, genial, brilliant Irishman', remembered him refusing to speak to a man who had made an unkind reference to Jane in print. Glover attempted to bridge the gap, but Willie was adamant. 'My dear James,' he said, 'there are certain circumstances which will ever prevent diplomatic relations being re-opened with your unpleasant friend and my equally unpleasant enemy . . . unless certain published apologies are forthcoming.'[28]

The brothers' mutual affection for Jane remained the real bond between them. She in turn could not bear it if either quarrelled with the other, and if she complained of one to the other it was with amusement rather than anger. Jane unquestioningly returned her sons' loyalty. Her admiration for Oscar remained high and she always thought Willie full of promise. She loved them both and, her sense of family being strong, liked nothing better than the three of them being together. In these early days in London, with the future still unknown, she was content to weave dreams for the two of them.

10

Feet in London, Eyes on America

JANE KNEW FEW people when she first arrived in London in 1879, but Oscar was quick to introduce her to his artistic circle. He would ask friends like the poet Frederick Locker to his Salisbury Street rooms to what he called 'Tea and Beauties', telling them he would have the pleasure of introducing them to his mother. 'The two beauties – Lady Lonsdale and Mrs Langtry – and Mamma, and a few friends are coming,' he told the actress Genevieve Ward.[1] He wrote to Harold Boulton, a friend at Balliol College, Oxford, to say that 'Any Saturday you are in London I hope you will call and see my mother who is always at home from five to seven on Saturday. She is always glad to see my friends, and usually some good literary and artistic people take tea with her.'[2]

Friends remembered the way he introduced them to Jane. Louise Jopling said she would 'never forget the proud and devoted tone of his voice as he said, "My Mother,"'[3] and Robert Sherard too said he recalled 'with what pride he said to me: "Robert, my mother!"'[4] In *De Profundis*, Oscar's long autobiographical prose essay written in jail, he wrote emotionally of Jane that she 'intellectually ranks with Elizabeth Barrett Browning, and historically with Madame Roland'.[5] Lord Alfred Douglas, with whom Oscar later had a passionate affair, recalled that it was 'a touching trait of poor Oscar's character that he always had an altogether exaggerated idea of his mother's mental powers and social standing. He really adored her and spoke of her always with the greatest reverence and respect.'

Jane held her own at Oscar's at-homes without difficulty. A letter to her from Edward Godwin said: 'I wish you had kept up the discussion you started; you were opposed by a painter. I had intended coming in at the finish in your support . . .'[6] Helena Sickert, the younger sister of Walter Sickert, the artist, remembered meeting Jane at Oscar's and her pushing the hair off Helena's forehead and saying, 'A highly intellectual countenance! I shall hear of you in the literary world.'[7] A contemporary of Oscar's at Oxford was equally taken aback when he visited Jane at Oscar's urging. She looked him straight in the face and said, 'You are a very young man, but before you are as old as I am you will know that there is only one thing in the world worth living for and that is sin.' Jane, like Oscar, delighted in making her conversation shock.[8]

Jane was pleased at the way both her sons had taken to London. She herself was preoccupied in completing the final section of Sir William's memoir of Gabriel Beranger from the notes left by her late husband and in 1880 she arranged the memoir's publication in book form. It included a lengthy tribute to her husband: a personal obituary. 'Sir William was no visionary theorist,' she wrote. 'His singularly penetrating intellect tested scrupulously everything that came before him . . . yet he was no dry and formal writer. His love of the antique past was an enthusiasm, and all that is strange and beautiful in the ancient art and architecture of Ireland touched him deeply.' She wrote of his unusual gifts, his marvellous memory, the way he went about the mammoth task of cataloguing the antiquities at the Royal Irish Academy – and attacked the Academy for being too apathetic to fund its completion.[9] To get reviews, Jane sent the book around to writers and friends in the way Oscar was to do with his poems. It was a successful move. One recipient said, 'You may depend upon my using what influence I possess to get it noticed.'

The book out of the way, Jane's thoughts returned to holding her beloved salons once more and she began sending out invitations to guests for Saturday afternoons. One visitor remarked that 'These certainly then unfashionable At Homes were, however, most original affairs . . . all belonged to the art, music or painting, dramatic or literary world . . . The dimness was to hide nothing else but the drear fact that in order to keep a London household in decent cleanliness rather more than the occasional domestic service was required. There were only chairs and tables – little tables – easily and constantly upset.'[10]

Many of the comments about the salons Jane held in London over the next fifteen years were unnecessarily spiteful. Most appeared in reminiscences written and published in the early twentieth century, when the name of Wilde was at its lowest ebb and the jackals were having a field day. A genuine friend of Jane's criticized these 'chroniclers of so-called autobiographies really made up of society gossip, who, for the sake of padding, no doubt, resorted to fictitious wit in the way of ridicule at her expense'.[11]

A number of well-known people were to attend Jane's salons, among them W.B. Yeats; the American authors and humorists Oliver Wendell Holmes and Brett Harte; Henry Ward Beecher, the opponent of slavery; Frances Hodgson Burnett, author of *Little Lord Fauntleroy*; George Moore, the Irish novelist, and women novelists Katharine Tynan, Marie Corelli and Ouïda. Ruskin and Browning appeared once, as did Eleanor Marx, daughter of Karl; while Bernard Shaw went to several of Jane's salons and although calling them 'desperate affairs', admitted that 'Lady Wilde was nice to me in London' during his impoverished early days there in the 1880s. He remembered dining with her and an ex-tragedy queen called Miss Glynn who had a head like a turnip and spent the time arguing that Gladstone's oratorical style was based on Charles Kean while Jane talked about Schopenhauer.[12]

Guests at Jane's salons commented with amazement or sarcasm on the clothes she wore. Her dress was defiantly in the style popular some twenty years previously. 'She seemed to wear two dresses,' said one guest. 'They were covered over with flounces in an entirely departed style, huge bodices with vast trimmings, draperies, caps, ribbons on her head – and her favourite colour seemed then mauve.'[13] Jane had indeed taken with her to London all the dresses she had worn in the heyday of her Dublin salons. She could afford few new clothes and in any case was impervious to current fashion and careless of the impression she made. Violet Hunt was taken aback to find Jane 'in an old white ball dress, in which she must have graced the soirees of Dublin a great many years ago',[14] while Katharine Tynan, seeing her in no doubt the same white dress, said she looked like a Druid priestess, with her hair hanging down her back.[15]

Another guest, a painter, admitted Jane looked more weird and imposing than ridiculous when she greeted him in 'a low-cut lavender-coloured silk dress over a crinoline, with a piece of crimson velvet about a foot deep round the skirt and a miniature, some six inches by four, pinned on her breast . . . Her hair was dressed in ringlets, surmounted by a high head-dress of lace, and hanging loosely round her waist was a Roman scarf which was bright green, with stripes of scarlet, blue and yellow.'[16]

Seeing Jane for the first time, one American visitor considered that her 'faded splendour was more striking than the most fashionable attire, for she wore that ancient finery with a grace and dignity that robbed it of its grotesqueness'. Jane greeted her in an old-fashioned purple brocade gown, a towering headdress of velvet, long gold earrings, a yellow lace fichu fastened with innumerable enormous brooches, huge bracelets of turquoise and gold and rings on all her fingers.[17]

Catherine Hamilton, the author of *Notable Irishwomen*, walked into Jane's salon to find her wearing a black and white chequered silk gown, with 'long white tulle streamers, mixed with ends of scarlet ribbons, floating down from the side of her head. She had a train of stiff amber silk and an overskirt of black. The large gold locket round her throat was nearly obscured by clouds of black lace.'[18]

The other aspect of Jane's salons that startled guests was her preference for keeping the lights so low they were practically non-existent. Katharine Tynan remembered going rather blindly towards a seat that Jane had indicated. 'A soft hand took mine and a soft voice spoke. "So fortunate," said the voice, "that no one could suspect dear Lady Wilde of being a practical joker! There really *is* a chair . . ."'[19]

Another guest noted the only light coming from 'candles with little red petticoats and alabaster vases with lights inside'.[20] Jane used to organize her few shaded candles to cast light only on the most prominent people. When she discovered a spectator in the outer darkness, she would blithely draw attention to their better points. 'My dear Miss Potter, you must not talk so much. Not with that face. You should be still – still and grave.' Other comments were, 'Such a beautiful long neck!' and 'Do you see the glint on her hair as she turns? I wish Oscar were here to see it.'[21]

Jane, always more at ease with the Irish than the English, kept in touch with her Dublin friends by correspondence and always asked them to her salon if they came to London. In 1880 Ireland was again in turmoil. Jane had been anxiously conscious of the situation for some time, writing to Lotten to say, 'Ireland is in a very unquiet state – I fear the people will now refuse to pay rents and whoever enforces payment will be assuredly shot – I despair of my beloved Irish at last – we want a strong hand like the Emperor Napoleon's over us.'[22]

The cause of the unrest was that cheap grain from America had forced down farm prices in Ireland and tenant farmers, unable to pay their rent, were being evicted in their thousands. Agitation for reduced rents and the transfer of land from landlord to tenant was being led by the republican Michael Davitt. He persuaded the MP for County Meath, Charles Stewart Parnell, to promote these views at a meeting of tenant farmers and from this was born the Irish National Land League. Its slogan was 'The Land for the People' and its president was Parnell. Posters went up around the countryside announcing, 'The Land War! No Rent!' The issue set the country alight and growing anger in western Ireland enabled Parnell to make a successful challenge in 1880 for the leadership of the Home Rule Party.

It was bad timing for Jane. She needed the rents from the Moytura estate to support her in London. She was nearly 59 and to uproot herself at that age was wearing enough without worrying over finances. Many of her Irish friends were also in similar financial difficulties. One expressed condolences to Jane about her deprivation of income and said he too had lost heavily in 1880 because his tenants 'yielding to evil counsel refuse to pay their rents'.

That summer Oscar and Frank Miles moved from Salisbury Street to 1 Tite Street, Chelsea, where the artist James Whistler was both neighbour and friend. Lady Augusta Fane recalled going to tea with the two of them there 'in their quaint little old house' where she was served by a maid, 'dressed in sage-blue and holding a lily in her hand – which got very much in her way when arranging the tea-table'.[23]

In need of money, Jane now turned her attention toward the London magazines. In January 1881, the *Burlington Magazine* published Oscar's poem 'The Grave of Keats' and reviewed G. Barnett Smith's *Irish Story and Song*, which praised 'Speranza'. The magazine considered Jane's 'thoughtful' poem 'Ruins' had a 'pathetic and eloquent' conclusion, with 'many lines worthy to be remembered, as: "The touch of a man's misdoings/Leaves more blighted tracks than time".'

As a result of this praise, Jane put herself forward as a contributor and soon wrote regularly for the *Burlington Magazine*. In the March issue she attacked the critics of *Endymion*, Disraeli's last completed novel: 'Why,' she said, 'should it be necessary for all the critics to rush at once upon a book, tear the heart and life out of it, and then fling it dead upon the shelf?' She went on to assess this 'thinly veiled autobiography', in which Endymion had 'no inheritance but his genius' and a twin sister, who was 'ever inseparable, all-daring, the sustainer of his courage, the inspirer of his life'. It was a theme that appealed to Jane, who could have visualized herself and her husband in those roles. She sympathized with Disraeli who died on 19 April 1881. 'Had he been given a few more years of power, he might have achieved something to satisfy even his ambition.'

In the May of that year Jane went with Oscar to visit Mary Atkinson, who had lived near the Wildes in Dublin and who introduced them to her granddaughter, Constance Lloyd. Jane, with Oscar's bachelor state in mind, invited Constance to her salons and Oscar in turn called on Constance frequently that summer at 100 Lancaster Gate, where she lived with her wealthy grandfather, John Lloyd, a QC.

Constance's father, Horace Lloyd, had been a highly successful barrister in London. He married Adelaide Atkinson, a Dublin girl from a military family, and the two set up house in London. Their first child was a boy, Otho, and their second, a girl, was Constance. The marriage was not a happy one and perhaps because of this Otho and Constance became very close. Horace Lloyd died comparatively young, at 46, and Adelaide married again, a George Swinburne King. The new couple did not wish to share their home with Constance and Otho, so the brother and sister had gone to live with their grandfather, John Lloyd.

Constance was 23 when she first met Oscar. She was a graceful, accomplished young woman with an eager mind, who had a gift for music, loved painting and poetry and read widely in French and Italian. She wrote to her brother, Otho, to say that Oscar had called on her begging her to see his mother again soon. 'I can't help liking him,' she said, 'because when he's talking to me alone he's never a bit affected and speaks naturally, excepting that he uses better language than most people.'[24] Oscar then asked her to go to *Othello* with him, and at another of Jane's salons, so she told her brother, Oscar had talked to her all the time, 'excepting when his mother seized on him for somebody else'.

In the May and July 1881 issues of the *Burlington Magazine*, Jane wrote a very lengthy two-part article on 'The Laws of Dress' – an odd subject to choose, given the way she flouted all the rules herself. She stated loftily that the dress of a woman of noble presence should express calm dignity, and she castigated artists for wearing sickly green because 'tints of decomposed asparagus and cucumber do not suit the long, pale English face'. After claiming that a bonnet tied directly under the chin 'shows reserve and dignity', she suggested rouge for ladies at London drawing rooms in February, to offset complexions 'made black and yellow by the livid light of their diamonds gleaming out of the foggy atmosphere'. In her view, the best 'writing dress' was black silk, 'for it is a non-conductor, and it is of the highest importance to preserve the electric fire, or the romance will have no interest, the poem no incandescent glow'.

That summer Oscar published his first book of poems, which was greeted with a mixture of hostility and approval. *Punch* wrote, 'The poet is Wilde,/But his poetry's tame,' while the *Athenaeum* regarded it as 'the evangel of a new creed . . . We fail to see, however, that the apostle of the new worship has any distinct message.' Ellen Terry (to whom two of the poems were addressed) praised Oscar highly, but the Oxford Union, having asked for a copy for its library, finally returned it because of its 'borrowings' from other poets. Writing to Oscar that August about his poems, the journalist and MP for Galway, T. P. O'Connor, said he felt 'your glorious mother's son must needs write well' and said even as he wrote there was in front of him a copy of the poems of Speranza ('what Irishman does not thrill to *that* name').[25]

The poems caused a crisis in Oscar's personal life that month. Frank Miles's father, a canon, disliked Oscar's sensual verse and complained to him that it was anti-Christian. He then wrote to his son and advised him to separate from Oscar. Frank, financially dependent on his father, had to obey and Oscar stormed out of the Tite Street house. He stayed a day or so with his mother then took furnished rooms in Charles Street, Mayfair.

Jane was busy reviewing a biography of Dr Doyle, one of the central figures of the Catholic emancipation movement in Ireland. It appeared in September in the *Burlington Magazine*. The biography was written by W. J. Fitzpatrick, an old friend of hers, to whom she sent another of Oscar's poems, 'Ave Imperatrix', which had been published in the *World*. Fitzpatrick pleased her by congratulating her on 'being the mother of two such gifted sons'. Jane was indeed delighted with Willie's progress in journalism and that Oscar had become a poet like herself.

The census for 1881 lists three people living at No. 1 Ovington Square, Chelsea: Jane, who gave her age as 57, despite being 59; Willie, who airily put down his occupation as barrister even though he had long stopped practising; and an Irish woman servant.[26] The servant was fortunate to find an Irish employer: many advertisements for domestics then ended, 'Irish servants need not apply.' A visitor of

Jane's at that time observed patronizingly that 'a single charwoman seemed to compose her domestic staff', and claimed that 'like many of her countrywomen, often devoid of the sense and understanding of common life, she was indeed the most unpractical of women.'[27]

By the end of 1881 Jane and Willie had decided to move to 116 Park Street, near Grosvenor Square. Although Chelsea was slowly becoming an acceptable, artistic neighbourhood, Jane wanted to hold her Saturday salons in a more fashionable and accessible area, and Park Street then was as smart as Park Lane. The new premises also had the bonus of being near to Oscar, and she immediately involved him in all its details, including her choice of wallpaper. 'I saw one that will do at Jackson & Grahams, Oxford Street – the best shop in London. It is *not* "sliced pickles powdered with dressed cucumber chopped fine," as a man described last night at the German circle, when he papered his room after the high art model "toned with mud mouldings." I have selected crimson and gold stars to give a genial glow.'[28]

Because property was extremely expensive in the West End, the Park Street house was tiny. One of Jane's eventual visitors there was Anna, Comtesse de Brémont, a young woman of Irish descent. She had met Oscar at a dinner party and he suggested to her that she visit his mother. The Comtesse was later to write a book on Jane, *Oscar Wilde and his Mother*, which in between meanderings on Oscar's feminine and Jane's masculine soul, gave a realistic picture of Jane's life. Calling on Jane for the first time, she was greatly disappointed at her unassuming small house, with its rusty knocker and murky interior. An Irish servant led her through a long dark hall into a large, low-ceilinged panelled room, dimly lit by red-shaded candles, saying, 'Shure, it's her ladyship that loves to turn daylight into candlelight.' When the Comtesse saw Jane, however, she was awed at 'the majestic figure standing in the centre of the obscurity'. It made her forget 'the dowdy maid, the poorly furnished room, the badly served tea, the dust and dinginess . . .'[29]

Constance also went with her mother to call on Jane and told her brother that they found her 'all alone in her glory in such wee rooms that mama and I puzzled internally how she had got into them'. Jane told them that Oscar's first play, *Vera or The Nihilists*, was to be given a one-off production on the afternoon of 17 December and said that Oscar was expecting Constance to go. 'I suppose she is trying to canvas an audience,' was Constance's comment.[30]

Oscar's political play, *Vera*, must have pleased Jane considerably, as in many ways it mirrored the scene in Ireland in 1848. In it, the Russians, subjugated by a tyrannical Czar, are swept towards republicanism by the fierce revolutionary, Vera Sabouroff. Like Jane's own call to arms in her notorious leader for the *Nation*, Vera says, 'I would fan the flame of this revolution into such a blaze that the eyes of all the kings in Europe shall be blinded.' She, like Jane, believes that liberty is worth dying for. And her brother's introduction to democracy ('I heard men talk of Liberty one night in a café. I had never heard the word before') recalls Jane's own conversion to the Young Irelanders, when, after reading a volume of *Ireland's Library*, she said, 'my patriotism was kindled'.

Oscar's dismissal of the 'dull Russian peasants' in *Vera* as being incapable of contributing to the revolution also recalls Jane's comment to a friend at the time of insurrection in Ireland: 'No Democracy. Why should a rude, uncultured mob dare to utter its voice?' And in falling in love with the new Czar, Vera's revolutionary fervour, combined with her feelings of submission, also has echoes of Jane's dual attitude towards marriage – a dislike of being dominated, yet a desperate adherence to it.

Visiting Jane in December 1881, Constance learned that Oscar had been invited to America to give fifty lectures, all expenses paid, which she thought 'not bad for him'. The invitation had come from the D'Oyly Carte New York office after Gilbert and Sullivan's *Patience* had been playing in America. The operetta had aroused the audience's curiosity as to what Bunthorne (the character that parodied Oscar walking down Piccadilly holding a lily) was really like and D'Oyly Carte decided a tour by Oscar would be useful publicity.

Oscar accepted the commission and left that December, planning only to stay till April. But he was asked to extend his tour and finally stayed a full year. The invitation came at a useful time: the money from the sale of his Bray houses and his occasional contributions to magazines was not proving enough. Throughout the time he was in America he wrote regularly to Jane ('I generally hear once a week,' she said, 'which is delightful') and sent her newspaper clippings of his reception. A letter of his in January 1882 asks the publisher of certain papers to send his mother three copies of particular issues.

Jane was in transports of delight throughout the whole tour, vicariously living his success and sending him the English and Irish papers, so that he in turn could read the comments on his tour. 'You will be the *first* apostle to the Gentiles,' she told him, 'and the Irish will love you.' What must have particularly pleased her was finding she was remembered by the Irish Americans. Oscar was greeted as 'Speranza's Son', and in Minnesota an Irish priest called him the son 'of one of Ireland's noblest daughters – of a daughter who in the troublous times of 1848 by the works of her pen and her noble example did much to keep the fire of patriotism burning brightly'.

Jane's chatty letters kept Oscar up to date with what was going on at home. Early in February 1882 she told him that his photographs 'are greatly admired here – especially the standing figure in the fur coat – they are beautifully executed. I only object to *the hair parted in the centre*. No newspapers have come since Philadelphia. I want Baltimore and Washington papers.' With a sudden change of mood she writes, 'I think of giving up *this house*. I cannot pay £200 a year.' The owner, she said, was willing to take it back at any moment. Then putting the problem aside, she launched into gossip. 'Lord Lonsdale is *dead*. She [Lady Lonsdale] was abroad and not with him, now she has arrived. He died in London. Who will she marry? Will you try your chance? If Willie marries he and Muriel will take a house – and *I* will take rooms. Life goes on the same. *Punch* has asked Willie to be dramatic critic and *he has accepted*. That is £100 a year.'[31]

Oscar was in Rochester that month and on 7 February his public lecture there was noisily disrupted by students who had arranged for an elderly black man to dance down the aisle holding a bunch of flowers and dressed in a parody of Wilde's clothing, including a white kid glove. The uproar wrecked the lecture. Jane wrote to Oscar on the 19th saying, 'What a tempest and tornado you live in!' adding, 'But you must give some *new lectures* on living and modern celebrities in England: poets and artists, writers and thinkers and philosophers . . . Ruskin – Mill – Carlyle. Your lecture is in *abstract*, nothing to catch the attention – give some personal *descriptions* – and extracts from poets and describe the schools of painting – Millais, B. Jones etc etc, and above all the Great Teacher – Ruskin.' She enclosed various papers, including the *Dublin Express* and the *Lady's Pictorial*, the latter having copied a whole page from an American paper. Telling Oscar admiringly that she had heard he had actually been to Niagara, she continued, 'The *Daily News* and the *Pall Mall* continue to be *sneering*, but still you are making way . . . Willie goes on just the same . . . don't rush about so rapidly – take more rest. La tua, La Madre.'[32]

Oscar ignored her advice and continued to follow a punishing schedule, often lecturing once a day in different cities. In March he wrote to Colonel Morse, the business manager for D'Oyly Carte who was organizing the tour, saying that he didn't know if he could stand the pace, but ending, 'Thank you for sending Lady Wilde the cheque . . . I will lecture as long as the public stands being lectured . . .'[33]

Jane read the papers Oscar sent in from cover to cover. 'The Chicago paper was very amusing, describing you – and pleasant without ill nature,' she wrote, continuing gleefully, 'The Prince [of Wales] shook hands warmly with Willie and asked at once for Oscar.' She was impressed how often Willie came across people who had met Oscar in America; but Oscar's celebrity was becoming hard for Willie to accept. Until now, he had been the elder brother, writing paragraphs about Oscar; suddenly Oscar had no need of him. The American trip changed the relationship between the brothers: they had been equals, but from now on Willie was to be in Oscar's shadow.

The year 1882 was one of Jane's happiest years in London: she was able to peacock around, glorying in the fact that Oscar's tour was fascinating London. She told Oscar with delight, mid-March, that 'Nothing is talked of but you. The *Chelsea Gazette* announces "Oscar Wilde has cut his hair".' She did not mention the full-page caricature in the *Lady's Pictorial*, entitled 'The Aesthetic Monkey' and picturing Oscar as a monkey dressed in velvet, with a white collar and sideburns, gazing at a sunflower with a lily on the table. Instead she reported that her Saturday salons were becoming crowded: 'Your photos excite great admiration.'

She added with a touch of the old Speranza spirit, 'They all say you are making heaps of money, and I smile and accept the notion – for it galls the Londoners.'[34] In a later letter she referred to his 'wonderful dollar success' and of hearing of this in so many quarters, that 'London *at last* is forced *to believe it*.' More practically, she mentioned a bill that had come for him for £10 and said, 'I advise you *pay all bills while you can.*'

Jane's travelling had been confined to Europe and she wrote to Oscar with amazement at the end of March to say, 'Your letter just arrived – telling of your going to the *Mormons* – what a tour!! What a book you might make of it! I feel as if you had gone out into the infinite – how changed you will be – I shall feel quite nervous having you to dinner in little Park Street.' She made similar comments several times while he was in America, saying he would now be 'self reliant and to the full stature of a man'. Meanwhile Oscar had been thinking of going on to Australia with a young painter, Spencer Blake, whom he had met in America and Jane agreed that this 'might be a good thing'.

A long essay of hers in praise of emigration to Australia appeared in the *Burlington Magazine* some six weeks later. She called emigration 'the one great remedial measure for the suffering classes of the Old World; for all who in our overcrowded cities and professions and trades are ever vainly seeking and hopelessly awaiting the employment that never comes, the income that never is realized'.[35] A George Shaw of the School of Law at Trinity College, Dublin, wrote to her to say he thought she had written 'with great power and beauty' even though he didn't believe in the practicality of her scheme. Jane had also sent her article to the Lord Mayor of London, J. Whittaker Ellis, who promptly wrote back to say that he had long thought that many of her views were 'the only solution of the difficulties of the day'.

Oscar had been in San Francisco in April, where he spoke to a mainly Irish audience on the Irish poets of the nineteenth century. He claimed that the conquering English may have destroyed the beauty of Irish art, but they had failed to destroy the poetry of the Celtic people. Speaking of the Young Irelanders of 1848 he said, 'I look on their work with peculiar reverence and love, for I was indeed trained by my mother to love and reverence them . . .' His words were greeted with applause and he went on to talk of Jane's involvement with the events of 1848, saying: 'Of the quality of Speranza's poems I, perhaps, should not speak, for criticism is disarmed before love, but I am content to abide by the verdict of the nation, which has so welcomed her genius and understood the song – noticeably for its strength and simplicity – that ballad of my mother's on "The Trial of the Brothers Sheares" in '98, and that passionate and lofty lyric, written in the year of revolution, called *Courage*. I would like to linger on her work longer, I acknowledge, but I think you all know it and it is enough to me to have had once the privilege of speaking about my mother to the race she loved so well.'[36]

Jane was deeply interested in the San Francisco papers he sent her, though saying anxiously: 'the interviewing is awful and how will you get through it?' Oscar told one paper there that he felt proud of his Irish birth and parentage. 'I live in London for its artistic life and opportunities,' he said, sounding like Jane. 'There is no lack of culture in Ireland but it is nearly all absorbed in politics. Had I remained there my career would have been a political one.'[37]

Ireland was currently in the news in England. Gladstone's Land Act the previous year had at last established the Irish tenants' demands for fair rent, fixity of tenure and free sale; but Parnell, in attempting to test the Act's effectiveness, had been arrested. After his release that April the Land Act was amended to protect tenants in arrears. Sadly for Jane, this meant she lost the legal right to collect any back rents due to her and inevitably tenants slipped yet further behind with payments.

Frank Harris recalled Willie taking him back to a crowded Park Street house one night at a time when Parnell was front-page news. The room was littered with empty teacups and cigarette ends, and Harris found Jane sitting 'enthroned behind the tea-table looking like a sort of female Buddha swathed in wraps – a large woman with a heavy face and prominent nose; very like Oscar indeed, with the same sallow skin which always looked dirty; her eyes too were her redeeming feature – vivacious and quick-glancing as a girl's. She "made up" like an actress . . . Her idealism came to show as soon as she spoke. It was a necessity of her nature to be enthusiastic; unfriendly critics said hysterical, but I should prefer to say high-falutin' about everything she enjoyed or admired. She was at her best in misfortune; her great vanity gave her a certain proud stoicism which was admirable.'

When Harris and Willie arrived, the Land League was being discussed along with Parnell's attitude to it. Harris found that Jane regarded him as 'the predestined saviour of her country. "*Par*nell," she said with a strong accent on the first syllable, "is the man of destiny; he will strike off the fetters and free Ireland, and throne her as Queen among the nations." '[38] Jane was quite prepared to talk about Parnell, but she wrote no campaigning articles about Irish politics in England. It was a wise move for someone hoping to get a civil list pension.

Jane became further preoccupied with Irish politics in May when what came to be called the Phoenix Park murders took place. On 6 May 1882 a previously unknown terrorist group, the Invincibles, assassinated the new Chief Secretary for Ireland, Lord Frederick Cavendish, and his permanent Under-Secretary at Dublin Castle, T. H. Burke, as they were setting out across the park. Burke had helped Jane in Dublin, after her husband died, when he tried to get support for a civil list pension for her. Writing to Oscar two days later, Jane said: 'All London is in horror over the two murders. Poor Tom Burke! What a fate! No one knows what will be next. Some papers think there will be a general massacre and smash. Today great work is expected in parliament. Callan the MP came here and O'Donnell . . . politics now are so interesting.'[39]

Oscar, asked his reaction to the murders, pleased Irish-American readers by saying, 'When liberty comes with hands dabbled in blood it is hard to shake hands with her . . . We forget how much England is to blame. She is reaping the fruit of seven centuries of injustice.'[40]

It was the kind of remark that echoed his mother's early writings and delighted her. Oscar never took up the Irish banner, but wrote articles condemning British policy in Ireland and also protested about the imprisonment of that champion of the Irish Nationalist Cause, Wilfrid Scawen Blunt, for his activities in the Irish Land League. He shared his mother's fellow-feeling for the oppressed, once going down to Lambeth in south London after the Thames flooded to see if he could help the homeless. Oscar ended his 'Sonnet to Liberty' with the words:

> . . . and yet, and yet,
> These Christs that die upon the barricades,
> God knows it I am with them, in some things.

During May Jane sent Oscar a 'nice notice' and commented, 'You see the *Wildes* are destined for celebrity and pinnacles. Nothing will put *us* or keep *us* under a Bushell.' She went on, 'You must do something wonderful on your return,' and added, 'Willie still "At the Play" [the name of *Punch*'s theatre column] and nothing else – very sad – if he would marry and go to the Bar I would be content. I want him to keep this house as it is and he and Hetty set up here for the present and I'll go off into space.' It was hard to keep up with the girls Willie was always about to marry. No wonder Jane ends her letter with a histrionic cry of 'All bewilderment before us – nothing but Death certain.'[41]

That month Violet Hunt, daughter of landscape artist Alfred Hunt and the novelist Margaret Raine Hunt, went to one of Jane's Saturday salons. Oscar had already met her in London, calling her 'the sweetest violet in England', and Jane wrote to him to say, encouragingly, 'Pretty Violet all eager to see you. We had 26 and when *you* come the rush will be tremendous.' Violet's diary entry for 27 May 1882 was cooler. It read: 'We called on Mrs Maxwell Lyte and Mrs Newall, whom we persuaded to come with us to Lady Wilde's who has actually got lodgings in Park Street. How they can afford, I can't tell! . . . Lady Wilde sits there . . . and talks about Oscar, his success in America, the costume "Oscar" which he has originated, and which all the young men of fashion are wearing there [and] showed us a photograph of him in his knee breeches, which looked very taking. William Wilde, the brother, has an agreeable manner and I should think is almost as clever as Oscar.'[42] Constantly being second-best must have been frustrating for Willie.

Placing little reliance on Oscar marrying Constance, Jane wrote to him while he was in Newport in July to say, 'Are you in love? Why don't you take a bride? Miss Howe was given to you by all the papers here . . .' Maud Howe was the daughter of Mrs Julia Ward Howe who said of the engagement rumour, 'If ever there were two people in the world who had no sympathy in common, they were the two.' Oscar wrote to his mother to deny the rumour, after which she reassured him that at her Saturday salon, 'I gave a decided contradiction to the report that you were to be married to the beautiful Miss Maud Howe,' signing her letter dispiritedly, 'La Povera Madre'.

Much of the large correspondence Jane received was in reply to her invitations to her Saturday afternoon salons. One woman asked Jane if she might bring a friend, a Miss Eleanor Marx, 'a very accomplished and clever girl and I believe as good as she is attractive', and ended, 'I wish you were in parliament or better still were premier while this Irish tragedy is playing.' The writer was envious of Jane's approaching visit to Ireland and said, in sudden imitation of Jane's own style, that she wished she could go 'among those poor evicted ones and return to sing their wrongs in burning verse to the guilty ears which heed them so little'.[43] Jane must have kept to the social circuit instead for she told Oscar on her return that 'Nothing is talked of in Dublin but the immense lot of money you have made! They are filled with envy.'

Oscar did at least have enough money to pay his debts. Early in September he sent Jane £80 to cover these, telling her to keep the remainder and give some to Willie – Oscar, when he had any money, was unfailingly generous to his mother and she loved him for it.

In return she sent Oscar a long list of the bills that she had paid with his money. 'That leaves me a large overplus,' she wrote. 'And so I'll hold on *here* for the *winter* at least and then see what fate brings. It is dreadful taking your money. Destiny does such very ill-natured things, whenever one member of a family works hard and gets any money immediately all the relations fling themselves on his shoulders.' She told him she expected Willie home several days ago but that he had neither come nor written and she had no idea where he was. When he did appear, she would give him the money Oscar had sent with his love ('this will please him'). Meanwhile, out of this money she had paid Willie's laundry bill – 'a great matter to have off our minds'.[44]

While Oscar was in America Constance had been attending art

school, but Jane wrote to Oscar late in 1882 to tell him that she had had an unexpected visit from Constance's great-uncle, Charles Hemphill, with whom she was slightly acquainted. He had once lived in Merrion Square and later became Solicitor-General for Ireland. Jane told Oscar that he had 'praised Constance immensely. I had nearly a mind to say I would like her for a daughter-in-law but I did not. It was Constance told him where we lived. I thought the visit looked encouraging. He said you were quite a celebrity now.' She had less hope of Willie, telling Oscar that he was going off to Ireland on 25 October – 'he has raised the money somewhere for I have none . . . I wish we could all join in a petition to sell Moytura. I still think it possible.'[45]

Oscar had taken with him to America a book of poetry called *Songs of the South* by his friend Rennell Rodd, an old friend and admirer from his Oxford days. He had promised Rodd to try and find him an American publisher and, on succeeding, wrote his own introduction for it. Rodd gratefully said he would dedicate the book to Oscar, who had renamed it *Rose Leaf and Apple Leaf*. When the book came out in October 1882, Rodd liked its sumptuous production but disliked certain parts of the introduction, in which Oscar claimed him as a disciple, and was dismayed at the dedication. Oscar had written this on his behalf and it read: 'To Oscar Wilde, Heart's Brother – these few songs and many songs to come.' It was based on a line in one of the poems, 'Shall we get hence? O fair heart's brother! . . .' Although Rodd had written these words privately in Oscar's copy of the English edition, the sight of their public airing as he was embarking on a career in the Foreign Office, sent a frisson through him.[46]

Willie wrote to Oscar in strong support: 'I read your introduction to Rodd's poems last night carefully. It is amazing (what a small creature he must be!), all it wants is (journalistic criticism) *more full stops*, sentences too long, think of this in your blank verse.' In a more depressed vein he continued, 'Go and burn a candle for me at some saint's shrine who . . . *knew remorse* and *hated harlots*. Can't you find out some battered old Carmelite? Some saintly swash-buckler that would teach me anodynes and sleeping-draughts and potions that would kill the past? Well dear old Oscar goodbye – you are working bravely and you are wise and you have not made devils for yourself as I have . . . say if you would like par[agraph] about *Vera* or the Duchess of Bally-Padua.'[47] Oscar had only just started writing *The Duchess of Padua*, a blank verse play; but *Vera*, his first play, had originally been scheduled to open in London in the spring of 1882. It was cancelled after the assassination of Czar Alexander II in March of that year.

While reviewers were mocking Rennell Rodd's book, Jane, aware of Lillie Langtry's success as Hester Grazebrook in Tom Taylor's *An Unequal Match* in New York, said, 'I wish you would act with her in America. Orlando and Romeo – you and she together would make fabulous scenes.' Day-dreaming was preferable to reality. Money was scarce again. 'I shall hold on to this house till March next,' she told Oscar, 'after that – chaos.' Meanwhile she wanted him to ask Roberts (the publisher who had brought out Oscar's *Poems* in America) if all her new poems, written for various periodicals, as well as her old ones, could be published as a complete volume; and what the terms would be.

Oscar did what he could, writing to John Boyle O'Reilly, the editor of the *Boston Pilot*, to ask if he could see him about his mother's poems and saying, 'I think your idea of a preface is excellent. She is very anxious to have them brought out, and if you will induce Roberts to do it she will send you her later work, which is so strong and splendid . . . I think my mother's work should make a great success here: it is so unlike the work of her degenerate artistic son.'[48]

Jane's hopes of making a little money this way come to nothing: there was to be no further edition. But she wrote to thank Oscar for all his suggestions about 'the vol', said she had just sent off another poem to O'Reilly and added, in her best grande dame manner, 'I would of all things like an introduction by him to the volume – showing the meaning and high tendency of my work by which I wish them judged.' In the same letter she told Oscar that Sir Charles Duffy had visited her: it had obviously brought back memories of her days as Speranza.[49]

Violet Hunt mentioned Jane again in her diary for 21 November 1882, when she said: 'I hear that Lady Wilde has got a new dress. Her last speech is, "I am tired of England, and must live somewhere else, where the men have courteous manners and splendid sins." I think Oscar and Willy might supply her in some sort of way.'[50] But Jane, like Oscar, often spoke for effect. Judging by her chatty letter to Oscar a couple of days later, she was happily caught up in London's social world, with no thought of leaving it: 'Although I wrote yesterday, I must write a line now to tell you the *last scandal*. Sir Coutts Lindsay [owner of the Grosvenor Gallery] has gone off with an *Italian model* and he has squandered all *his wife's fortune* – she does not choose to get a divorce, as he would then marry the model – but she has given up her house and gone to a *flat in Sloane Street*.'⁵¹

Jane would have scorned the idea of writing for the tabloid press, but she was well suited for it. She claimed she couldn't write 'about such things as Mrs Green looked very well in black, and Mrs Black looked very well in green', but she was fascinated by other people and their lives and through her numerous letters and salons heard what was going on. In this same letter she added, 'Lady Colin Campbell has gone off, they say, with someone and there will be a trial', and gave details of the failure of the spectacular at the Globe: 'They are losing £500 a week . . . they now build up hope on Wills's play of Jane Eyre, to be brought out at once.'

Jane's final letter to Oscar that year was to tell him his two valises and two hatboxes had arrived and she would take care of them. She ended by offering up fervent prayers for his prosperity, safety and success. While he had been away she had treated Oscar like a diary, peppering him with the weekly minutiae of what she, Willie and their friends were doing. She told him of Willie's visits to the pawnbroker; provided a four-page detailed critique of his poem, 'Magdalen Walks', adding that she hated the title and suggesting he call it 'Primavera'; claimed she was now great friends with a rich woman called Mrs Bloomfield; and said that Ruskin had come up to her at one of her salons and said, 'Give Oscar my love.'

In January 1883, Jane wrote an article in the *Gentlewoman* on 'A New Era in English and Irish Social Life'. It was a salvo in praise of the Married Women's Property Act, which she called 'an important and remarkable epoch in the history of women' as women would no longer enter marriage 'as a bond slave, disenfranchised of all rights over her fortune . . .' She welcomed the end of 'the whole cumbersome and involved arrangements of settlements' and 'that peculiarly humiliating form of provision for a wife's personal expenses called pin money', paid from her own property, with 'the husband reserving all the rest for himself and giving the wife no account for it'. She castigated the way husbands scrutinized the bills, 'a season of much torture and an ordeal of terror to the wife', and ended by saying that women were going to need training in self-assertion to 'become worthy of the nobler life of freedom'. It was a subject on which Jane felt strongly, given the way her husband had used part of her own settlement.⁵²

The *Lady's Pictorial* sniped at Oscar that same month, even before his ship returned to England: 'Poor Oscar: so his mission has failed, or, at all events, has not been a triumphant success. The banner of the lily and sunflower is not to be carried to Japan or Australia and he has left New York sorrowfully. The Bothnia is bearing him back to our shores and we can but hope the Wild waves of the Atlantic will treat him mercifully.'[53] He returned, however, an established celebrity and his arrival home was greeted by a poem in the *Whitehall Review* called 'The Returning of Oscar'. He went straight back to Charles Street where he had lived since leaving Chelsea. Restless after a year away, and having signed an agreement to finish *The Duchess of Padua* by 31 March 1883, he left for Paris at the end of January.

It was an enjoyable time for him: his writing went well and, armed with introductions and confident after his American tour, he met a number of French writers and artists including Victor Hugo, Zola, Degas, Alphonse Daudet, Pissarro and Edmond de Goncourt. He also made friends with a young Englishman called Robert Sherard, great-grandson of Wordsworth, who was to become a lifelong, loyal friend and Oscar's first biographer.

Oscar was soon a recognized figure in Paris, not least as a result of his outrageous clothes. Jane wrote to him to say the *Lady's Pictorial* had reported that his 'sleeves and trousers are so tight that you are remarked on the boulevards. You see you cannot escape notoriety.' She went on to praise him extravagantly: 'Your French letters are worthy of Balzac, so pure and eloquent – capital practice. In hateful London nothing is to be learned.' She then descended to more pressing matters. 'The *creditori* are dreadful – as to Willie I give him up – his debts are now about £2,000.' She ended crossly, 'I am very stupid and sick and dull and weary.'[54] It would have been more truthful to admit she was getting weary of Willie. She needed a son to look after her and pay her own debts; instead he worsened their disastrous financial position and, despite his 30 years, caused Jane constant worry.

He was in Scotland when Jane wrote, possibly to avoid the *creditori*, then crossed to Ireland. From here he sent Oscar a note, asking if *Vera* was in print as he wanted a copy, and saying how glad he was that it was to be produced in America with 'London to be conquered subsequently'. He went on to mention his own work. 'My little play was a one-act comedy I wrote for Compton . . . it is only a sketch, not fanciful . . .' With Oscar moving now with authority on the French literary scene, Willie, alone at Illaunroe, asked him, 'Send me a French paper – *Figaro* – anything – send me a desperate novel – send *here*.'[55] It was a plea to be part of the world Oscar was inhabiting, from a man aware of an isolation not solely attributable to being in a remote part of Ireland.

Jane must have sensed Willie's feelings: she remained, on the whole, unendingly patient with him. She was saddened by his immature behaviour, but loyally supported him to outsiders: any criticism was only for Oscar's ears. While Willie had always fled any kind of commitment, Oscar on the other hand was now seriously thinking of marriage. A stable element in the lives of both her sons, as Oscar became more preoccupied with his own relationships, so Jane found Willie clinging to her more and more strongly.

11

'A Violet-eyed Artemis'

DURING OSCAR'S ABSENCE in America and Paris, Jane had made a
point of keeping in touch with Constance. Constance's brother, Otho,
when writing to his fiancée Nellie Hutchinson on 28 February 1883,
described a visit he and Constance had made to Lady Wilde. 'I think
she would kill you with laughing,' he said. 'I came away not quite
certain whether I liked her or not. In appearance she is an enormous
woman with a face like the face of an eagle and she talks like a book.'
A woman guest there had asked him if he painted, because, she told
him, 'when one comes to Lady Wilde's afternoons one always expects
to find people there who can paint or do something clever'. Otho admitted he had enjoyed the salon. 'What a talk we all had afterwards about
the Irish,' he told Nellie, 'though Lady Wilde would speak of little
else than her son Oscar, whom she calls As-car.'[1]

He and Constance and their mother went to another of Jane's salons
in May, shortly before Oscar returned from Paris. Otho told Nellie
that Lady Wilde had taken a great fancy to Constance; 'she is a kind
friend to girls, with all her oddities, especially if they have brains.' He
gave her a light-hearted account of the next hour or so, which mostly
found him being whisked around the room by Jane: 'Now, Mr Lloyd,
whom shall I introduce you to? An old lady or a young lady?' Otho,
introduced to one or the other, had no chance to speak. 'No sooner
had we bowed than we could get no further; a tall old man rose to go
away; he and Lady Wilde who takes up some square yards of room
swept in between us, and there for what seemed five minutes these two

stood saying good-bye and paying each other compliments.' He retired defeated to a dark corner but 'Lady Wilde routed me out'. He went into the back room to talk to Constance, but 'presently I see Lady Wilde again drawing towards my quarter . . .' Willie was at the afternoon salon and Otho described him briefly as 'a plausible well-spoken fellow, with better manners than he used to have; but I do not like him.'[2]

Oscar returned from Paris that month with a new Neronian coiffure. Laura Troubridge, who met him at a mutual friend's house, said disparagingly: 'He is grown enormously fat, with a huge face and tight curls all over his head – not at all the aesthetic he used to look.'[3] For a while he stayed with Jane at 116 Park Street. He was hard up now, facing previous bills as well as present ones. He had finished *The Duchess of Padua* while in Paris but the actress Mary Anderson, who had requested it, felt the part did not fit her and rejected it.

Jane's solution to the money problem – one that she was constantly urging on both her sons – was to marry well. Constance was expected to inherit money from her grandfather and Oscar was already interested in her. The two now met increasingly. Marriage had another advantage to Oscar: it would silence the snide remarks about his effeminacy that his flamboyant dress style in America and Paris and his new hairstyle only helped confirm.

Otho, writing to his fiancée again in May, said, 'You will think that we must be becoming very intimate with the Wildes, when I tell you that we have been to their house again today, Constance and I . . . Oscar Wilde had a long talk with Constance; it was of art, as usual, and of scenery; he so amused me when he called Switzerland "that dreadful place, Switzerland, so vulgar with its ugly big mountains, all black and white, like an enormous photograph".' The tiny rooms had been packed, he told Nellie, 'with Lady Wilde, gigantic as ever and this time also with a great head-dress upon her head, moving about like an unquiet dream'.[4]

Robert Sherard, attending one of Jane's receptions, was rather impressed: 'Her hair was dark and in ringlets, and her broad face, with its massive features, was illuminated by her magnificent eyes.' But he was taken aback when she handed him a bunch of narcissi, repeating 'Flowers for the poet,' after Oscar had told her that Sherard had just written a volume of verse.[5] Willie's clipped comment on this collection in *Vanity Fair* was that Sherard had rightly called it *Whispers* as it would make no noise in the world.[6]

Oscar gave his mother a great deal of information about his American trip which enabled her to write an article for an American magazine, in May 1883. The article was headed by an editorial rider stating that 'The following notes by the distinguished mother of Oscar Wilde, appearing so soon after the return of the latter to London, will naturally be traced to his recitals.' It was a necessary rider as Jane airily implied that she herself had been to America. The article was light-hearted, chiefly comparing the women in different American cities. In Boston (the 'city of advanced intellects and the emancipated woman'), she admired the literary salons held by writer Margaret Fuller, which were full of intellectual women who proudly disdained 'the fashion, follies and dress of New York'. Philadelphia was the Quaker city, where ladies 'make no effort to heighten the charm of their pretty faces by the adventitious aid of rouge or pearl powder', whereas in grand and courtly Washington 'every young lady looks forward, confidently, to being elected to the English peerage'. But Jane was impressed by American women demanding perfect equality with men, including the right to vote and be elected to Congress. Though European women had made great strides, she felt they still lagged behind.[7]

In order to earn some money, Oscar had arranged to tour Britain giving two lectures: one on his impressions of America, the other on 'The House Beautiful'. He called his progress 'civilizing the provinces'. He lectured eloquently, without notes, and the audiences and local press, though equally interested in the style of his hair and clothes, enthusiastically applauded him. Throughout June and July he managed to make trips back to London and he and Constance met frequently. Otho had to apologize to his fiancée Nellie for his letters being almost exclusively about the at-homes held by his family, friends or by Jane.

Early in June he reported with delight on a most successful afternoon at the Lloyds, when sixty people had turned up, including Oscar and his mother. Constance had sat out all the time with Oscar, but Otho told Nellie that 'I don't believe that he means anything; that is his way with all girls whom he finds interesting; and Constance told me afterwards that they had not agreed upon a single subject.' A day or two later he and Constance were accompanying Oscar on an outing to the Fisheries Exhibition, with Oscar talking throughout. Constance, dining with an aunt that evening, said to her thankfully, 'Oh, how delightful it is to see you, Aunt Carrie, after spending three hours and a half with a clever man.'[8]

Constance was now a weekly visitor at Jane's Saturday salons, and each time Oscar deliberately sought her out. Jane, used to him playing joint host, was not always pleased. Once, in early July, when Oscar was deep in conversation with Constance, Otho noticed Jane come up to him; 'with a glare at Constance [she] remarked, "Now Oscar, I hope that you are doing your duty." "Oh yes mamma," replied Oscar with an amused laugh, turning to speak again to Constance, at whom Lady Wilde cast another glare, while to Oscar she said, "Don't you think Oscar that you had better speak to Miss Smith" – who is the ugly disagreeable old woman whom everybody shuns.' Oscar, however, refused to move. When he left later on, he bade Jane a stately farewell, pressing her hand and saying several times how sorry he was to leave, 'while she, like a Spartan mother sending him forth to the wars, repeated, "Well, go along then." '[9]

Otho was acutely conscious of the particular attention Oscar was paying to Constance. 'Wherever she went, there followed he, and when he could not approach her then with his eyes he followed her.' He admitted that 'If the man were anyone else but Oscar Wilde, one might conclude that he was in love.'

Oscar broke off this growing intimacy with Constance to sail for America on 2 August 1883 in order to be present at the first night of his play *Vera* at the Union Square Theatre in New York on 20 August. Writing to him the day before the opening, Jane said, 'I hope you have not been arrested – such a long silence . . . Everyone asks for you and about the play, send me back the American paper with *Vera* . . . send me a line, *all alone* here. I feel so nervous and anxious if I don't hear.' She mentioned that Willie, in Ireland, had had a cold, and seemed rather low and depressed.[10]

It was then Oscar's turn to feel low, for *Vera* only lasted a week before closing. The Comtesse de Brémont, who was there, put its failure down to a second-rate company, the off season and the heat. Nevertheless many of the reviews were good. The *New York Mirror* admitted the audience had come to laugh, but continued: 'They remained to applaud . . . *Vera* is a really marvellous production . . . finely written.' Oscar returned to England in September and the London magazine *Entr'Acte* ran a caricature of Willie consoling him – both men looking like Sumo wrestlers.[11]

That year, 1883, Sir Charles Gavan Duffy published his book, *Four Years of Irish History*, and sent a copy to Jane. She wrote back to thank him, saying, 'I have read it with tears and trouble and memories and despair – our Irish nationality is such a beautiful legend – such a fairy dream – and this all to end. It is the horrible reality of the Phoenix Park . . .' She added that Willie was in Ireland looking after their property – 'but nothing is paid, the horizon is very dark for all of us'.[12]

Willie was at least earning some money from his light-hearted writing in the *World*. Jane cut out one of his stories, 'A Witless Thing', which appeared that October, and pasted it into a family scrapbook she was keeping. It was full of articles by Oscar, some of Willie's, reviews of Oscar's work and her own, and one or two pictures of her husband.[13] The story told of the muscular Lord Grayton, 'strong as a horse, buoyant as a balloon', who attended a dance at a private asylum and thought the attractive woman volunteer there was an inmate. There could have been a hint of autobiography in the character of Lord Grayton, who 'felt oddly morbid as he thought of his own lonely life. He had once loved and given his heart to a woman whom he had both idealized and idolized . . . she turned out to be as loveless as she was lovely.'[14]

Oscar was having more luck. Although busy with lecture engagements around the country, he returned to London mid-October for a weekend and saw Constance on the Saturday at his mother's salon and again on the Sunday. Otho wrote to Nellie to say that Oscar admitted he was in Brighton one day, the next in Edinburgh, then Penzance, then Dublin. 'He laughed a good deal over it and he said that he left it entirely to his manager.' Oscar gave Constance *Vera* to read, although he was greatly mortified by its lack of success in America, and she told her brother she thought it 'very fine'. In Otho's eyes, parts of it, like the curate's egg, were 'wonderfully powerful and thrilling'.

In November Oscar went over to lecture in Dublin. It was a busy time for him: he gave a poetry recital, addressed the Royal Academy and took part in a public debate with Mahaffy, his old tutor. He went to see Constance, at her invitation, as she was over there visiting her grandmother, Mary Atkinson, who lived at Ely Place near the Wildes' old house in Merrion Square. Writing to Otho about the visit, Constance said that 'though decidedly extra affected, I suppose partly from nervousness, he made himself very pleasant.' In another letter to Otho Constance admitted she was being chaffed about Oscar's attentions. 'Such stupid nonsense,' she ended.

On 25 November 1883, Oscar proposed and Constance, by now very much in love, accepted. She wrote to her brother to say, 'Prepare yourself for an astounding piece of news. I am engaged to Oscar Wilde and perfectly and insanely happy.'[15] Her letter crossed with one of his telling her of a story critical of Oscar. Constance brushed it aside, telling her brother that even if it had any foundation, she would not allow anything to come between them.

Oscar was equally happy, describing Constance to Lillie Langtry as 'a grave, slight, violet-eyed little Artemis, with great coils of heavy brown hair which make her flower-like head droop like a blossom and wonderful ivory hands which draw music from the piano so sweet that the birds stop singing to listen to her'.[16]

Apart from the couple themselves, no one was in a higher state of excitement than Jane, who wrote to Oscar on the 27th to congratulate him and tell him her plans for his future:

I am intensely pleased at your note of this morning – You have both been true and constant and a blessing will come on all true feeling.

But one feels very anxious . . . It always seems so hard for two lovers to get married. But I have hope all will end well.

Willie is greatly pleased, but says he feels so old and venerable – *quite* shelved by 'the young people'. What endless vistas of speculation open out. What will you do in life? Where live? Meantime you must go on with your work. I enclose another offer for lectures. I would like you to have a small house in London and live the literary life and teach Constance to correct proofs and eventually go into parliament.

May the Divine Intelligence that rules the world give you happiness and peace and joy in your beloved. La Madre.[17]

The idea of Parliament was not just one of Jane's fond ideas. The *Lady's World* mentioned in January that year that Oscar, asked what career he intended to pursue, had replied that he was still undecided whether to go into Parliament, go on the stage, or marry. The magazine commented acidly, 'What a choice! One is inclined to wonder whether a grateful country would appreciate the youth with lovelocks and lace ruffles among its rulers, whether he would be welcome behind the footlights, and why marriage should figure as his *arrière pensée*.'[18]

Jane's parliamentary hopes for him were not to be realized, though Oscar did once tell W. B. Yeats that he had been offered a safe seat in Parliament and, had he accepted, might have had a career like Disraeli's. But he wrote in *An Ideal Husband*, 'Only people who look dull ever get into the House of Commons, and only people who are dull ever succeed there,' and once said that he had considered entering English political life, but that it was too much a matter of catchwords. In 'The Soul of Man Under Socialism' he stated, 'High hopes were once formed of democracy, but democracy means simply the bludgeoning of the people by the people for the people.'

Oscar wrote to Constance's stepfather, George Swinburne King, to ask for formal permission to marry Constance, and so too did Jane. Thanking her for her letter, he said, 'Both are, as you say, young, gifted . . . I was very pleased that you should write so highly of your son, though not surprised since I have often thought what a fine, noble, good countenance he has.'[19]

Still in a state of euphoria, Jane wrote again to Oscar to ask him when he was coming, and to tell him that she had written both to Constance and to Constance's stepfather. She was still forming plans for his future: 'I wish you would take a small house in Green Street – all the relations will furnish it – and begin a settled life at once. Literature and lectures and parliament – receptions 5 o'clock for the world – and small dinners of genius and culture at 8 o'clock. Charming this life, begin it at once – take warning by Willie.'[20]

Willie, unbothered by his mother's warnings, was delighted with Oscar's engagement. He wrote to him saying, 'My dear old Boy, this is indeed good news, brave news, wise news and altogether charming and amazing in the highest and most artistic sense. I do indeed congratulate you from the bottom of my heart. She is lovely and loveable and all that is sweet and right and she is a lady . . . and a love from a good pure girl like her is ever a refining sunbeam in a man's life . . . it is splendid. God bless you always, affectionately, Will.'[21]

It was a time of general happiness. The couple went to the theatre constantly and were regarded as minor celebrities: in December, at a play at the St James's Theatre, the cast rushed to a spy-hole in the curtain at the intervals to see what Constance looked like. At the theatre again the following night, Otho noted that 'Willie and Oscar were like two boys together, full of chaff and fun; they are very affectionate brothers.'

The Wilde family at the time were perilously on the edge of financial disaster, apart from Willie who was forever falling over the brink. The lack of rents from Moytura was a devastating blow to Jane. She was forced to rely on Willie, who preferred to spend his money enjoying himself rather than on household bills. Oscar was in debt to a moneylender, but was paying him back slowly through his lecture fees.

Constance's grandfather, John Lloyd, was a wealthy man and as part of Constance's marriage settlement put £5,000 into a trust fund and arranged for the interest to be paid to Oscar and Constance as an annual income. When he died, the £5,000 would be deducted from Constance's share of his will.

Constance received a further £500 as her dowry and this the couple put aside to purchase the lease of a house. In March they looked at 16 Tite Street in Chelsea and decided to take it. Oscar made the expensive choice of asking Edward Godwin, the fashionable architect, to oversee the redecoration. Godwin had redesigned No. 1 Tite Street, where Oscar had lived with Frank Miles, as well as designing the White House for Whistler.

After Oscar's engagement, Jane resumed a long broken-off correspondence with her two Swedish friends. She wrote to Rosalie Olivecrona to tell her of Oscar's marriage plans, and said Willie was still unmarried and living with her, being 'given up to journalism which is his passion. He is a brilliant and topical writer and has many good openings.' She admitted that since giving up her home in Ireland she had had many troubles and anxieties: 'London is a good focus of life and intellect. I have met all the celebrities – Ruskin and Browning and Matthew Arnold and others. But still I dislike London, the life is too ponderous and expensive and *expense* is troublesome now – for since the troubles began in Ireland I have not been paid any rents and have received nothing for the last four years from the property in Mayo which should pay me £200 a year. Ireland is in a bad state, all the gentry are ruined and the shops are bankrupt.'[22]

At the end of February 1884, in a letter to a friend of hers in Dublin, Jane was still very depressed about her lack of money. 'I have no receptions now,' she told her, 'I was too triste and low all the winter and I have no heart for anything, but I see a friend or so on Saturdays in the little study. The drawing rooms are turned into a lumber of books – that I meant to arrange, but time and courage failed me – so there they are covering the floor and I think they will never be settled till Willie's wife comes – I am too weary of everything to make any exertion – It is a dreadful thing to have my whole income stopped from Ireland – I receive *nothing* and the little that is paid in is stopped for government charges – we have to pay for all the murders and outrages, and the police etc, and so *nothing's left*. Can you wonder if I am triste?'[23]

Jane went on to chat about acquaintances, telling her that she sometimes saw Mrs [Bram] Stoker, although Mrs Stoker never visited

Jane. 'Bram is always very attentive and kind when I meet him at the theatre.' Oscar, she went on more cheerfully, was doing splendidly and everyone was greatly pleased at his engagement to Constance, 'a very nice, pretty, sensible girl – well connected and well brought up – and a good fortune, about £1,000 a year'. Willie, she said, 'is at journalism, a very profitless profession. I don't like it – he ought to be at the Bar – he has splendid talents for public life – but he wants *patient industry*.' Willie, however, was quite content with journalism. Ambition was all on his mother's side: he put his energies into enjoying life, not in climbing the legal or political ladder she envisaged for him.

While Oscar continued lecturing up and down England, Jane wrote to Lotten to say that she was now well settled in London. 'My sons like it and I do not now much mind where I live . . . and I sometimes write. That is my chief amusement when I have time. Both my sons are very literary and do not like professional work, only journalism and lectures and poetry. One cannot help the bent of minds – they go their own way, but they are a fine pair of young men – clever and distinguished.'

Telling Lotten that she had been looking over her notes on Sweden, which she said she meant to publish in some magazine, she asked her for any news that could be usefully added to these. 'Is literature flourishing? And the drama? . . . Did not *you* found a Scholarship for Women? And can women now take a degree at Uppsala University? I would like to know how the women's question is going on.'[24]

She wrote again shortly, telling her enthusiastically – and incorrectly – that 'Oscar and his bride will visit Stockholm . . . to meet your distinguished circle of *Les Ames d'Elite*.' In a change of mood, she added, 'Life grows sad as years go on – and my life was rent and broken when Sir William died.'

In reply to Jane's request Lotten sent her information about a debate on women's franchise, and Rosalie forwarded the paper she had written on the condition of women in Sweden. With her Swedish connections renewed, Jane decided to turn her notes on her travels in Sweden into a book called *Driftwood from Scandinavia*. Her publishers were Richard Bentley of New Burlington Street, 'Publishers in Ordinary to the Queen's Most Excellent Majesty' – a distinction which must have appealed to her. When returning the agreement on 7 April 1884, witnessed by Willie, she enclosed a paper written by her husband on some Scandinavian antiquities discovered at Islandbridge, near Dublin, which she asked to be included as an appendix.[25] The publishers paid

Jane fifty guineas for the first printing of 1,000 copies and promised a further fifty guineas if there should be a second edition.

The book, published that year, was the first Jane had written – apart from her poems and the conclusion of her husband's memoir on Beranger – that was not a translation. Her eye was acute and she was fascinated by the linked history, legends and antiquities of Scandinavia and Ireland, writing in her most dramatic style about Viking invaders like terrible Turgesius the Dane. Catherine Hamilton in *Notable Irishwomen* pointed out that Jane's style became less inflated with age, but recalled her outpouring of adjectives in her Scandinavian sketches when she spoke of 'poor dyspeptic, nervous, depressed, worn-out hypochondriacal humanity'. The reviewer of *Driftwood* for the *Academy* magazine loathed it and said so scathingly: 'The title of this book is somewhat misleading. It is "driftwood" undoubtedly, and that of a quality which, perhaps, it was hardly worth while to collect and preserve; but very little of it comes "from Scandinavia" . . . almost every page contains the most startling inaccuracies and exaggerations . . .'

The *Academy* reviewer gave examples of Jane's high-flown writing, but failed to realize that in the criticized passages Jane was gently mocking much of what she saw. She sympathized, for instance, with the Berlin ladies for being 'doomed to wear huge, ungainly bonnets' because their heads are 'globular' instead of being 'ophidian'; and remarked that: 'Germany is the sandy deposit of an ocean which once must have overflowed it, and out of the sediment the German population has evidently been formed, mere rolled-up balls of sand, heavy and colourless, without type or form or feature worth mentioning.'

Jane had a strong sense of the ridiculous which constantly comes to the fore in the book. She tried reindeer meat in Denmark, but found 'it suggested too forcibly sliced boot'. At Copenhagen, she noticed the beer had a peculiar flavour: 'it seemed to me as if a cat had been drowned in it. Next day it was worse; the kittens seemed added.' At Christiana, in Norway, the huge pillows used meant 'you are almost forced to stand in bed'; and in Sweden the old Queen Desiree so hated state ceremonial that after arriving at a ball, concert or pageant, she 'seated herself comfortably in the state chair, huddled up in her little black dress, and fell fast asleep'.

Even the *Academy* reviewer ultimately admitted that it was easier to laugh when reading the book than to ponder its merits or literary power, and that when the author laid aside her fine writing for 'a bright and chatty style', she was far more pleasing.[26] In the event Jane had the satisfaction of being able to tell Lotten with some truth that 'The book has had a good success here and the publishers are very content with the sale.'

She had taken the opportunity in *Driftwood* of pointing out how highly literary women were regarded in Sweden, and attacking the way 'the female writers of England work in obscurity, live undecorated, unrecognized, and unhonoured, and die without any national tribute to their genius or memory'. She cited the neglect of Mrs Browning: no statue or even a bust of her in Westminster Abbey. Jane was still petitioning for a civil list pension at the time and was delighted to make a public point about what she considered – certainly in her own case – a disgraceful situation.

Although Jane regarded herself as a feminist, she never took to the campaign trail herself. It was certainly not for lack of causes. On her arrival in London, Josephine Butler was crusading against white slave traffic, while Annie Besant needed support after shocking the public with a high-minded bombshell on sex and contraception, *The Fruits of Philosophy: the private companion of young married people.* Jane was quite prepared to welcome women with such views at her salons – she had been delighted to have Mrs Fawcett visit in Dublin – and would happily air her own opinions on any subject in conversation or in print; but she was not one to go out on the hustings.

A female reporter who interviewed Jane commented that though her life had been one of intellectual activity, 'she has none of the zeal of those whom Mrs Lynn Linton [the author] dubs "The Wild Women".' The reporter must have been reeling from some of Jane's more reactionary remarks. 'If I were a dictator,' she had said, 'no girl should be taught to read and write. It is women's mission to adorn life, to impart beauty to the commonplace . . . No woman if I had my way should have to work for her livelihood; it is simply terrible to think of girls wasting youth and beauty in hard toil.'[27]

Jane's dual attitude towards women had her at one moment arguing that they should be mere ornaments, then extolling the Swedish methods of educating women. She saw no irony in this and genuinely managed to believe in both arguments at once. Although, like Oscar, she put a high premium on beauty, no one challenged her as to what her own life would have been like had she not been taught to read and write.

Feminists aside, the views of the majority of women then were reactionary. The journalist Ella Curtis, who had covered a large-scale suffrage meeting for the *Lady's Pictorial*, told Jane that though the women spoke well, she did not care whether or not they got the vote. 'I fancy the majority of women are guided in this matter by the opinion of some man in whom they believe . . . if I had a vote I should probably vote for the man who sent me to the poll in his carriage! That, of course, would be highly immoral.'[28]

Early in April 1884, when at one of Jane's salons, Otho Lloyd met Katharine Tynan who impressed him with her fair colouring, eye glasses and rich Irish brogue. Katharine Tynan had been amazed to find Jane lived in such a little house 'wedged in between another little house and a big public house at the corner'. She admitted she had not realized that Park Street, Grosvenor Square, W., was a place to live, regardless of whether there was a pub next door and you couldn't swing a cat in the rooms.

That afternoon the latest beauty, a Miss Craigie Halkett, was present as well as the fashionable actress Miss Fortescue, who had just been involved in a breach of promise case against Lord Garmoyle. When Oscar turned up Katharine Tynan saw 'how like he was to the photographs of him which were all about the room, full-face, half-face, three-quarter face; full-length, half-length, three-quarter length; head only; in a fur coat; in a college gown; in ordinary clothes. He came and stood under the limelight so to speak, in the centre of the room . . .' With him came 'poor picturesque pretty Constance Lloyd, dressed all in brown, a long brown cloak, a wide brown velvet hat with a plume . . . a delicate charming creature . . .'[29]

Introduced to Oscar, Katharine Tynan found him pleasant, kind and interested, with 'an immense fat face, somewhat pendulous cheeks, and a shock of dark hair'. She remembered how Jane in turn had introduced him to a Hannah Lynch. 'This is Miss Hannah Lynch, Oscar: a young Irish genius,' she had said. Oscar replied, 'Are not young Irish geniuses as plentiful as blackberries?' Willie was there too and though Katharine Tynan said he was eclipsed by Oscar, family friends had told her he was as amusing as his brother and quite as brilliant.

Despite Jane being superstitiously opposed to Constance and Oscar marrying in May, the couple were married on 29 May 1884 at St James's Church, Paddington, by special licence. The *World* explained that 'Owing to the illness of the bride's grandfather the ceremony was meant to be of a rather private nature.' It added that 'All most intimately concerned in the affair seemed thoroughly pleased.'[30] Jane certainly was in her element.

The wedding was at 2.30 p.m., with admittance by ticket only, and a large crowd gathered to watch. The *Queen*, under its 'Fashionable Marriages' column, reported regretfully that 'The muster in the church was not distinguished by the presence of many social, artistic, or literary celebrities, invitations to the bride's home, in Lancaster Gate, being strictly confined to near relations.' It described the bride's clothes, including Oscar's gift of a beautifully worked silver girdle, and reported that punctually at half past two Oscar could be seen standing at the altar, 'a rose in his buttonhole, a touch of pink in his neck tie'. Willie acted as best man and Jane stood near Oscar, wearing 'a handsome costume of silver-grey brocaded silk and satin; on the bodice was fastened a large spray of roses and pink carnations; grey and pink feathers trimmed her hat.'[31] The *Canterbury Times* reported that 'Lady Wilde "snatched" her new daughter to her heart with some effusion.'[32]

Oscar and Constance left from Charing Cross station at 4.30 p.m. for a honeymoon in France, unperturbed by it being the year of the great cholera scare. *Tinsley's Magazine* later looked back on the summer with a shudder, reporting that 'Italy was closed to us; on the frontiers of Switzerland lurked a shadowy quarantine of doubt; France was suspect; and indeed, the whole continent was under an imaginary reign of terror.'[33] The couple didn't care: to them, the future was bright.

12

A Surrogate Daughter

CONSTANCE WAS TO get on very well with Jane and a strong affection developed between them based on a genuine liking for each other and their mutual love of Oscar. Constance in no way posed a threat to Jane: much though she loved Oscar, she respected the bond between him and his mother and would never have attempted to break this.

Her quiet good manners, gentleness and charm appealed to Jane, for whom in many ways she took the place of her dead daughter, Isola. Jane foresaw a happy and socially successful future for the newly married couple. Delighted to hear that on their honeymoon they had given a dinner party at their Paris hotel for various friends, she wrote to Constance there to say:

> You are a most charming letter writer and Willie is going to get you appointed special correspondent to one of the leading weeklys.
> Miss Lloyd paid me a visit yesterday and looked well and happy. We had a crowd – all eager in enquiries about the Bridal pair. Mrs Ashton Dilke was here. The *Queen* has a nice account, also the *Lady's Pictorial*. I hear the Dublin *Freeman* had a grand account. It is to be sent to me – I have never been out since the wedding . . . I got a Dutch paper with a long account of the wedding – your dress was greatly admired – Miss Drake was at the church – Willie and she are good friends but I see no further tendresse – your *first dinner* was very nice. I'm glad you have begun the social duties.[1]

Jane was used to telling Oscar that he should do this or that and had no qualms in giving Constance a list of instructions for him: he was to telegram the landlord of his previous lodgings in Charles Street to say where his belongings should go; he must visit a certain Madame Adam in Paris; and he should send her the *Journal des Modes*. She ended her letter in the same way as she did to Oscar, 'Ever your devoted La Madre'.

When, after a further week spent in Dieppe, Constance and Oscar returned to London on 24 June 1884, their planned 'House Beautiful', at 16 Tite Street, was still being beautified by Godwin. It was not to be finished for another seven months. Willie had booked the couple into the Brunswick Hotel, but at two guineas a night this was too expensive for a stay of more than a day or so and they were forced to ask Constance's Aunt Emily, who lived at Lancaster Gate with Constance's grandfather, John Lloyd, if they could stay there.

The day after their return, Constance wrote to her brother Otho to say, 'Tonight we dine with Mme Gabrielli [a well-known hostess] and go to the Avenue Theatre. She seems smitten with Willie; in fact it is an extraordinary friendship and it's a pity there is an ancient nonentity called Mr Gabrielli in the background somewhere. She sends W. a horse every morning and they ride in the row together; she sends him wine, cigarettes, even *tonics* I believe.'[2] It was said that when Willie wore a bangle she gave him, he commented: 'I wear it because it's the gift of the Gab.'

There was a wave of interest in the occult at the time, with practitioners in palmistry and planet-reading being in hot demand. The *Lady's Pictorial* of 5 July 1884 described in detail the fashionable thought-reading experiments that took place at Mrs Gabrielli's supper party. The magazine noticed that: 'William Wilde did not choose either Oscar or his bride as mediums.' After having no success with two of the ladies present, Willie finally succeeded with a third. He looked carefully at the object she chose – a silver bonbonnière – before leaving the room. 'The box was at once hidden on a chair behind a curtain at a long distance from the door and Mr Wilde called in blindfolded, being met by his medium on the threshold. He seized her hand, pressed it to his forehead thrice, then, without a second's hesitation, led her to the end of the room where the silver box was hidden, and in a very few seconds had found it.' He must have enjoyed being the centre of attention for once, rather than Oscar.

Palmists, clairvoyants, astrologers and fortune-tellers were much in vogue also and both Oscar and Constance were greatly intrigued by them. Oscar later had his palm read by the palmist Cheiro, who told him, 'The left hand is the hand of a king, but the right that of a king who will send himself into exile.'[3] Another fashionable fortune-teller, a Mrs Robinson, told him, 'I see a very brilliant life for you up to a certain point. Then I see a wall. Beyond the wall I see nothing.'[4]

Constance's grandfather John Lloyd died on 18 July 1884, and on the following day the couple moved out of the Lancaster Gate house. Oscar was fortunately able to lease again his old lodgings at 9 Charles Street where he and Constance stayed until their Tite Street home was ready early the following year.

Willie was currently dramatic critic of *Vanity Fair* and when he took a break in August that year, Oscar stood in for him. Two months later Oscar embarked on a further lecture tour around Britain. This time he spoke on two other subjects: 'The Value of Art in Modern Life' and 'Dress'. As far as dress was concerned, he was in favour of simplicity and against bustles, corsets and high heels. One of Jane's salon guests, looking at the outrageous clothes she liked to wear, commented that she 'was a walking contradiction to every dawning notion of the day led by her son'.

Oscar's views naturally influenced what Constance wore. Marie Belloc Lowndes, who had known the Wildes in Dublin in the mid-sixties, remembered Constance dressing very simply at home in the type of dress becoming known as a teagown, but that in public 'she would appear in what were regarded as very peculiar and eccentric clothes. She did this to please Oscar and not to please herself.'[5] But Constance soon became more assured and within three years was editing the Rational Dress Society's *Gazette*.

Jane's views on dress were tongue-in-cheek. She accepted the practicality of modern dress, which she described as 'short, hard, concise as a telegram', but decreed that 'literary dress' should be free, untrammelled and unswathed: 'No stiff corselet should depress the full impulses of a passionate heart. There should be no false coils upon the head to . . . mar the cool logic of some grand, deep thought. And the fewer frills, cuffs and cascades of lace the better, for . . . in moments of divine fury or feverish excitement the authoress is often prone to overturn her ink-bottle.' Variety in dress she thought essential: 'A woman should never appear twice in the same dress, except, of course, at lectures on primary molecules or the revolution of atoms.'[6]

An article by Oscar suggesting 'More Radical Ideas upon Dress Reform' appeared in the *Pall Mall Gazette* in November 1884 and shortly after, to supplement his decidedly thin income, he became a regular contributor to the *Gazette*. Jane, in equal need of money, wrote for any magazine that would take contributions: these included the *Pall Mall Gazette*, *St James's Magazine*, the *Lady's Pictorial*, *Burlington Magazine* and the *Queen*.

Few of Oscar's letters to Constance remain as most of these were destroyed, either by Constance herself or by her family. But one he wrote to her in December 1884, while lecturing in Edinburgh, shows that he was still romantically in love. Perhaps she kept it for nostalgic reasons.

Dear and Beloved, Here am I, and you at the Antipodes. O execrable facts, that keep our lips from kissing, though our souls are one.

What can I tell you by letter? Alas! nothing that I would tell you. The messages of the gods to each other travel not by pen and ink and indeed your bodily presence here would not make you more real: for I feel your fingers in my hair, and your cheek brushing mine. The air is full of the music of your voice, my soul and body seem no longer mine but mingled in some exquisite ecstasy with yours. I feel incomplete without you. Ever and ever yours

OSCAR.[7]

The couple had been going through a harassing time with their new house in Tite Street. Oscar had refused to pay one of the builders as his work was below standard, and the builder not only sued him but took possession of some of the new furniture. The matter was settled out of court, but it added to mounting bills. They were only now about to move in.

Jane wrote to her friend Lotten in January 1885 to say, 'My son Oscar and his wife are well and happy and have taken a home in London to be fitted up in *true aesthetic style*.'[8] It was indeed quite different from the standard Victorian house, traditionally full of heavy furniture, dark wooden panelling and ornate hangings. The Tite Street house was full of light. The walls and ceilings of the staircase were yellow, the woodwork white: the dining room had white chairs and upholstery. Constance's bedroom on the second floor, alongside Oscar's dressing room, was again mainly white, with a particularly beautiful white silk counterpane embroidered in gold. Oscar's study was on the ground floor, its prize possession being Carlyle's desk.

Constance held her at-homes in the drawing room on the first floor, which had a spectacular ceiling designed by Whistler featuring gold dragons and real peacock feathers. Jane was often present at these occasions when Constance was also to act as hostess to such varied guests as Sarah Bernhardt, Mark Twain, Herbert Beerbohm Tree, A. J. Balfour, John Ruskin, Lillie Langtry, Robert Browning, Algernon Swinburne, Henry Irving and Ellen Terry. As a very small boy, Oscar's younger son Vyvyan also remembered the Pre-Raphaelite artists coming and he and his brother Cyril being invited to children's parties at their houses and studios.[9]

Jane, writing to Lotten, said that although she was in good health, 'London demands too much of one's time, the circle of acquaintances is so wide and always increasing.' She said she still saw visitors herself every Saturday from 4 to 7 p.m., 'but reserve all the other days to myself. I want to bring out another book – "Studies of Men, Women and Books". [She did, but not until 1891.] Nothing amuses me except History.' She went on to say that 'Willie is not married – he says he never will – he has thrown himself quite into journalism.'[10]

Willie was fond of Constance and during Oscar's extensive lecture tour of Britain in the early months of 1885 he wrote affectionately to her from Brighton to say: 'The big brother is very sorry that you are for the moment deserted and left all alone – and he comforts you with the best box in the house for Court on Friday night. I have had real quiet here . . . I write all day and go in to Brighton to swim or see people I like. I am *delighted* to hear of all Oscar's work. It will do him a world of good . . . and show people how earnest he is in the work he has taken up . . . Once you are settled in the sweet little nest in Tite Street, he can and will I know sit down and write more testing work than lectures.'[11]

On 5 June 1885, Oscar and Constance's first child, Cyril, was born. Constance recovered well and was very happy; so was Oscar, despite an acid comment on his son's Wagnerian crying habits. Jane was as thrilled as the new parents with her first grandchild; Constance would bring Cyril round to visit her, and Jane adored him and followed his progress with interest.

Jane now allowed herself no reservations in her dealings with Constance, even to the extent of borrowing money from her. She had grown increasingly fond of her daughter-in-law and depended on her for both friendship and practical help. They saw each other frequently and often went out together. Once, after admitting she was a 'little knocked up' after getting up very early to see Willie off to Brighton, she told Constance, 'I don't feel well enough to go out today, and I send word that you may not have a wet walk or a drive . . . If tomorrow is fine you might come here and we could go to the Holborn Shop.'

Constance was often in her thoughts: she recommended servants to her and enquired anxiously after her health. 'My Dear, Darling Constance,' she wrote on one occasion, when Constance had gone down to the Isle of Wight, 'I hope you have arrived safely and that *the cold* has vanished. I was miserable when Oscar told me you were ill – you must take care and avoid draughts and air – you are so susceptible to cold.' She went on chattily to tell her that Willie was touring through Switzerland and was sending her a postcard daily from the Alps, with his love to 'Alcibiades and Lady Constance', his postcard names for Oscar and Constance.[12] Oscar would have known that Alcibiades was a brilliant but irresponsible Greek leader.

On another occasion she wrote to Constance to say, 'I hope you are not the worse for our dissipation', and enclosed some tickets she had just been sent with the words, 'I wish Oscar could go – and you – I cannot, I am too tired.' She was often subject to tiredness and depression. Thanking Oscar for sending her one of Tolstoy's novels, she said, 'I have read it all through and feel better and stronger after it to face the despair of life.'

Delighted though he was with his new son, Oscar was still occupied in 1885 with his lecture tour. Realizing the importance of a regular income, he tried that summer to get a post as a school inspector. His money problems were intensified by his mother's own applications to him for money. Although Willie was earning a reasonable amount from his journalism, he casually ignored the household bills when he went off on holidays abroad or to Ireland to stay at the hunting lodge at Illaunroe, leaving Jane to do her best to settle them. On one of these occasions, Jane admitted to Oscar that she had not had a line from Willie, 'so I am obliged to apply to you much *à contre coeur* to ask you to lend me £2 which *I shall return* as soon as Willie sends me anything – perhaps you would call today with it. I had to borrow from Teresa and must pay her back. Would you buy a dressing table and glass – I'll sell mine for £2 10*s* – it cost £5.'[13]

The following year, 1886, Jane was forced to start selling her books. The Irish editor and poet T. D. O'Sullivan discovered this when in a London second-hand bookshop he came across a book he had given

Jane, a valuable first edition, complete with his inscription. Amused, he wrote a further inscription and handed it back to Jane, asking her to read both inscriptions and the different dates. Jane did so and without embarrassment said, 'And a very useful book it proved, my friend, for it served, like Caesar's dust, to fill up a hole in my purse.'[14]

Jane sold her books through the bookseller, Walter Spencer, who remembered the episode well:

In 1886 Lady Wilde ordered some books on Irish antiquities from one of my catalogues and when acknowledging their receipt she invited me to view her library. I called at the house and was shown into a room whose walls were crowded with books from floor to ceiling, and in many places along the floor.

Lady Wilde received me in state: that is, she welcomed me from a dais at the far end of the room, like a queen on a throne. 'Look round, Mr Spencer,' she said regally, 'and tell me what you would wish to buy.'

I picked out a good few volumes, including Browning's *Bells and Pomegranates*. I said, 'What will you take for these, your ladyship?' She answered with splendid indifference, 'Whatever you offer, Mr Spencer, whatever you offer.'

So I suggested £10. She seemed pleased and accepted it readily, saying that I might visit her once a fortnight at eleven in the morning as long as I felt there was a parcel worth giving £10 for. Thus it came about that I saw a good deal of the pathetic, faded old lady.[15]

Jane was 64 at the time. Her financial plight might have rendered her pathetic but the Comtesse de Brémont who saw her then found her by no means faded, saying, 'Never before, nor since, have I met a woman who was so absolutely sure of herself and of what she was. I felt an absorbing respect for her courage in being herself.' The Comtesse was moved by 'the evidences of womanly coquetry in the arrangement of her hair and those little aids to cheat time and retain a fading beauty. Yet age could not deprive the brow, nose and chin of their classic lines.' Jane still, she noticed, posed 'like the *grande dame* that she was by right of intellect . . .'[16] Oscar, a grand poseur himself, could take his mother as a model.

Constance became pregnant again in 1886 and in the November gave birth to their second son, Vyvyan. She was not to have another child. Oscar had been disgusted by the physical signs of pregnancy: 'How can one desire what is shapeless, deformed, ugly?' he asked Frank Harris, telling him that women were not 'good instruments' for passion and love, but were made to be mothers: 'When I married, my wife was a beautiful girl, white and slim as a lily, with dancing eyes and gay rippling laughter like music. In a year or so the flowerlike grace had all vanished; she became heavy, shapeless, deformed. She dragged herself about the house in uncouth misery with drawn blotched face and hideous body, sick at heart because of our love. It was dreadful. I tried to be kind to her; forced myself to touch and kiss her, but she was sick always, and – oh! I cannot recall it, it is all loathsome . . . I used to wash my mouth and open the window to cleanse my lips in the pure air.'[17]

Oscar had long admired the beauty of young boys, who never aroused his distaste by becoming pregnant. He wrote the following poem for the Trinity College magazine, *Kottabos*, though he carefully changed the sex of the subject to 'A Lily-girl', and called it 'Madonna Mia' when he included it in a collected volume of poetry:

> A fair slim boy not made for this world's pain
> With hair of gold thick clustering round his ears
> Pale cheeks whereon no kiss hath left its stain,
> Red under-lip drawn in for fear of Love,
> And white throat whiter than the breast of dove . . .

Jane once wrote prophetically, that 'Reason can do little against the force of beauty; the first impulse, the irresistible instinct of a man's nature is the homage to physical beauty. It has a mystic power that sweeps down all before it, the strongest and wisest.'[18]

The letters Oscar wrote to Harry Marillier, a Bluecoat Boy who lodged at 13 Salisbury Street when Oscar was living there with Frank Miles, and was now at Cambridge, again show the intensity of feeling a beautiful youth could inspire in him, even though in those days men as well as women wrote to each other with an open, innocent romanticism that would be viewed far more cynically nowadays. Jane's letters to her friend Lotten were highly affectionate and full of praise for her face and figure. In those days romantic friendship between women was quite acceptable.

Oscar ended one of his letters to Marillier in 1885: 'When am I to see you again? Write me a long letter to Tite Street, and I will get it when I come back. I wish you were here, Harry. But in the vacation you must often come and see me, and we will talk of the poets and forget Piccadilly!! I have never learned anything except from people younger than myself and you are infinitely young.'

Although Oscar had not yet committed himself to having a homosexual affair, he told Marillier, 'I myself would sacrifice everything for a new experience . . . I would go to the stake for a sensation and be a sceptic to the last! Only one thing remains infinitely fascinating to me, the mystery of moods. To be master of these moods is exquisite, to be mastered by them more exquisite still.'[19]

It was in 1886, following Constance's two successive pregnancies and his revulsion from her, that Oscar first met Robert Ross, the 17-year-old son of Canada's Attorney-General. Ross was a homosexual and was later to tell his close friend Christopher Millard that it was because he was the first to have led Oscar 'astray' that he felt responsible for Cyril's and Vyvyan's welfare, and indeed as Oscar's literary executor he settled Oscar's debts after his death and recovered his copyrights on the children's behalf.[20] Arthur Ransome, in his study of Oscar, relied on Ross's information when he claimed that Oscar 'first experimented with the vice in 1886; it became a habit in 1889.'[21] Oscar himself said to his friend, the journalist Reggie Turner, 'Who do you think seduced me? Little Robbie.'[22]

Oscar knew the dangers of being a professed homosexual. When he was at Oxford an undergraduate known to him, William Hardinge, had been sent down for writing homosexual sonnets. Oscar was more circumspect in those days, writing of another student he had seen with a choirboy that though he 'only mentally spoons the boy', he was 'foolish to go about with one'.[23] Yet he increasingly, and more and more openly, flirted with danger.

In Victorian times, the family was all-important and any deviant sexual behaviour was hushed up – which is why Oscar's flaunting of his later relationship with Lord Alfred Douglas outraged so many. Men, through public school experience and gossip and innuendo in clubs and pubs, were aware of homosexuality even if not involved, but the average woman hardly knew it existed. It was not a subject for polite society and men would never dream of enlightening their wives or women friends. In 1893, the Comtesse de Brémont was at an Authors' Society dinner when Oscar came over to speak to her. Her escort immediately left her table and when she later asked him why, he replied, 'Don't ask me for any further explanation. I could not give you one.'

Because the subject of homosexuality was taboo there was a great deal of ignorance about it. When Queen Victoria signed the Criminal Law Amendment Act in 1885, prohibiting gross indecency between consenting adults, it was pointed out to her that women had been omitted from the definition. She replied, or so it is claimed, 'No woman would do that.'

Constance would have known nothing about male homosexuality and over the years remained ignorant of Oscar's growing involvement. He had always needed intellectual stimulation and although Constance was hurt at his continually seeking this away from home, she accepted it. She was also understanding when Oscar claimed he needed peace to work and stayed at London hotels. She always drew the most innocent conclusions from his actions and saw nothing wrong with him being constantly in the company of individual men. She had had two sons by him and had no reason to doubt his nature.

On one occasion, according to the young French poet and writer Pierre Louÿs who was there, Constance turned up at the Albemarle Hotel where Oscar was staying with Bosie. She took Oscar's mail up to the room the two men were sharing, having not seen him for some time, and could hardly have missed the sight of a double bed with two pillows. Although she seemed not to understand its significance, she begged Oscar to come home. He refused, jokingly pretending that he couldn't remember the number of the Tite Street house as it was so long since he had been there; Constance was visibly upset.[24] Jane with her classical background would have known about homosexuality, but that does not mean she would have recognized her own son's sexual ambivalence and his gradual change to a homosexual lifestyle. Like Constance, she was never to see Oscar 'feasting with panthers', as he himself put it, under the pink-shaded lights at Kettner's.

During Oscar's absences, the two women came increasingly to depend on each other for company. But now, with her grandchildren just born and her son and daughter-in-law apparently set for a long and happy marriage, Jane had no worries apart from lack of money. There was only one thing she could do to bring in some much-needed income. She closeted herself in her house and returned with energy to writing.

13

The Writing Wildes

'CONGRATULATIONS ON YOUR delightful and recondite book on Celtic lore,' wrote a friend to Jane in February 1887.¹ The book, published late the previous year, was *Ancient Legends, Mystic Charms and Superstitions of Ireland, with sketches of the Irish past.* Her nationalism of the revolutionary days of the 1840s had turned to the quieter channels of Irish folklore. W. B. Yeats was to say of her collection: 'The best book since Croker [Thomas Croker, the Irish folklorist] is Lady Wilde's *Ancient Legends*. The humour has all given way to pathos and tenderness. We have here the innermost heart of the Celt in the moments he has grown to love through years of persecution, when, cushioning himself about with dreams, and hearing fairy-songs in the twilight, he ponders on the soul and on the dead. Here is the Celt, only it is the Celt dreaming.'²

In writing up the legends, Jane used the abundant material collected by her late husband for his book, *Irish Popular Superstitions*. 'He had a passion for such research,' she said. In a preface, signed Francesca Speranza Wilde, she regretted such legends were dying out: 'the old race is rapidly passing away to other lands.'³ Her introduction to the book was a book in itself. She traced the movement of myths and legends from the East to Ireland; argued whether the Egyptian lamentation *Hi-loo-loo! Hi-loo-loo!* was the original form of the Irish wail *Ul-lu-lu*; and told of the custom on the west coast of Ireland for no funeral wail to be raised for three hours from the moment of death, as the sound of the cries would stop the soul from speaking to God.

Jane had a journalistic eye for the graphic, and a poet's ear, as is evident from the example she cited of Irish keening by a bereaved mother:

> O women, look on me! Look on me, women! Have you ever seen any sorrow like mine? Have you ever seen the like of me in my sorrow? Arrah, then, my darling, my darling, 'tis your mother that calls you. How long you are sleeping. Do you see all the people round you, my darling, and I sorely weeping? Arrah, what is this paleness on your face? Sure there was no equal to it in Erin for beauty and fairness and your hair was heavy as the wing of a raven, and your skin was whiter than the hand of a lady. Is it the stranger must carry me to my grave, and my son lying here?

The *Legends*, starting with the Horned Woman and ending with the Skelligs of Kerry, are absorbing to read. But they were not greeted with universal praise. The *Athenaeum*, whose reviewer seemed blind to the book's imagery, said: 'We find among them [the legends] little trace of the fantastic and original imagination which abounds in the old Celtic romances . . .' though admitting they were told 'with great simplicity, charm, and raciness.'[4]

The *Academy* thought the legends interesting and beautiful but ridiculed the preface, of which its reviewer complained: 'Lady Wilde writes, "The three great sources of knowledge, respecting the shrouded part of humanity, are the language, the mythology, and the ancient monuments of a country." I felt puzzled when first I read this sentence, and I am puzzled still. What does "the shrouded part of humanity" mean? Does it refer to physical qualities, or to mental qualities? Can it mean little-known obscure nationalities? Is it a euphemistic term for the Irish race?'[5] The reviewer hadn't bothered to read Jane's preface to the book, in which she specifically explained that the phrase referred to a country's language, mythology and ancient monuments. She ended by saying the legends expressed 'my love for the beautiful island that gave me my first inspiration, my quickest intellectual impulses, and the strongest and best sympathies with genius and country possible to a woman's nature'.

Other reviewers were more appreciative. Jane wrote to Constance cheerfully to say, 'There is a nice notice in the *World* of today, so altogether I have been fortunate and the *St James's* is nice also. I return the *Athenaeum* with thanks and I send you a clever pamphlet to read, *Esoteric Christianity*.'[6] Jane's Dublin friends, too, all welcomed the book. One told her it had 'excited much interest among your old friends and admirers here', and another took the opportunity of chiding her for not accepting invitations. A letter from a woman called Helen Reins to Willie, asking for tickets to the next Lyric Club meeting, also bewailed the fact that 'your mother never comes to see us now'.[7]

Jane now preferred to stay at home and write. In a leader on 'Clever Women' written for the *Queen* in April 1887, she pointed out that all the most popular novelists of the age were women, who should 'assert their claim to national recognition'. She argued provocatively that if these women were silenced, and only male sages like Huxley, Tyndall and Darwin were left, there would be nothing to talk about 'save the history of anthropoid apes, the habits of ants, the galvanism of frogs, the evolution of atoms, palaeolithic man, and old red sandstone'.

Gathering steam, she demanded a female university, staffed entirely by women, as a fitting tribute for the Queen's imminent Jubilee celebrations. She also called for money and an Order of Merit exclusively for eminent women of intellect and genius. These, she said, could wear their badge on their shoulder where it would be immediately recognized as a sign 'of intellectual distinction, and entitle the wearer to an honourable place in social circles'. She was confident that her own place was assured.[8]

Always anxious for journalistic work, Jane must have been delighted at her own prospects, as well as Oscar's, when in April 1887 he was offered the editorship of the *Lady's World: a magazine of fashion and society*. The news was also welcomed by the *Pall Mall Budget* which said, 'Oscar's star has been low in the horizon since he cut his hair and became "Benedict the married man". Of late I have seen certain signs in the heavens from which I divine that the star is ascending once more . . .'[9]

The proprietors of *Lady's World*, a monthly journal which was part of Cassell's publishing firm, appointed Oscar as editor rather than making the more obvious choice of a woman, in the expectation that Oscar would reinvigorate the magazine. His ideas for reconstructing it were very much in line with his mother's beliefs. He told Wemyss Reid, manager of Cassell's, that the *Lady's World* should represent 'women's opinions on all subjects of literature, art, and modern life'.[10] He thought there should be news from the women's colleges at Oxford and

Cambridge, and listed a regiment of literary women he hoped would contribute.

He insisted on changing the magazine's name from *Lady's World* to the *Woman's World*, telling Reid its present name had 'a certain taint of vulgarity about it . . . it will not be applicable to a magazine that aims at being the organ of women of intellect, culture, and position.' Payment was to be a guinea a page, average for the time, while the editor was paid £6 a week, giving him at last some regular money of his own.

Jane was very conscious that any money coming to her would have to derive from writing and not from her Irish rents, as Ireland was once again in turmoil. A. J. Balfour, Lord Salisbury's nephew, was Irish Secretary and had earned the nickname 'Bloody Balfour' in 1887 by introducing the Irish Crimes Act, which made it illegal for Irish tenants to resist eviction however high the rents. There was an immediate return of violence in an attempt to force landlords to accept reductions in rent. Charles Stewart Parnell, 'the uncrowned king of Ireland' who had been unsuccessfully trying to steer the Home Rule Bill through the Commons, deplored the return of violence, but could not prevent it.

Although forty years had passed since her Speranza days, Jane was still a keen follower of Irish politics. As *Irish Society* was to say in its issue of 31 December 1892, 'She pleaded in prose and verse for the liberation of the Fenian prisoners in '67; she sympathized with the Land League movement and now the Home Rule cause has in her an ardent supporter.'[11]

In April 1887, therefore, Jane was riveted by the uproar when *The Times* published a facsimile of a letter, allegedly written by Parnell, which condoned the 1882 Phoenix Park murders – murders which at the time he had vociferously condemned. After publication of the letter, *The Times* ran a series of articles on 'Parnellism and Crime', accusing Parnell of inciting political murder. A follower of Parnell, F. A. O'Donnell, was mentioned in these articles and promptly sued the newspaper for libel. Other letters, also allegedly by Parnell, were produced by the defence and Parnell, denouncing them all, called for a select committee to investigate the matter. Instead the government appointed a special commission of three judges.

Oscar, Willie and Jane were strongly on Parnell's side and both brothers attended meetings of the commission. Indeed, Willie's articles on the hearings in the *Daily Telegraph* were hailed as his best work.

Ella Curtis, the novelist, wrote to Jane at the time to say, 'The Parnell Commission is more interesting than any of our novels at present.'[12] The letters allegedly by Parnell were finally found to have been forged by an Irish journalist called Richard Pigott, and Parnell was completely vindicated, only to have his career wrecked within a year by his affair with Kitty O'Shea.

Jane liked attending the relevant debates in Parliament. John O'Connor, a loyal Parnellite, occasionally wrote to her from the House of Commons to offer her a seat in the Ladies' Gallery, which she refused on one occasion, saying, 'I am not equal to any exertion and must content myself with reading the speeches in place of hearing them.'[13] Another friend asked her to join a private discussion with other sympathizers on the Irish question, with I. P. Gill, the MP, in the chair. 'Perhaps you know of it and are already going,' he wrote, 'but if not I am urged to bring friends and you are my friend, are you not, Speranza?' J. D. Sullivan (Jane wrote 'Poet and Patriot' at the top of his letter) told her he was working hard towards a settlement of the Irish question which 'the Irish people can accept without any sacrifice of honour. I know how great a joy it would be to you to witness such a consummation as that.'[14]

However, Jane told D. J. O'Donoghue, who was compiling an anthology of Irish poets and poetry in 1887, that 'I have recently devoted myself more to literature than to politics.' She added that 'Nationality was certainly the first awakener of any mental power of genius within me, and the strongest sentiments of my intellectual life, but the present state of Irish affairs requires the strong guiding hand of men, there is no place any more for the more passionate aspirations of a woman's nature.'[15]

Jane's devotion to literature meant that she spent more and more of her time reading at home. But in May the social correspondent from the *London Figaro* went to Upper Phillimore Place to 'one of those interesting At Homes at which one sees everybody, and much to my satisfaction I saw Mr Rider Haggard . . . and Mr and Mrs Oscar Wilde . . . and Lady Wilde, one of the most popular of matrons.'[16] Marie Corelli went to the same 'grand crush' and said of Oscar Wilde that he 'kept me no end of time talking on the stairs. Lady Wilde, his mother, was there in a train-dress of silver grey satin, with a hat as large as a small parasol and long streamers of silver grey tulle all floating about her! She did look eccentric.'[17]

The first instalment of Oscar's 'Lord Arthur Savile's Crime' appeared in the *Court and Society Review* that month. The story contained a light-hearted description of a London gathering which was a gentle mockery of Jane's salons: 'Gorgeous peeresses chatted affably to violent Radicals, popular preachers brushed coat-tails with eminent sceptics, a perfect bevy of bishops kept following a stout prima-donna from room to room; on the staircase stood several Royal Academicians, disguised as artists, and it was said that at one time the supper room was absolutely crammed with geniuses.'

Jane wrote admiringly to Oscar to say, 'The story is most brilliant and attractive. It ought to run *at least three numbers*. There is such a thrilling mystery to be worked out – all your epigrammatic style tells in this kind of work – you could be the D'Israeli of fiction if you choose – and all your social knowledge comes in so well. Especially your women.' Less fortunate with her own manuscript for the *Court and Society Review*, she said crossly that she wished they would return it, as it would do for the *Lady's Pictorial*, and ended, 'I hope you and Constance will be here tomorrow, though I suppose the Queen will carry off all my people.'[18]

She was referring to the attention focused on Queen Victoria's Golden Jubilee, which fell on 21 June 1887. The magazine the *Queen* exclaimed at the number of fancy dress balls being held by London hostesses, while the *World* complained that as the service was going to cost the country £20,000 and nobody would see anything of it except the 'representative congregation', the Queen should drive to the Abbey by a circuitous route. A row broke out over the procession: should foreign royals be in closed carriages? Should the Queen wear white and not black? In the event, she wore black trimmed with white *point d'Alençon* and vast crowds, forgetting their irritation with the Widow of Windsor, cheered her as she rode in a gilt landau drawn by six cream ponies on her way to the Abbey.

Succumbing to the festivities of the London season, Jane made another rare outing. The actress Elizabeth Robins saw her at a reception given by Lady Seton at Durham House, which was crowded with people, bric-à-brac and pictures, and remembered her as 'tall, dark-eyed, with a big nose and heavily rouged under a double white gauze veil drawn close like a mask over the features'. Jane pleased her by telling her she had a dramatic face.[19]

Constance was more caught up in domestic anxieties than the social whirl. She wrote to her brother in August to say, 'My little Vyvyan is so very tiny, and I fear still very delicate, but he may get stronger when he has teethed. We have never let our house yet, and I wish we could, for I am obliged to have two nurses on account of Baby and expenses grow!' She added more optimistically, 'Oscar and I are very happy together now and Cyril is delightful.'[20]

The emphasis on gaiety, receptions and fancy dress balls in London during 1887 concealed an undercurrent of violent socialist and radical agitation. The number of unemployed was growing and early that year an organized demonstration of unemployed workmen rioted in Pall Mall. More trouble arose in November 1887, fuelled by an Irish demonstration in Mitchelstown against land evictions which turned into a riot. Led by the powerful street orator, John Burns, there was such a serious riot in Trafalgar Square that 200 people ended up in hospital and two died. It was remembered as 'Bloody Sunday'.

Constance's concerns remained domestic. In another letter to her brother, she said: 'Baby's birthday was last Thursday and tho' he is small I think he is quite strong now. He is *frightfully* spoilt and very self-willed and does not say one mortal word! Cyril grows a greater darling every day. But Baby is his father's pet.'[21]

The first issue of the *Woman's World* under Oscar's editorship was published in November 1887. It was a handsome edition on good paper with illustrated drop initials for the articles; and Oscar had collected an impressive bunch of contributors. He had also commissioned top illustrators like John Tenniel, Walter Crane and Dante Gabriel Rossetti. Although Oscar considered the insurrectionary subject of the unemployed unfit for the world of women, some of the articles he commissioned as editor on women's work and their position in politics were far in advance of the thought of the day. Subjects ranged from 'Drama in Relation to Art' to 'The Fallacy of the Equality of Woman' and Oscar himself wrote acerbic and amusing Literary Notes.

The magazine was well received. The *World* said of its contents: 'Mrs Annie Thackeray gossips delightfully about Madame de Sévigné's grandmother; Mrs Francis Jeune relates more of her experiences among the poor children of London; Mrs Bancroft chirrups with greatest good humour about Pontresina and its environs; there is the commencement of a serial story by George Fleming, a sonnet by Violet Fane . . .'[22]

Jane later contributed Irish peasant tales and a 250-line poem on 'Historic Women' written in her most flamboyant into-battle style. The author Edward Maitland, having read this poem, praised her imagination and ability to move from the material to the spiritual plane.

'Whether or not your son Oscar has inherited it through you, and will some day develop and manifest it, I cannot say, but as yet he is woefully devoid of it and hence is utterly unable to appreciate writings in which you and I agree in finding so much.'[23]

As Jane considered she had a proprietary interest in both the *Woman's World* and its editor, she was shocked by Oscar's long review of Mrs William Sharp's anthology, *Women's Voices*, in the first issue, in which he queried why certain women writers had been excluded from it; she wrote to him sharply to say, 'Dear Mr Editor . . . Why didn't you name *me* in the review of Mrs Sharp's book? *Me* who holds such an historic place in Irish literature! And you name Miss Tynan and *Miss Mulholland*! The *Hampshire Review* gives me splendid notice – *you* – well, 'tis strange.' Typically, Jane was far more upset at a professional slur than a personal one, particularly from her own son of whom she expected the loyalty that she unquestioningly gave him.

She went on rather waspishly to say, 'Lady Archie [Lady Archibald Campbell] is the best of your women essayists – George Fleming begins interestingly – and is good – but women in general are a wretched lot.' Jane was clearly writing in pique. She had very decided views about the abilities of writers, both male and female, but she was not the type of woman who ridicules all rivals while outwardly supporting the woman's cause. Enquiring if Oscar had read an article of Willie's on soda water ('it is so brilliant'), she went on to ask him to come round for a talk the following Sunday evening. 'I have so little time left now,' she said, determined to alarm him for treating her the way he did, 'for I must certainly drown myself in a week or two – life is quite too much trouble. La Madre Dolorosa.'[24]

Oscar had troubles enough of his own towards the end of 1887, explaining to the actress Mrs Bernard Beere that Vyvyan had been so ill that he and Constance had feared for his life. 'I was so unhappy over it that all my duties and letters escaped me,' he said. However, he at least returned to favour with Jane when he reviewed W. B. Yeats's *Fairy and Folk Tales of the Irish Peasantry* in the *Woman's World* and quoted the extract in which Yeats praised the pathos and tenderness of Jane's work in *Ancient Legends*.

Constance wrote to her brother on 7 March 1888 to say that 'Oscar is overworked and is very miserable at times and needs a change of air very badly. I wish I could get him away.' She also told him that 'I have been political lately. It has become the fashion to have political parties in London and some of the swells managed to get Gladstone . . .'

Unable to resist mentioning her children, she tells him that 'Cyril adores me and Vyvyan more or less dislikes me and adores his father, but I suppose this will come right in the end.'[25]

Oscar was an excellent father. He adored his two sons and established a strong rapport with them. Like his brother Willie he had in many ways a childlike nature and Vyvyan recalled that 'he would go down on all fours on the nursery floor, being in turn a lion, a wolf, a horse, caring nothing for his usually immaculate appearance.' One day he turned up with a toy milk-cart, drawn by a horse which had real hair, and to the children's delight went down to the kitchen and filled all the milk churns with real milk.[26]

He was intensely amused by them, repeating their remarks to friends in the way of all fond fathers. Once Cyril, refusing to pray to God to make him good, compromised by asking Him to make his baby brother good instead. Another time Cyril asked his father what he dreamed about and Oscar came up with a stream of velvet phrases about 'dragons with gold and silver scales'. Cyril was patently bored. Oscar asked what he dreamed about. To his delight the reply was 'Pigs.'[27]

Having children turned Oscar's mind to fairy tales. That May he published a collection of them, called *The Happy Prince and Other Tales*. These tales, he said, were 'an attempt to mirror modern life in a form remote from reality'. Jane keenly followed his work and Oscar bore all her comments with good humour. In one letter she instructed him to write another story soon, 'something as tender and touching as *The Happy Prince*', and in another she said, 'Suppose you lay the plot of your story in the Isle of Wight? Lady – – will tell you some striking incidents of her life as a beauty and you can work them up.' She added some advice all writers could profit by: 'Begin – the first sentence is everything.'

On one occasion, she wrote to tell Oscar she had found some old letters of his in her hoarded treasures: 'You ought to work them up and weave them into *a Blackwood's story* – but, cielo! can it be that we are all 14 years older since they were written.'

Jane herself was now writing regularly for the *Pall Mall Gazette*. An article of hers on 'The Story of St Patrick' in which she described how St Patrick prayed against 'the spells of women, smiths and druids', was followed by another in May called 'Whitsuntide in Ireland', when she warned of the danger of water at Whitsun, when no one should bathe, or sail in a boat 'unless a bride steers'.[28]

She continued also to hold her weekly salons. A new visitor in July
was the poet, W. B. Yeats, with whom she shared a deep interest in
Irish history and folklore. Yeats had already attempted to call on Jane
one Sunday afternoon but told his friend Katharine Tynan that 'She
was not visible – being not yet up, needing, as the servant put it, "a
great deal of rest". I wonder if I shall find her as delightful as her book
[*Ancient Legends*] – as delightful as she is certainly unconventional.'²⁹
Now both were highly pleased to meet, and Jane was to greet him
fondly on his successive visits with the words, 'My Irish poet!'

Jane wrote to Yeats from time to time over the next seven years. She
pleased him by her comments on Katharine Tynan's prose ('Every
sentence was so beautifully poised') and constantly praised his own
work. 'Lady Wilde has written me an absurd and enthusiastic letter
about it [his book *John Sherman*],' he told Katharine Tynan. 'She is
queer enough to prefer it to my poems.'³⁰

Meanwhile money, or the lack of it, was worrying Jane. The Park
Street house, though small, was in an expensive part of town and this
must have been the deciding factor in her decision to return to
Chelsea – a move which suited the landlord who had other plans for
the house. When the Comtesse de Brémont happened to call on Jane
at Park Street she found the household in disarray. Willie blithely
apologized to her for the state they were in, explaining that the move
had turned everything topsy-turvy. Jane told her they were leaving
'owing to the deterioration [*sic*] of our landlord – he has developed
commercial instincts, and is desirous of converting the place into a
shop – or pulling it down to make way for a more profitable building
than it is at present.'

The Comtesse thought that Willie, whose breezy cordiality differed
markedly from Oscar's stately manner, lacked his brother's boldness
and originality. But she considered him just as brilliant a speaker and
polished a writer. To her, Willie 'was a man, in the true sense of the
word, working valiantly in the hardest worked profession in the world,
hiding his resentment against reverses of fortune under a gallant front,
and perhaps fighting hardest against himself . . . his faults and his
failures belong to influences and adverse circumstances.'³¹

She noticed that Willie never mentioned Oscar during her visit, but
there was no aggravation between the brothers. They got on well, even
if Oscar could rarely resist a quip at Willie's expense. He once said of
Willie's attempts to sculpt that 'his brother's statues showed palpable
signs of death, but no hopes of living.'³² He was no kinder to Willie's

profession. In his essay 'The Decay of Lying' he said: 'Lying for the sake of a monthly salary is, of course, well known in Fleet Street, and the profession of a political leader-writer is not without advantages. But it is said to be a somewhat dull occupation, and it certainly does not lead to much beyond a kind of ostentatious obscurity.'

In October 1888, Oscar heard that the mother of the poet and journalist William Henley was ill and wrote to him to commiserate: 'All poets love their mothers,' he said, 'and as I worship mine I can understand how you feel.'[33] He could be taken at his word. That month he was busy trying to get Jane a grant from the Royal Literary Fund, as well as to secure for her a civil list pension: writing about this to Theodore Watts, the poet and critic, he admitted, 'It takes a long time and there are many applicants, though few I think with my mother's claims.'[34] Oscar told Watts that the poet and critic Algernon Charles Swinburne, whose affairs Watts managed, had gratified Jane by his immediate response to the request for a sponsor. Oscar also thanked Edward Dowden, the Irish writer and critic, for signing his mother's application for a pension, adding he had 'some hopes of success'.

That same October Jane and Willie moved from Park Street to 146 Oakley Street, only a few minutes' walk from where Carlyle had lived. Oakley Street then was a pleasant, quiet road, linking the King's Road in Chelsea to Albert Bridge. The houses there were comfortable and old-fashioned, some covered in ivy. The drawing room in the house was downstairs, leading off the small, narrow hallway, but Jane usually held her salons in the rooms on the first floor. This caused an immense crush as people going up the stairs jostled those going down. Outside in the street stood a long line of hansom cabs and broughams, their descending occupants adding to the crowd.

Jane liked living near the Thames. 'All London comes to me by way of King's Road,' she said impressively, 'but the Americans come straight from the Atlantic steamers moored at Chelsea Bridge.' Ever since Oscar's tour of the United States, American visitors had queued up to visit Jane, with the hope of seeing Oscar. She told Constance that seven new Americans had come to visit her after hearing Oscar lecture: 'all came in at once in a long line.'

The Comtesse de Brémont claimed that London society first took Oscar seriously when he started to edit the *Woman's World*. This had caused 'a flutter in the boudoirs of Mayfair and Belgravia' and it had become 'very intellectual to frequent Lady Wilde's crushes' by 'ladies of high degree and ladies of no degree – poets and painters,

artists and art critics, writers and scribblers, all eager to attain a place
in the pages of the new magazine'.[35]

Both Oscar and Willie always attended their mother's salon if they
were in London. The Comtesse remembered Oscar sauntering in and
'after saluting his mother, take a position by the chimney piece and
strike a graceful pose'. Because of the rush to see Oscar, Jane was
acclaimed by one paper as 'one of the most popular hostesses in
London' with her black glossy hair, 'combed straight back to fall over
her ears', and her usual voluminous robes of violet, lavender or old
gold satin covered with Irish lace. Her Saturday afternoon salons
became so full that she decided to be at home on another day as well
for select friends like Tom Taylor, the editor of *Punch*, and the
Shakespearean actress Helen Faucit, now married to Sir Theodore
Martin, the biographer of Prince Albert.

Catherine Hamilton described a visit to one of Jane's salons at this time
in her book *Notable Irishwomen*. On knocking at the door (the bell
was broken), she saw the narrow hall was heaped with wraps. 'The
maid opened a door which led into two small rooms with folding doors
between' and the company there, squashed against each other, was
mainly Anglo-Irish and American-Irish literary people, 'to say nothing
of a sprinkling of brutal Saxon'. When she saw Jane, she thought her
a strikingly handsome woman, even though Jane was then 68. She
commented on her 'glorious dark eyes' and despite Jane's shoulders being
slightly bent with rheumatism, claimed, 'It is easy to see that Speranza's
spirit lives still and that her mental energies are still as strong as ever.'

Jane, Catherine Hamilton noticed, had a horror of the 'miasma of
the commonplace'. She once asked her the time, as she needed to catch
a train: 'Does anyone here,' asked Lady Wilde, with one of her lofty
glances, 'know what time it is? We never know in this house about
Time.'[36]

Oscar was equally bored with the mundane. When an acquaintance
of his said he was leaving London for Liverpool, Oscar replied,
'largely, vaguely and inquiringly, "Where is Liverpool?"' The acquaintance, aware he was only talking for effect, quickly replied, 'Nowhere.
Never mind. Goodbye.'[37]

On another occasion, Jane took against a guest and requested the
friend who brought her not to do so again. The friend protested that this
particular guest, an American singer, was a most respectable woman.
'*Respectable!*' repeated Lady Wilde. '*Never use that word here.* It is only
tradespeople who are respectable. We are above respectability!'[38]

Many openly laughed at Jane for such comments. 'Whether she was conscious of that ill-bred ridicule is difficult to say,' said this same friend, 'as she comported herself with the same stately dignity and hospitality to all. She possessed the supreme tact of appearing to ignore any *gaucherie* on the part of her guests, and she had the admirable faculty of appearing not to understand that which did not please her.'

Another guest at Jane's salon was the painter Herbert Schmalz, who was amazed at how she had succeeded in collecting so many literary and artistic notables, as well as political and aristocratic celebrities. He described Jane as 'a tall, elderly lady of austere aspect', and found the atmosphere of her rooms was 'made more mysterious by pastilles burning on the mantelpiece and by large mirrors being placed between the floor and the ceiling, with curtains over the edges, so that when crowded with people you could not see where the actual room left off'. When he took his leave, Jane quizzed him about the painting he had in the Royal Academy. Schmalz said he hoped she liked it and she replied, 'I have not seen it, but Oscar shall guide me to it! Oscar shall guide me to it!'[39] Although she had forthright views of her own, Jane turned to Oscar in all matters of aesthetic taste.

Although pleased to be back in Chelsea and even nearer to Oscar, the move initially added to Jane's financial problems. She wrote to Constance from Oakley Street to say, 'We arrived here *yesterday* and I have no end of work and expense to get it in order and I have no money except this cheque which will you kindly cash for me as soon as possible, all in gold. But *now* can you lend me one sovereign for present expenses – that makes *three* I have borrowed from you, which please deduct from the £10 cheque. If possible send me the *£1 now* by Mrs Faithful, as I have nothing in hand.'[40]

Needing money and having heard that *Ancient Legends* was being sold in America, Jane wrote to the publishers, Ward & Downey, to see if any was due to her. They slapped down her hopes in the kind of reply authors hate, pointing out that all they had done was to sell some of their 6/- edition on sheets cheaply to Ticknor & Co. in America, so she could hardly expect a percentage on these, and adding: 'The book has not unfortunately been a success (from our point of view) – the entire sales of the 6/- edition (including the copies sold to Ticknor) being only 355 copies.'[41]

Oscar was also facing financial difficulties, writing to the Inland Revenue in the spring of 1889 to say, 'I wish your notices were not so agitating and did not hold out such dreadful threats.'[42] Perhaps financial pressure was behind his extraordinary run of work that year. January saw the publication of two essays, 'Pen, Pencil and Poison' in Frank Harris's *Fortnightly Review* and 'The Decay of Lying' in *Nineteenth Century*; in March his story of 'The Birthday of the Infanta' appeared in *Paris Illustré*; and by the end of the year he was working on *The Picture of Dorian Gray*.

His story, 'The Portrait of Mr W. H.', was also published that July in *Blackwood's* magazine. It was about the young actor, Willie Hughes, who, Oscar argued, was Shakespeare's boy lover. He had shown it to Jane late the previous year and she had been delighted with it, writing from Park Street just before she moved to say, 'Your essay on Shakespeare is learned, brilliant, flashing with epigrams and most *perfectly written*.'[43] It aroused a storm of conflicting opinions in which Oscar revelled.

Jane was busy at the time writing a long review of a collection of *Irish Minstrelsy* for the *Pall Mall Gazette*. It gave her a chance to look back on the fiery days of the Young Irelanders, when 'even the peasants and artisans of the time became poets', and she nostalgically recalled the leaders of the movement. She enjoyed the whole collection, from 'the rollicking humour of such ballads as "The night before Larry was stretched"', to 'the weird fancies of Clarence Mangan', and argued that the literary value of the songs remained, even if 'the passionate dreams of political enthusiasts pass away'.[44]

She was still in touch with Sir Charles Gavan Duffy, a link to her life as Speranza, and now wrote to thank him for his most generous gift (presumably money). 'Mine is indeed a sad case,' she said, explaining that there was no money coming in from the Moytura estate and that 'Willie has nothing but his salary from the *Daily Telegraph* and on that it is difficult to keep himself, and the home, and myself.' She went on to report on her efforts to get a grant from the Royal Literary Fund, saying that her claim was supported by a number of influential people. Oscar had canvassed widely for her and signatories were Lords Lytton, Spencer and Coleridge, Sir Theodore and Lady Martin, A. C. Swinburne, G. O. Trevelyan, John Lubbock, Archibald Sayce, J. S. Blackie, J. P. Mahaffy, Richard Quain, Edward Dowden and J. B. Burke. 'The *only refusal* came from Mr Gladstone who refused to sign as I had "two sons who ought to provide for me." How ill-natured of him! Whereas Lord Spencer wrote that "he was most happy to show his appreciation of Speranza".'[45]

Jane based her formal application to the Royal Literary Fund for a grant on the 'state of affairs in Ireland', which, she said, deprived her of her income of £200 a year and resulted in her entire receipts from the Irish property from 1880 to 1888 amounting to only £150. 'Her son, Mr Oscar Wilde,' read the statement, 'has on many occasions given her help and assistance but she is anxious now to secure some small independence of position until the Irish property is placed under more favourable conditions.' The application was dated November 1888 and in it Jane gave her age as 67, her place of birth as Dublin and her birthdate as 27 December 1821.[46] She was a month off 67, but the older she seemed the more sympathy she might be expected to elicit: until then, she had always manipulated her birthdate to appear younger.

Sir Theodore Martin, the writer, stressed in his letter of support that Lady Wilde was 'an authoress both of poetry and prose of an excellent quality . . . through a long series of years', adding that she would only have made such an application 'under the pressure of extreme necessity'. He did not exaggerate and Jane's letter dated 16 November 1888 thanking the Literary Fund for its 'liberal donation of £100 sterling' was heartfelt. She wrote to Sir Theodore to thank him, as she later told Oscar, and had a nice note back. 'He says he was present at the committee and spoke and was supported by Mr Lecky and the grant was given at once. I added also that *you* felt his kindness in this matter very gratefully – and he seems much gratified.'

She went on to discuss Oscar's current projects: 'Now as regards your essays, both are *admirable* – your style is . . . original, the perfect diction, the subtle criticism, the unexpected humour – all – delightful – on Mr Browning you are splendid – and my lines read gloriously! Then, *on models* is capital – and *modest* also. Willie was highly appreciative of it. I am so glad you have "struck oil" in Literature – I know of no other at once so strong and so beautiful – except Ruskin.'[47] Of Browning Oscar had written, 'The only man who can touch the hem of his garment is George Meredith. Meredith is a prose Browning, and so is Browning. He uses poetry as a medium for writing in prose.'

Jane told Oscar at the end of the year that 'Willie is delighted with your article in the December *Woman's World*. [Oscar had reviewed W. E. Henley's *A Book of Verses*.] He says it is "a perfect Literary Critique" – thoughtful, cultured, eloquent, etc . . . come tomorrow, Saturday, and have a talk. I am in the *Queen* of last week. And now – what shall I do? I think of an article on English and American women.'[48] She only had to unearth the one written for an American magazine some six years previously.

Her article in the *Queen* had been on 'Hallow-Tide in Ireland': it gave the history of Hallow-Eve, the last day of October, which is known as *La-Samnah* in Ireland and is regarded as the first day of winter; November, which ushered in the weird winter season of drear and ill-omen, being called 'the month of mourning'.[49] Such Irish seasonal stories had featured in her book on legends and Jane extracted many for use in magazines.

Although Oscar was still editing the *Woman's World* in 1889, his interest in the enterprise was fading. He started by going in twice a week, on Tuesdays and Thursdays, but gradually turned up later and later. A colleague, Arthur Fish, recalled him coming in, glancing perfunctorily at proofs and layout, and saying, 'Is it necessary to settle anything today?' before putting on his hat, with a languid 'Good morning', and trailing out.[50]

That year Oscar saw a great deal of John Gray, a fair, good-looking young man of 23, who had contributed to the *Dial*, a magazine launched in August 1889 by the artists Charles Ricketts and Charles Shannon. When Frank Harris met Gray, he considered him to have 'great personal distinction' and a marked poetic gift. 'It seemed to me,' he said, 'that intellectual sympathy and the natural admiration which a young man feels for a brilliant senior formed the obvious bond between them.'[51] Oscar was to use his surname for Dorian Gray, but there is no proof Gray was intended as the original character.

Oscar was still very fond of Constance, but his early physical passion had faded. He made no attempt to hide his intimate friendship with Gray and was seen frequently at places like the Café Royal amid a circle of other admiring young men. He went out less with Constance, a pattern which Frank Harris believed he had set early on in his marriage, saying, 'His wife would certainly have been invited with him if he had refused invitations addressed to himself alone; but from the beginning he accepted them . . .'[52] *The Picture of Dorian Gray* contains comments by the character Lord Henry Wotton which rather paralleled the situation at Tite Street: 'I never know where my wife is, and my wife never knows what I am doing. When we meet – we do meet occasionally, when we dine out together, or go down to the Duke's – we tell each other the most absurd stories with the most serious faces. My wife is very good at it – much better, in fact, than I am. She never gets confused over her dates, and I always do. But when she does find me out, she makes no row at all. I sometimes wish she would, but she merely laughs at me.'

Constance showed a certain cool irony over her husband's behaviour. Once, at a dinner party the two attended, Oscar was asked where he had been that week and replied, at 'an exquisite Elizabethan country house, with emerald lawns, stately yew hedges, scented rose-gardens, cool lily ponds, gay herbaceous borders, ancestral oaks, and strutting peacocks'. 'And did she act well, Oscar?' asked Constance. Oscar had been to a play.[53]

Although Constance may not have appeared outwardly distressed, her husband's increasing absences did upset her. Once, when talking to the singer Nellie Melba about his two sons, Oscar said: 'I was telling them stories last night of little boys who were naughty and who made their mother cry, and what dreadful things would happen to them unless they became better; and do you know what one of them answered? He asked me what punishment could be reserved for naughty papas, who did not come home till the early morning, and made mother cry far more?'[54] Elizabeth Robins recalls dropping in at Tite Street to see Oscar and finding Constance there, a lonely figure in white muslin. Constance admitted to her she had no idea where Oscar was.

Jane was close enough to Constance to have been aware of her loneliness and unhappiness during Oscar's absences. She was genuinely concerned at the solitary existence Constance led without him and always pleaded with Oscar to come home when he was away for long. Both women supported each other during his increasing absences and loyally defended him to outsiders.

Although Jane missed Oscar too, she was preoccupied in 1889 with many activities – preparing for publication her next book on ancient Irish cures, holding her salons, and keeping up her voluminous correspondence. Many of her letters were to other writers. 'But why are you so sad?' she wrote to one woman who had sent her newly published book to Jane. 'You are yet too young to have passed into the shadow.' The author J. S. Stuart Glennie wrote from Lincoln's Inn with gritted teeth, to acknowledge the 'friendly frankness with which you have spoken of the obscurity of many passages' of his book.[55]

In late July Oscar resigned from the *Woman's World*, cutting off a market for Jane. It returned to being a less highbrow magazine, concentrating on fashion and society news, but folded the following year. A Mr Alfred Harmsworth, launching a new type of cosy magazine, *Home Chat*, which was not Jane's style, successfully cornered the women's market.

Cyril had been ill that summer and Oscar excused himself from visiting a friend saying 'terror for Cyril' had kept him away. The two were very close; Constance wrote to a friend in the September to say that Cyril had 'cried bitterly in a room by himself because I told him in a joke that his father had eaten my bread and butter'.[56] Jane adored both the children and proved an affectionate grandmother. 'Love to Prince Cyril,' she once wrote to Constance, 'I meant to buy a little wooden horse to have here to amuse him.' And, 'Cyril looked lovely today – quite a young prince and dressed to perfection.'

That month Constance 'dragged Oscar to the Park' to see a vast meeting in support of the London dock strike. Thousands turned up with their banners to hear the powerful orator John Burns. Constance was intrigued by the representatives of different societies: 'One cart,' she reported, 'contained a Neptune with a long beard and a trident and a crown, a Minerva with a moustache and a helmet, two polar bears and a barber . . . and others had effigies of coal-porters climbing ladders.'[57]

W. B. Yeats concentrated on the London social scene in September when writing for the American readers of the *Boston Pilot*, a magazine for which Jane had also written. She was known for her work as Speranza by its editor, John Boyle O'Reilly who, together with Yeats's friend John O'Leary, had been imprisoned and exiled from Ireland for political activities. Yeats said of Jane: 'Lady Wilde still keeps up, in spite of London's emptiness, her Saturday afternoon receptions, though the handful of callers contrasts mournfully with the roomful of clever people one meets there in the Season. There is no better time, however, to hear her talk than now, when she is unburdened by weary guests . . . When one listens to her and remembers that Sir William Wilde was in his day a famous *raconteur*, one finds it no way wonderful that Oscar Wilde should be the most finished talker of our time.'[58]

The Comtesse de Brémont agreed with his praise of Jane's conversation. She once watched Oscar, as he leant on the mantelpiece toying with the jewelled charms around his neck, and thought he effaced himself so that 'his mother might display her brilliant wit and hold everyone by the charm of her conversation'. Jane, like Oscar, delighted in epigrams. Her Irish turn of phrase added to her salty remarks. 'There has never been a woman yet in the world,' she once said, 'who wouldn't have given the top of the milk jug to some man if she met the right one.'[59]

Yeats considered Jane was doing good work in getting down in good English her husband's store of folklore and legends: 'Lady Wilde is now preparing for the press a new volume taken from this great collection. It will be of some size and deal mainly with charms and spells.'[60] *Ancient Cures, Charms and Usages of Ireland: contributions to Irish lore* was published early in 1890. A companion to *Ancient Legends*, the book was much lighter in substance, and comprised a miscellaneous and amusing collection of cures and charms against every imaginable ailment from being 'fairy-stricken' to hydrophobia – recovery invariably involved having to recite some strange incantation or swallow something mildly unpleasant, like the blood of a crowing hen.

The *Lady's Pictorial* called it a 'curious and interesting book', and the *Athenaeum* said Jane had a pleasing way of telling a story; but the *Academy*, Jane's usual adversary, led with a right: 'Everything which real students most desire – mention of authorities, local touches, chronological and topographical details; anything that would render it possible to separate genuine ancient legend from modern invention or artistic embellishment – all these are either carelessly omitted or carefully suppressed.'[61] Jane would have had difficulty in providing these. Yeats described how Sir William asked everyone all over Ireland to let him know of any charm or fairy tale they knew, and old men and women, after leaving his hospital cured, 'would ask leave to send him eggs or fowl, or some such country gift, and he would bargain for a fairy tale instead'.[62]

To extend the book Jane had included some earlier articles of hers, including her long article on 'The American Irish', first written in 1878. In this piece Jane had resumed her role of Speranza, lambasting the English in both poetry and prose. She welcomed a suggestion 'that America should purchase Ireland from the English Government in a peaceable, orderly way' and the *Athenaeum* countered, 'By whom and to whom this remarkable suggestion was offered the author does not vouchsafe to say.'[63] Jane further claimed that Irish poets were far better than any England had produced and her examples drove the *Academy* to say that Jane herself ranked higher than her mediocre selection. The *Athenaeum*, unaware the article was written when Jane was still living in Dublin, said, 'It is sad to think that all the years that Lady Wilde has dwelt in London have taught her nothing but hatred.'

Although Jane could be sarcastic about London and the Londoners, she was firmly settled there. The thought of returning to Ireland

and leaving her sons never entered her head. After interviewing her, one magazine writer even said, 'I suspect from her talk that she has, notwithstanding patriotic sentiment, a sneaking love for the cockney city.'[64] Her most serious complaint against her adopted country was her failure so far to get a civil list pension. Her Literary Fund grant was most welcome, but would not last long. She wrote to Oscar to say, 'I am very miserable about the pension. A blank silence – and I don't know what I am to do about it. I wrote to the Chief Clerk explaining that I resided entirely in London . . . but no answer has come as yet. If not by Monday, I think I better go to the office – Whitehall – myself.'

But the same letter had other news to relate. 'WCK [Willie],' she went on, 'has almost fixed to go to the U.S. with Mrs Frank Leslie and give three lectures – he can return in three months – it would do him a deal of good.' Jane could see that Willie was in need of a new direction. At 38, he was still showing few signs of maturity. He would shout instructions to the actors from his box when watching a play and that year, 1890, at the opening night of *Ravenswood* on 20 September at the Lyceum, he started an argument with an American man in the interval, then came to blows with him, with 'both parties fighting a running engagement as they left the theatre'.[65] His interests remained superficial. He had been quick to join the fashionable new Pelican Club the previous November, which was associated with the start that month of the *Pelican*, a magazine for men-about-town for which Willie wrote occasionally, although not enough to bring in sufficient income on which to live. A club member commented that he was a 'very brilliant writer, when he chose to take a little trouble with his work', but added that though he could work quickly, 'he was not at all keen about working often, or indeed at all'.[66]

The widowed Mrs Frank Leslie was a wealthy American newspaper proprietor. Jane, always with an eye to helping her sons, had spotted her potential long ago and written to Oscar, when he was still attempting to make his name, advising him to call on her while she was in London. 'She is going to organize a London issue of her journal and you should cultivate the press of all nations.'

Mrs Leslie was a tough woman. Her early beginnings were shrouded in mystery. Rumour had it that she was the illegitimate daughter of an African slave and that her mother had run a New York brothel. She had already married four times and had inherited seven newspapers from her last husband, Frank Leslie. A forceful, energetic woman, her

London appearances and the jewels she wore were faithfully reported in the press. She often visited Jane's salons and had also been to Constance's at-homes. Jane admired her, writing in an article that 'The most important and successful journalist in the States is a woman – Mrs Frank Leslie . . . With her many gifts, her brilliant powers of conversation in all the leading tongues of Europe, her splendid residence and immense income, nobly earned and nobly spent, Mrs Frank Leslie may be considered the leader and head of the intellectual circles of New York.'[67]

Nothing came of Willie's lecture tour to America, but the project at least succeeded in bringing him into close contact with Mrs Frank Leslie. Jane urged on Willie's growing involvement with her, hoping at last to see her cherished ambition of a wealthy bride for him realized. Meanwhile she was further cheered by an improvement in her own financial situation. After telling Oscar that 'at last I think the pension will be paid, for the income tax has been allowed for exemption', on 24 May 1890 she was finally awarded a civil list pension of £70 a year.

Her delight at this was enhanced when Oscar's story *The Picture of Dorian Gray* was published in the July issue of *Lippincott's Magazine*. It caused a sensation and brought Oscar all the attention he could want. Frank Harris said it represented months of Oscar's witty talk and believed it the first piece of work in which he had at last found his true vein. Jane wrote to Oscar ecstatically to say, 'It is the most wonderful piece of writing in all the fiction of the day. I put down my thoughts as I read and will ask WCK to see if they can be put in the *Daily Telegraph* as a short review. I have just had a note from WCK from Margate and he says "Oscar's second letter is thought highly of and he is now considered to have won the victory." The story is tremendous; I nearly fainted at the last scene.' She asked him to come over for a talk, 'as all has to be done for the pension – up to 11 o'clock at night you will find me up.'[68]

Some reviewers found the book repellent and charged him with immorality. The *Scots Observer* declared the subject matter was 'only fitted for the Criminal Investigation Department', while the *Daily Chronicle*, a normally liberal paper, said it was 'a tale spawned from the leprous literature of the French *decadents* – a poisonous book, the atmosphere of which is heavy with the mephitic odours of moral and spiritual putrefaction'. This provoked Oscar to reply, 'It is poisonous, if you like; but you cannot deny that it is also perfect, and perfection is what we artists aim at.'

Oscar also published the first of his two essays on criticism in July, 'The True Function and Value of Criticism: with some remarks on the importance of doing nothing: a dialogue'. The writer Katherine Bradley (one half of 'Michael Field') had visited him while he was writing it and noted in her diary, 'He is at his best when he is lying on a sofa thinking.'[69] It brings to mind Jane lying on her sofa in Merrion Square, reading Greek philosophy, while the puzzled bailiffs looked on.

Oscar was becoming increasingly in demand. He was normally assiduous in attending his mother's salons, but when the Comtesse de Brémont turned up later that year at one of Jane's salons after a trip to South Africa, she was disappointed to find very few people there and no sign of Oscar. Without his presence Jane looked a rather solitary figure, though she was quick to tell the Comtesse that: 'Oscar does not come when I have people here. He is so very much in demand everywhere, and he prefers to come when I am alone, as he has so little time now for me that he wishes to have me all to himself.' The Comtesse stayed on for supper – cold beef and salad, with a glass or two of white Italian wine – forgetting 'the gaucheries of the unkempt servant . . . under the spell of her charming talk'.[70]

The following year, 1891, saw an extraordinary starburst of work from Oscar. In January, his verse tragedy, *The Duchess of Padua*, was produced in New York, anonymously, under the title of *Guido Ferranti* – so that reviewers would not associate it with *Vera*, which had had such a short run. The play got reasonably good reviews though one of the reviewers disclosed the author as Oscar. It ran for about three weeks, quite acceptable to Oscar, and after it closed he asked Henry Irving to stage it in London. Irving, however, declined and Oscar offered it to George Alexander, the actor manager who took over the St James's Theatre that year and was on the lookout for new plays. Alexander wanted a lighter, more topical play and commissioned Oscar to write one.

Oscar first wrote his political essay, 'The Soul of Man under Socialism'. He was moved to do this, so Bernard Shaw was told, after hearing Shaw deliver an address on socialism at a Fabian Society meeting in Westminster, at which Oscar himself spoke.[71] The essay, in which Oscar argued for artistic freedom and the reconstruction of society 'on such a basis that poverty will be impossible', appeared in the *Fortnightly Review* in February 1891. The *Weekly Dispatch* commented: 'He wants the world to be all Oscar Wilde,' and the Tory *Spectator* said, 'The article, if serious, would be thoroughly unhealthy.'

Such radical ideas had always appealed to Jane. She had earlier asked the Honorary Secretary of the Fabian Parliamentary League, I. Brailsford Bright, for a copy of the League's manifesto. Sending it to her, he replied to a question of hers, confirming that 'Bernard Shaw *is* a leading member of our party and of my own particular group of constitutional or political workers. The "Queen's Speech" of which I forward you a copy under wrapper may amuse and interest you. I understand it is G. B. Shaw's composition.[72]

Oscar revised *Dorian Gray* in book form that year with six extra chapters and a new preface; refurbished two essays on criticism for his volume *Intentions*; nearly completed *Salome*; and published two books of short stories. Yet even before embarking on all this he felt overworked and ill. He told George Alexander that he couldn't get a grip on the new play he was writing for him and went to Paris for a change of scene and inspiration. Writing to five-year-old 'dearest Cyril' on 3 March 1891 he told him he felt much better, and explained how he was spending his time ('I go every day and drive in a beautiful forest called the Bois de Boulogne'). He promised to bring both boys some chocolates on his return and said, 'I hope you are taking great care of dear Mamma. Give her my love and kisses, and also love and kisses to Vyvyan and yourself. Your loving Papa.'[73]

Jane was busy while he was away compiling a number of her reviews and essays. The collection was published that July under the title, *Notes on Men, Women and Books*. She was pleased with it and donated a copy to the Chelsea Library. The book is a tribute to Jane's impressively wide reading. In it she discussed English writers of the eighteenth century, claiming the literature of that era swung from 'sensuous and material' to 'vapidly didactic', and went on to praise the Irish writer Dean Swift, 'the leading genius of his country'. When reviewing in erudite detail the literary work and lives of writers like Alfred Tennyson, George Eliot, Harriet Martineau, Wordsworth, Leigh Hunt, Thomas Moore, Bulwer Lytton and Disraeli, she enlivened the collection by her strong personal views and descriptions – calling the writer Harriet Martineau, for instance, 'cold, bitter, sarcastic, unlovely and unloving' and taking an unexpected swing at George Eliot for her 'language of oracular obscurity' and the way *Middlemarch*, in particular, 'exhausts our patience by page after page of pretentious commonplace'. She told the 'mournful tale' of the life of the 'beautiful Marguerite, Countess of Blessington, loved, worshipped, even adored . . .' and why she was forced to write 'trash and twaddle';

and berated English novelists for not seeing 'the superior force, beauty, and power of the French style of writing, where a line, a word, is made to unfold a character or express a dramatic situation' as opposed to 'the long-winded descriptive sentences of English writers, with their numerous clauses and concatenations'.

When she tackled 'World Leaders' through the centuries, however – from 'the inspired, doomed Dominican' Savonarola to 'the gloomy relentless bigot' Philip of Spain – her own prose occasionally descended into oracular obscurity. Her last essay was a forceful assessment of Richard III as played by Charles Kean, in which Jane argued that Kean was right to portray the powerful Richard as a passionless man, 'calm, cold and relentless as fate'. You might not agree with Jane, but she was a provocative, challenging writer.

The *Athenaeum*'s reviewer for once let her off fairly lightly, saying there was plenty of ability in her collected articles. 'One of the best is an essay on Calderón, although . . . it is a mistake to say, "He seems not to have been much of a warrior" . . . no one, however, with a reputation to lose as a critic would venture to call *Lalla Rookh* [by Thomas Moore] a perfect poem.'[74]

Jane wrote to Oscar in July to say that she was glad a dinner Willie had given for him had been a success. She then wrote again in distress, to say that she had muddled up something Willie had said, which had obviously angered Oscar. 'He only mentioned that the boy at the hotel said, "Mr Oscar Wilde was there and had a gentleman to dinner." Something else put *twelve* men into my head . . . I hope I have not entirely ruined the peace of the family. I feel dreadfully wretched and quite unfit to live. Of course I don't expect ever to see you again. La povera Madre.'[75]

That summer Lionel Johnson, a poet, critic and friend of Oscar's, introduced him to Lord Alfred Douglas, known as Bosie. Johnson, a homosexual, had been at Winchester with Bosie, who was a slim, girlishly pretty 20 year old with a fair fragility that strongly appealed to Oscar's love of beauty. In describing his first meeting with Oscar, Bosie later said that 'Oscar took a violent fancy – it is no exaggeration to describe it as an infatuation – to me at sight.'[76] According to Frank Harris, Oscar told him after meeting Bosie that the boy had frightened him as much as he attracted him, 'and I held away from him. But he wouldn't have it; he sought me out again and again and I couldn't resist him.'[77]

Constance met Bosie on that first occasion, as the three men took tea with her in Tite Street. Bosie insisted that she liked him. 'She told me, about a year after I first met her, that she liked me better than any of Oscar's other friends.'[78] If that was the truth she was unaware, like Oscar, of the fact that Bosie's angelic face hid intense selfishness and a neurotic personality. Bosie must have met Jane too at some point, though she did not comment on him in any of her letters to friends. He sent her a photograph of himself, and she in turn thanked him for his 'admirable portrait'.

Oscar saw Bosie again in July and the younger man boastfully claimed that 'From the second time [Oscar] saw me, when he gave me a copy of *Dorian Gray*, which I took with me to Oxford, he made overtures to me. It was not till I had known him for at least six months and after I had seen him over and over again and he had twice stayed with me in Oxford, that I gave in to him.'[79]

That same month Oscar first met the spectrally lean artist Aubrey Beardsley at Edward Burne-Jones's house and described him as having 'a face like a silver hatchet, with grass green hair'. They got on well initially, and Beardsley's disturbingly erotic drawings were to illustrate *Salome*, the play Oscar was currently planning. In July, too, *Lord Arthur Savile's Crime and Other Stories* was published in book form and Constance was delighted when Oscar gave her a presentation copy, signed 'Constance from Oscar, July '91'.

Jane was immensely proud of Oscar's outpouring of work and she was further cheered by a letter from a journalist friend of hers, Charlotte Eccles, who worked for the Dublin magazine, the *Lady of the House*, to say that in a prize competition to name the greatest living Irishwoman, 78 per cent of the votes were in her favour.[80]

That September she told Oscar that Willie intended to sail for New York on the 23rd: 'You might come for a parting shake hands with him. He would like it,' she said. Then, to her delight, on 4 October 1891 – four days after his arrival – Willie married Mrs Frank Leslie in New York at the Church of the Strangers.

Willie was 39 when he married in the October; his bride was 55. He may have looked on her as a surrogate mother; he certainly regarded her as a provider. But he had made a poor choice: Mrs Leslie was not to repeat his mother's uncritical love. Oscar's friend Robert Sherard recalled Oscar's percipient remark that Willie had acted very foolishly in not insisting on a settlement before he married his wealthy bride: 'When she has glutted her lust on him and used him up, she'll pitch him his hat and coat and by means of an American divorce get rid of him legally and let him starve to death for all she'll care.'[81]

Reporting on the marriage, which was a quiet one, the *New York Times* said Mrs Leslie had not immediately accepted Willie's first proposal in August that year. 'He corresponded with her, however, and the result was that he arrived in this city last Thursday. Arrangements were made at once for an immediate marriage.' Mrs Leslie wore a Worth costume of pale grey satin for her wedding and for their honeymoon the couple planned to go up the Hudson and visit Niagara, before they returned to live at Mrs Leslie's apartment on West 27th Street. Oscar, who dismissed Niagara Falls as 'simply a vast unnecessary amount of water going the wrong way and then falling over unnecessary rocks', also said that 'every American bride is taken there and the sight of the stupendous waterfall must be one of the earliest, if not the keenest, disappointments in American married life.'

The *New York Times* described Willie as a 'London journalist of reputation', and said his mother was a 'close and respected friend' of Mrs Leslie's. Willie, in addition, was reported to be 'a fine pianist and also has done some artistic work on canvas in oils'. His well-built figure was praised, along with his clear blue eyes, dark hair, moustache and whiskers. The paper also claimed that 'the groom will at once enter into editorial work in connection with the Leslie publications.'[82]

Mrs Leslie must have been responsible for announcing this. She was a hard worker herself: 'She rose early, enjoyed or endured a cold bath, did physical exercises, turned up at the office at nine a.m. arrayed in black silk.'[83] She was obviously unaware that Willie preferred to spend his time blowing cigar rings. His reply, when asked what he was working at, was, 'At intervals.' He was turning down a great opportunity: he could now have been writing for, or managing, a newspaper empire. But as one of his London friends said, when Willie found himself married to a wealthy proprietor, 'he appeared to consider that there was no need for more than one of the combination to hustle; and that perhaps he had better not be the one.' He was quickly nicknamed 'Wuffalo Will' on the grounds that he was totally unlike the hardy Buffalo Bill, apart from his height and hair.[84]

Jane wrote optimistically to Oscar on 13 October to say, 'No letter today – of course they are at Niagara . . . I have written both to WCK and to Mrs William C. Kingsbury Wilde, but I don't know yet what name she will adopt for her cards.' She added, 'I hope you write to Willie – he seems in radiant health, hope and happiness. God keep them happy and wise and loving in truth and trust. I think it is altogether a fine and good thing for Willie. Her influence may work great good in him and give him the strength he wants.'[85]

Willie, as Jane could see, needed help to progress in his career and not to slide down the path of amiable drinking. He had done well in London with the *Daily Telegraph* and different magazines until resigning to leave for America; but his work as leader writer, critic and short story writer, however talented, was anonymous and difficult to identify and it failed to build his name and reputation. He must have been keenly aware that even in Fleet Street he was known chiefly for being the brother of Oscar; and, as far as success was concerned, an unbridgeable gap was opening between the two of them.

Jane had an iron belief in Willie's talent and had he only shared this he might well have challenged Oscar. Instead, lacking ambition, he made no effort to make a success of himself. Once Oscar, listening to a young man being told to begin at the bottom of the ladder, said, 'No, begin at the top and sit upon it.' Willie now had the chance to make his name and his fortune, but he failed to live up to Jane's hopes that he would be fired with some of his wife's energy.

Oscar meanwhile was thinking of writing an introduction to two plays by Maeterlinck. When on the 16th of that month the publisher William Heinemann came to Tite Street to discuss the idea, he found Oscar wearing black, in deep mourning for it being his thirty-seventh birthday. His mother would have understood. Oscar constantly returned to the subject of youth in his works, endorsing Lord Henry Wotton's comment in *The Picture of Dorian Gray*: 'When your youth goes, your beauty will go with it, and then you will suddenly discover that there are no triumphs left for you . . .'; and Lord Illingworth's remarks in *A Woman of No Importance*: 'To win back my youth, Gerald, there is nothing I wouldn't do – except take exercise, get up early, or be a useful member of the community.'

That month Oscar had completed his new play for George Alexander. Having worked on it while staying in the Lake District, he called the main character Lady Windermere, after the principal lake there. When he asked Alexander if he liked it, Alexander replied, 'Like it is not the word, it is simply wonderful.'

Oscar now went off to Paris to finish *Salome*. He at once became involved in an exhausting social round, dining out constantly with new friends – the poet Pierre Louÿs, Marcel Schwob, the symbolist writer, and André Gide, the novelist. He also met Marcel Proust, among many others, and saw old friends like Robert Sherard. The French press, as his mother recorded, was quick to report on his work and activities.

Figlio mio carissimo [wrote Jane], Your fame in Paris is becoming stupendous. A column in the *Figaro*! And then a charming sketch in the *Echo de Paris*. I have sent both papers on to WCKW and hope it will stimulate him to action. The sketch is written very nicely, so appreciative, and also written with knowledge and with a kind of awe in approaching you – you are really favoured to have had such articles about you in the greatest and most cultured city in the world – and now we may expect your dramas – you are indeed taking a high place in the literature of the day and I am very proud of you.

Still I would like you home. I want to see my poet son and Constance would like you back. She is very lonely. Finish your dramas *now* and come back to us, though London is very dull and dark and wet and cold and foggy – WCKW is well.

I heard from both of them yesterday – he doesn't seem to care for Americans, the *men* only talk business and the *women* he doesn't like – and the newspapers he says are simply diabolic – all personalities . . . I want Willie to start a Literary Journal. He is living in idleness and that is quite absurd – idleness and pampered luxury. I want you to go and see Henri Gaidoz, editor of *Mélusine*. He is an old friend of mine and sends me the journal regularly . . . *Mélusine* is devoted to popular superstitions and essays and I am often quoted in it. In the December number I am in. A story from Kerry . . . no I am not named.[86]

Despite his mother's pleas, Oscar was to stay two months in Paris. He was enjoying himself immensely, was obsessed with *Salome* and had made several drafts of the play. He was writing it in French and had private hopes that Sarah Bernhardt might play the leading role.

November 1891 saw the publication of *A House of Pomegranates*, which Oscar dedicated to Constance. It was a collection of four stories, 'The Young King', 'The Birthday of the Infanta', 'The Fisherman and his Soul' and 'The Star-Child'. Although none of these stories is directly taken from the myths and legends that so fascinated his father and mother, Oscar had been brought up on Gaelic myths since childhood and these strange, imaginative stories must have exerted a great influence on him.

A House of Pomegranates was reviewed in the *Bookman* by Walter Pater, Fellow and Tutor of Brasenose College, Oxford and one of the founding fathers of the aesthetic movement. On reading his review, Jane wrote at once to Oscar to say that Pater 'evidently has a high appreciation of you, but his style is not as beautiful as usual – involved, laboured – whereas *your style* is always clear and sparkling as a diamond – so, I used to hope you would equal Pater, *now* I think you are far beyond and above Pater.'

She went on to tell him a touching story about the last tale, in which the Star-Child, set by his master to find a piece of gold three days running or face being whipped and killed, had then mercifully given each piece of gold he found to a leper.

> Yesterday as I had just finished reading that touching and pathetic story of the Star-Child, who should come in but Bessie Byrne – all in a flutter – 'Oh, Lady Wilde, I have come to borrow 30s. Can you give it to me at once?'
>
> Well, to lend to Bessie Byrne was not to be thought of and so I set my face hard. But then I thought of the Star-Child and how he gave the white gold piece to the leper and my heart melted – and actually – yes, actually – I drew the £1 10s from my purse and handed it to Bessie Byrne! Think of that! All your doing and of course I shall never hope to see my £1 10s again. But see what you can do!
>
> Now is this not a beautiful comment on your style – better than Pater's sentiment.[87]

Jane and Constance were both delighted at Oscar's growing fame. 'All the papers mention your play that you are writing,' Jane ended a letter to him – in fact you are the leading man of England, as Willie is of New York.'

It took a doting mother to regard Willie as New York's finest. He had started his married life as he meant to continue it – staying in bed until noon or one o'clock, then thoughtfully calling for his wife at the office mid-afternoon and taking her for a drive. He would then have pre-dinner drinks, followed by more drinks at dinner, before going on to really serious drinking at his favourite clubs: the Century or the Lotus.

Jane's hopes for him persisted. She wrote to Oscar on 1 December 1891 to say that she had sent Willie a review of *A House of Pomegranates* by the *Star*, which 'touched all the chief points so well and with such fine appreciation . . . I hope he will order the book. I told him to do so. I also want him to establish either a Literary Review, edited by himself, or a literary column in one of Frank Leslie's seven journals – he seems to be getting on well and he has been well received. The Bar and the press and the journalists all gave him dinners and it is pronounced that "Sir Edwin Arnold and Wilde are the only good writers in America."'

She went on to say that she had had a nice letter from Mrs Frank Leslie. 'She wants to send me £400 a year, but I said *no*, if she sent anything, £100 would be enough to help me to keep on the House.'[88] Jane had a strong sense of morality and was very straight in her dealings. Deeply in need of that extra £300, she unhesitatingly turned it down as she felt she could not justify taking it; she was happy to take the £100 on the grounds that she could offer the couple her house to stay in when they were in England.

She couldn't resist telling Oscar once again that 'Your book [*A House of Pomegranates*] is beautiful, most beautiful. Jewels of thought set in the fine gold of the most exquisite words – and yet it all seems written with the most unconscious grace, without strain or effort – and no matter how strange and fantastic the incidents, yet the pathos, the human pathos is always real, as in the tale of the Dwarf . . . you have quite taught the age the meaning of a really beautiful book.' Finally she asked him when he was coming back. 'I am very lonely without my two sons,' she admitted, 'and the weather is wretched. Constance is looking well and is much pleased at the dedication to her.'[89]

Jane wrote a further plea to Oscar on 3 December about his prolonged visit, telling him that Constance had visited her the evening before. 'She is so nice always to me. I am very fond of her – *Do* come home. She is very lonely and mourns for you . . .' But Oscar, unconcerned, preferred his life in Paris, where he dined most evenings with André Gide and between intense bouts of writing *Salome* was fêted by a coterie of the leading writers of the day. He returned to London late in December 1891. Earlier that month, *L'Echo de Paris* had called him *le 'great event'*: the next four years took him to heights that not even Jane had imagined.

14

'A Leaning Tower of Courage'

LADY WINDERMERE'S FAN opened at the St James's Theatre on 20 February 1892 and took London by storm. Writing to Oscar from what she called 'Oakley Hermitage', Jane told him, 'Truly you are a startling celebrity!!!', adding, perhaps wistfully with her own remembered fame in mind, 'I must now pose as "the Mother of Oscar".'

She was relieved everything had gone so well. Before the play was staged she had written censoriously to him to say, 'The *Sunday Sun* gives the name of your play and I do not like it – *A Good Woman*, it is mawkish. No one cares for a good woman. *A Noble Woman* would be better. [The published play was finally called: *Lady Windermere's Fan: a play about a good woman*.] Also do try to be *present yourself at the first performance* – it would be right and proper and Constance would like it. Do not leave her all alone. Then you might be of real use, if any hint was wanting behind the scenes to the actors and it is really better and *more dignified* for you to be present – it would give courage to everyone and I advise you to keep on good cordial terms with your manager, Mr Alexander – if you go away, it will look cowardly, as if you feared the result.'[1]

Jane had an abhorrence of cowardice and could not bear to see it in her sons. She also believed strongly in close family bonds and was upset at the way Oscar continued to absent himself from Tite Street. In her letter she went on to say that she had just written to Willie to tell him that Oscar's new play was about to be staged, and admitted, 'I am very anxious about it and for you and for Constance, whose whole heart is in the success – and I have every hope it will be a success. I believe in you and in your genius.'

Oscar dutifully squired Constance to the first night of *Lady Windermere's Fan*, telling a friend, 'she will be very nervous probably.' Bosie and Robbie Ross were also there, and so were Lillie Langtry and Henry James – the latter thinking the play 'infantine'. At the interval Frank Harris discovered that most of the critics disliked it, but the audience cheered loudly and called for the author. Oscar, cigarette held in mauve-gloved hand, and wearing a green carnation, came to the front to say, according to Harris, 'I am so glad, ladies and gentlemen, that you like my play. I feel sure you estimate the merits of it almost as highly as I do myself.'[2] They did: people talked only of the play and Oscar became the idol of smart London.

The poet Richard Le Gallienne remembered telling Oscar on the first night of *Lady Windermere's Fan* that he was writing an essay on loving his enemies. Oscar said he would like to write on that, but 'all my life I have been looking for twelve men who didn't believe in me . . . and, so far, I have only found eleven.' When Le Gallienne later heard of Oscar's prison sentence, he said, 'Poor Oscar! he has found his twelfth man.'[3]

Jane dashed off further letters to Oscar, all expressing the same delight about the play: 'You have had a splendid success and I am very happy and very proud of you'; 'I warmly give you my congratulations. *You are the great success of the day*'; 'Pray come in Saturday next: the people languish for you – and I want you sadly, badly, madly to help me to talk.' She asked him for seats for all her friends, and collected up the reviews. 'I thought the *World* very good and the *St James's* and *Observer*. Only the *Referee* was bad and spiteful and the *D.T.* was *mean* and *poor*. I sent all to Willie except the *Referee* – that I threw in the fire . . . I thought *The Times* had some good criticism and it was not rude like the *Referee*.'[4] Oscar was to give her a copy of the play inscribed, 'To my dear wonderful mother with my love, Oscar Wilde '93'.[5]

Willie, reading of his brother's success, must have drawn a parallel with his own life. Perhaps it accounted for his growing abusiveness, which was understandably horrifying his wife. He openly mocked her when she gave public recitations and was insulting to her at home. When he had accompanied her on a press trip to San Francisco in January 1892 – Mrs Leslie having a drawing room on the train and Willie being confined to a section 'just outside' – she told an interviewer that she was not taking the name of Wilde until 'by dint of industry and perseverance he makes a name in the world of American journalism as I have'. She ended the interview with a shrewd hit at Willie by remarking, 'I really think I should have married Oscar.'[6]

Early that year Jane had become concerned for Oscar's health, writing anxiously to say that she hoped he was better: 'Do keep well and strong.' Oscar had indeed felt ill after the strain of the rehearsals, which he had attended every day, although the success of the play had swept his malaise away.

And there were other diversions: it was at this time that Bosie introduced Oscar to the world of boy prostitutes. After going down to Torquay briefly to finish *Salome*, Oscar spent much of January and February that year staying at the Albemarle Hotel ('the drains at Tite Street have gone wrong'). He recklessly invited several youths to visit him there and was openly seen with them. One of those was Edward Shelley, a clerk at the publisher John Lane's office. Shelley went to the first night of *Lady Windermere's Fan*, sitting next to Pierre Louÿs, the French writer who helped correct *Salome*, and was one of twelve boys whom Oscar was later in court accused of soliciting to commit sodomy – in Shelley's case on 26 February, a week after the play opened. Almost all the allegations regarding these boys related to dates in 1892 and 1893.

Victorians were careful to keep their liaisons secret. If Oscar had concealed his casual affairs, he would have avoided prosecution. Instead he got a perverse satisfaction from being seen publicly wining and dining his latest young man, making no attempt to hide his amorous intentions. Such impudent flouting of the moral laws of the time made many privately hope for his downfall. The narrow attitudes of the period were underlined by Ben Webster, on tour with *Lady Windermere's Fan* that summer, when he wrote to his wife from Liverpool to say, 'The play went exceedingly well . . . I actually got some laughs; though my remark that "the devotion of a married woman is a thing no married man knows anything about" is still received with the stony silence of moral disapprobation.'[7]

On 22 February 1892, the *Daily Telegraph* published a poor review of the play ('the play is a bad one but it will succeed'). The review was anonymous and has been attributed to Willie who, staring at disaster in his own marriage, may well have grudged Oscar his success. But he could not have been present at the first night as he was in America.

Jane wrote to tell Oscar that Willie and his wife were thinking of

coming over for a visit and Willie would be going to Moytura. 'I think
that would be right and proper,' she said, adding that she had just
received a cheque for £20 for the Moytura rent, the first payment that
year. Oscar must have lent his brother some money before he left for
America as Jane went on to assure him that Willie 'hoped to be able
to pay his debt to you *soon*, or some of it at all events'.

It must have been a serious disappointment to Willie when he found
that his wife not only intended to keep tight control over her fortune,
but soon took the wise step of reducing his allowance. He was forced
to earn some money by writing four articles, called 'Willie Wilde's
Letter', in the *New York Recorder*. The first, appearing on 20 March
1892, began in typical Willie style: 'At the very serious risk of permanently imperiling that hard-earned reputation for cultivated
indolence bestowed on me so lavishly by certain candid critics, I must
perforce acknowledge that the *Recorder* has with a falconer's voice
lured this tasseled gentle back to the old familiar paths that he fears
may ultimately lead to honest toil.'

Mrs Leslie was to say of Willie that if he had only deigned to work
in her office, she would have given him a good place on her payroll.
Unfortunately, all Willie did was 'spend his time at the Century Club
and inform people that what New York lacked was a leisured class and
that he, Willie Wilde, was determined to introduce such a class'.[8]
After only five months of marriage, Mrs Leslie had had enough of
Willie. She told her friends, regarding their planned visit to England
in the spring of that year, 'I'm taking Willie over, but I'll not bring
Willie back.'[9] Once in England, she asked her London solicitors to
have Willie watched by a private enquiry agent. It turned out to be the
start of her divorce proceedings.

In a letter to Oscar shortly after the start of *Lady Windermere's Fan*,
Jane wrote optimistically that a woman friend had told her 'that you
will make a *fortune* by a successful play. She expects *thousands* will
come into the family and that we shall be located soon in Belgrave
Square, all on your play!' Oscar, who had refused George Alexander's
offer of £1,000 for the play and had instead opted for taking a
percentage, did indeed make £7,000 in its first year.

But Jane was not to see Belgrave Square. Oscar, up to now, although
careless about money, had not been a spendthrift: but during the year
1892, the expenses of his changing lifestyle grew. That spring, Bosie
asked Oscar's help over a blackmailing letter and Oscar paid the
sum required, £100. In June he agreed to pay the costs of publishing

John Gray's book, *Silverpoints*; and the following month he went to
Bad Homburg in Germany with Bosie, whose bills he paid. Bosie's
extravagance at Oscar's expense became staggering: after losing when
gambling, he would telegraph Oscar to deposit the amount owing in
his bank account. In *De Profundis*, Oscar was to write to Bosie that
'When I tell you that between the autumn of 1892 and the date of my
imprisonment I spent with you and on you more than £5,000 in actual
money, irrespective of the bills I incurred, you will have some idea of
the sort of life on which you insisted.'[10]

Constance wrote to her brother in June 1892 to say that although
Oscar had been ordered to Carlsbad by his doctors to take the
waters for his health, he had decided to stay in London because Sarah
Bernhardt had agreed to play the leading part in his play *Salome*.
Rehearsals stopped abruptly, however, when the play was banned by
the Lord Chamberlain because it contained religious characters.
Furious, Oscar threatened to take out French citizenship and go and
live in France. 'Mr Oscar Wilde Angry', said the papers, quoting Oscar
as saying, in echo of his mother, 'I have English friends, to whom I
am deeply attached, but as to the English, I do not love them.'[11] He
left immediately to visit Bad Homburg with Bosie. Constance wrote
with amusement to her brother to say that he was now under a strict
regime of drinking the waters, getting up at 7.30 a.m. and smoking
hardly any cigarettes; 'I only wish I was there to see it.'[12]

Jane was in lower spirits, perhaps because she had cancelled her
salons. She told Oscar, 'I have no *Saturdays* now – I am too weary of
life and like *Rest* and settling all my papers and books.' She was
irritated by an annual pension regulation which required her 'having
to send for a man to see if I am alive' and was concerned at having
no further news from Willie in America.[13]

In August and September Oscar went to a farmhouse in Norfolk to
work on *A Woman of No Importance* – a play he had promised to
Herbert Beerbohm Tree, the manager of the Haymarket Theatre. Bosie
visited him there and their relationship intensified over the next three
months, when they were hardly ever apart. It was in January 1893 that
Oscar wrote the notorious letter to him that began 'My Own Boy, Your
sonnet is quite lovely, and it is a marvel that those rose-leaf lips of
yours should have been made no less for music of song than for
madness of kisses. Your slim gilt soul walks between passion and
poetry . . .'[14] – the letter which was to feature so prominently in the
sequel of events.

Yet despite their passionate attachment, Oscar and Bosie continued to have transient affairs. Bosie had met a 17-year-old clerk, Alfred Wood, and that February passed him on to Oscar. Oscar met Wood at the Café Royal and the two went back to Tite Street together, Constance being away. Bosie continued to see Wood himself and gave him some old clothes, in the pockets of which were some letters from Oscar. Wood and two confederates then blackmailed Oscar for the return of these letters and were given £30 for them. But the letter referring to the 'rose-leaf lips' was kept by Wood who made a further attempt to extort money from Oscar. It failed and Wood then merely returned the letter to Oscar. However, Bosie's father, Lord Queensberry, managed to get hold of copies of some of the letters, including that one, which was later read out in court. Oscar was to deny that it was open to any unclean interpretation.

The French version of *Salome* was published in February 1893 and Jane told him, 'It is so audacious a thing to write in French – I hope you sent a copy to Swinburne,' adding, 'You really might give a small talk on *Salome* here, next Saturday, and show its inner meaning.' She also asked him to cash two cheques for her, explaining, 'One is an *Irish* cheque and they [the tradespeople] are all strong against the Irish specially and won't have it at all.'

By now Willie too had returned to England and she told Oscar that he was going off to the American Consulate to question some witnesses but, she said, 'will not resist the divorce . . . if you call on Tuesday you will get the latest.' She mentioned having heard from Constance who, having left the children in Oscar's care, was now in Florence on a European tour and about to go on to Switzerland, and added, 'I trust the dear children are well – Cyril must be quite a companion now.'[15]

Writing back to 'dear darling Constance', to thank her for her letter, Jane said affectionately, 'I trust God will keep and bless you and yours through all the parting weeks, when I am never to behold you.' She thanked Constance for enclosing some letters from the children, say-ing, 'Why Cyril is splendid, a capital hand and excellent orthography and little Vyvyan is sweet.' She went on to tell her that she 'was daily expecting the legal announcement of the *divorce*. Meantime, all Willie's allowance is stopped. However, he has been working well and has got an offer to be Editor of *Piccadilly*. I wish him to accept but he seems disinclined.'[16] After keeping Constance up to date with the latest gossip ('They say that Prince George will *not* marry Princess May and he dislikes all idea of any marriage') she told her the main news, as far as she was concerned, which was that the publishers Ward & Downey had taken her new book, *Social Studies*, 'and are much pleased with it'. It was to come out in the Easter of 1893.

Social Studies was a collection of Jane's published articles. Containing also two stories translated from Spanish and German, it was an eclectic mixture. Her freely paraphrased study of a poem by Victor Hugo, 'The Vision of the Vatican', sat a trifle uneasily with 'Social Graces', in which, among other subjects, she discusses the charm of the French mouth. Jane liked tackling large issues and this collection included 'The Destiny of Humanity', 'Genius and Marriage' and 'Irish Leaders and Martyrs'.

Though her arguments could be serious – in 'The Poet as Teacher', for instance, she discussed the powerful educational influence of poetry, particularly on children – her sense of fun still showed through. Much of her essay on 'American Women' was devoted to caricaturing Englishwomen – though considering how rarely she went out, it is surprising she knew any: '[English] girls are dull, diffident and monotonous, with their pale eyes, pale hair and sealskin jackets, one might gather a thousand, or fifty thousand of them together, and they would all be found precisely alike.' American women, she claimed, having heard Oscar on the subject, 'are learned as well as being admirable housekeepers. They can extract square roots as well as pickle them . . .'

In her essay on 'Venus Victrix' she gently mocked the 'model woman' for the way she 'carries a cigarette in her mouth, a whip at the end of her parasol, a stiletto in her fan, and in her hand is the roll of resolutions she is to enforce at the next public meeting upon a crowd of men'.

Jane's views could still startle her friends. In another essay on 'Suitability of Dress', she decreed that 'Black is unlovely and unbecoming to everyone, especially to English women . . . with the murky grey of the atmosphere . . . nothing can be more dreary at afternoon teas than rows of opaque, black bundles along the walls of a drawing-room, like masses of hummocky ice.'

Maria La Touche, who had known Jane in Dublin, wrote to an acquaintance to say, 'I've also been reading *Social Studies* by Lady Wilde. There are some good things in the book, but she says we ought none of us to wear black when we are in mourning! The older and uglier we are the more it becomes our duty, in her opinion, to contribute agreeable colour and pleasant light to our surroundings. And there should not be black draperies grouped about a drawing-room. I am not converted, or else I might wear a green and yellow bonnet, with a pink-satin cloak, and a sky-blue gown, scarlet shoes and gloves, so as to give lots of agreeable colour to Carnalway Church!'[17] More coolly, the *Athenaeum*'s reviewer, on 12 August 1893, considered the book 'a clever set of essays, not with much substance, but showing a good deal of observation' and rapped Jane's knuckles over occasional lapses of grammar.

While Constance was on her European tour, Oscar and the two children had been down in Devon staying at Babbacombe Cliff, a large, rambling house belonging to Lady Mount-Temple, a distant cousin of Constance's. There they were joined by Bosie. Oscar went up to London occasionally in response to Jane's letters, one of which read: 'You really *must* come to *your mother's* receptions, surely. You won't have me long and you might give me some time now . . .' It was emotional blackmail. Jane exerted stronger pressure on Oscar than Constance ever dared and sometimes demanded more from her son than he was prepared to give. But neither Oscar nor Willie ever expressed a word of criticism about their mother.

In this instance, Oscar quickly retrieved his position and on 30 March Jane wrote, 'Dear, darling Oscar, your visit made me very happy last night – and do believe in my love for my brilliant son Oscar and my warm sense of his kind thought and generous consideration of La Madre.'[18] Willie – now once again living with her – had her love too, but showed her less generous consideration. 'As to the American business,' Jane told Oscar, 'it is a crisis and a catastrophe which I cannot help thinking of.' She cheered up when Willie was offered £10 a week to write two articles from London for an American paper 'and expects to make £30 a week soon'.

Oscar was beginning to show signs of wear and tear. Max Beerbohm told a friend that he had seen him 'in a hopeless state of intoxication' and was afraid he was drinking far more than he ought. 'He has deteriorated very much in appearance: his cheeks being quite a dark purple and fat to a fault. I think he will die of apoplexy on the first night of the play.'[19] The actress Elizabeth Robins, meeting Oscar after a lapse of time, was also shocked by his appearance, commenting that she was sure that if Oscar cut himself he would 'bleed absinthe and clotted truffles'.[20]

A Woman of No Importance opened on 19 April 1893 at the Haymarket Theatre. It was a glittering first night. A number of politicians including Balfour and Chamberlain were there and Oscar wore a white waistcoat and a bunch of small lilies in his buttonhole. The Prince of Wales went to the second performance and chatted to Oscar at the end. Jane was even more ecstatic than before, writing to him a few days later to say:

> You have had a brilliant success! and I am so happy. I receive many notes of congratulations . . . *the Prince* [of Wales] was very nice and you ought really to go to the Levee. I hope you have all the notices. I have only seen half a dozen or so – they all want *more plot* and more human feeling. So in your part, strengthen the plot and heighten the human interest. I had a crowd here on Saturday and many had seen the play and nothing else was talked of . . . I would so like to see you. You are now the great sensation of London and I am very proud of you – you have made your name and taken your place and now hold a distinguished position in the circle of intellects – *that* all your critics acknowledge tho' they are a little sharp on some points.
>
> Take care of yourself and your health and keep clear of suppers and late hours and champagne. Your health and *calm* of mind is most important.[21]

Oscar ignored her advice. In May he paid a lengthy visit to Bosie, who was up at Oxford and for once not playing truant, and was involved in a non-stop round of festive dinners. Jane wrote euphorically to tell him the *Telegraph* had said his play was the greatest success of the Haymarket. 'You have indeed a glorious triumph and your name is now made. Go on, achieve more conquests while the vivid power of youth is upon you.' She told him that 'When I see you knighted, I shall be happy,' adding, 'I have now so many cares, and the moving must begin, and my intellect is all too dark to go and enjoy your brilliant play as yet.' The move she referred to was her return to 146 Oakley Street. She had told Oscar early that year that No. 146 'must be put in entire repair – foundation sinking', and while it was being done she had moved to No. 26 Oakley Street.

On 25 May the evidence collected against Willie by the private enquiry agent was presented to Mrs Leslie's solicitors. There was a clear case for divorce on grounds of drunkenness and adultery. Mrs Leslie's domestic staff corroborated allegations that Willie was prone to 'gross and vulgar intemperance and to violent and profane abuse of and cruel conduct to the plaintiff'. He was also charged with consorting

with 'women of disreputable character' in places 'of low resort'.[22]
W. B. Yeats later reported Willie as commenting, at the time of Oscar's
trial, 'Thank God my vices were decent.'

On 10 June 1893 Willie was formally divorced by Mrs Leslie, who
announced that he 'was of no use to me either by day or by night'. Her
marriage, she said, had been 'a blunder'.[23] Jane was wretched at the
whole affair but laughed over the newspaper reports of the divorce, telling Oscar that 'Most are very amusing – one is headed in large capitals
TIRED OF WILLIE and then a synopsis of the divorce case is given. All
because "Willie Won't Get Up and Won't Work". Mrs Leslie has *stopped
all his allowance* – so he has nothing now but what he earns.'[24]

Sherard believed it had been a disastrous marriage for Willie. 'He
went out to America a fine, brilliantly clever man, quite one of the
ablest writers on the press . . . [Mrs Frank Leslie] sent him back to
England a nervous wreck, with an exhausted brain and a debilitated
frame . . . it soon became apparent that his power for sustained effort
was gone.' Oscar used to explain Willie's occasional absences by saying
he had been on an 'alcoholiday'. But it was said of Willie with reason
now that he had gone to America a drinker and returned to England
a drunkard.[25] Oscar when he saw him asked if his marriage had
indeed broken up. 'No, it has broken down,' said Willie. 'What is the
difference?' said Oscar. 'She is up, I am down,' was the reply.[26]

Although Oscar was irritated at Willie failing to come out of his
marriage solvent, the brothers were on perfectly good terms. Oscar
wrote to him in July from a house in Goring on Thames, which Bosie
had liked and persuaded Oscar to rent. Willie wanted to come down,
unaware that Bosie was there, and Oscar told him regretfully that he
couldn't put him up that Saturday, as 'people are staying here and
things are tedious'. He added that he was sorry Willie had missed the
regatta's fireworks and told him solemnly that he was 'greatly distressed
to hear you and the fascinating Dan [an unknown friend] are smoking
American cigarettes – you really must not do anything so horrid –
charming people should smoke gold-tipped cigarettes or die – so I
enclose you a small piece of paper – for which reckless Bankers may
give you gold – as I don't want you to die. With best love . . .'[27]

Jane needed some small pieces of paper too. She wrote to Oscar to say,
'I am submerged with claims. Today came bill for £2 10s for repairs of
water pipes. So I venture to ask you for the balance due – £2 10s – on the
pension quarter. This will just pay the water pipes.' She told him she had
'given up *the Saturdays* till October and am all alone'.

Oscar turned up at the last night of *A Woman of No Importance*, on 16 August 1893, defiantly wearing clusters of vine leaves and accompanied by Aubrey Beardsley, Robbie Ross and Bosie. Late that month he went off to Dinard, this time alone. 'I required rest and freedom from the terrible strain of your companionship,' he was to tell Bosie in *De Profundis*.

Jane wrote to him, very upset, on 28 August and yet again on 9 September, telling him that she had received a summons from the agent who had leased her the property at No. 26 Oakley Street, claiming money for 'injuries' to the house. Jane disputed the amount claimed, and told Oscar he was not to pay it. 'I would rather go into court, *on oath* . . . the charges made are all *utterly absurd* . . . it would grieve me to think you were so fraudulently treated.' She added, 'Come and see me when you can – I am poorly – but always better for a flash of intellect, so light me up. Come in the *evening* if you can as I am not down till late.'

Her indignant twelve-page reply to the agent refuting the charges shows the conditions in which she, Willie and a maidservant had lived at the rented property. The house, she said, had not been cleaned down for her occupation, after having been unlet for eight months. 'The kitchen was in a particularly bad state of *rust* and *neglect* . . . none of the articles named "Missing" were taken away by Lady Wilde or her servant.' Of the three bedrooms, she pointed out that two were never occupied and in the third, the carpet had been very shabby, and had not been made worse in any way: 'the fire place never touched or injured – no fires lit [this was winter] . . . blankets *never used*, Lady Wilde had her own . . . muslin curtains *very soiled* and no clean ones were put up . . . as Lady Wilde only stayed by the week . . . the table with leather top *never used or stood upon* . . . only the knob of the wardrobe was broken off and glued on for 6*d*.'

The carpets and rugs on the landing, Jane insisted, were very shabby on arrival, she had never used the hip bath and had only entered the drawing room three times during her stay. 'Lady Wilde had the piano tuned at cost of 3/6*d* – but it was never used except once . . . the stairs [had] *grease spots* for as all the bells were broken in the house, candles had to be carried up and down.' While living there, Jane had cancelled her salons and therefore, she explained, the red curtains had never been touched and neither had the hall mats, 'as there was no traffic through the hall . . . so few people came to the house'. The kitchen was in a particularly bad state: 'all the saucepans rusted and *no oven* . . . Lady

Wilde brought over her own coffee pot, kettle, china, glass, cutlery, spoons and jugs. No fish kettle or frying pans were used . . . she considers that the payment of 25 guineas for two months' occupation of the house by only three persons ought to be quite sufficient.'[28]

Oscar nevertheless settled the account and Jane wrote to him at Goring on Thames on 18 September to say, 'Best and most generous of sons! I am *truly grateful* for your great kindness and your letter was a most pleasant surprise – to find it all settled! This was truly something though I must regret all the money I have cost you and which you have paid so freely and generously. Again and again I thank you dear Oscar – you have always been my *best and truest help* in everything.'[29]

She told him she was glad 'dear Cyril' was with him and that Willie was with her, 'in high spirits and writing order' and with his eye already turning to other women. 'He seems bent on Lily Lees – and who can say how all will end?' said Jane. Sophie (Lily) Lees was Irish, the youngest daughter of a certain William Lees of Dublin. Willie had only recently met her but where he met her and whether Jane knew the family is unknown.

The day before she wrote, Willie was formally expelled from New York's Lotus Club for non-payment of dues. The report in the *New York Times* of 18 September 1893, headlined 'Mr William Wilde Forgot a Little Matter of $14', explained in large type that Willie was 'Known to Fame as Oscar, the Aesthete's, Brother, as Mrs Frank Leslie's Ex-Husband, as Having Been "Born Tired," and as Chronically Willing to Drink All Night at Somebody Else's Expense'.

The paper went on to quote a club member, who said Willie was, beyond question, 'the very laziest man that ever went around in shoe leather'. Willie, the Lotus Club member then revealed, 'owed most of his celebrity to his height and his easy-going manner and, above all, to his excellent imitations of his brother, the Aesthete. These latter were simply killing. You know, Oscar had a fat, potato-choked sort of voice and to hear Willie counterfeit that voice and recite parodies of his brother's poetry while he struck appropriate and aesthetic attitudes was a rare treat.' Willie's jeering impersonation of his brother revealed his impotent anger at Oscar's outstanding success. Satire was the only weapon available to Willie and he used it mercilessly.

The *New York Times* soon reached London and the account of his brother's impersonations of him appalled Oscar when he read it. He was already contemptuous of Willie's idleness and constant drinking and his battening upon their mother with whom he had returned to live. Constance was later to write about how Oscar 'used to go on about Willie's extravagance and about his cruelty in forcing his mother to give him money'. Willie seemed to have picked up his father's worst habits: apart from drinking heavily, he was equally careless of his appearance. Oscar said cuttingly of him, 'He sponges on everyone but himself.'

After the newspaper account, there was an open breach between the brothers. Oscar regarded Willie's parody of him as treachery, while Willie failed to understand why Oscar felt deeply betrayed merely at being mimicked at the Lotus Club. He told a friend that the only trouble between him and his brother 'was caused by Oscar's inordinate vanity in the period before his conviction', and that in his opinion Oscar had surrounded himself 'with a gang of parasites who praised him all day long, and to whom he used to give his cigarette-cases, breast pins, etc. in return for their sickening flattery. No one, not even I, his brother, dared offer any criticism on his works without offending him.'[30]

In many ways, Willie was at that time a darker image of Oscar. Max Beerbohm, writing in September to Reggie Turner, his friend and regular correspondent, said, 'Broadstairs are *very triste* indeed and I long for London; my only consolation has been Willie Wilde, the brother of Oscar, of whom I have seen a great deal. He is very vulgar and unwashed and inferior, but if I shut my eyes I can imagine his voice to be the voice of Oscar. Who was it that said, "Scratch Oscar and you will find Willie?" It is a very pregnant saying: if Oscar had not been such a success as he has been, he would be the image of Willie. It was Willie, by the way, who was found by his host in the smoking room, filling his pockets with handfuls of cigars – wasn't it dreadful.'[31]

On 30 September 1893, a friend of Jane's, a Miss Mynous, wrote dramatically to Constance Wilde to tell her that she had heard from her friend Mrs Faithful about a terrible state of affairs, and that 'Lady Wilde will utterly break down and die if something is not done to prevent the tormenting worry. It seems that Miss Lees has confessed that she and Mr W. Wilde have been living together as man and wife at Malvern and Broadstairs and the wretched woman has actually asked Mrs –– to give her a powder to prevent the birth of a baby! And she says he has treated her with great brutality . . .' She added that Willie 'is always asking his mother for money and stamps his foot and swears at her if she hesitates'. Lady Wilde, she said, had asked her to call, but when she did so, 'I was sorry to find her in bed and suffering . . . you

and Mr Oscar are so good to her, but she conceals the state of affairs
. . . the house is not safe and wholesome, Lady Wilde is always being
asked for money and *worried to death* . . . please destroy this letter.'[32]

Constance instead promptly showed the letter to Oscar, to whom it
was the last straw. He sent an angry letter to Willie and also wrote to
his mother. On 8 October Jane replied soothingly, trying as usual to
calm matters between her sons. 'It was Miss Lowe told Henriette who
told Miss Mynous who then spoke to Mrs Faithful and wrote to you,'
she told Oscar. 'This is how it all travelled – however, I am not at all
miserable about the affair, for *I don't believe it* . . . I believe Miss L
[Lily Lees] set up the whole story just to try and force on the marriage
which will *never be* now – Willie was very angry with her . . .'[33]

Willie wrote to apologize to Oscar. Jane, in his defence, wrote again,
saying, 'So I think there is no occasion for you to be angry with him
and this sad dissonance between you and Willie is very distressing to
me. I would rejoice much to see you both on friendly terms. Do try
and be more kind and conciliatory with Willie and help him with your
advice. This would do him good, but coldness and hostility do no good
to anyone.' She also told Oscar that she had shown Willie the American
cutting 'and he says it is *all lies*. He *never* used the words about you
and *never* tried to imitate your recital of a poem. It is all lies, lies,
lies – indeed, Willie has always a good word for you and I never heard
him say anything against you in my life.'[34]

Oscar, however, had finished with Willie and wrote as much to his
mother. Jane replied that she had read his letter carefully, but begged
him to reconsider. Her very lengthy letter was high on pathos as she
told him how desolate she was to know that when he and Willie met
in society, they were hostile and did not exchange a word, causing
sneering watchers to make sarcastic remarks:

Already several have done so and it is commonly said that *you hate*
your brother. Now this does *not* make me happy. Nor to find that
you will not come here for fear of meeting him . . . I would suggest
quite a different line of conduct on your part. Try and *do Willie
good* – be a friend to him, speak truly and wisely, but *kindly*. He
is very susceptible to kindness and he would greatly appreciate your
taking interest in him. He feels your coldness most bitterly . . . *Come*
here, hold out yr hand to Willie and say, Let us be friends as brothers
should. Give him good advice . . . He is reckless and extravagant,
preach to him, but do it *kindly*. Willie has some good points and

do try and help him to be better. I am *miserable* at the present position of my sons . . . give up all bitter thoughts . . . try and do him good by kindly advice and live as brothers: it is a sacred relationship . . .

She tried to alleviate Oscar's anger at Willie's financial demands on her by adding, 'I pity Willie in this that he does not get a sixpence from Moytura and so I am content to give him what I can. At my death he will at least have something – but till then I try and help him a little . . . He has a high opinion of you but feels bitterly your open and profound hatred . . . *He has never injured you.* Why should you hate him? If he has taken help from me in money, why that *does not injure you* and I don't want you to hate Willie on my account.'

Putting on the pressure, she begged him, 'Do as I ask – come to the house here and be *friendly* and let the past bitterness die. Otherwise, *I shall die* of utter despair. I cannot live and see you and Willie hostile to each other and I know that you could if you chose greatly influence Willie for good by simple friendly kindness. You will both have to meet by my coffin and I want you to meet before that in friendly feeling. Come then and offer him your hand in good faith and begin a new course of action. Not insulting him by coldness before your friends . . . I shall hope to see you soon – if not I'll die of grief.'[35]

Karl Beckson points out, in a study of the antagonism between the two brothers,[36] that Jane clearly believed 'that the bad Willie needed the aid of the good Oscar'. It was a theme taken up by Oscar in *The Importance of Being Earnest*, which he was to write the following year: a play based on the brotherly relationship between the responsible Jack Worthing and the younger brother he invents, the idle wastrel Ernest.

There are decided echoes of Jane's letter in the text. When Jack's ward Cecily intervenes with him to forgive his brother, who is being impersonated by Jack's friend Algy Moncrieff, she says, 'However badly he may have behaved to you in the past he is still your brother. You couldn't be so heartless as to disown him.' She then makes two references to handshaking. The first is, 'I'll tell him to come out. And you will shake hands with him, won't you, Uncle Jack?' Then, again, 'Uncle Jack, you are not going to refuse your own brother's hand?' Jack's reply is: 'Nothing will induce me to take his hand.' Algy later says, 'Of course I admit that the faults were all on my side. But I must say that I think that Brother John's coldness is to me peculiarly painful.'

In a fourth act, later dropped, Algy is even arrested for debt – an always likely happening with Willie, who was constantly borrowing money. Jack says to him, 'Personally, if you ask me, I don't see any use in having a brother. As for paying your bill, I have not the smallest intention of doing anything of the kind.' In reply to Algy's remark that 'No gentleman ever has any money,' the solicitor replies, 'My experience is that it is usually relatives who pay.' In a comment which might be said to summarize Oscar's present attitude to Willie, Gwendolen, Jack Worthing's intended, remarks, 'I have never heard any man mention his brother. The subject seems distasteful to most men.'

Jane's efforts to reconcile her two sons were in vain: they had parted for good. Yet an undated letter exists from Willie to Oscar which shows that he had no wish to break with his brother. It is a sad, revealing letter, poignantly showing Willie's affection and his need of Oscar's friendship:

> My darling Boz, forgive me. You have no notion of the fuss and fever I am in till all this is done – we have hot tempers *all* of us, but we love each other – God grant it – all through. I did *not* know, when you spoke to me of 'annoyance' that you had not heard the reason of there being no matinee today and I thought it selfish of you to be annoyed – it was stupid of me – I cried when I came up here like a baby.
>
> I am much more lonely in the world than you are Oscar and I fret over things – that is all . . . a quarrel would be a device of the devil – I am older than you are and my words are the wrong ones . . . and so forgive me for the sake of the love we have for each other . . . affectionately always. Willie.[37]

In the late autumn of 1893, Oscar, working hard on his new play, *An Ideal Husband*, was made constantly aware from his mother's letters of her near-bankrupt situation. The relatively small amounts she asked him for were an undoubted lifesaver when they came. 'How good and generous you are!' she wrote on 16 October 1893, thanking him for a cheque. 'All my help comes from you, ever since you began an income in America you have always thought of me with the most loving consideration and I am most grateful and most gratified at this proof of your affection and interest . . . La Devotissima Madre.'

Oscar paid many of his mother's accounts. There was a small lacquer rack hanging over the mantelpiece in the downstairs room of Oakley

Street, into which all the bills were put. 'Whenever Oscar called on his mother, before going upstairs to her private suite, he invariably used to enter this front room, cross over rapidly to the fireplace, and examine the unpaid bills. He had sufficient experience of financial emergencies to be able to decide which of Lady Wilde's liabilities it was urgent to discharge, and then and there on the marble mantelpiece the necessary cheque would be written.'[38]

Seen through her doting eyes, Oscar was her financial saviour and she was pathetically grateful to him. Yet knowing his mother's increasingly desperate situation, and fond of her as he was, it seems heartless that he continued to spend so much on Bosie when giving his mother a regular allowance would have made all the difference to her financially. Jane was a proud woman, however, and may have demurred. While Bosie talked of the 'sweet humiliation' of asking Oscar for money, Jane hated having to do so. Her poverty, however, and the ever-present threat of the bailiffs, gave her no option. As she once wrote to Oscar: 'Dare I ask for a little help? I know it is very dreadful to ask you to give or lend money – but I am helpless. £5 or £10 would be salvation to me . . . I am poorly and have not left my room.' On another occasion, she wrote: 'I am in much trouble, overwhelmed with threatening letters for rent . . . and nothing to meet them except my grant and pension . . . I therefore reluctantly ask you for the sum of £10 to help me over the difficulties and I shall be ever grateful.' She went on to tell him that she was happy he was profiting from his work. 'It is reported that you have made thousands from *The Fan*. I hope so. You deserve it all. You are an earnest worker and keep up the honour and glory of the family.'[39]

But Bosie's demands were fast eating away the money that Oscar made. Once, after Oscar, Constance and the boys came back to London from a stay at the Goring on Thames house, the butcher refused to give them a joint until they had paid his bill and Oscar had to drive round in a hansom and settle up.[40]

Jane faced a further financial crisis in December 1893 when a writ was served over a debt of Willie's. Oscar, without sufficient funds to meet this, could think of no solution other than cabling Mrs Leslie for a loan. Jane wrote anxiously to Oscar, hoping the matter would be settled quickly, 'for I dread the bailiff coming in'. Mrs Leslie paid up but wrote to Jane crossly to say that she had made a loss on cashing up securities 'to take up Willie's note' and to make matters worse had also received 'two of the rudest and most under-bred letters from Willie

. . . who put *you* forward to ask a service from me and then proceeded to pelt me with abuse'. She told Jane she would no longer send newspaper clippings to 'amuse you in your desolate life, as this furnishes food for Willie's malevolence'. As to the invitation to holiday on the Continent this had not been seriously meant: 'I should as soon think of hoping to move the Obelisk from its Embankment home as to tempt you from yours when you will not go out for even a drive once in a year.'[41]

This was true: Jane now rarely left her house. She was 72, and the struggle to manage financially had taken its toll. Oscar was away so much, and, fond though she was of Willie, having him back again to live with her was an added burden. In an interview she gave that autumn she spoke about the visual susceptibility which caused her to shun strong light, and the physical weakness which made walking tiring. 'I have not been out of doors for weeks,' she said. '. . . I much prefer my friends coming to see me to going to see them. Then if I can only get a good book and a good fire I am perfectly happy – I want nothing more. In society you are never given the divine thoughts that great writers give you. Who is there that can speak as Ralph Waldo Emerson speaks to you?'[42]

Willie, according to Max Beerbohm, found on his return to England after the divorce that 'the *Telegraph* no longer wanted him. He began doing drama criticism for unimportant papers and writing general articles in which he would mention tradespeople and get perquisites.' Beerbohm remembered meeting Willie once at a restaurant where the waiter, an old friend of them both, was called Bismarck. Willie asked Beerbohm to lend him ten shillings and when Beerbohm did so, Willie in a flush of affluence decided to order something and whistled for Bismarck. The action annoyed the waiter, who told Willie never to whistle for him again: he wasn't a dog. 'Everything went out of Willie,' Beerbohm related. 'He began to stammer out apologies to the waiter. "But, my dear fellow," he kept mumbling, "my dear fellow . . . I didn't mean . . . I meant nothing . . ." It was awful, you know – that sudden capitulation. In that moment, I believe, he really saw, and perhaps for the first time, the dingy failure of his life; even behind the bulwark of that ten shillings, he saw himself facing tragedy and defeat, he saw that there was nothing ahead for him, that he would never recover, that he would never find a clearing in the shambles he had made for himself. He saw the end, and I saw it, too. It was very painful.'[43]

Jane at least had some good news: she was given £25 for selling the rights of *Sidonia the Sorceress* to William Morris. That December he produced a superb new edition of the book, with a vellum cover and ingenious illustrations, printed by the Kelmscott Press. Jane wrote to him to say that she had received 'with extreme pride and pleasure the splendid artistic copy of *Sidonia*', adding, 'My son, W. C. K. Wilde is enchanted with it, for he has the artistic soul and fully appreciates the delicate beauty of the lettering, the binding and general arrangement.'[44] Jane clung to her belief in Willie's artistic soul, ignoring his more obvious physical deterioration.

A calling card from Jane, scribbled to Miss May Morris and asking her to a Saturday *conversazione*, shows that Jane was continuing, as of old, to hold her salons.[45] Gertrude Atherton, the novelist, went to visit her with Henriette Corkran. Henriette took with her a large plum cake, explaining that 'Lady Wilde is frightfully poor, her sons do little or nothing for her. Her friends don't dare offer her money or real food, for she's very proud, so we always take her a cake, which we beg her to "try as we have made it ourselves". I only hope the gas isn't turned off, and you will be able to see her.'[46]

Gertrude Atherton was another of those writers whose memoirs were written over forty years after the event in a climate hostile to the Wildes. She called Jane a 'crumbling wreck' forgotten by time – as now Atherton is herself. After commenting dismissively on the eight-foot-square drawing room (the rooms in Oakley Street were decidedly larger than this) and the 'miserable slavey' who ushered them in, she drew a fairly waspish picture of Jane:

> . . . the strange figure that rose as we entered received us with the grand air. She might have been a queen graciously giving a private audience. In her day she must have been a beautiful and stately woman; she was still stately, heaven knew, but her old face was gaunt and grey and seamed with a million criss-crossed lines, etched by care, sorrow and (no doubt) hunger. Her dress was a relic of the 'sixties, grey satin trimmed with ragged black fringe over a large hoop-skirt. As her hair was black it was presumably a wig and it was dressed very high, held in place by a Spanish comb from which depended a black lace mantilla. She pressed her withered lips to Henriette's red cheek, and extended to me a claw-like hand . . . She received the cake graciously, but put it aside without a glance. Poor thing, no doubt she devoured it whole as soon as we left; but her manner was lofty and detached, almost complacent. She always remains in my mind as a leaning tower of courage.[47]

Early in 1894, Jane's financial position, if possible, worsened as her allowance from Mrs Leslie stopped. Her conviction that Willie would not marry Lily Lees proved wrong: the two married in a register office mid-January. Willie had chosen better this time. Lily was a kind woman, who was fond of him and was less fearsomely ambitious for him than his first wife. It was hard to see what Lily herself gained from the marriage, as Willie was now drinking steadily. She was later to admit sadly that he had not lived up to his potential.

On 4 February 1894, while Oscar was in Brighton working on *An Ideal Husband*, Jane wrote saying she needed to talk to him about family matters:

> Willie is *married* to Miss Lees – though not yet publicly announced as her stepmother objects . . . and they look forward to come *to live here* in March next *with me*, but as they will have no income, I am alarmed at the prospect – and I feel so bewildered and utterly done up that I would be glad to have a talk with you all about it.
>
> I am also dreadfully hard up as to income for Mrs Leslie has quite stopped the allowance and the loss of the £100 a year is very dreadful – I have ever so many bills to meet and unless I can get at least £30 to meet them I shall be utterly crushed – what is to be done? Willie is utterly useless – and now, just when my income has fallen so low, he announces the marriage and the whole burden of the household to fall upon me . . . Miss Lees has but £50 a year . . . she can give nothing to the house and Willie is always in a state of utter poverty. So all is left *upon me*.
>
> I sometimes think of taking apartments for myself and leaving the house and furniture for I have an immense dislike to sharing the house with Miss Lees, with whom I have nothing in common . . . The idea of having her here is quite distasteful to me . . . La Madre Dolorosa.[48]

Oscar was otherwise occupied. Within a week of her letter, *Salome* was published in English, with Aubrey Beardsley's compelling, erotic illustrations. The background had been stormy: the previous year, Oscar had asked Bosie to translate the play, which he had done that summer. But it was poorly done, Bosie's French proving inadequate, and his version was unacceptable to Oscar. Oscar had been obliged to alter much of it, and the two quarrelled violently over the translation, and much else, through late 1893 and the early months of 1894.

Jane wrote to Oscar again on 17 February, saying that she had had a threatening notice over the house rates and asking him to lend her £10, or at least £5. She mentioned that he appeared in the literary column of that day's *Telegraph* and added wistfully, 'Why don't you make as much as Pinero? You are more celebrated, yet he has made £40,000 by his plays.' Her finances hadn't improved by 29 March, when she wrote to Oscar to say, 'I am in dreadful financial difficulties and have literally not a shilling in the world . . . *could you advance me £20?*'

She was further upset by the continuing breach between her two sons. In the same letter she said, 'I am truly sorry to find that you and Willie meet as enemies. Is this to go on to my death? Not a cheering prospect for me to have my two sons at enmity and unable to meet at my deathbed.' She asked Oscar if he could not possibly write a few words to Willie offering once more to be friends. 'Can you not do it to oblige me? There need be no intimacy between you, but at least *social civility.*'[49]

The next day she wrote again to thank Oscar for his promise to give her £20, and told him she had now heard she would get no Moytura rent before mid-May. 'In fact I am plunged in total ruin for I owe two quarters rent already and I give up this house the end of June – so ends my eventful history. But again I must thank you for your ready help.' The day after she gratefully acknowledged the arrival of the £20.

For the last six months Oscar had been living in rooms at St James's Place in order to work. Bosie's emotional demands on him had become intolerable and he was deeply thankful when that spring Bosie left for Egypt. Oscar refused to answer any of his letters and Bosie was finally driven to approach his own mother to intercede for him with Oscar; and then even wrote to Constance begging her to get Oscar to write. Out of kindness, she did. In *De Profundis* Oscar wrote, 'Our friendship had always been a source of distress to her, not merely because she had never liked you personally, but because she saw how your continual companionship had altered me and not for the better; still, just as she had always been gracious and hospitable to you, so she could not bear the idea of my being in any way unkind . . .'

Oscar agreed to meet Bosie in Paris in March 1894 and there they became reconciled. On his return, Constance, keeping her brother up to date with her children's activities, told him that 'their father brought them lovely toys from Paris and Cyril is in the 7th heaven of joy with regiments of French and Algerian soldiers. He is so sweet and he says, "My father is the greatest man in the world." '[50]

Two days after Oscar and Bosie returned to London at the end of March, they lunched at the Café Royal and were there seen by Bosie's father, the Marquess of Queensberry. Angered already by their association, he wrote at once to his son to say, 'With my own eyes I saw you both in the most loathsome and disgusting relationship as expressed by your manner and expression. Never in my experience have I ever seen such a sight as that in your horrible features. No wonder people are talking as they are.' He told his son the relationship must end, 'or I will disown you and stop all money supplies'.[51] His son stoked his father's fury by sending him a telegram in reply saying, 'What a funny little man you are.'

The following month Jane resigned from the Irish Literary Society. Along with Oscar and Willie she had been a founding member, but she told W. B. Yeats that she could now no longer attend any meetings. She enclosed a copy of her book *Social Studies* for the library, so that members would not forget her. The committee refused to accept her resignation, however, and elected her an honorary member. Thanking them, Jane wrote on 13 April 1894 to say that she much regretted that her 'very uncertain health' would prevent her from going to the lectures.[52]

Oscar went to Paris briefly at the end of April 1894, then on to Florence where he had arranged to meet Bosie. He returned to London in June. André Gide, who came across Oscar by chance in Florence, found an unattractive change in him. He wrote, 'One felt that there was less tenderness in his looks, that there was something harsh in his laughter, and a wild madness in his joy. He seemed at the same time to be sure of pleasing and less ambitious to succeed therein. He had grown reckless, hardened and conceited . . .'[53]

But Jane, writing to Oscar on 8 June to thank him gratefully for his generous present of £5, as well as a gift of some excellent champagne, saw her son through a mother's loving eyes and ended her letter, 'Dear Oscar, my love and thanks. I hope to see you soon – and you never looked so perfectly well, young and handsome.'

That May, Constance and Oscar decided to send their two sons away to boarding school. Cyril, now aged nine, was sent to a rather spartan school at Haywards Heath in Sussex, which prepared boys for a naval career while Vyvyan, seven, went to a preparatory school at Broadstairs in Kent. Both were reasonably happy, but it left Constance alone at Tite Street with even more time on her hands.

Jane's own grasp on life was weakening. Writing to Bosie in July

1894 to say how much he missed 'your grace, your boyish beauty, the bright sword-play of your wit, the delicate fancy of your genius', Oscar went on to tell him that, after working that day, he then 'went and sat with my mother. Death and Love seem to walk on either hand as I go through life: they are the only things I think of, their wings shadow me.'[54]

Oscar spent August to October in Worthing with Constance and the boys. Vyvyan recalled him being at his best at the seaside, taking them fishing and helping them make sandcastles. At the time Oscar had just embarked on writing *The Importance of Being Earnest*, for which he had been paid an advance, and it was going well. He told Bosie that he was overdrawn at the bank and when Constance wrote to her brother on 31 August she mentioned that it was costing the two of them £10 10s 0d a week. It was a happy letter: Cyril, she said, had gone out with Oscar in a boat and Oscar had given her a plot for a book she was planning.

Despite Jane's earlier conviction that, for financial reasons, she would be forced to give up her house, she managed to cling on with Oscar's help. But her letters to him for the rest of that year continued to be about money. In September she wrote telling him how unhappy she was at being without a shilling in the world and that even when her pension arrived in October, it would only pay the rent.

She had just read *The Green Carnation*, a novel on fashionable London society written by Robert Hichens and published that month, and said she found it 'very clever and not ill-natured. It is very amusing altogether.' She was quite unaware of how much it had damaged Oscar. It contained a highly recognizable portrait of him (as the dominant Mr Amarinth) and of Bosie (as his susceptible follower, Lord Reggie). Even Willie was introduced in the guise of 'Teddy'. ('Do you know, Mr Amarinth,' says a character called Madame Valtesi, 'I am almost afraid I shall have to put down my carriage or your brother. I cannot keep them both up . . .' Mr Amarinth replies: 'Poor Teddy! Have his conversational powers gone off? I never see him. The world is so very large, isn't it.')[55]

The book cast doubts on the morality of the two main characters and acted as a confirmation of the suspicions and rumours current in London clubs of Oscar's homosexual leanings. It infuriated the Marquis of Queensberry, already angry at Oscar's Svengali influence over his son. That summer he had visited Oscar at Tite Street, a scene recalled by Oscar with horror in *De Profundis*: 'waving his small hands in the air in epileptic fury, your father . . . had stood uttering every foul word his foul mind could think of, and screaming the loathsome threats he afterwards with such cunning carried out . . .'

Two more events happened in October that fuelled Queensberry's incandescent rage: first, his second marriage was annulled, with his wife alleging 'malformation of the parts of generation' and 'frigidity and impotency'. Secondly, his eldest son died – with suicide suspected – thus avoiding what Queensberry was certain was a homosexual scandal.

Oscar meanwhile, to scotch the rumour that he himself had written *The Green Carnation*, wrote to the *Pall Mall Gazette* in October 1894, disclaiming this. Jane wrote to tell him that 'Willie was delighted with your letter in the *Pall Mall*. Thought it so cleverly sarcastic.' She also thanked her 'best and kindest of sons' for his contribution of £15 to her 'dilapidated affairs'. He had, she assured him, been her 'best aid and comforter'.

He was also acting as best aid, comforter and banker to Bosie. The same month, October, the two were together in Brighton, at the Grand Hotel. Bosie fell ill and was nursed by Oscar, the two of them then moving into lodgings so that Oscar could continue work on *The Importance of Being Earnest*. However, when Oscar fell ill Bosie walked out, returning to the hotel and maliciously charging all his expenses there to Oscar. He wrote to Oscar spitefully, saying, 'When you are not on your pedestal you are not interesting. The next time you are ill I will go away at once.'

An Oxford undergraduate journal, the *Chameleon*, came out in December with a poem in it by Bosie which ended with the line, 'The Love that dare not speak its name'. Oscar, caring less and less for convention, seemed determined to let it be spoken.

15

Triumph and Tragedy

AN IDEAL HUSBAND opened on 3 January 1895 before an audience that included government ministers such as Balfour and Chamberlain, as well as the Prince of Wales – who assured Oscar, when he remarked on the length of the play, that he should not cut a word. It was greeted rapturously and Bernard Shaw, now dramatic critic of the *Saturday Review*, wrote: 'In a certain sense Mr Wilde is to me our only thorough playwright. He plays with everything: with wit, with philosophy, with drama, with actors and audience, with the whole theatre . . .' He played too with elements of his own life, hinting at the fear of blackmail, and the dire consequences that past actions laid up in store for the future.

Jane had written previously to Oscar to say she trusted all would go well with his new play. He had sent her, possibly for Christmas, a number of gifts and she said she had been 'overwhelmed by a crowd of the most charming presents and know not how to thank you enough for your beautiful thought about me'. Everything he had given her, she said, was both lovely and useful. 'The rug is superb, the pillow delicious and *two* fitted covers, and the shawl is splendid. Then my oriental carpet is brilliant and beautiful and is immensely admired. I never had so many pretty and useful things given to me before and all so eloquent of your kind consideration for me. I am indeed truly grateful and proud of my son.'[1]

At the time his play opened, Oscar was living mainly at the Albemarle Hotel. Although his next play, *The Importance of Being*

Earnest, was already in rehearsal, he left for Algiers with Lord Alfred Douglas later in January. He explained his journey to Ada Leverson by saying, 'I begged him [Douglas] to let me stay to rehearse, but so beautiful is his nature that he declined at once.'[2]

Constance wrote to her brother on 22 January to tell him that Oscar had gone to Algiers and that her darling Cyril had gone back to school. She said he was growing sweeter by the day, 'though his father does his best to spoil him and Cyril told me himself that he was growing perfectly reckless like father!' She closed by saying she was just off to see Lady Wilde.[3]

That month, alone at Tite Street, Constance slipped on a loose stair carpet at the top of the stairs and fell down the whole flight to the bottom. It was a very bad fall and she injured her spine and her right hand. The damage to her spine later led to serious complications. Not knowing Oscar's address in Algiers, she wrote to Robbie Ross asking him to pass on various messages, including the fact that as she was unable to walk after her accident she could not go to Oakley Street to see Jane, 'but I will leave directions about his mother having everything that she needs'.[4]

Her concern about Jane at a time when she was in undoubted pain shows the closeness of her relationship with her mother-in-law. But despite Constance's accident Oscar, who knew about it, did not return to London until early February and then went to the Avondale Hotel. There after a fortnight or so Douglas joined him and, by inviting a third young man to join them, ran up a large hotel bill which Oscar had to pay.

The Marquis of Queensberry had meanwhile been 'stamping round the West End of London vowing vengeance against Wilde, defaming his character, and threatening to shoot, thrash, assault, fight, ruin, disgrace, or otherwise incommode him'.[5] His actions naturally caused gossip, though many still did not suspect the truth about Oscar. Even man-about-town Frank Harris was amazed to hear Oscar admit it when the two were talking a few months later: 'I did not believe the accusation. I did not believe it for a moment,' he said.[6] Both Shaw and Sherard said they were also unaware of it. When Ellen Terry heard Oscar say to the young actress, Aimée Lowther, 'If only you were a boy, how I would adore you,' she was mystified and asked him if he really meant it.[7]

Willie, whose life was one of gossip in the clubs, must surely have heard the innuendoes about Oscar's relationship with Bosie made by those who had heard Queensberry's fulminations against Oscar. He was also likely to have seen Oscar with Bosie, or another youth, at well-known haunts like the Café Royal. He would hardly have told his mother, though, and neither would her women friends, if indeed they had heard the gossip. Jane remained incarcerated in her house, unaware of tension.

The Importance of Being Earnest opened at the St James's Theatre on 14 February 1895 during one of the worst snowstorms for years. Oscar, in a coat with a black velvet collar and wearing a green carnation, had been warned that Queensberry intended to create a disturbance and had arranged for him to be refused entry to the theatre. His plans balked, Queensberry had a bunch of carrots and turnips – what Robert Sherard called 'a phallic bouquet' – delivered to Oscar at the stage door.

The play was greeted rapturously by both audience and reviewers. Jane wrote to him the next day to say, 'You have had a splendid success and I am so glad. Someone said you were now the foremost man of the day and I am very proud of you. If you can send me the typewritten copy I would be glad to read the play with all the brilliant dialogue . . . I have seen many of the reviews for the new play. All good. You are indeed the success of the day and no one gets such long notices.'[8]

It was sad, extraordinary even, that Jane never saw a single one of Oscar's plays; but leaving her solitary existence for the brouhaha of a first night would have been too overwhelming. She was used to the grand entrance, but could no longer make the effort. She was now 74 and had gradually withdrawn further and further from the world, holding no more salons and writing no more for publication. Even writing letters to her friends had become an effort and she did not encourage visitors, preferring to look at the world through papers and magazines. She avidly read Oscar's reviews, rejoicing in them and writing to tell him of her delight.

Even her flow of letters to Oscar, once happily full of gossip about friends and her own and Willie's affairs, was now drying up. As she rarely went out to friends she could no longer pass on their gossip and Oscar had no wish to hear about Willie – who was spending all his time at his drinking clubs. Preoccupied with her lack of money, Jane had taken the decision to retreat from the unkind real world. Oscar wrote of her at this time: 'My mother, who knew life as a whole, used often to quote to me Goethe's lines – written by Carlyle in a book he had given her years ago, and translated by him, I fancy, also:

> Who never ate his bread in sorrow,
> Who never spent the midnight hours
> Weeping and waiting for the morrow –
> He knows you not, ye heavenly powers.'

These particular lines, Oscar explained, were said by the Queen of Prussia 'in her humiliation and exile' after her brutal treatment by Napoleon: 'They were the lines my mother often quoted in the troubles of her later life.'[9]

Jane's grandson, Vyvyan, said his own recollection of her, when taken to see her as a very small boy in her Oakley Street house, was 'of a terrifying and very severe old lady seated bolt upright in semi-darkness'. He remembered her being dressed 'like a tragedy queen, her bodice covered with brooches and cameos', all the curtains permanently drawn and the drawing room 'lit by guttering candles arranged in the corners of the room, as far away from my grandmother as possible, so that the heavy make-up with which she tried to conceal her age could not be detected'. He hated going there and protested strongly each time he was forced to make a duty visit.[10]

Queensberry, infuriated by the success of *The Importance of Being Earnest*, went to the Albemarle Club on 18 February to leave a visiting card on which he had written, 'To Oscar Wilde posing as a somdomite' – his spelling echoing his distraught state – or possibly his illiteracy. Oscar, visiting friends in the country, did not see it until 28 February. After reading it, he wrote a letter to Robert Ross, asking him to come over and see him at the Avondale Hotel, saying, 'I don't see anything now but a criminal prosecution, my whole life seems ruined by this man.'[11] Oscar had reached the end of his tether: taking legal action against the Marquis and thus bringing the matter to a head was preferable, in his eyes, to being constantly hounded by the man. He went to Marlborough Street police station on 1 March and swore out a warrant for Queensberry's arrest on a charge 'that he did unlawfully and maliciously publish a certain defamatory libel of and concerning one Oscar Wilde'.

After a preliminary hearing on 9 March the trial began on 3 April 1895 at a densely crowded Old Bailey. It must have been a severe shock to Jane. She would have read the newspaper coverage and been devastated at the revelation of her adored son's relationship with paper-boys, stableboys and waiters; at the public airing of his love letters, poems and presents; at the explicit questions about whether he kissed this or that young man. Willie must also have passed on the latest news. Oscar was to comment, 'My poor brother writes to me that he is defending me all over London; my poor, dear brother, he could compromise a steam-engine.'[12] And indeed, according to Bernard Shaw, Willie told him 'with maudlin pathos' that 'Oscar is not a man of bad character. You could have trusted him with a woman anywhere.'[13]

Oscar joked in the witness box – when asked if he had kissed a certain boy, he replied, 'Oh dear no! He was a peculiarly plain boy' – and turned up each day in a carriage and pair with liveried attendants. But in reality he was deeply worried. As a result, Sir Edward Clarke, appearing for Oscar, requested on his behalf to withdraw from the prosecution to save 'going through day after day, it might be, matters of the most appalling character'. Discharging Queensberry, the judge directed the jury to return a verdict that the libel was true. Within hours a warrant was issued for Oscar's arrest.

In a letter Oscar wrote to the editor of the *Evening News* on 5 April he gave his reasons for closing the case as wanting to avoid putting Lord Alfred Douglas in the witness box against his father.

That afternoon he went to the Cadogan Hotel, where Bosie was staying. His friend Robbie Ross was with him and Oscar asked him if he would tell Constance what had happened. Ross did so and Constance, already in a state of fear and trepidation, burst into tears, saying that she hoped her husband would leave the country before the warrant was served.

Oscar was arrested at the Cadogan Hotel at 6.20 p.m. that evening. He was taken to Bow Street police station, charged and put in a cell where reporters peered at him through the grille. Refused bail, he was lodged at Holloway Prison pending trial. Ross's relatives were upset when the press revealed that he was with Oscar at the time of his arrest, and Ross was also forced to leave some of his clubs. He later wrote, 'My mother promised that if I would go abroad for a few weeks she would contribute to the expenses of Wilde's defence, which she did; and that she would assist Lady Wilde (who was entirely dependent on her son Oscar), which she did until Lady Wilde's death . . .'[14]

Meanwhile, a vicious campaign of denigration was carried out against Oscar. His name outside the theatres where his highly successful plays were running was covered up by strips of paper; his books were removed from bookshops; and acquaintances, out of fear, destroyed quite innocuous letters. Yet at the time homosexual practices were widespread in London and during the 1890s the police had knowledge of some 20,000 male homosexuals. Willie worsened matters for Oscar, who wrote to Ada Leverson from Holloway Prison to say, 'Willie has been writing me the most monstrous letters, I have had to beg him to stop.'[15]

Because of the outcry, Constance decided that month to remove Cyril and Vyvyan from their schools in Sussex and Kent and bring them back to London. It bore out Macaulay's remark that '. . . once in six or seven years our virtue becomes outrageous . . . accordingly some unfortunate man . . . is singled out as an expiatory sacrifice. If he has children, they are to be taken from him. If he has a profession, he is to be driven from it. He is cut by the higher orders, and hissed by the lower . . .'[16]

Vyvyan was to say that he remained unaware of the nature of his father's offences until he was 18. Cyril later told him that he had seen a placard headlining his father's name when he returned to London from school, and never rested until he found out what had happened. Shortly after, on being sent to stay with his mother's cousins in Ireland, he read the newspaper accounts. Adoring his father, he was desperately upset. To shield the boys, Constance engaged a French governess who took them both to Switzerland.

She, meanwhile, stayed on in Tite Street. Oscar was committed for trial on 26 April, charged with committing indecent acts. Bosie had frequently visited Oscar in jail but on the advice of Oscar's lawyers left England for France at the end of April.

Lord Queensberry in the interim had claimed costs against Oscar and deliberately and spitefully forced a bankruptcy sale of his possessions. Two days before the trial, the bailiffs entered Tite Street. The catalogue of the bankruptcy sale of the house contents shows how the place was ripped apart. Oscar's son Vyvyan said with justification that the sale was a scandalous piece of barefaced robbery.

Souvenir hunters joined in the free-for-all, with the result that Oscar's and Constance's possessions were ravaged: first editions of Sir William Wilde's books, inscribed to Jane, Willie and Oscar, disappeared or, along with others which had particular associations, were sold in bundles for a few pounds. Manuscripts and Constance's letters from Oscar were pillaged. All the children's toys went for a few shillings. Somehow Jane's letters to Oscar over a period of twenty years, all of which he had kept, managed to survive.

At the end of Oscar's first trial, the jury failed to reach agreement and a new trial was fixed for 20 May. As Oscar left court – having this time been allowed bail – to take up residence at a hotel, he was pursued by Queensberry's bully boys who threatened trouble at any hotels that consented to give him a room. According to Robert Sherard, 'Long past midnight, his brother Willie heard a knock at the door of the house in Oakley Street. When he had opened the door, Oscar Wilde, pale as death, dishevelled, unnerved, staggered into the narrow hall, and sinking exhausted into a chair cried out, "Willie give me shelter or I shall die in the streets." '[17] Afterwards, said Sherard, Willie often related the incident, mixing his metaphors for greater effect: 'He came tapping with his beak against the window-pane, and fell down on my threshold like a wounded stag.' He offered Oscar a small camp bed in a corner between the fireplace and the wall in a poorly furnished room.

After all Oscar's preaching at him, Willie must have felt revenged. Yeats believed Willie was secretly pleased: 'His successful brother who had scorned him for a drunken ne'er-do-well was now at his mercy.' Yeats also alleged that Willie refused to sit at the same table as Oscar, and instead 'dined at some neighbouring hotel at his brother's expense'.[18] Willie was to say of Oscar, 'It is his vanity that has brought all this disgrace upon him; they swung incense before him. They swung it before his heart.'

Frank Harris, who went to Oakley Street to take Oscar out to lunch, reported Oscar as complaining that 'Willie makes such merit of giving me shelter.' When Harris strongly urged Oscar to jump bail and go abroad, he claimed that Oscar told him that such was the enmity between him and his brother that if he did not go back to Oakley Street that night, Willie would tell the police. 'You don't know Willie,' Harris claimed he continued, 'he has made my solicitors [Humphreys] buy letters of mine; he has blackmailed me.'[19]

Sherard, however, attacked Harris for this story, saying he couldn't conceive why he had invented it, unless he had a grudge against Willie who, in Sherard's view, 'stood by his brother most loyally all through his time of trouble'. Years later Sherard wrote to Humphreys to find out if the remark about Willie using blackmail was true, and Humphreys had answered that he had no recollection of the incident.[20] Rumours, though, were rife at the time, Max Beerbohm claiming, for example, that 'Willie has been extracting fivers from Humphreys.'[21] But even if Willie had felt a flash of triumph that his celebrated brother had been brought down, he was essentially a kind man and rumours of blackmail were palpably untrue. Despite this, his estrangement from his brother remained.

Oscar was under pressure to flee the country from friends like Sherard and even one of his bail guarantors, Lord Douglas of Hawick, Bosie's brother, was prepared to forfeit his bail money if Oscar left the country. Constance, too, pleaded with him to go. But Jane felt passionately that Oscar should stay. According to Yeats she told Oscar, 'If you stay, even if you go to prison, you will always be my son, it will make no difference to my affection, but if you go, I will never speak to you again.'[22] Her Irish pride was still strong and she would not expect her son, the son of Speranza, to lack moral courage. She would hate the thought of losing a battle with the English by default. Perhaps she remembered her own witness box appearance in the Travers *v.* Wilde trial some thirty years before, when she successfully survived her skirmishes with the prosecution and the plaintiff was only awarded damages of a farthing. It would have seemed unlikely to her that her son could possibly lose a court case.

Willie, too, was adamant that Oscar should stay, believing like his mother that for a Wilde to run away was cowardly and far more disgraceful than being convicted and imprisoned – no remarkable occurrence in Ireland. He believed the honour of the family would be compromised if Oscar fled and kept repeating, 'He is an Irish gentleman, and he will face the music.'[23]

Unsure how Oscar felt, Willie made certain he stayed. Yeats came to visit Oscar in Oakley Street at this time, and the Irish servant who opened the door, with 'her face drawn and tragic as in the presence of death', told him that he could not see Oscar, but only Willie. Willie greeted him with 'Who are you; what do you want?' and when Yeats said he had brought some letters from Ireland for Oscar said, 'Do these letters urge him to run away? Every friend he has is urging him to, but we have made up our minds that he must stay and take his chance.'

Yeats said the letters were only of sympathy and Willie admitted his brother would be glad to get them, but added he would 'keep them from him if they advised him to run away'. He was convinced, he said, that Oscar would lose every friend he had if he left the country. Speaking emotionally he continued, 'He could escape, O yes, he could escape – there is a yacht in the Thames . . . but he has resolved to stay, to face it out, to stand the music like Christ . . .'[24] Oscar, sounding like his mother, wrote to Douglas to say, 'I decided that it was nobler and more beautiful to stay.'[25] He hated the thought of a 'dishonoured name'.

The events were a severe strain on Jane. According to Sherard, 'during all those dreadful days in May, 1895, when I was a constant visitor to my friend [Oscar], who had been released on bail, she [Lady Wilde] was confined to her room, indeed to her bed.'[26] The Comtesse de Brémont recalled 'a mournful train of friends that went silently to the closed door of the house in Oakley Street to drop a word of tender enquiry or reassurance into the letter-box'.[27]

After a further few days at his mother's Oakley Street house, Oscar's friend Ada Leverson, the novelist, noticing that 'he seemed so unhappy with his family at this time', asked him to stay with her and her husband. Oscar remained there until his new trial on 20 May. Sherard said that the night before he spent 'a long hour with the mother, deeply loved and deeply honoured, whom he was never to see again'.

The Comtesse de Brémont called on Jane unsuccessfully during the next few days, then by chance came across Willie while he was pacing up and down in the gardens of the Middle Temple. She asked him how Jane was managing. 'Mother is bearing up bravely – she hopes for the best,' he said. 'It was so good of you to call, but she cannot see any one, no matter how dear a friend.' Willie left her saying, 'Oscar will need me when the verdict is given. I must take care of my poor brother – for, one way or another, he will be a wreck after this terrible business!'[28]

On Saturday 25 May, Oscar was convicted and sentenced to two years' hard labour. He began his sentence in Pentonville Prison.

The blow to Jane must have been almost as shattering as it was to Oscar. Despite the newspaper coverage, and all the sordid details, she would loyally have retained her belief in his innocence and must have been devastated by the harsh sentence. According to Robert Sherard, when the final verdict was communicated to her, 'she only turned over on her side in bed and said, "May it help him!"' This could have been just a rumoured remark. It isn't clear what Jane meant by it and she was more likely to fire up in Oscar's defence than condone his sentence.[29]

She had not left her house for some time, but from then on she did not even leave her room. She remained there as isolated as Oscar was in his cell. Oscar, according to Sherard, had often dwelled on her serenity. She now needed to draw deeply on this. She had written some prophetic comments and aphorisms on several pages of the manuscript copy of a long and ambitious early poem by Oscar, possibly written when he was about 16. One of these comments expressed her present mood: 'Life is agony and hope, illusion and despair – all commingled, but despair outlasts all.'[30]

After Oscar was sentenced, Constance left England to join her sons in a hotel near Lake Geneva. The manager of the hotel shortly realized who the family was and asked them to leave. They went on to Nervi in Italy, some eight miles from Genoa, where Constance had friends. Then, in the early summer of 1895, Constance took the boys to stay with her brother in Switzerland while she went to England to settle up some business affairs. The hotel incident made her decide to change their surname by deed poll from Wilde to that of Holland.

Bosie, who had been in Rouen since fleeing the country in April, petitioned the Queen in June for clemency for Oscar, but was unsuccessful. Oscar was still in Pentonville Prison then and Lily Wilde, heavily pregnant, wrote to the governor there asking him to give her 'unhappy brother-in-law' her 'fondest love' and to tell him 'what perhaps will give him the most pleasure, that his mother is wonderfully well'.[31]

This must have been deliberately said to give solace to Oscar. In fact Jane's health was deteriorating. She was suffering from respiratory problems and her energy and interest in life was on the wane. Already in April that year, Edmond de Goncourt mentioned in his diary that he had met Sherard, who told him Lady Wilde was sick and about to die. Oscar had been her mainspring and without him her spirit had gone. She did not wish to see or talk to friends. Her letter-writing days were now over. She lived entirely in solitude, defending herself against the harsh realities of life.

She had once written to a friend, 'Well, one must die at last, but this dying is a sad process though I do not dread death. I rather long for it with an eager yearning for the Higher Life beyond. But what is so wonderful in our mystic dual nature is that the soul knows no change and lives in an eternal present. My soul remains unchanged – all my life seems to me but one long yesterday.'[32]

Willie was drinking more than ever. In July, an old acquaintance of Oscar's arranged for some wine to be sent anonymously to Jane. He told the intermediary that he wanted it to be sent 'with a letter saying that you wish her [Lady Wilde] and not Willie Wilde to have it'.[33] According to an unsubstantiated and malicious entry in his diary for 28 May, Edmond de Goncourt claimed he was told by Alphonse Daudet, in London at the time, that Lady Wilde was always drunk on gin and the bedroom was full of bottles.

On 11 July 1895, Lily Wilde's baby was born. The child, a girl, was christened Dorothy Ierne Wilde. Jane had at least lived to see her first granddaughter. Willie, irresponsibly, did not even have enough money to pay his wife's doctor. Oscar was to tell Robert Ross later on, 'I paid out of my own pocket *since my imprisonment* all the expenses of her confinement, to the extent of £50 . . .' The money came from the sum of £1,000 given to him when he was on bail by a friend and held on Oscar's behalf by Ernest Leverson. Oscar told Leverson that the money was primarily for his mother's wants and Jane received about £280. Oscar also paid £39 13s 6d in rent for Oakley Street.[34] Willie and his wife and baby continued to make their home at the Oakley Street house. They needed somewhere to live and Jane, no longer able to afford a servant, could not now manage on her own.

Oscar, who had been moved to Wandsworth Prison in July, was only allowed to write one letter every three months and Jane was obviously hoping his first would be to her. She was to be disappointed. Oscar had to write instead to his solicitors about business matters and also to Constance, who was still living in Switzerland with Cyril and Vyvyan. Oscar had been told that if she did not hear from him she would petition for a divorce, which would mean his being parted from her and the boys. Constance, under pressure from Sherard to attempt a reconciliation, finally relented, however, and told Oscar she had dropped the divorce proceedings and had forgiven him. She was shortly to ask the governor of Wandsworth Prison for permission to see him, which was granted. Bosie, who asked permission to write to Oscar, was unsuccessful.

On 29 August Jane wrote to Ernest Leverson to say: 'Accept my grateful thanks for your kind attention in bringing me news of dear Oscar, as I am myself very poorly and unable to see friends or to leave my room . . . I thought that Oscar might perhaps write to me after the three months, but I have not had a line from him, and I have not written to him as I dread my letters being returned.'[35]

Jane could not stand the humiliations of the prison system coming between her and Oscar. Over the remaining months of 1895, she sat alone in her dimly lit room in Oakley Street, a silent, Miss Havisham-like figure, with only the grandeur of her memories to comfort her. In January 1896, she became ill with bronchitis. As her condition worsened, she asked if Oscar could be brought from prison to see her. She was told this was impossible.[36] On Monday, 3 February, she died, her death certificate recording the cause of death as sub-acute bronchitis. She had once told a friend, 'How can people weep at Death? To me it is the only happy moment of our miserable, incomprehensible existence.'

Willie had black-edged cards printed with the words, 'In Memoriam JANE FRANCESCA AGNES SPERANZA, Lady Wilde, Widow of Sir William Wilde, MD, Surgeon Oculist to the Queen in Ireland, Knight of the Order of the North Star in Sweden. Died at her residence, 146 Oakley Street, Chelsea, London, Feb 3rd 1896.'[37] Where had the Agnes come from? Speranza, too, was only a pseudonym. And Jane had almost certainly, long ago, altered the family name of Frances to the more interesting Italian version, Francesca. The list represented a life-long mixture of fantasy and reality.

According to Jane's friend, Henriette Corkran, Jane had said that 'she hoped that when she died her body would he thrown in the sea, or buried near a rock on some wild coast. She loathed the idea of being buried in a London cemetery.'

Her funeral, nevertheless, took place at Kensal Green Cemetery on Wednesday 5 February, two days after her death. There was just the one hearse, the mourners being Willie and his wife Lily. The small funeral was at Jane's particular request. Lily wrote to More Adey, a close friend of Robert Ross's, to say that Jane 'left us a private letter expressing very strongly the wish to be buried *quite privately* and for no one to come to her funeral'. She thanked him and Oscar's friends for the very beautiful wreath they had sent. She also said that she would like to see him the following day to explain their plans for breaking the news to Oscar: 'I fear it will be terrible for him in his state of health.'[38] Oscar was later to write to More Adey, thanking him for being 'so kind to my mother, so sympathetic and gentle in your delicate attentions to her up to the last . . .'[39]

Although Willie arranged the funeral, he could not afford to pay for it and Oscar had to meet the bills out of the money Leverson held in trust for him. Oscar asked Leverson to go to Oakley Street and remove 'the books of *my own writing* I gave my dear mother'. Petitioning the Home Secretary, in the third person, on 2 July 1896 for his release he adverted to 'the despair and misery of this lonely and wretched life having been intensified beyond words by the death of his mother, Lady Wilde, to whom he was deeply attached . . .'[40]

The love Jane's two sons expressed for her at her death was an exceptional tribute. She had given them her absolute loyalty and support all her life; and both recognized the anchor they had lost. Willie wrote to More Adey to say:

I thank you sincerely and all good friends of Oscar's for the token of sympathy with me in my sorrow deeper than you can imagine, for my dear mother was more than a mother to me – she was the best and truest and most loyal friend I had on earth – her loss is irreparable. She was quite conscious up to an hour before her passing.

It is useless to disguise from you and Oscar's friends that his sad fate saddened her life. With all his faults and follies, he was always a good son to her and even from the prison walls managed to help and assist her, as he always did when he was among us all. This must ever stand to his credit.

Willie told More Adey that he and his wife had consulted Ernest Leverson about the best way to tell Oscar and it was decided to ask Constance if she would carry out this task. It might reconcile them, Willie thought, thanking Adey for himself offering to tell Oscar. 'For many reasons he will not wish to see me,' said Willie.[41]

Constance wrote back from Genoa to 'Dearest Lily' to say she had immediately applied for leave to visit Oscar. Being more aware than almost anyone of the closeness of the bond between Jane and Oscar, she told Lily: 'I quite agree with you that it must be broken to him and I believe it will half kill him . . . I am not strong but I could bear the journey better if I thought that such a terrible thing would not be told him roughly. I am indeed sorry for you and Baby.'[42] Constance managed the journey, despite her ill-health. It was to be the last time she ever saw Oscar.

Oscar, highly superstitious, had already had two 'warnings' of disaster. A warden had killed a spider in his cell shortly before he heard the news, which he was sure augured some terrible happening; and his friend Vincent O'Sullivan claimed that Oscar had told him quite seriously that the night she died she had appeared to him in his cell. 'She was dressed for out-of-doors, and he asked her to take off her hat and cloak and sit down. But she shook her head sadly and vanished.'[43]

Jane had shown unending loyalty to Oscar and this was fully returned. 'No one knew better than you,' he wrote to Alfred Douglas in *De Profundis*, 'how deeply I loved and honoured her. Her death was terrible to me . . .' In an access of remorse at his mother's death, he continued:

I, once a lord of language, have no words in which to express my
anguish and my shame. Never even in the most perfect days of my
development as an artist could I have found words fit to bear so
august a burden; or to move with sufficient stateliness of music
through the purple pageant of my incommunicable woe. She and my
father had bequeathed me a name they had made noble and
honoured . . . I had disgraced that name eternally . . . What I suffered then, and still suffer, is not for pen to write or paper to record.

In the same letter he writes of 'the intolerable burden of misery and
remorse that the memory of my mother placed upon me, and places
on me still'. He believed that his mother 'died broken-hearted because
the son of whose genius and art she had been proud, and whom she
had regarded always as a worthy continuer of a distinguished name,
had been condemned to the treadmill for two years'.[44]

Jane was buried in plot 127 at Kensal Green. Willie never bought
a headstone for her grave and as no payment was made for a permanent
sepulture, her remains were removed after seven years and nothing
marks the place of her interment. But what the writer Henriette
Corkran said of her could stand as an epitaph:

If her talk was often foolish and even reprehensible, her own life was
honourable and courageous, and never mean. Though she liked
interchange of thought she never gossiped or listened to scandal. She
was fond of solitude; she realized that joy comes not from outer
things, but from the depths of the inner being. Her talk was like
fireworks – brilliant, whimsical and flashy. She was most inconsis-
tent, and in many ways very foolish. But in great adversity she was
brave, indeed heroic, and went through terrible ordeals; and though
she felt the sharp pinch of poverty she was always ready to help those
who were worse off than herself.[45]

Jane wrote once, 'I have a habit of looking at souls, not forms. Alas
now, I only feel the agony and loss of all that made life endurable, and
my singing robes are trailed in London clay.'[46] It was an aptly poetic
comment on the path her own life had taken, conjuring up a picture
of a Celtic muse finally bogged down by an English pragmatism that
did not concern itself with souls. And it had been an extraordinary life.

The obituary writers were kind to Jane. The correspondent for
the *World* wrote: 'The note of her character was loftiness; she did not

perceive small things; her soul was as high as her imagination was fervent, her enthusiasm fresh, and her heart tender and true . . . the motto upon her seal, "Fidanza, Constanza, Speranza", expressed her nature and her strength.' The *Pall Mall Gazette* praised her poetry and the *Westminster Gazette* thought she was 'exceptionally highly dowered intellectually'.

The *Athenaeum*, never a friend in life, relented at her death. It referred to her Dublin days, 'when her eccentricities excited little comment and her talents commanded much appreciation', and noted that 'she professed to value intellectual culture not only above all else, but as the only object in life.' It continued, 'Those of us who can testify from intimate knowledge of her sentiments and who had reason to probe her inmost feelings when the strain of society was not upon her, know well that, under the mask of brilliant display and bohemian recklessness, lay a deep and loyal soul and a kindly and sympathetic nature.' It sympathized with her having to bear 'her heavy cross in silence and stoical patience under the cover of darkness and the cloak of oblivion'.[47]

The *Telegraph* only gave her a few lines, but *The Times* wrote at length, calling her 'a distinguished member' of the Young Ireland party and praising her verse 'of virile and passionate rhetoric'. Like a number of other papers, and as Jane had earlier forecast with amusement, it repeated the heroic but apocryphal story of her standing up in court at Gavan Duffy's trial to take the blame for the seditious leader, protesting, 'I am the culprit, if culprit there be.'

The *Chelsea News* said that despite increasing infirmity, Jane had 'maintained to the last the interest in literature that had been an absorbing passion of her life and she was, as we learn, projecting a new book of collected essays when the Death Angel came for her . . . the end was perfectly peaceful and she retained mental consciousness to the last.'[48]

The Irish papers devoted columns to her, recalling that she was one of the best known and most popular figures in Dublin society and lavishly praising her poetry. The *Freeman's Journal* called her 'A woman of the most versatile attainments, genuine intellectual power and commanding character'. There were only sidelong references to Oscar's disgrace; the *Dublin Evening Mail* was typical in saying that Jane had 'a great deal of the shadows of this life to encounter'.[49]

After Jane died, Lily wrote to More Adey from 146 Oakley Street to tell him that 'Owing to Lady Wilde's death we are leaving this house and going into a few small rooms.' She enclosed a box of Oscar's shirts which he had asked Lily to keep for him and some of his play manuscripts, saying that 'I feel sure now his mother is dead he will not wish to hold any further communication with us.'[50]

The one item Lily did not return was his fur coat. Willie had pawned it. The news upset Oscar, who told Robert Ross, 'I have had it for twelve years, it was all over America with me, it was at all my first nights, it knows me perfectly, and I really want it.' Unable to bring himself even to mention Willie's name, Oscar wrote to More Adey on 1 May 1897 to say that 'These people who disposed of my fur coat' also had other belongings of his, like rugs and two portmanteaux. He asked More Adey to get them back and said he only wished he had been told about the fur coat the previous year, after his mother died.[51]

Even if he had known, it is unlikely he could have stopped Willie from pawning everything in sight at Oakley Street, including the rugs and portmanteaux. 'These people will probably try to annoy me,' Oscar said – but Willie sensibly kept out of his way.

Oscar was released from prison on 19 May 1897 and crossed to Dieppe on the night boat. Sad at not being allowed to see his sons ('I want my boys,' he told Robert Ross), he then alienated Constance and lost all chance of meeting his sons by reuniting with Bosie in Rouen that summer.

Constance, on returning to Italy from her visit to Oscar after Jane's death, had sent her sons to a school in Germany. Vyvyan, unhappy there, was transferred to one in Monaco. It was a time of constant change and bewilderment for the two boys: according to Vyvyan, Cyril 'had already started on his determined mission in life to rehabilitate the family name by sheer force of character . . .'[52]

During 1896 and early 1897, Constance's health seriously deteriorated. Her spine and right arm, hurt in her Tite Street fall, were becoming gradually paralysed. She was living tranquilly in an attractive apartment in the Genoa area and the last letter she wrote to Vyvyan said: 'Try not to feel harshly about your father; remember that he is your father and that he loves you . . . whatever he has done he has suffered bitterly for.'[53] Shortly afterwards Constance went into a nursing home near Genoa to have what proved to be an unsuccessful spinal operation. On 7 April 1898 she died.

Cyril and Vyvyan, then aged 13 and 12, were sent back to England, where they were looked after by Constance's aunt, Mary Napier. It was a moral household: their father's name was never mentioned to them.

Barely a year after Constance's death, on 13 April 1899, Willie was to die, aged 46. His death certificate gave his address as 9 Cheltenham Terrace in Chelsea, where he and his wife and daughter had moved after Jane's death, and the cause of death as 'hepatic and cardiac disease'. Willie's liver had finally given up. There was a three-line obituary notice in *The Times* and the *Daily Telegraph*. The *New York Times* put a news item about his death on the front page, mentioning his American marriage and adding, 'He was a fine pianist and had also done some artistic work in oils.'[54]

Oscar, by then in Switzerland, was telegraphed the news of Willie's death by Robert Ross and wrote back saying, 'I suppose it had been expected for some time. I am very sorry for his wife, who, I suppose, has little left to live on. Between him and me there had been, as you know, wide chasms for many years. *Requiescat in Pace.*'[55]

He was quite right about Lily Wilde, who was left too poor by Willie to bring up their child, Dorothy. She wrote to Oscar on 7 May to say, 'One has always sad memories of what Willy might have been instead of dying practically unknown and leaving his child to be supported by my sister. She is well and happy in a country convent and I think will have a good share of the family brains.'[56]

After Jane's death, the Moytura estate had reverted to Willie, and Lily told Oscar that the Irish tenants had at last paid up £93 arrears of debt. Considering how Jane, and then in turn Willie, whose journalistic earnings at the end completely dried up, so needed this money, it was ironic that it only arrived after both had died.

Willie's first wife, Mrs Frank Leslie, told Robert Sherard that when she next visited England after Willie's death she tried to find out where he was buried as she wanted to place a wreath on his grave. She could not trace it.

Oscar himself died in Paris in November 1900. The Comtesse de Brémont, who saw him on his deathbed, said, 'The beauty of his youth had returned, while his striking likeness to the face of his mother smote my heart with a pang of remembrance.'[57]

It seems incredible that little after five years from the opening night of Oscar's most brilliant play, *The Importance of Being Earnest*, all those in the Wildes' immediate family circle – Jane, Willie, Oscar and Constance – were dead. The party that had been going at full tilt came to a sudden stop. The lights went out. No more letters, no more witty conversation, just silence.

Oscar was survived by his two sons, Cyril – who fell to a sniper's bullet in the First World War – and Vyvyan, who became a writer and translator and died in 1967, leaving a son, Merlin, who in turn has a son, Lucian.

Lily, Willie's wife, was to remarry within eighteen months of Willie's death. Her second husband was Alexander Teixeira de Mattos, of Portuguese-Jewish descent, who translated continental writers like Maeterlinck. Dorothy (Dolly), the daughter of Lily and Willie, inherited her father's bright blue eyes and mass of dark hair, as well as his indolence. She went to live in France in a literary, lesbian circle which included Natalie Clifford Barney, Gertrude Stein and Alice Toklas.

Returning to England at the outbreak of the Second World War, Dorothy died in the spring of 1941 when only 46, exactly the same age at which both her father and Oscar had died. She herself claimed that her father was even wittier than Oscar, 'except that the drink had taken him early before anybody had time to get it all down on paper'. Introducing a book of memorial essays on her, Natalie Clifford Barney said that with her death, 'a certain quality of laughter – of Wildean laughter – has gone out of our world'.[58]

Constance's grave, as Oscar noticed with sadness when he visited it in February 1899, merely had the words, 'Constance Mary, daughter of Horace Lloyd QC' on it and a verse from the Book of Revelation. 'I was deeply affected,' he told Robbie Ross, 'with a sense, also, of the uselessness of all regrets.' It was over fifty years before the words, 'wife of Oscar Wilde', were added to Constance's grave. No plaque was put up to Oscar at his Tite Street house until 1954: a day or so later it was sprayed with paint.

The plaque on the old family house in Dublin, No. 1 Merrion Square, commemorates only the achievements of Sir William Wilde, not those of Jane. Yet her impact during the famine as the fiery poet, Speranza, was immense. Her feelings often overruled her judgement, but the families who emigrated to America during the famine remembered her name for generations. She deserves a place of honour in the history of Ireland.

In England she is forgotten, except peripherally as the mother of Oscar. Her Chelsea house at 146 Oakley Street, now No. 87, is quite unknown and the ghostly procession of those who flocked there to her salons can no longer pay tribute to this outstandingly erudite, witty, eccentric and gifted woman.

Appendix: The Ancestry of Jane Francesca Elgee

JANE ELGEE'S ROMANTIC dreams of an Italian ancestry were only dreams. More prosaically, as Brian de Breffny has shown in his account of the family, 'Speranza's Ancestry: Elgee – the Maternal Lineage of Oscar Wilde', the Elgee family originally came from the Durham area of England, their name being spelled Elgie, Elgey, Elegg and Ellge. The men in the family worked mainly as farmers, labourers and stonemasons.

Parish records for Staindrop, in Raby, Co. Durham, show a James Elgie marrying for the first time in 1657 and for the second in 1667. Two of his grandchildren, Charles Elge (a bricklayer, builder and carpenter) and William Elgie (a builder and carpenter), went over to work in Dundalk, County Louth, Ireland during a building boom there in the early 1730s. Work went well and they decided to stay.

Charles married and he and his wife Alice had eight children. Only one of the sons, John, survived and he went into the Church. In 1779 his signature as curate appeared in the church registers of Wexford. It was a good place to choose: Wexford was known as a religious and moral town and one of the strongest Protestant settlements outside Ulster.

John was appointed Rector in 1795, but three years later nearly lost his life in the ferocious Wexford Rising of 1798, when martial law was declared in Ireland to suppress the followers of the Society of United Irishmen. Founded in 1791 in Belfast, the society aimed to unite the Presbyterians of the north with the Catholics of the south and, with the aid of the French, overthrow the government and establish a republic. The government panicked and sent in the army to terrorize the southern Catholics. In mid-May 1798 the Wexford–Wicklow border became a blood-bath: men were flogged, pitch-capped and half-strangled to make them reveal names of insurgents. The massacre and execution which followed caused the Wexford Rising. The rebels retreated to the town and the troops following them burned the hospital, its eighty sick and wounded inmates, and all the nearby houses.

In later years Jane Elgee, the granddaughter of John Elgee, told how he had avoided being killed at a time when few escaped butchering. The Rector was taking a service in his church when the rebels burst in, but 'one of them turned away their pikes and related a great kindness which the clergyman had rendered to his family. It was at once resolved that he and all his belongings should be untouched and a guard was placed at his home for its protection.'

John Elgee's sister Anne wrote to him from Dundalk on 29 June 1798, in relief at having heard from him: 'I received your unexpected Letter with more joy than language can express . . . I watched the papers daily but there was no consolation for me; in them was mentioned the most horrid massacres and other depredations shocking to humanity . . . We waited in anxious expectation to hear from you as it was rumoured that you and family had gone off with other fugitives but when there came no letter I knew the report was groundless, and to think what might be your fate by staying in Wexford distracted me. All the hope we had left rested in the love and respect the inhabitants had for you . . .'

John Elgee was promoted to Archdeacon in 1804. His wife had had seven children by then, the eldest son being called Charles. Charles took up the law as a career, married a Sarah Kingsbury, and had four children: Emily Thomasine, John, Frances (who died as an infant) and Jane Elgee.

In the windswept churchyard of St Bridgid's Church, Rathaspeck, a few miles out of Wexford, the memorial to John Elgee's 'beloved and lamented' wife stands alongside six other memorial tombstones to the many Elgees who died in Wexford and were all buried at Rathaspeck. The churchyard provides over a century's record of the Elgee family history. Only one descendant now bears the Elgee name – Edith Elgee, a great-granddaughter of Archdeacon John Elgee.

The Archdeacon's only surviving daughter, Jane, married a Captain

Robert McClure, of the 89th Regiment, in 1806 and by him had one child, born posthumously: Robert John le Mesurier McClure. He became an explorer of the Arctic regions and was associated with the discovery of the North-West Passage while on the ship *Inventor*. Although born in Wexford, he never returned there and was buried in Kensal Green Cemetery – strangely, the same place where Jane Elgee, then Lady Wilde, was also to be buried.

Bibliography

LADY WILDE: LITERARY WORKS

1849 *Sidonia the Sorceress*, translated from J. W. Meinhold, The Parlour Library, vol. 29/30; 2nd edition, Kelmscott Press, 1893; 3rd edition, Reeves and Turner, 1894

1850 *Pictures of the First French Revolution*, translated from Alphonse de Lamartine, Simms & McIntyre

1851 *The Wanderer and His Home*, translated from Alphonse de Lamartine, Simms & McIntyre

1852 *The Glacier Land*, translated from Alexandre Dumas père, Simms & McIntyre

1853 *The Future Life*, translated from Emanuel Swedenborg, John McGlashan (there is doubt over the authorship of this translation)

1863 *The First Temptation or 'Eritis Sicut Deus'*, translated from Wilhelmine Canz, T. Cautley Newby

1864 *Poems*, James Duffy; 2nd edition, Cameron & Ferguson, 1871 and 1883; 3rd edition, M. H. Gill, 1907

1880 Introduction to William Wilde's *Memoir of Gabriel Beranger*, M. H. Gill

1884 *Driftwood from Scandinavia*, Richard Bentley & Son

1887 *Ancient Legends, Mystic Charms and Superstitions of Ireland*, Ward & Downey

1890 *Ancient Cures, Charms and Usages of Ireland*, Ward & Downey

1891 *Notes on Men, Women and Books*, Ward & Downey

1893 *Social Studies*, Ward & Downey

OTHER SOURCES

Anne Clark Amor, *Mrs Oscar Wilde*, Sidgwick & Jackson, 1983
Gertrude Atherton, *Adventures of a Novelist*, Jonathan Cape, 1932
Natalie Clifford Barney (ed.), *In Memory of Dorothy Wilde*, privately published

Karl Beckson, 'The Importance of Being Angry: the mutual antagonism of Oscar and Willie Wilde' in Norman Kiell (ed.), *Blood Brothers: siblings as writers*, International Universities Press, 1984
Mrs Claude Beddington, *All That I Have Met*, Cassell, 1929
Max Beerbohm, *Letters to Reggie Turner*, ed. Rupert Hart-Davis, 1964
S. N. Behrman, *Conversation with Max*, Hamish Hamilton, 1960
Lady Benson, *Mainly Players*, Thornton Butterworth, 1926
Arthur Binstead, *The Works of Arthur M. Binstead*, T. Werner Laurie, 1927
John Stuart Blackie, *The Letters of John Stuart Blackie to His Wife*, William Blackwood, 1910
David Hunter Blair, *In Victorian Days*, Longmans, 1939
Trevor Blakemore, *The Art of Herbert Schmalz*, George Allen, 1911
Frank M. Boyd, *A Pelican's Tale*, Herbert Jenkins, 1919
Brian de Breffny, 'Speranza's Ancestry: Elgee – the Maternal Lineage of Oscar Wilde', *Irish Ancestor*, vol. 4, 1972
——— 'The Paternal Ancestry of Oscar Wilde', *Irish Ancestor*, vol. 5, 1973
Anna, Comtesse de Brémont, *Oscar Wilde and His Mother*, Everett, 1911
Patrick Byrne, *The Wildes of Merrion Square*, Staples Press, 1953
Mary Campbell, *Lady Morgan*, Pandora, 1988
David Cecil, *Max*, Constable, 1964
Cheiro (Count Louis Hamon), *Cheiro's Memoirs: the reminiscences of a society palmist*, William Rider, 1912
Davis Coakley, *The Irish School of Medicine*, Town House, 1988
William Cobbett, *Rural Rides*, ed. G. D. H. and Margaret Cole, Peter Davies, 1930
Henriette Corkran, *Celebrities and I*, Hutchinson, 1902
Thomas Cromwell, *Excursions through England and Wales, Scotland and Ireland* (12 vols), Longman, Hurst, Rees, Orme & Brown, 1818–22
William Dillon, *Life of John Mitchel*, Kegan Paul, Trench, 1888
Lord Alfred Douglas, *Oscar Wilde: a summing up*, Duckworth, 1940
——— *Without Apology*, Martin Secker, 1938
Charles Gavan Duffy, *Four Years of Irish History*, Cassell, Petter, Galpin, 1883
——— *Young Ireland, 1840–1845*, M. H. Gill, 1884
——— *My Life in Two Hemispheres*, T. Fisher Unwin, 1898
Richard Ellmann, *Oscar Wilde*, Hamish Hamilton, 1987
Lady Augusta Fane, *Chit-Chat*, Thornton Butterworth, 1926
Martin Fido, *Oscar Wilde*, Hamlyn, 1973
W. J. Fitzpatrick, *The Life of Charles Lever*, Downey, 1896
Harry Furniss, *Some Victorian Women: good, bad and indifferent*, John Lane The Bodley Head, 1923
Regenia Gagnier, *Idylls of the Marketplace: Oscar Wilde and the Victorian public*, Scolar Press, 1987
André Gide, *Oscar Wilde*, Paris, 1938
Rosa Mulholland Gilbert, *Life of Sir John T. Gilbert*, Longmans, Green, 1905
James M. Glover, *Jimmy Glover his Book*, Methuen, 1911
Edmund Gosse, *Leaves and Fruit*, Heinemann, 1927
Robert Graves, *Life of Sir William Rowan Hamilton*, Hodges, Figgis & Co., London, Longmans Green, vol. 3, 1889
C. J. Hamilton, *Notable Irishwomen*, Sealy, Bryers & Walker, 1904
Frank Harris, *Oscar Wilde: his life and confessions*, published by the author, 1918
Rupert Hart-Davis (ed.), *The Letters of Oscar Wilde*, Rupert Hart-Davis, 1962

——— (ed.), *More Letters of Oscar Wilde*, John Murray, 1985

Harold Hartley, *Eighty-eight Not Out*, Frederick Muller, 1939

Edward Hayes (ed.), *The Ballads of Ireland*, A. Fullerton, 1859

H. G. Hibbert, *Fifty Years of a Londoner's Life*, Grant Richards, 1916

Merlin Holland, 'What Killed Oscar Wilde?', *Spectator*, 24/31 December 1988

Vyvyan Holland, *Son of Oscar Wilde*, Rupert Hart-Davis, 1954

James Edward Holroyd, 'Brother to Oscar', *Blackwood's Magazine*, March 1979

Jacqueline Hope-Nicholson (ed.), *Life Amongst the Troubridges*, John Murray, 1966

Mrs Desmond Humphreys, *Recollections of a Literary Life*, Andrew Melrose, 1936

H. Montgomery Hyde, *Oscar Wilde: the aftermath*, Methuen, 1963

——— *Oscar Wilde*, Methuen, 1976

——— *Lord Alfred Douglas*, Methuen, 1984

Leonard Cresswell Ingleby, *Oscar Wilde: some reminiscences*, T. Werner Laurie, 1912

Laurence Irving, *Henry Irving*, Faber and Faber, 1951

G. P. Jacomb-Hood, *With Brush and Pencil*, John Murray, 1925

Louise Jopling, *Twenty Years of My Life, 1867–1887*, John Lane The Bodley Head, 1925

Norman Kiell (ed.), *Blood Brothers: siblings as writers*, International Universities Press, 1983

Norbert Kohl, *Oscar Wilde: the works of a conformist rebel*, Cambridge University Press, 1989

Mary M. Lago and Karl Beckson, *Max and Will (Max Beerbohm and William Rothenstein) 1893–1945*, John Murray, 1975

Lillie Langtry, *The Days I Knew*, Hutchinson, 1925

W. R. Le Fanu, *Seventy Years of Irish Life*, Edward Arnold, 1894

Richard Le Gallienne, *The Romantic '90s*, Putnam, 1951

Susan Lowndes (ed.), *Diaries and Letters of Marie Belloc Lowndes 1911–1947*, Chatto & Windus, 1971

Seamus MacCall, *Irish Mitchel*, T. Nelson, 1938

Martin MacDermott, *Songs and Ballads of Young Ireland*, Downey, 1896

Stuart Mason, *Bibliography of Oscar Wilde*, T. Werner Laurie, 1914

Charles Maturin, *Melmoth the Wanderer*, Richard Bentley, 1892

W. B. Maxwell, *Time Gathered*, Hutchinson, 1937

Dame Nellie Melba, *Melodies and Memories*, 1925

Eamonn Mulligan and Brian McCluskey, *The Replay: a parish history*, privately published, 1984

Luther Munday, *A Chronicle of Friendships*, T. Werner Laurie, 1912

D. J. O'Donoghue, *Transactions of the Royal Society of Literature*, vol. XVII, 1895

——— *The Life of William Carleton*, Downey & Co., 1896

——— *The Poets of Ireland*, Hodges Figgis, 1912

——— *The Irish Book Lover*, vol. XII, 1921

Vincent O'Sullivan, *Aspects of Wilde*, Constable, 1936

Norman Page, *An Oscar Wilde Chronology*, Macmillan, 1991

Hesketh Pearson, *The Life of Oscar Wilde*, Methuen, 1946

——— *The Pilgrim Daughters*, Heinemann, 1961

Peter Raby, 'The Making of *The Importance of Being Earnest*: an unpublished letter from Oscar Wilde', *Times Literary Supplement*, 20 December 1991

Lord Rathcreedan, *Memories of a Long Life*, John Lane The Bodley Head, 1931

Elizabeth Robins, *Both Sides of the Curtain*, Heinemann, 1940

Rennell Rodd, *Social and Diplomatic Memories 1884–1893*, Edward Arnold, 1922

A. H. Sayce, *Reminiscences*, Macmillan, 1923

Willem Scholten, *Charles Robert Maturin, the Terror-Novelist*, Garland Publishing, 1980

Horst Schroeder, *Additions and Corrections to Richard Ellmann's Oscar Wilde*, privately published, 1989

Robert Harborouh Sherard, *Oscar Wilde: the story of an unhappy friendship*, Greening, 1905

—— *The Life of Oscar Wilde*, T. Werner Laurie, 1906

—— *The Real Oscar Wilde*, T. Werner Laurie, 1917

—— *Bernard Shaw, Frank Harris and Oscar Wilde*, T. Werner Laurie, 1937

Ian Small, *Oscar Wilde Revalued*, ELT Press 1993

Ethel Smyth, *Impressions That Remained*, vol. 1, Longmans Green, 1919

Walter T. Spencer, *Forty Years in My Bookshop*, Constable, 1923

W. B. Stanford and R. B. McDowell, *Mahaffy: a biography of an Anglo-Irishman*, Routledge & Kegan Paul, 1971

Marguerite Steen, *A Pride of Terrys*, Longmans, Green, 1962

Madeleine B. Stern, *Purple Passage: the life of Mrs Frank Leslie*, University of Oklahoma Press, 1953

A. M. Sullivan, *New Ireland*, Sampson Low, Marston, Searle & Livingston, 1877

T. D. Sullivan, *Recollections of Troubled Times in Irish Politics*, Sealy, Bryers & Walker, 1905

A. M., T. D. and D. B. Sullivan (eds), *Irish Penny Readings*, Dublin: M. H. Gill & Son, 1904

H. M. Swanwick, *I Have Been Young*, Gollancz, 1935

W. M. Thackeray, *The Irish Sketch Book*, Smith, Elder, 1892

Laura Troubridge, *Life Amongst the Troubridges*, John Murray, 1966

Katharine Tynan, *Twenty-five Years: reminiscences*, John Murray, 1913

Bertha Vyver, *Memoirs of Marie Corelli*, Alston Rivers, 1930

Terence de Vere White, *The Parents of Oscar Wilde*, Hodder & Stoughton, 1967

—— 'Speranza's Secret', *Times Literary Supplement*, 21 November 1980

Oscar Wilde, *De Profundis*, Methuen, 1949

William Wilde, *Irish Popular Superstitions*, James McGlashan, 1852

T. G. Wilson, *Victorian Doctor*, EP Publishing, 1974

George Woodcock, *The Paradox of Oscar Wilde*, T. V. Boardman, 1949

Horace Wyndham, *Speranza*, T. V. Boardman, 1951

J. B. Yeats, *Letters to His Son W. B. Yeats and Others 1869–1922*, ed. Joseph Hone, Secker & Warburg, 1983

W. B. Yeats, (ed.) *Fairy and Folk Tales of the Irish Peasantry* (Walter Scott, 1888)

—— *Tribute to Thomas Davis*, Cork University Press, 1965

—— *Autobiographies: reveries over childhood and youth* and *The Trembling of the Veil*, Macmillan, 1955

—— *Letters to Katharine Tynan*, ed. Roger McHugh, Clonmore & Reynolds, 1953

—— *Letters to the New Island*, Oxford University Press, 1970

Notes

1: GROWING UP IN DUBLIN

1. *Freeman's Journal*, 6 February 1896.
2. Deed held at Henrietta Street Archives, Dublin.
3. Letter in possession of Mrs Richard Elgee, Wexford.
4. Rosa Mulholland Gilbert, *Life of Sir John T. Gilbert*.
5. Charles Maturin (preface), *Melmoth the Wanderer*.
6. *Hearth and Home*, 30 June 1892.
7. Charles Gavan Duffy, *Four Years of Irish History*.
8. Thomas Cromwell, *Excursion through Ireland*.
9. Charles Lever, *Jack Hinton the Guardsman* (1843).
10. Lady Wilde, 'Social Graces' in *Social Studies*.
11. Charles Maturin (preface), *Melmoth the Wanderer*.
12. Mary Campbell, *Lady Morgan*.
13. William Cobbett, *Rural Rides*, ed. G. D. H. and Margaret Cole.
14. *Hearth and Home*, 30 June 1892.
15. Lady Wilde, 'Irish Leaders and Martyrs' in *Social Studies*.
16. Charles Gavan Duffy, *Young Ireland 1840–1845*.
17. Seamus MacCall, *Irish Mitchel*.
18. Charles Gavan Duffy, *Young Ireland*.
19. *Hearth and Home*, 30 June 1892.
20. W. B. Yeats, *Tribute to Thomas Davis*.
21. 'Irish Poets of 1848' (lecture given by Oscar Wilde at Platt Hall, San Francisco, 5 April 1882).
22. *Hearth and Home*, 30 June 1892.

2: SPERANZA OF THE *NATION*

1. *Freeman's Journal*, 4 February 1896.
2. *Ibid*.

3. *Ibid.*
4. Charles Gavan Duffy, *Four Years of Irish History*.
5. *Dublin Review*, April 1865.
6. *Transactions of the Royal Society of Literature*, vol. XVII, 1895.
7. *Irish Fireside*, 2 September 1885.
8. Letter from John MacCorry at William Andrews Clark Library, University of California at Los Angeles.
9. William Dillon, *Life of John Mitchel*.
10. Letter to an unknown correspondent, University of Reading.
11. *Ibid.*
12. Charles Gavan Duffy, *Four Years of Irish History*.
13. *Nation*, 27 June 1846.
14. Charles Gavan Duffy correspondence, National Library of Ireland.
15. Charles Gavan Duffy, *Four Years of Irish History*.
16. Charles Gavan Duffy correspondence, National Library of Ireland.
17. A. M., T. D. and D. B. Sullivan (eds), *Irish Penny Readings*.
18. Lady Wilde, 'Australia: a plea for emigration' in *Social Studies*.
19. Rosa Mulholland Gilbert, *Life of Sir John T. Gilbert*.
20. A. M. Sullivan, *New Ireland*.
21. C. J. Hamilton, *Notable Irishwomen*.
22. Letter to an unknown correspondent, University of Reading.
23. Charles Gavan Duffy, *Four Years of Irish History*.
24. Letter to an unknown correspondent, University of Reading.
25. Terence de Vere White, 'Speranza's Secret', *Times Literary Supplement*.
26. Letter to an unknown correspondent, University of Reading.
27. *Ibid.*
28. William Carleton correspondence, National Library of Ireland.
29. Letter to an unknown correspondent, University of Reading.
30. William Carleton correspondence, National Library of Ireland.
31. Charles Gavan Duffy, *My Life in Two Hemispheres*.
32. John O'Donovan correspondence, National Library of Ireland.
33. Letter to an unknown correspondent, University of Reading.
34. *Nation*, 8 July 1848.
35. A. M. Sullivan, *New Ireland*.
36. W. R. Le Fanu, *Seventy Years of Irish Life*.
37. Charles Gavan Duffy, *My Life in Two Hemispheres*.
38. William Carleton correspondence, National Library of Ireland.
39. *Freeman's Journal*, 20 February 1849.
40. A. M. Sullivan, *New Ireland*.
41. Letter to an unknown correspondent, University of Reading.
42. *New York Nation*, December 1848.
43. Letter to an unknown correspondent, University of Reading.
44. *Irish Society*, 31 December 1892.
45. *Daily News*, 23 February 1849.
46. *Freeman's Journal*, 21 February 1849.
47. *Saunders's News-Letter*, 20 February 1849.
48. Letter to an unknown correspondent, University of Reading.
49. *Ibid.*
50. *Ibid.*
51. Charles Gavan Duffy, *My Life in Two Hemispheres*.

3: 'IN LOVE I LIKE TO FEEL MYSELF A SLAVE'

1. Letter to an unknown correspondent, University of Reading.
2. Sir Edmund Gosse, *Leaves and Fruit.*
3. George Bernard Shaw, 'My Memories of Oscar Wilde' in Frank Harris's *Oscar Wilde: his life and confessions.*
4. William Wilde, *Irish Popular Superstitions.*
5. Letter to an unknown correspondent, University of Reading.
6. Rupert Hart-Davis (ed.), *The Letters of Oscar Wilde.*
7. A. M. Sullivan, *New Ireland.*
8. Harry Furniss, *Some Victorian Women.*
9. *Irish Fireside*, 2 September 1885.
10. Letter to an unknown correspondent, University of Reading.
11. *Ibid.*
12. *Ibid.*
13. *Ibid.*

4: 'GENIUS SHOULD NEVER WED'

1. Terence de Vere White, 'Speranza's Secret', *Times Literary Supplement.*
2. Letter to an unknown correspondent, University of Reading.
3. Lady Wilde, introduction to William Wilde's *Memoir of Gabriel Beranger.*
4. Rosa Mulholland Gilbert, *Life of Sir John T. Gilbert.*
5. W. J. Fitzpatrick, *The Life of Charles Lever.*
6. Lady Wilde, 'The Bondage of Women' in *Social Studies.*
7. Letter to an unknown correspondent, University of Reading.
8. Letter to Lotten von Kraemer, Royal Library of Sweden.
9. *Hearth and Home*, 30 June 1892.
10. Lady Wilde, 'Venus Victrix' in *Social Studies.*
11. Lady Wilde, 'Alfred Tennyson' in *Notes on Men, Women and Books.*
12. Lady Wilde, 'The Girondins' in *ibid.*
13. Lady Wilde, 'Genius and Marriage' in *Social Studies.*
14. *Ibid.*
15. MSS, Trinity College, Dublin.
16. Letter to an unknown correspondent, University of Reading.
17. *Ibid.*
18. *Ibid.*
19. *Dublin University Magazine*, March 1853.
20. Letter to an unknown correspondent, University of Reading.
21. Rosa Mulholland Gilbert, *Life of Sir John T. Gilbert.*
22. Terence de Vere White, 'Speranza's Secret', *Times Literary Supplement.*
23. Letter to an unknown correspondent, University of Reading.
24. *Ibid.*
25. Robert Perceval Graves, *Life of Sir William Rowan Hamilton.*
26. *Ibid.*
27. *Ibid.*
28. Lady Wilde, 'The Bondage of Women' in *Social Studies.*
29. Robert Perceval Graves, *Life of Sir William Rowan Hamilton.*
30. Sir William Rowan Hamilton correspondence, National Library of Ireland.
31. *Ibid.*
32. *Ibid.*

33. Katharine Tynan, *Twenty-five Years: reminiscences.*
34. Letter to an unknown correspondent, University of Reading.
35. *Ibid.*

5: FEMINIST FRIENDS

1. Auctioneer's catalogue of the Library of the late Sir William Wilde, 24 April 1879.
2. Letter to an unknown correspondent, University of Reading.
3. Lady Wilde, introduction to William Wilde's *Memoir of Gabriel Beranger.*
4. Luther Munday, *A Chronicle of Friendships.*
5. Robert Sherard, *The Life of Oscar Wilde.*
6. Lady Wilde, *Driftwood from Scandinavia.*
7. *Ibid.*
8. *Ibid.*
9. Lotten von Kraemer, 'Forfataren Oscar Wilde's Foraldrahem i Irlands Hufvudstad, Ord och Bild' (1902) translated by Christine English.
10. Letter to Lotten von Kraemer, Royal Library of Sweden.
11. Robert Perceval Graves, *Life of Sir William Rowan Hamilton.*
12. Letter to an unknown correspondent, University of Reading.
13. Lady Wilde, *Driftwood from Scandinavia.*
14. Letter to Lotten von Kraemer, Royal Library of Sweden.
15. *Ibid.*
16. Letter to an unknown correspondent, University of Reading.
17. 'Irish Poets of the Nineteenth Century', unpublished lecture notes of Oscar Wilde, ed. Michael J. O'Neill, *University Review*, vol. 1, no. 4, 1955.
18. Letter from Reginald Turner to A. J. A. Symons, 26 August 1935, William Andrews Clark Library.
19. Robert Sherard, *The Life of Oscar Wilde.*
20. *Ibid.*
21. *Ibid.*
22. Rosa Mulholland Gilbert, *Life of Sir John T. Gilbert.*
23. *Ibid.*
24. Letter to Lotten von Kraemer, Royal Library of Sweden.
25. *Irish Times*, 28 August 1954.
26. Richard Ellmann, *Oscar Wilde.*
27. Revd Lawrence Charles Prideaux Fox, 'People I Have Met' in *Donahoe's Magazine*, Boston, May 1905.
28. Letter to Lotten von Kraemer, Royal Library of Sweden.
29. Letter from Henriette Corkran to Jane Wilde, William Andrews Clark Library.
30. Letter from Christopher O'Keeffe to Jane Wilde, William Andrews Clark Library.
31. *Ibid.*
32. Walter Nelson, 'Oscar Wilde's Parents and the Congress in Dublin 1861', privately published.
33. Letter to Rosalie Olivecrona, National Library of Ireland.
34. Walter Nelson, 'Biographical Research on Oscar Wilde, from a Swedish Point of View', private mss.
35. Letter to Madame Lundberg, Royal Library of Sweden.

36. Horst Schroeder, *Additions and Corrections to Richard Ellmann's Oscar Wilde.*
37. *Athenaeum*, 20 June 1863.
38. *Duffy's Hibernian Magazine*, vol. IV, 1863.
39. *Saunders's News-Letter*, 20 December 1864.
40. Rupert Hart-Davis (ed.), *The Letters of Oscar Wilde.*
41. Letter to Lotten von Kraemer, Royal Library of Sweden.

6: LOYALTY ON TRIAL

 1. *Saunders's News-Letter*, 29 January 1864.
 2. Letter to Sir William Wilde from W. Carleton, 6 February 1864, at William Andrews Clark Library.
 3. Richard Ellmann, *Oscar Wilde.*
 4. Richard Le Gallienne, *The Romantic '90s.*
 5. *Irish Times*, 29 January 1864.
 6. *Irish People*, 2 May 1864.
 7. *Freeman's Journal*, 8 December 1864.
 8. *Dublin Review*, April 1865.
 9. *Athenaeum*, 18 March 1865.
10. Letter to Lotten von Kraemer, Royal Library of Sweden.
11. Letter from Christopher O'Keeffe to Lady Wilde, at William Andrews Clark Library.
12. *Ibid.*
13. Letter to Rosalie Olivecrona, National Library of Ireland.
14. Letter to Lotten von Kraemer, Royal Library of Sweden.
15. *Ibid.*
16. Letter to Rosalie Olivecrona, National Library of Ireland.
17. Letter from Robert Travers to Thomas Jones, Librarian, Cheetham's Library, Manchester.
18. *Dublin Evening Mail*, 15 December 1864.
19. *Morning Post*, 16 December 1864.
20. *Dublin Evening Mail*, 15 December 1864.
21. *Freeman's Journal*, 17 December 1864.
22. *Freeman's Journal*, 15 December 1864.
23. *Irish Times*, 14 December 1864.
24. *Commercial Journal*, 20 June 1863; letter from its publisher to editor of *Irish Times*, 17 December 1864.
25. *Dublin Evening Mail*, 15 December 1864.
26. *Freeman's Journal*, 16 December 1864.
27. Pamphlet, *Florence Boyle Price, or A Warning. By Speranza*, quoted in *Freeman's Journal*, 14 December 1864.
28. *Freeman's Journal*, 16 December 1864.
29. *Morning Post*, 16 December 1864.
30. *Freeman's Journal*, 16 December 1864.
31. *Florence Boyle Price* pamphlet.
32. Letter signed 'Inquirer' in *Saunders's News-Letter*, 29 April 1864.
33. *Irish Weekly Advertiser*, 2 and 9 March 1864.
34. *Dublin Evening Mail*, 12 December 1864.
35. *Morning Post*, 19 December 1864.

36. *Freeman's Journal*, 14 December 1864.
37. *Florence Boyle Price* pamphlet.
38. *Freeman's Journal*, 15 December 1864.
39. *Freeman's Journal*, 16 December 1864.
40. *Freeman's Journal*, 14 December 1864.
41. *Ibid.*
42. *Freeman's Journal*, 17 December 1864.
43. *Morning Post*, 17 December 1864.
44. *Caledonian Mercury*, 22 December 1864; *Lancet*, 24 December 1864; *Dublin Evening Post*, 20 December 1864.
45. Frank Harris, *Oscar Wilde*.
46. Robert Sherard, *Bernard Shaw, Frank Harris and Oscar Wilde*.
47. Lord Rathcreedan, *Memories of a Long Life*.
48. Letter to Rosalie Olivecrona, National Library of Ireland.
49. *Ibid.*
50. T. G. Wilson, *Victorian Doctor*.

7: 'A SWORD THROUGH MY HEART'

1. Letter to Mrs Perinetta, Royal Library of Sweden.
2. T. D. Sullivan, *Recollections of Troubled Times in Irish Politics*.
3. Letter to Mrs Perinetta, Royal Library of Sweden.
4. Letter to Lotten von Kraemer, Royal Library of Sweden.
5. Article in *New York Herald*, 18 August 1881, signed E.R.F.
6. *Ibid.*
7. Letter to Lotten von Kraemer, Royal Library of Sweden.
8. *Ibid.*
9. Minutes of the Medico-Philosophical Society, Dublin.
10. Letter to an unknown correspondent, University of Reading.
11. Letter to Rosalie Olivecrona, National Library of Ireland.
12. Rupert Hart-Davis (ed.), *The Letters of Oscar Wilde*.
13. Frank Harris, *Oscar Wilde*.
14. James M. Glover, *Jimmy Glover His Book*.
15. Portora School bill, William Andrews Clark Library.
16. Letter from C. Purser to A. J. A. Symons, 28 January 1932, William Andrews Clark Library.
17. Edward Sullivan in Frank Harris's *Oscar Wilde*.
18. Alfred Douglas, *Oscar Wilde: a summing-up*.
19. MSS, William Andrews Clark Library.
20. Letter to Lotten von Kraemer, Royal Library of Sweden.
21. Henriette Corkran, *Celebrities and I*.
22. 'Catling Card', British Library.
23. Letter to Lotten von Kraemer, Royal Library of Sweden.
24. *Irish Times*, 11 March 1878.
25. W. B. Yeats, *Letters to the New Island*.
26. C. J. Hamilton, *Notable Irishwomen*.
27. *Ibid.*
28. 'Oscar Wilde and His Mother' in *T.P.'s Weekly*, 25 April 1913.
29. C. J. Hamilton, *Notable Irishwomen*.
30. Lady Wilde, 'Lady Blessington' in *Notes on Men, Women and Books*.

31. Letter from James Bourke to Lady Wilde, William Andrews Clark Library.
32. Letter from J. D. Sullivan to Lady Wilde, William Andrews Clark Library.
33. *Ibid.*
34. Frank Harris, *Oscar Wilde.*
35. George Bernard Shaw, in *ibid.*
36. Eamonn Mulligan and Brian McCluskey, *The Replay: a parish history.*
37. T. G. Wilson, *Victorian Doctor.*
38. J. B. Yeats, *Letters to His Son W. B. Yeats and Others 1869–1922.*
39. *Northern Standard*, 25 November 1871.
40. Letter from R. P. Graves to Lady Wilde, 11 August 1873, William Andrews Clark Library.
41. John Stuart Blackie, *The Letters of John Stuart Blackie to His Wife.*
42. George Bernard Shaw, 'My Memories of Oscar Wilde' in Frank Harris's *Oscar Wilde.*
43. T. G. Wilson, *Victorian Doctor.*
44. David Hunter Blair, *In Victorian Days.*
45. Letter to Oscar, William Andrews Clark Library.
46. Letter to Lotten von Kraemer, Royal Library of Sweden.
47. *Ibid.*
48. Letter from Oscar to Sir William Wilde, William Andrews Clark Library.
49. Letter from Oscar to Lady Wilde, William Andrews Clark Library.
50. Letter to Rosalie Olivecrona, National Library of Ireland.
51. *Ibid.*
52. Letter to Oscar, William Andrews Clark Library.
53. Ethel Smyth, *Impressions That Remained.*
54. Letter to Longfellow, Houghton Library, Harvard University.
55. Letter to Oscar, William Andrews Clark Library.
56. *Ibid.*
57. Letter to Sir Thomas Larcom, National Library of Ireland.
58. T. G. Wilson, *Victorian Doctor.*
59. Robert Sherard, *The Life of Oscar Wilde.*
60. *Express*, 24 April 1876.
61. *World*, 26 April 1876.
62. *Dublin University Magazine*, May 1875.
63. *Freeman's Journal*, 20 April 1876.

8: THE LAST DAYS IN DUBLIN

1. Letter to Lotten von Kraemer, Royal Library of Sweden.
2. Letter to Sir Thomas Larcom, National Library of Ireland.
3. *Ibid.*
4. Letter to Oscar, William Andrews Clark Library.
5. Letter to Charles Gavan Duffy, National Library of Ireland.
6. Letter to Oscar, William Andrews Clark Library.
7. Letter to Sir Thomas Larcom, National Library of Ireland.
8. Letter to Oscar, William Andrews Clark Library.
9. Letter from Sir Thomas Larcom, National Library of Ireland.
10. Letter to Sir Thomas Larcom, National Library of Ireland.
11. *Irish Times*, 11 March 1878.
12. Norbert Kohl, *Oscar Wilde: the works of a conformist rebel.*
13. Letter from C. Limerick to Sir Thomas Larcom, National Library of Ireland.

14. Letter from J. W. Burke to Sir Thomas Larcom, National Library of Ireland.
15. Letter to Oscar, William Andrews Clark Library.
16. *Ibid.*
17. Letter to Sir Thomas Larcom, National Library of Ireland.
18. Letter to Lotten von Kraemer, Royal Library of Sweden.
19. *Ibid.*
20. 'The Fairy Mythology of Ireland' in *Dublin University Magazine*, July 1877.
21. Letter from Keningale Cook to Oscar, William Andrews Clark Library.
22. Letter from Oscar to Keningale Cook, William Andrews Clark Library.
23. Letter to Oscar, William Andrews Clark Library.
24. James Edward Holroyd, 'Brother to Oscar' in *Blackwood's Magazine*.
25. Rupert Hart-Davis (ed.), *The Letters of Oscar Wilde*.
26. *Freeman's Journal*, 15 June 1877.
27. Agreement dated 4 October 1877, Henrietta Street Archives, Dublin.
28. Letter to Longfellow, Houghton Library, Harvard University.
29. Letter to Oscar, William Andrews Clark Library.
30. *Ibid.*
31. Letter from Willie to Margaret Campbell, William Andrews Clark Library.
32. *Ibid.*
33. Lady Wilde, *The American Irish*, pamphlet, 1878.
34. *Sentinel*, 1 January 1879.
35. Rupert Hart-Davis (ed.), *The Letters of Oscar Wilde*.
36. Robert Sherard, *The Life of Oscar Wilde*.
37. Letter to Oscar, William Andrews Clark Library.
38. A. H. Sayce, *Reminiscences*.
39. Letter to Oscar, William Andrews Clark Library.
40. Letter to Mrs Knott, New York Public Library, Berg collection.
41. Letter to Oscar, William Andrews Clark Library.
42. *Ibid.*
43. Letter to Rosalie Olivecrona, National Library of Ireland.

9: THE TWO SONS

1. Letter to Oscar, William Andrews Clark Library.
2. Lady Augustus Fane, *Chit-Chat*.
3. Leonard Cresswell Ingleby, *Oscar Wilde: some reminiscences*.
4. H. G. Hibbert, *Fifty Years of a Londoner's Life*.
5. Arthur Binstead, *The Works of Arthur M. Binstead*.
6. Luther Munday, *A Chronicle of Friendships*.
7. Leonard Cresswell Ingleby, *Oscar Wilde*.
8. Robert Sherard, *The Life of Oscar Wilde*.
9. *Ibid.*
10. Letter from Yates to Willie Wilde, William Andrews Clark Library.
11. Richard Ellmann, *Oscar Wilde*.
12. *Punch's* Fancy Portraits No. 37, June 1881.
13. Letter to Margaret Campbell, William Andrews Clark Library.
14. James Edward Holroyd, 'Brother to Oscar' in *Blackwood's Magazine*.
15. *Ibid.*
16. Arthur Binstead, *The Works of Arthur M. Binstead*.
17. Leonard Cresswell Ingleby, *Oscar Wilde*.
18. Mary M. Lago and Karl Beckson (eds), *Max and Will*.

19. Letter to Otho Lloyd's fiancée, Holland family private papers.
20. Luther Munday, *A Chronicle of Friendships*.
21. Frank Harris, *Oscar Wilde*.
22. S. N. Behrman, *Conversation with Max*.
23. Max Beerbohm, *Letters to Reggie Turner*.
24. Leonard Cresswell Ingleby, *Oscar Wilde*.
25. Arthur Binstead, *The Works of Arthur M. Binstead*.
26. *Ibid*.
27. S. N. Behrman, *Conversation with Max*.
28. James Glover, *Jimmy Glover His Book*.

10: FEET IN LONDON, EYES ON AMERICA

1. Rupert Hart-Davis (ed.), *The Letters of Oscar Wilde*.
2. *Ibid*.
3. Louise Jopling, *Twenty Years of My Life, 1867–1887*.
4. Robert Sherard, *The Real Oscar Wilde*.
5. Oscar Wilde, *De Profundis*.
6. Letter from Edward Godwin, William Andrews Clark Library.
7. H. M. Swanwick, *I Have Been Young*.
8. Harold Hartley, *Eighty-eight Not Out*.
9. Lady Wilde, introduction to William Wilde's *Memoir of Gabriel Beranger*.
10. 'Oscar Wilde and His Mother', *T. P.'s Weekly*, 25 April 1913.
11. Anna, Comtesse de Brémont, *Oscar Wilde and His Mother*.
12. George Bernard Shaw, 'My Memories of Oscar Wilde' in Frank Harris's *Oscar Wilde*.
13. 'Oscar Wilde and His Mother', *T. P.'s Weekly*, 25 April 1913.
14. Extract from Violet Hunt's diary, Cornell University papers.
15. Katharine Tynan, *Twenty-five Years*.
16. Trevor Blakemore, *The Art of Herbert Schmalz*.
17. Anna, Comtesse de Brémont, *Oscar Wilde and His Mother*.
18. C. J. Hamilton, *Notable Irishwomen*.
19. Katharine Tynan, *Twenty-five Years*.
20. Trevor Blakemore, *The Art of Herbert Schmalz*.
21. Katharine Tynan, *Twenty-five Years*.
22. Letter to Lotten von Kraemer, Royal Library of Sweden.
23. Lady Augustus Fane, *Chit-Chat*.
24. Letter to Otho Lloyd, Holland family private papers.
25. Letter from T. P. O'Connor, William Andrews Clark Library.
26. Census for 1881, Public Record Office, London.
27. 'Oscar Wilde and His Mother' in *T. P.'s Weekly*, 25 April 1913.
28. Letter to Oscar, William Andrews Clark Library.
29. Anna, Comtesse de Brémont, *Oscar Wilde and His Mother*.
30. Letter to Otho Lloyd, Holland family private papers.
31. Letter to Oscar, William Andrews Clark Library.
32. *Ibid*.
33. Rupert Hart-Davis (ed.), *The Letters of Oscar Wilde*.
34. Letter to Oscar, William Andrews Clark Library.
35. Lady Wilde, 'Australia: a plea for emigration' in *Burlington Magazine*, May 1882.

36. 'Irish Poets of 1848' (lecture given by Oscar Wilde at Platt Hall, San Francisco, 5 April 1882).
37. *Daily Examiner*, San Francisco, 27 March 1882.
38. Frank Harris, *Oscar Wilde*.
39. Letter to Oscar, William Andrews Clark Library.
40. *Philadelphia Press*, 9 May 1882.
41. Letter to Oscar, William Andrews Clark Library.
42. Extract from Violet Hunt's diary, Cornell University papers.
43. Letter from Zadel Gustafson, William Andrews Clark Library.
44. Letter to Oscar, William Andrews Clark Library.
45. *Ibid*.
46. Rennell Rodd, *Social and Diplomatic Memories 1884–1893*.
47. Letter from Willie Wilde to Oscar, William Andrews Clark Library.
48. Rupert Hart-Davis (ed.), *The Letters of Oscar Wilde*.
49. Letter to Oscar, William Andrews Clark Library.
50. Extract from Violet Hunt's diary, Cornell University papers.
51. Letter to Oscar, William Andrews Clark Library.
52. Lady Wilde, 'A New Era in English and Irish Social Life', in *Gentlewoman*, January 1883.
53. *Lady's Pictorial*, 6 January 1883.
54. Letter to Oscar, William Andrews Clark Library.
55. Letter from Willie Wilde to Oscar, William Andrews Clark Library.

11: 'A VIOLET-EYED ARTEMIS'

1. Letter to Nellie Hutchinson from Otho Lloyd, Holland family private papers.
2. *Ibid*.
3. Laura Troubridge, *Life Amongst the Troubridges*.
4. Letter to Nellie Hutchinson from Otho Lloyd, Holland family private papers.
5. Robert Sherard, *The Real Oscar Wilde*.
6. *Ibid*.
7. Lady Wilde, 'American Traits: women and society in the States' in *Home Journal*, New York, 2 May 1883.
8. Letter from Constance Lloyd to Otho Lloyd, Holland family private papers.
9. Letter from Otho Lloyd to Nellie Hutchinson, Holland family private papers.
10. Letter to Oscar, William Andrews Clark Library.
11. *Entr'acte*, 1 September 1883.
12. Letter to Sir Charles Gavan Duffy, National Library of Ireland.
13. Scrapbook, according to Stuart Mason's *Bibliography of Oscar Wilde*, 'once belonging to Lady Wilde', in Robert Ross Memorial Collection, Bodleian Library, Oxford.
14. William Wilde, 'A Witless Thing' in *World*, 24 October 1883.
15. Letter to Otho Lloyd, Holland family private papers.
16. Lillie Langtry, *The Days I Knew*.
17. Letter to Oscar, William Andrews Clark Library.
18. *Lady's World*, 19 January 1884.
19. Letter from George Swinburn King to Lady Wilde, William Andrews Clark Library.
20. Letter to Oscar, William Andrews Clark Library.
21. Letter from Willie Wilde to Oscar, William Andrews Clark Library.

22. Letter to Rosalie Olivecrona, National Library of Ireland.
23. Letter to Mrs Knott, New York Public Library, Berg Collection.
24. Letter to Lotten von Kraemer, Royal Library of Sweden.
25. Agreement, dated 4 April 1884, between Lady Wilde and Richard Bentley & Son, William Andrews Clark Library.
26. *Academy*, 2 May 1885.
27. *Kentish Mercury*, 2 September 1892.
28. Letter from Ella Curtis to Lady Wilde, William Andrews Clark Library.
29. Katharine Tynan, *Twenty-five Years*.
30. *World*, 4 June 1884.
31. *Queen*, 7 June 1884.
32. *Canterbury Times*, 16 August 1884.
33. *Tinsley's Magazine*, January 1885.

12: A SURROGATE DAUGHTER

1. Letter to Constance Wilde, William Andrews Clark Library.
2. Letter from Constance to Otho Lloyd, Holland family private papers.
3. Cheiro, *Cheiro's Memoirs*.
4. Rupert Hart-Davis (ed.), *The Letters of Oscar Wilde*.
5. Susan Lowndes (ed.), *Diaries and Letters of Marie Belloc Lowndes 1911–1947*.
6. Lady Wilde, 'The Laws of Dress', part 2, *Burlington Magazine*, May–August volume, 1881.
7. Rupert Hart-Davis (ed.), *The Letters of Oscar Wilde*.
8. Letter to Lotten von Kraemer, Royal Library of Sweden.
9. Vyvyan Holland, *Son of Oscar Wilde*.
10. Letter to Lotten von Kraemer, Royal Library of Sweden.
11. Letter from Willie Wilde to Constance, William Andrews Clark Library.
12. Letter to Constance, William Andrews Clark Library.
13. Letter to Oscar, William Andrews Clark Library.
14. Anna, Comtesse de Brémont, *Oscar Wilde and His Mother*.
15. Walter T. Spencer, *Forty Years in My Bookshop*.
16. Anna, Comtesse de Brémont, *Oscar Wilde and His Mother*.
17. Frank Harris, *Oscar Wilde*.
18. Lady Wilde, 'Venus Victrix' in *Social Studies*.
19. Rupert Hart-Davis (ed.), *The Letters of Oscar Wilde*.
20. Letter from A. J. A. Symons to Reginald Turner, William Andrews Clark Library.
21. *Ibid.*
22. Letter from Reginald Turner to A. J. A. Symons, William Andrews Clark Library.
23. Rupert Hart-Davis (ed.), *The Letters of Oscar Wilde*.
24. G. P. Jacomb-Hood, *With Brush and Pencil*.

13: THE WRITING WILDES

1. Letter from John Dunne to Lady Wilde, William Andrews Clark Library.
2. Quoted in *Woman's World*, February 1889.

3. Lady Wilde, preface to *Ancient Legends, Mystic Charms and Superstitions of Ireland*.
4. *Athenaeum*, 27 August 1887.
5. *Academy*, 14 May 1887.
6. Letter to Constance, William Andrews Clark Library.
7. Letter from Helen Reins to Willie Wilde, William Andrews Clark Library.
8. *Queen*, 2 April 1887.
9. *Pall Mall Budget*, 22 September 1887.
10. Rupert Hart-Davis (ed.), *The Letters of Oscar Wilde*.
11. *Irish Society*, 31 December 1892.
12. Letter from Ella Curtis to Lady Wilde, William Andrews Clark Library.
13. Letter to John O'Connor, William Andrews Clark Library.
14. Letters from Zadel Gustafson and J. D. Sullivan, William Andrews Clark Library.
15. Letter to D. J. O'Donoghue in Robert Sherard's *The Life of Oscar Wilde*.
16. *London Figaro*, 21 May 1887.
17. Bertha Vyver, *Memoirs of Marie Corelli*.
18. Letter to Oscar, William Andrews Clark Library.
19. Elizabeth Robins, *Both Sides of the Curtain*.
20. Letter from Constance Wilde to Otho Lloyd, Holland family private papers.
21. *Ibid.*
22. *World*, 26 October 1887.
23. Letter from Edward Maitland, William Andrews Clark Library.
24. Letter to Oscar, William Andrews Clark Library.
25. Letter from Constance Wilde to Otho Lloyd, Holland family private papers.
26. Vyvyan Holland, *Son of Oscar Wilde*.
27. Richard Le Gallienne, *The Romantic '90s*.
28. *Pall Mall Gazette*, 17 March and 21 May 1888.
29. W. B. Yeats, *Letters to Katharine Tynan*.
30. *Ibid.*
31. Anna, Comtesse de Brémont, *Oscar Wilde and His Mother*.
32. Lady Augusta Fane, *Chit-Chat*.
33. Rupert Hart-Davis (ed.), *Letters of Oscar Wilde*.
34. *Ibid.*
35. Anna, Comtesse de Brémont, *Oscar Wilde and His Mother*.
36. C. J. Hamilton, *Notable Irishwomen*.
37. 'Oscar Wilde and His Mother', *T. P.'s Weekly*, 25 April 1913.
38. Robert Sherard, *The Real Oscar Wilde*.
39. Trevor Blakemore, *The Art of Herbert Schmalz*.
40. Letter to Constance, William Andrews Clark Library.
41. Letter from Ward & Downey, William Andrews Clark Library.
42. Rupert Hart-Davis (ed.), *The Letters of Oscar Wilde*.
43. Letter to Oscar, William Andrews Clark Library.
44. *Pall Mall Gazette*, 29 November 1887.
45. Letter to Charles Gavan Duffy, National Library of Ireland.
46. Royal Literary Fund Archives, British Library.
47. Letter to Oscar, William Andrews Clark Library.
48. *Ibid.*
49. Lady Wilde, 'Hallow-Tide in Ireland', *Queen*, 24 November 1888.
50. Arthur Fish, 'Oscar Wilde as Editor', *Harper's Weekly*, 4 October 1913.
51. Frank Harris, *Oscar Wilde*.

52. *Ibid.*
53. Mrs Claude Beddington, *All That I Have Met.*
54. Nellie Melba, *Melodies and Memories.*
55. Letter from J. S. Stuart Glennie, William Andrews Clark Library.
56. Letter from Constance to her friend Emily, William Andrews Clark Library.
57. *Ibid.*
58. W. B. Yeats, *Letters to the New Island.*
59. Robert Sherard, *The Real Oscar Wilde.*
60. W. B. Yeats, *Letters to the New Island.*
61. *Academy*, 27 September 1890.
62. W. B. Yeats, *Letters to the New Island.*
63. *Athenaeum*, 29 March 1890.
64. *Kentish Mercury*, 2 September 1892.
65. Laurence Irving, *Henry Irving.*
66. Frank M. Boyd, *A Pelican's Tale.*
67. Lady Wilde, 'American Women' in *Social Studies.*
68. Letter to Oscar, William Andrews Clark Library.
69. Michael Field (Katherine Bradley and Edith Cooper), *Works and Days: from the journal of Michael Field.*
70. Anna, Comtesse de Brémont, *Oscar Wilde and His Mother.*
71. George Bernard Shaw, 'My Memories of Oscar Wilde' in Frank Harris's *Oscar Wilde.*
72. Letter from J. Brailsford Bright, William Andrews Clark Library.
73. Letter from Oscar to Cyril Wilde, William Andrews Clark Library.
74. *Athenaeum*, 8 August 1891.
75. Letter to Oscar, William Andrews Clark Library.
76. Lord Alfred Douglas, *Oscar Wilde: a summing-up.*
77. Frank Harris, *Oscar Wilde.*
78. Lord Alfred Douglas, *Oscar Wilde: a summing-up.*
79. H. Montgomery Hyde, *Lord Alfred Douglas.*
80. Letter from Charlotte Eccles, William Andrews Clark Library.
81. Hesketh Pearson, *The Life of Oscar Wilde.*
82. *New York Times*, 5 October 1891.
83. Hesketh Pearson, *The Pilgrim Daughters.*
84. Frank M. Boyd, *A Pelican's Tale.*
85. Letter to Oscar, William Andrews Clark Library.
86. *Ibid.*
87. *Ibid.*
88. *Ibid.*
89. *Ibid.*

14: 'A LEANING TOWER OF COURAGE'

1. Letter to Oscar, William Andrews Clark Library.
2. Frank Harris, *Oscar Wilde.*
3. Richard Le Gallienne, *The Romantic '90s.*
4. Letter to Oscar, William Andrews Clark Library.
5. *Lady Windermere's Fan*, 1893.
6. Madeleine B. Stern, *Purple Passage: the life of Mrs Frank Leslie.*
7. Margaret Webster, *The Same Only Different.*

8. Hesketh Pearson, *The Pilgrim Daughters*.
9. Madeleine B. Stern, *Purple Passage*.
10. Oscar Wilde, *De Profundis*.
11. *Pioneer*, 22 July 1992; *Gaulois*, July 1992.
12. Letter from Constance Wilde to Otho Lloyd, Holland family private papers.
13. Letter to Oscar, William Andrews Clark Library.
14. Rupert Hart-Davis (ed.), *Letters of Oscar Wilde*.
15. Letter to Oscar, William Andrews Clark Library.
16. Letter to Constance, William Andrews Clark Library.
17. *The Letters of a Noble Woman (Mrs La Touche of Harristown)*, ed. Margaret Ferier Young.
18. Letter to Oscar, William Andrews Clark Library.
19. Max Beerbohm, *Letters to Reggie Turner*.
20. Unpublished memoir by Elizabeth Robins, New York University.
21. Letter to Oscar, William Andrews Clark Library.
22. Madeleine B. Stern, *Purple Passage*.
23. *Ibid*.
24. Letter to Oscar, William Andrews Clark Library.
25. Robert Sherard, *The Real Oscar Wilde*.
26. Hesketh Pearson, *The Pilgrim Daughters*.
27. Letter from Oscar to Willie, William Andrews Clark Library.
28. Inventory to agent, William Andrews Clark Library.
29. Letter to Oscar, William Andrews Clark Library.
30. Frank Harris, *Oscar Wilde*.
31. Max Beerbohm, *Letters to Reggie Turner*.
32. Letter from A. Mynous to Constance Wilde, William Andrews Clark Library.
33. Letter to Oscar, William Andrews Clark Library.
34. *Ibid*.
35. *Ibid*.
36. Karl Beckson, 'The Importance of Being Angry: the mutual antagonism of Oscar and Willie Wilde' in Norman Kiell (ed.), *Blood Brothers: siblings as writers*.
37. Letter from Willie Wilde to Oscar, William Andrews Clark Library.
38. Robert Sherard, *The Real Oscar Wilde*.
39. Letter to Oscar, William Andrews Clark Library.
40. Richard Ellmann, *Oscar Wilde*.
41. Letter from Mrs Frank Leslie, William Andrews Clark Library.
42. *Kentish Mercury*, 2 September 1892.
43. S. N. Behrman, *Conversation with Max*.
44. Letter to William Morris, William Andrews Clark Library.
45. MSS, British Library, calling card.
46. Gertrude Atherton, *Adventures of a Novelist*.
47. *Ibid*.
48. Letter to Oscar, William Andrews Clark Library.
49. *Ibid*.
50. Letter from Constance Wilde to Otho Lloyd, Holland family private papers.
51. Frank Harris, *Oscar Wilde*.
52. D. J. O'Donoghue, *The Irish Book Lover*.
53. André Gide, *Oscar Wilde*.
54. Rupert Hart-Davis (ed.), *The Letters of Oscar Wilde*.
55. Robert Hichens, *The Green Carnation*, The Pioneer Series, 1894.

15: TRIUMPH AND TRAGEDY

1. Letter to Oscar, William Andrews Clark Library.
2. Rupert Hart-Davis (ed.), *The Letters of Oscar Wilde*.
3. Letter from Constance Wilde to Otho Lloyd, Holland family private papers.
4. Letter from Constance Wilde to Robbie Ross, William Andrews Clark Library.
5. Hesketh Pearson, *The Life of Oscar Wilde*.
6. Frank Harris, *Oscar Wilde*.
7. Marguerite Steen, *A Pride of Terrys*.
8. Letter to Oscar, William Andrews Clark Library.
9. Robert Sherard, *The Life of Oscar Wilde*.
10. Vyvyan Holland, *Son of Oscar Wilde*.
11. Rupert Hart-Davis (ed.), *The Letters of Oscar Wilde*.
12. W. B. Yeats, *Autobiographies*.
13. George Bernard Shaw, 'My Memories of Oscar Wilde' in Frank Harris's *Oscar Wilde*.
14. H. Montgomery Hyde, *Lord Alfred Douglas*.
15. Rupert Hart-Davis (ed.), *The Letters of Oscar Wilde*.
16. Thomas Babington Macaulay, *Literary Essays*.
17. Robert Sherard, *The Life of Oscar Wilde*.
18. W. B. Yeats, *Autobiographies*.
19. Frank Harris, *Oscar Wilde*.
20. Letter from Robert Sherard to C. O. Humphreys, William Andrews Clark Library.
21. Max Beerbohm, *Letters to Reggie Turner*.
22. W. B. Yeats, *Autobiographies*.
23. Robert Sherard, *The Life of Oscar Wilde*.
24. W. B. Yeats, *Autobiographies*.
25. Rupert Hart-Davis (ed.), *The Letters of Oscar Wilde*.
26. Robert Sherard, *The Real Oscar Wilde*.
27. Anna, Comtesse de Brémont, *Oscar Wilde and His Mother*.
28. *Ibid*.
29. Robert Sherard, *Oscar Wilde: the story of an unhappy friendship*.
30. MSS, New York Public Library.
31. Letter from Lily Wilde to the Governor of Pentonville Prison, William Andrews Clark Library.
32. Letter to an unknown correspondent, University of Reading.
33. Letter from Sebastian Bowden to More Adey, William Andrews Clark Library.
34. Rupert Hart-Davis (ed.), *The Letters of Oscar Wilde*.
35. *Ibid*.
36. Frank Harris, *Oscar Wilde*.
37. Robert Sherard, *The Life of Oscar Wilde*.
38. Letter from Lily Wilde to More Adey, William Andrews Clark Library.
39. Rupert Hart-Davis (ed.), *The Letters of Oscar Wilde*.
40. *Ibid*.
41. Letter from Willie Wilde to More Adey, William Andrews Clark Library.
42. Letter from Constance Wilde to Lily Wilde, William Andrews Clark Library.
43. Vincent O'Sullivan, *Aspects of Wilde*.
44. Oscar Wilde, *De Profundis*.
45. Henriette Corkran, *Celebrities and I*.

46. MSS, New York Public Library.
47. *World*, 12 February 1896; *Pall Mall Gazette*, 6 February 1896; *Westminster Gazette*, 5 February 1896; *Athenaeum*, 8 February 1896.
48. *Daily Telegraph*, 5 February 1896; *The Times*, 7 February 1896; *Chelsea News*, 7 February 1896.
49. *Freeman's Journal*, 6 February 1896; *Dublin Evening Mail*, 6 February 1896.
50. Letter from Lily Wilde to More Adey, William Andrews Clark Library.
51. Rupert Hart-Davis (ed.), *The Letters of Oscar Wilde*.
52. Vyvyan Holland, *Son of Oscar Wilde*.
53. *Ibid*.
54. *New York Times*, 14 March 1899.
55. Letter from Oscar Wilde to Robert Ross, William Andrews Clark Library.
56. Letter from Lily Wilde to Oscar Wilde, William Andrews Clark Library.
57. Robert Sherard, *The Real Oscar Wilde*.
58. *In Memory of Dorothy Ierne Wilde* (privately printed).

Index